HOME FREE

An American Road Trip

ETHAN CASEY

www.ethancasey.com

BLUE EAR BOOKS

First published in 2013 by
Blue Ear Books
7511 Greenwood Ave. N, Box 400
Seattle, WA 98103
USA

Revised Second Printing January, 2015

ISBN: 978-0-9844063-3-3

Credits:

Cover Painting:
  Marquin Campbell, www.marquindesigns.com
Cover Design:
  Jason Kopec, tojasonkopec@gmail.com
Book Composition:
  Jennifer Haywood, Blue Ear Books, Seattle, WA
Printer:
  Scott Morris, Morris Printing Services, Arkansas City, KS, www.morrisprint.com

CONTENTS

My spiritual preparation for what was ahead was almost equally inadequate. Is it not said that in peacetime the chiefs of staff always prepare their armies as well as possible—for the previous war? I cannot judge the truth of that, but it is certainly true that conscientious parents always educate their sons for the era that is just over.

— *Sebastian Haffner*

CHAPTER 1

GOING HOME AGAIN

"We could use more rain, put it that way," Barry Ott told me. We were standing in his dry soybean field on a warm, sunny September day. "But we're okay. Just south of here, like in Pittsfield, there's people that didn't get nearly what we got, in terms of yield."

I had driven all the way from Seattle to meet Barry on his farm outside Marshfield, in central Wisconsin. Barry was husky and weathered as you would expect a farmer to be, and he was wearing shorts and a faded Mountain Dew t-shirt. Marshfield didn't answer my idyllic image of a Midwestern small town; it was sprawling and a little ragged, with railroad tracks and scruffy motels and fast food. It was a working market town for farmers in its part of Wisconsin. It also had the Marshfield Clinic, whose catchment area covered a radius of several hours' drive. Barry said, laughing, that when he was a kid he hadn't understood why people came to Marshfield for medical care from as far away as Michigan's Upper Peninsula. Why didn't they just go to the similar clinics that they surely had in their towns? Only as an adult had he realized that the Marshfield Clinic was a pretty big deal.

"We just milk a hundred cows," he was saying. "We got a cash crop and milk cows, and they kinda go good together. What makes the yield is the size of the bean." He pulled open a soybean husk to show what he meant. "That's what makes the yield. Now, this year it's really dry out. Some years you're walkin' in mud out here."

I asked if the summer's Midwestern heat wave had hurt his crop.

"Not necessarily," he said. "The biggest thing was the moisture. If we woulda had more moisture, we woulda had crops outta this world." He and his brother Steve planted eighty acres to soybeans and corn.

I asked Barry about his family.

"Yeah, my dad farmed since he was a little kid," he said. Yeah, the family was German, since of course Ott was a German name, but he didn't know much more than that, or really care. "We have family reunions and that, but history and all that I can't get into." Anyway, what they were was farmers. Family life had always been all about working hard, on the farm, all day, every day. "If we went fishing one day the whole summer, that was like our vacation. This is what I was always gonna do. And now I'm too old to do anything else. My wife's a schoolteacher. She teaches third grade. But the next generation, after me and Steve, they're not real interested." Barry's high school-age son, for example, wasn't real interested. "It used to really bother me, I'll be honest with you. But he helps me out, don't get me wrong."

The Otts had bought this farm from the family of my friend Jeb Wyman, who taught at a community college in Seattle. "I've got two older sisters, and they babysat here a lot," Barry said. "Jeb's mom and dad planted all these pine trees. They kinda border the whole farm. They were pine-tree crazy." He showed me the barn that Jeb remembered from childhood. One wing of it had been dismantled, and the lumber salvaged, by local Amish, but the rest of it still stood.

Then I got in my rental car and followed Barry a few miles to his other farm. "That's the drive I make every morning," he said when we got there. "I get up about four-twenty in the morning. I'm here by five o'clock. Dad bought this farm. He grew up right across the road there. His dad, my grandpa, was a farmer too." He showed me his tractors and other machinery in a big shed and the calves he was starting to raise for beef and, inside the barn, the milking equipment. "This is like a million years old. If you're really serious about milking cows, you don't do it this way."

Barry had a generous, open manner and a cheerful, candid demeanor. What I liked most about him was that he seemed self-reliant and unsentimental. "I couldn't work for anybody else," he said.

My own hometown, Oconomowoc, was partly a farming town, but it was also a bedroom community at the far edge of metro Milwaukee, and it nursed an attitude from having been a resort town for tycoons back in old-timey times. Oconomowoc had lakes with boating and water-skiing, and a manmade ski hill. But if you were looking for an honest-to-gosh working Wisconsin farmer, Barry Ott sure gave the impression of being the real deal. Growing up in the 1970s and early 1980s, I had felt disoriented watching farms around Oconomowoc morph into subdivisions, though as a town kid I had not experienced directly the upheaval in Midwestern family farming. I asked Barry about it.

"There was a lot of guys around here who didn't make it farming," he said matter-of-factly.

"So what happened to those farms?"

"Well, the farms are empty."

His brother Steve had joined us. "We were okay," said Steve. "We didn't have a lot of debt."

"A lot of things in life are just timing," said Barry.

"What's your attitude toward the guys who didn't make it?"

"I can kinda see why they didn't make it," he said bluntly. "You gotta be a good manager, you gotta be good with a pencil. There's a lotta things you gotta do. You can say you got hired help, but hired help isn't family. At the end of the day, they're here for the paycheck."

Like any middle-class American couple, Barry and his wife worried about things like sending their kids to college. "It's way outta whack," he said. "Since they were born we been saving. And they all work summer jobs. I don't mind helpin' kids that help themselves." Barry's father was in his nineties but still involved in the farms. "Do you still take advice from your father?" I asked.

"Oh, he gives it to ya whether ya ask for it or not. He'll say things like, 'You guys shouldn't be spending money on that.' Farming's what he knows. He only reads farming magazines, reads farming papers, and farms. He doesn't watch TV or game shows or do anything else. You know, change is hard. And as you get older, it gets even harder."

Near the end of our couple of hours together, I asked Barry about Scott Walker, the Republican governor whose attempt to ban collective bargaining by Wisconsin state employees had led to one of the most dramatic confrontations in recent American political history: the occupation of the state capitol building in Madison by upwards of 80,000 protesters, in sub-freezing weather, during February and March 2011. The occupation was already eighteen months in the past at this point, the June 2012 attempt to recall Walker in a special election had ended with a whimper, and I was starting to wonder what the longer arc of history would make of it. I was proud, as a Wisconsinite, of what the occupation had expressed and represented. Anymore, though, I didn't feel sure I knew where it would lead, or even where it should lead. Two things I did know were that Madison and Wisconsin are not the same thing, and that around half of Wisconsinites disagreed with the occupiers' premises and goals. Right or wrong, that was something some of us were going to have to put in our pipe and smoke.

"I tell ya," said Barry, "my wife's a schoolteacher, so she hates Walker. I think what he's doing is just fine. Everybody's gotta pull together and sacrifice. I'm not a big union guy. I think they protect the people who are poor workers. I tell my wife, 'You stick with me, and I'll bail you out.'" He laughed. "She says, 'You wait and say that when we're not gettin' my salary.'"

Throughout the rest of my long drive around America, this factoid about the Ott family stuck in my mind. Evidently Barry and his wife disagreed on a fairly basic level about a fairly important matter regarding the ordering of society. I wasn't privy to their family councils or even their dinner-table conversation, but from what I could glean it was also evident to me that they loved and supported each other, lived together, and shared a concern for their children's future. If they could disagree and surely argue, maybe even bitterly for all I knew, yet respect and live with each other, maybe the rest of us could too.

I felt sheepish putting Barry on the spot about something so public and divisive, because he was so evidently just a guy who did his thing, which was farming. He might have his views on other things, and if you asked he would tell you what they were, because he was a polite Midwesterner, but otherwise he just got on with doing his thing. But putting people on the spot was my thing and, in the service of that, I was not above enlisting my own Midwestern politeness.

Walker, said Barry, "got the state of Wisconsin back into the black again, and that's important."

"Hopefully he'll keep us in the black, and we won't end up like California," added Steve. "Or Illinois."

*

At the moment when everything had seemed to be at stake in the capital of Wisconsin, I was in the capital of Pakistan. I had been visiting Pakistan ever since 1995, originally as a reporter for newspapers, and had written two books about my adventures in that interesting country. In early 2011, my purpose was to visit communities affected by the previous summer's severe flooding, when twenty percent of Pakistan had been underwater and some two million people left homeless. One thing I had learned over years as an international journalist was that, as soon as you focused your attention somewhere, something was bound to happen somewhere else. Still, to read in Islamabad about upheaval in Madison felt odd. And it was somehow in the moment of that juxtaposition that my inchoate notion of one day driving around America and writing a book about it began coalescing into an intention.

My father had thrown me in at the world's deep end by taking me to Haiti at age sixteen. That had led to a college year in Nepal; back to northern Wisconsin and then southern Ohio; to California, Central Europe, Washington, D.C., and Detroit; to five years in Bangkok as a journalist; to seven or eight restless and frustrating years trying too hard to be at home in an English suburb; then at age forty to Seattle, for no better reason than that it seemed like a good idea at the time. Many of my major life decisions had been made on whims and hunches, and some had blown up in my face, but all had been productive, and Seattle turned out to be the happiest decision of all. By forty I had learned not to chase after stasis, but in Seattle I did find love and stability and a home. But I couldn't buck my longtime habits, which is why I found myself in Pakistan in early 2011, wondering from afar what exactly was going on in Wisconsin.

The uprising in Egypt was also going on then, and the *New York Times* was tossing off glib and patronizing headlines like "Cairo in the Midwest." Some of the protesters, for their part, were encouraging parallels, and the magic of social media was also somehow supposed to be part of the change for the better that was felt to be in the offing. But I had made a personal byword of something a journalist friend in Thailand had said to me: "There's no substitute for the sniff on the ground." Ideologies and theories and scholarship and digital media were well and good, but what you knew was real was what you saw for yourself. No single traveler could see it all; in fact, you were bound to miss most of whatever was going on, regardless. But if you showed up, paid attention, and took notes, you could at least sit down later and stitch together a story that rang true.

That was what I had been trying to do ever since those Bangkok days of the 1990s, and I had done it at book length about what I had seen and heard over years in Haiti and Pakistan. When I landed in Seattle in 2006, I thought I was coming in from the cold. I even tried going straight and cashing in on the tech boom with a soulless but well-paying office job. But Microsoft Corporation and I didn't get along very well and, like Barry Ott, I was too set in my ways to do anything other than what I had been doing all those years. And I found that my eye had changed. I now saw the world and my own country differently. The quality and extent of the change were not easy to define, but what I knew I could do was what I had learned to do overseas: show up, meet people and take an interest in them, ask questions, take notes.

✳

"When you hear somebody saying, 'This time is different,' that's when you run for the hills," George was saying. "Institutions are failing. The credibility of institutions is gone. What you're seeing is the last gasp of white privilege. This is their Alamo." The problem, said Janine, was "structural as well as ideological." If memory serves she meant the problem with American higher education in particular, but she might well have been speaking of the country as a whole. "It's not sustainable," said Larry. "We live in a global world like it never was before, and I don't think the American empire is sustainable."

The setting was Dr. John Bryant Wyman's dinner table in Fitchburg, just outside Madison, and everyone present had some sort of connection to the University of Wisconsin. Bry, as he wanted to be called, was my friend Jeb's father. The family was educated and, as Jeb described them, local gentry in Marshfield, where I had just been. Bry's brother, Mark Wyman, was a professor who had written distinguished works of history with titles like *The Wisconsin Frontier* and *Hoboes, Bindlestiffs, Fruit Tramps, and the Harvesting of the West*. Bry was portly and affable, still practicing medicine at the university medical center at age 79. "I don't have any committee work or anything," he told me.

"Because you didn't want to?"

"Yeah, I didn't want to. I just wanted to take care of people and read."

"How do you feel about the cost of medical care?"

"The costs I can't do anything about, but it's the greed of my colleagues that disturbs me." He had stopped doing surgical procedures at 70, mainly because of his bad knee, and he had started requesting an hour for each new patient. "In my old age I've learned that you have to listen to people to determine what's going on," he said.

George had a lot to say. I didn't catch it all. Janine Veto was director of development at the University of Wisconsin Foundation. Larry Nesper was a professor of anthropology studying Great Lakes Indian law and politics. Bry's daughter Mary and her husband were there too, and a few others, and my wife Jenny, who traveled with me as far as Milwaukee. It was an enjoyable gathering of alert, intelligent liberal white people. Jenny asked me afterwards why I hadn't taken more notes that evening. Part of my answer was that you don't just show up at someone's dinner party and whip out your pen and notebook. But it also had to do with pacing myself; I would be taking a lot of notes over the next three months. "You're trying to drink from a fire hose," George rightly observed.

And Madisonian political chitchat wasn't high on my to-do list. I had taken part in many such conversations, ever since arriving in Madison as a freshman in 1983. And not only in Madison. I now lived in a bigger and, in some ways, even more isolated self-selecting liberal enclave. In Pakistan, if you weren't careful, you could waste a lot of time assessing the perpetually grim scenarios there over tea and snacks, and end up getting nowhere but down. A driving purpose of this trip was to get away from the echo chambers of received opinion, so I could hear myself think.

It had taken Jenny and me ten days to get this far. We had done a spectacular fifteen-mile hike across the Continental Divide in Glacier National Park. We had driven through Great Falls and Livingston and out the east side of Yellowstone to Thermopolis and from there through Sioux Falls and Fargo to the Boundary Waters in northern Minnesota. I'm content, as John Steinbeck daintily phrased it in *Travels with Charley*, to draw a veil over those ten days of personal time. But our route is worth noting, because it was dictated partly by locations of personal significance.

Among my first adventures in childhood were annual driving trips from Wisconsin to southern Colorado, where we spent a couple of weeks with my mother's parents in a remote and staunchly unfashionable mountain valley. Cuchara was private, ours, the only place I felt uncomplicatedly at home. I didn't know then that to have such a refuge is a privilege of social class. My grandfather owned an advertising agency in Dallas, and my mother had grown up in the upmarket enclave of Highland Park. My father's working-class parents had moved to the less affluent bordering town of University Park so he could attend Highland Park High School, and that was where they met. He was co-captain of the HPHS baseball team. He also, by virtue of being young and white as well as intelligent and athletic in postwar America, enjoyed the chance to earn a liberal-arts education at a good university. He ended up with three master's degrees and a stable career, making himself useful to local communities in Wisconsin and Colorado as an Episcopal parish priest with, eventually, a pension and a paid-off house and a stable middle-class way of life into old age. My mother likewise did her professional thing as a reading specialist and principal in public schools. My parents did everything that middle-class Americans are supposed to do, and they did it well.

Many years later, when my dad and I made a sentimental visit to the Highland Park High School baseball field and saw the banners behind center field honoring past state championship teams, he exclaimed, "'Fifty-four! They remembered us!" But he also told me that same day that Highland Park High School was where he began feeling the way he had felt ever since: out of place. Teammates and classmates had gone on to be things like partners in leading Dallas law firms, but he and my mother had opted out of Texas, and he at least had never really looked back. He told me that, if his parents had not made his and his sister's education their top priority, he probably would have ended up a machine-tools inventory guy in a factory, like his father. "I love them for it," he said.

But as a kid I wasn't yet equipped to connect these dots. Many of the well-off Texans in Cuchara socialized with each other back home the rest of the year. When it's 110 degrees in Dallas it's much nicer, if you can afford it, to be at 8,500 feet in the Rockies. My parents and brother and I were included in that circle, once a year for a week or two, by dint of being family. So every July or August, we would pack ourselves into the Volvo station wagon that a salesman had persuaded my father against his better judgment to buy, and drive two long days across the Great Plains. On one of those trips we stopped in Thermopolis, Wyoming, and on another at Wall Drug in western South Dakota. So Jenny and I spent two nights at the Paintbrush Inn in Thermopolis and enjoyed the free public sulfur pool at Hot Springs State Park, then headed east again. Wall Drug was even more of what it had always been: an unabashed tourist trap developed during the Depression out of sheer American gumption and a highway sign promising FREE ICE WATER. Now it was staffed by young guest workers from China and Belarus. What was personally important to me was that it was at Wall Drug, the summer I was twelve, that my father bought me off the paperback rack a copy of *The Big Sky* by A.B. Guthrie Jr., the great American novel about a young man who leaves his ma behind in Kentucky and heads west on his horse to have adventures and be a mountain man. I read the book and got the message.

*

"They're putting millions of people out of work in order to get one man out of a job," George was saying. "And it ain't gonna work. It's gonna be close, but it's not gonna work." The presidential election was less than two months away.

Then Bry caught my attention by asking: "Is this occupation going to have a legacy?"

One day in February 2011, returning for a family visit to Marshfield, Jeb Wyman had caught a connecting flight in Detroit. His seatmate taught at the university, and before the flight landed in Madison she had persuaded him to join the occupation at the capitol. "Jeb is really the instigator of my involvement," Bry said. "I've been in the privileged class since birth. Somehow I got the idea of medicine in high school and just kept going. And I've always been on a salary. And all this came to my awareness, that many people don't have this. So I'm grateful that Jeb grabbed me. He didn't have to drag me. He just said, 'Dad, we're not going to Marshfield. We're going to the capitol.' I think I said, 'You oughta have a recorder, Jeb.'" The occupation, said Bry, "was not joyful, but it certainly was happy. They would move in portable stands. When Jeb was here it was very pleasant: sunny, bright, not snowy. But then there were days when it was snowing, and man, I was buttoned up." He showed us the sandwich sign he had carried. It read, on one side:

SOME OF MY PATIENTS
CAN'T AFFORD THEIR PRESCRIPTIONS

And on the other:

GOVERNMENTS EXIST
TO SERVE THEIR CITIZENS

"Were there counter-protests?" asked Jenny.

"The Koch brothers brought in Sarah Palin. I really can't say I was much involved, other than walking around with a sign. I was just there as a body. And identifying myself as a physician, thinking I would have more influence as a physician than as a union member. That's why I wore a tie. I thought that if a physician announced that he was unhappy, it might influence more people who were not physicians. I wasn't involved in the decision-making or anything. My decision was, 'What time am I going to go up to the capitol?' I would walk around once, and then I would stand or sit. And people would signal me with the thumbs-up or whatever. Usually I wouldn't go around more than once or twice, because of this knee. I'm in photographs on Facebook, and I just don't know how to get that. People have come up to me and said they've seen me there. I'm not computer illiterate, but I am computer impaired."

"Why did you come down on that side?" I asked.

"Because my patients were not being cared for. Couples would say, 'This month is his turn to get medicine, and next month is mine.' And that really disturbed me. At about the same time as the protests, the great University of Wisconsin said, 'We can no longer give samples to patients.' That angered me. I had email communications  with the executive director of whatever, and his justification was, 'This is just the way it is.' I had Crohn's disease and irritable bowel patients that were saving hundreds of dollars from samples. I'm sure there are some that haven't returned, because Badger Care, which used to cover 62,000 Wisconsin residents, has now been cut down to 26,000."

"Where is this headed?"

"Well, as George said, the pendulum will swing and come back. Hopefully there'll be a change of parties in the state assembly in November."

"What's the legacy of the occupation?"

"The circuit judge has just said that the law is unconstitutional. So some brave people have pressed on, with a lawsuit. Maybe this is a victory. Which will be appealed, of course." Given how divided the state was, any victory was sure to be equivocal and compromised. "I'm disappointed," said Bry. "I grew up with a liberal father. Even though Mother didn't express herself, Dad did. And Dad said, 'Wisconsin politics are clean. It's nothing like Illinois.' And you know, workmen's compensation was developed in Wisconsin. So that's how I grew up. I'm disappointed in what's happening to Wisconsin now, with its long history that I was educated in by my dad. So now we have a governor who lies, and this new pants-on-fire evaluation scheme. He's got his pants on fire much of the time."

"You've got to explain that to me," I told him.

"I read that recently about Ryan," he said, meaning Congressman and vice presidential candidate Paul Ryan, Republican of Wisconsin. "That his speech had six pants on fire, or something like that."

I was trying to understand why the special election to recall Walker, which had been conceived as a way to press home the occupation's momentum, had failed so miserably. The Democratic Party had put up against Walker the same lukewarm candidate, Milwaukee mayor Tom Barrett, that Walker had defeated in 2010, and he had defeated him again, by a wider margin. Attempts had been made to recruit instead former U.S. Senator Russell Feingold or former Congressman David Obey, to no avail. "Why did Obey and Feingold decline?" I asked Bry.

"I didn't read any excuses, except that they were tired," he answered. "They may have worried about defeat."

"Aren't you mad at Feingold for not stepping up?"

"No. He served well."

We were out and about in Madison, the day after the dinner party. He showed us the new business school building: "This is a product of the Badger football team winning." They hadn't won much back when I was a student; in my day, the football Badgers were reliably ninth in the Big Ten, ahead of Northwestern. Union South, which I remembered, had been torn down. "It was a hideous thing," said Bry. "It was built during the Vietnam War, so the buildings were barricades. Vilas Hall is here. Another of those Vietnam buildings." He indicated a new building. "This is a private apartment building. This is what student affluence has allowed." Along Johnson Street we passed the high-rise Southeast dorms. "Some of these are scheduled to be torn down." And passing Sterling Hall, the physics building bombed by antiwar radicals in 1970, he told an anecdote: "I had a woman faculty member as a patient. And I suggested something and suggested she return in three months or six months or something. And then a colleague asked me,

'Have you read *RADS*?'[1] So I went down to Borders and bought it and read it, and read about the graduate student who was killed. And when my patient came back I said, 'Are you …?' And she said, 'Yes, I'm his widow.' And she said, 'Students today have no knowledge of what went on on campus.'"

✳

As near in time to the fabled sixties as 1983 I had arrived in Madison myself, with little knowledge of all that had gone down. You heard about Sterling Hall, and you saw the actual building, and you were told that the bombing had had to do with the war in Vietnam. And you were made to feel that you had shown up late. Eventually I learned some of what I needed to know, but only because I did my own self-directed reading and then actually went to live in Southeast Asia. My first inkling came in 1985, when I saw *The Killing Fields* with a college friend whose father had been one of South Vietnam's biggest bankers. But I had too little prior information. Born in the year the first U.S. combat troops went to Vietnam, I had grown up in a strange vacuum of silence about the war. By the time I got to Madison, the famous generation gap had been superseded by a new one: Americans old enough to remember the sixties had all staked out their positions and retreated into partisan enclaves, and none of them were explaining any of it to me. Only years later, and only after I goaded him, did one friend erupt in bitter exasperation: the sixties, he said, were about "how the blood of the war got on everyone's hands, and we couldn't wash it off. It's still all over the place."

So, living in Bangkok a decade after seeing the movie and two decades after the fact, I went to see the war's aftermath for myself. "Killing field open tomorrow," said the moto taxi driver on the street outside my hotel in Phnom Penh. "Close today. Flea. Look, no pay." But you paid for the ride there, just like at any tourist site. An Australian colleague and I were in town to write journalism, not history, but when we had a morning free we hired two moto guys to take us to Chheng

---

1 *RADS: The 1970 Bombing of the Army Math Research Center at the University of Wisconsin–Madison and Its Aftermath* (HarperCollins, 1992) by Tom Bates.

Oek, some fifteen kilometers south of the city on bad roads. Mine was a mild-mannered fellow named Leap who told me, when I summoned the nerve to ask, that he was thirty-eight years old. That meant he had been eighteen in 1975, when Phnom Penh fell. His brother had been killed by the Khmer Rouge, who accused him of being with the CIA. "But not true," insisted Leap. "He *not* with CIA!" Leap became a friend, and later he took me to his home village in southeastern Cambodia, the area that had borne the brunt of the secret bombing as the Americans laid the groundwork for their withdrawal from Vietnam. He shared with me then his childhood memory of seeing KR fighters in the tops of palm trees, shooting AK-47s at U.S. helicopters. "Oh, crazy time!" he said.

At Chheng Oek human skulls had been stacked in a wooden tower, and nearby were half a dozen pits, remnants of mass graves. Bones and bits of clothing still littered the ground. Only thirty then, I was cultivating a penchant for seeking out such scenes, not yet knowing how it would leave me bruised. Haitians had told me about a place called Ti Tanyin, where soldiers serving their country's coup regime dumped bodies in mass graves. In disputed Kashmir I had visited the town of Charar-e-Sharief, where the 535-year-old shrine of Sheikh Noorud-din Wali had been destroyed by two fires of disputed origin. And I had seen the factory for disassembling human beings at Auschwitz, which made me feel that if being human means anything, it means to be somehow greater than the sum of our parts. On display were the parts: 12,910 pairs of glasses, 4,358 pairs of trousers, 49,865 teeth. Human hair, shaving brushes, cans of shoe polish, kitchen utensils, artificial legs, crutches, corsets, suitcases.

The other moto driver, Mr. Elephant, began unbidden to tell us stories. His nickname was Elephant because he belonged to the Phnong ethnic minority, so he was bigger than Khmers, with darker skin and a bigger nose. He was my age. He remembered being made to work long into the night in the fields during the Khmer Rouge time, on two small bowls of rice every day. People were so hungry, he said. If you were working away, planting or harvesting rice, and you happened on a lizard or a frog, you would hide it as best you could—he made sneaky, comical pantomime gestures—until you could convince the supervising cadre that you had to go to the bathroom. Then you would slip away and eat it. He had been of foot-soldier age in the years after the Vietnamese invasion of 1979 ended the terror, only to begin the new horror of a civil war that lasted throughout the 1980s. I asked if he had been a soldier. No way, he said. After slaving for the Khmer Rouge, he wasn't about to spend any more of his life working to support anyone in power. When the conscriptors came to his house, his mother told them he wasn't home and—more gestures—"Psht, I go out back door."

"This happened in Europe too," I reflected.

"I know," said Mr. Elephant. "Germany. But they kill another people."

My Australian friend observed that Communists always kill their own people, as the Bolsheviks had done. Same with the Khmer Rouge.

"But democracy alway kill another people," said Mr. Elephant.

＊

The fact that the Badgers were chronically ninth in the Big Ten helped inoculate me against the compulsion to care about the football team. But I was proud of the university itself, and especially of the fact that it was only an hour down the highway from home. I thought it was cool that Rodney Dangerfield came to campus while I was there, to film *Back to School*. More significantly it meant something to me that, as a Wisconsin resident and a good-enough student in a good-enough public high school, I could lay claim to attendance at one of the best universities in America almost as a birthright. If memory serves, my parents paid as little as $700 per semester for my tuition. I didn't know how good I had it. I was determined not to major in history, because that was what my father had majored in, but by my junior year I had taken so many history classes that it was too late for me to major in anything else.

My third year in Madison, I lived in rooms connected to the Episcopal church off campus on University Avenue. Part of the deal was that you understood that the parish was active in the underground railroad harboring refugees from the right-wing regimes in Central America. The rector was a local celebrity and often on the TV news, holding press conferences with our resident refugees, who went by pseudonyms and obscured their faces with bandanas. All of which was fine until one of them started sleeping with one of the female students, with predictable results. When her parents drove down from whatever little town they lived in up north to ask the priest what he was going to do about his refugee impregnating their daughter, he didn't exactly step up to the plate. The daughter was a friend of mine, and I've looked askance ever since at the political left's arrogation of the moral high ground.

I experienced a similar dilemma myself that year but got off the hook when my girlfriend and I walked, on a bitterly cold day in January, to the clinic for a pregnancy test. The store-bought test we had already done had come back positive, and she was six days late. We walked in, and the lady gave her a little plastic cup. She emerged from the restroom a minute later and exclaimed, "I just got my period!" That was my last happy moment with that particular girlfriend.

The possibly unrelated wrenching separation that came a few weeks later propelled me halfway around the planet. It was during that pain-laden next semester that I happened past a bulletin board and saw a flyer pitching COLLEGE YEAR IN NEPAL. Why not?

Kathmandu led eventually to many other Asian adventures. But in the short term, when I returned to the States the next spring, I found that my parents had moved to Colorado. I later realized that that kind of thing happens to a lot of young people while they're off at college, though most aren't as far from home as Nepal. When I returned years later, Madison felt like an abandoned stage set for outdated dramas. Multiple more recent cohorts of students had already churned through and fanned back out around Wisconsin and the world; whatever was now going on in Madison had little to do with me; my favorite professor had left. I had become better equipped to see Madison for what it is: "a giant suburb with a university in the middle."[2]

✻

"Where's that voice?" said John Riggs. "I keep waiting for that voice to come back. It was powerfully current in a lot of people's minds. I had

2 Writer Frank Bures coined that very apt phrase in a terrific article, "The Fall of the Creative Class": http://thirtytwomag.com/2012/06/the-fall-of-thecreative-class/.

the most wonderful conversations with people during that show, and a good eighty percent of them ended up in tears. Now it's like, 'What was that that happened, sometime back there?' I think a lot of people are dealing with that feeling. I think that explains the result of the recall, and I think it explains the fact that the right is going to get its ass whooped in the state of Wisconsin."

I had looked up John the previous spring after learning about his photo book *Inside, at Night – Origins of an Uprising*, a compilation from an exhibition of photos of the occupation, by several photographers. We were sitting in his Tamarack Studio on East Washington Avenue in Madison. John had retired from an engineering career and was now doing photography full time. His former company, Isthmus Engineering, had been featured in Michael Moore's film *Capitalism: A Love Story*. "It was organized as a workers' cooperative," he explained. His next photographic installation was to be called *Letting Go – A Meditation on the Tamarack Tree, Its Environment, and the Meaning of Loss*. "The tamarack bog is one of the last places where I can feel like civilization has never been here, and might never be here," he told me. "I'm going to take the risk and go out on a limb and put myself out there emotionally. Isn't that what artists are supposed to do? I'm on the leading edge of the baby boom. I'll be seventy years old in a couple of weeks. As a photographer, as an artist, and just as a human being, I feel a sense of responsibility. There are a lot of issues that I'm facing in my personal life that have got to be out there all over the place. How do you deal with these things? I'm just going on faith that it won't be embarrassing to deal with intensely personal things."

In the coming election, John was cautiously enthusiastic about a woman named Tammy Baldwin, who was running for a U.S. Senate seat against the Republican former governor and Bush cabinet member Tommy Thompson. "Is she going to win?" I asked him.

"Well, it's looking like she and Obama are cresting the same wave. She was behind, and now she's pulled even and it looks like she's pulling ahead."

I had met John and his son, Arthur Kohl-Riggs, back in the spring, before the recall vote. Art was 23 years old, boyish and lanky, and sported a reddish beard-without-mustache to cultivate a vague resemblance to Abraham Lincoln. The legacy of the great Wisconsin governor "Fighting Bob" La Follette was back in currency, and Art's idea had been to run against Walker in the primary as a self-styled "Lincoln-La Follette Republican." His thinking was that defeating Walker in the Republican primary would obviate the need for a recall. Art didn't win, but he sure had a good idea. He had been written about in *The New Yorker*. He gave me a brochure and an "Art for Gov" campaign button.

John was extremely proud of Art. "He had hundreds of people lining up to help, and simply because he was willing to step up ahead of the crowd," he said. "That's what leadership is, standing up ahead of the crowd. He firmly believes that to get through to people who believe differently than you do, the only way to do it is through humor. And that's why he dressed like Abe Lincoln."

I asked Art and his girlfriend, Harriet, to explain the recall result to me.

"I think I saw it coming," said Harriet.

"My efforts were focused on ..." said Art.

"Getting yourself elected!" said Harriet.

"Yeah, getting myself elected, and exposing the lies of Walker."

"It was literally the same campaign as it was two years ago," said Harriet. "And there was a reason Walker won that time, too."

"Exactly the same," agreed Art. "Barrett made a point of not being labor's candidate. So he did not make any union issues his issues. He announced that he was running for governor just after Rahm Emanuel

came to Wisconsin and hosted a fundraiser for him. He wasn't particularly the champion of anything that the people participating in the recall movement would have wanted. Except for not being Walker. Had Barrett won the recall, a lot of people would have felt good about getting rid of Walker, and Barrett wouldn't have done much to change anything."

"Do you wish that Feingold had run?"

"If he had played an entirely different role," said Art. "If he had from the beginning taken a forward role. But he had kind of denounced the whole thing and said, 'I'm stepping back.' The crackdown at the capitol has been going on," he added.

"You mean with the Capitol Police?"

"Yeah. And I think that's a pretty good frame for looking at Walker from." New policies were in place limiting public access to the building. "Both the *State Journal* and the *Journal-Sentinel* had op-eds saying that it's going too far. It really shows Walker's disregard for Wisconsin traditions and values." And a new prohibition against carrying signs was being harshly enforced. People had been arrested for holding an 8½"-by-11" sheet of paper with the article of the Wisconsin state constitution guaranteeing right to peaceable assembly printed on it. "I was arrested for holding a sign saying 'We [heart] blood donors,'" said Art.

"People think the Capitol Police are just, like, building guards," he went on. "In reality, they have jurisdiction all around the state." During the occupation, there had been "hundreds of police there at any one time. It was a show of force. But they were entirely hands-off throughout the occupation. After that the chief of police started getting a lot of politics that 'He's being too nice to the protesters.' A friend of ours was strapped to a gurney for taking part in drumming. At the time, they said it was standard protocol for someone being non-compliant."

"I'm sad that we left, in retrospect," said Harriet. "It didn't feel good. It felt like we were being told to leave or we would get charged with felonies."

"Most recently they're going to people's homes and workplaces," said Art, "targeting people who held up banners. The police don't stop them from doing it at the time, but afterwards they show up at people's houses."

"Boy, that's intimidating!" I said.

"Yes, very much so. Last week a disabled veteran, this woman, her name's Dawn, was sort of shipping out of the building, the police kind of bum-rush her. I found out yesterday that a woman who filed a complaint got a citation in the mail for obstruction, for an incident where the police shoved her and she complained about it. And presumably the only reason they knew her name and address was because she filed a complaint. There were two women who were holding t-shirts. The blood drive was going over here. Her and this other woman were both handcuffed and taken downstairs and told they would be arrested."

Art and Harriet had put videos of this sort of thing on YouTube. "Can you share some of this video with me?" I asked.

"Yep," said Art. "It's got 41,000 views in the couple weeks since I put it up. One of my more popular videos."[3]

Harriet told me that if you googled her name, Harriet Rowan, the first item that came up would be a ten-minute video that she had shared with Amy Goodman's group Democracy Now! "I got to show them a lot of things that other people didn't get to see," she said.

"Somebody was arrested for holding a crucifix," said Art.

"Our friend Craig," said Harriet. "He was kind of violently arrested, too."

"They dragged him over these rows of chairs, and he had horrible bruises all over him," said Art.

"You can wear a t-shirt," Harriet explained. "You can pin or sew a sign onto your t-shirt. But if you hold a sign, you get arrested. It's ridiculous."

✳

Driving east on Interstate 94 from Madison through rural Jefferson County, beside the freeway was one of those American warehouse appliance and electronics stores. In later years they spread around the country, but when I was growing up it was American of Madison, and the owner was Crazy TV Lenny. He did his own commercials: "Get a bike, get a bike, get a bike! Buy a refrigerator—*get a bike!* Buy a TV—*get a bike!*" I also drove now past pro-Walker and anti-Obama billboards, some of them homemade and stuck in the ground on private land. Off the last freeway exit heading east in Jefferson County is Watertown. They used to be our high school football rivals, probably still are:

---

3 "Wisconsin Capitol Police Abridge Freedom of Speech" on YouTube account arthurkr222. See also the Wisconsin Citizen Media Coop, wcmcoop.com.

I'm a raindrop, I'm a raindrop,
I'm a raindrop falling down
But I'd rather be a raindrop
than a drip from Watertown.

Then, just over the line in Waukesha County, is Oconomowoc. You can tell it's coming up by the manmade ski hill that looms out of nowhere over the otherwise gently rolling landscape. Looming now on the other side of I-94, where a cornfield used to be, is a huge new hospital opened in 2010 by the Aurora Health Care system. Thirty miles further east is Milwaukee on the shore of Lake Michigan, and that's part of the point of Oconomowoc: to be near enough to Milwaukee that you can get there if you want to, say for a Brewers game or for Summerfest, but far enough away that you can ignore and disavow the things and people there that you don't like. There are towns like Oconomowoc in suburban counties all over America.

But there's only one actual Oconomowoc. I felt at home there when I was growing up largely, I now think, by force of will, because I felt a need to feel at home somewhere. My parents strove to emphasize that it wasn't really our home, and ultimately they, and the passage of time, got the point across. But change is hard, as Barry Ott pointed out to me, and a lot of things have changed since 1974.

That's the year we moved to Oconomowoc from the lakeshore suburb of Whitefish Bay. We had moved to Whitefish Bay three years earlier from New Hampshire because University School of Milwaukee, the local private school, offered my dad a job as head of the history department. Many years later he reflected that he should have known that to be a dumb move, even to become a department head, because the school he left was one of the most prestigious boarding schools in New England. "You don't ask to be traded from a pennant winner," he said. But he and my mother hadn't felt at home at Exeter anyway: "We were country cousins." It didn't matter after all, though, because within three years he had left teaching. We moved to Oconomowoc so he could attend the Nashotah House seminary and become an Episcopal priest. We lived in a rented duplex at 1100A Lowell Drive, behind the Whitman Park shopping center. In 1977, the year he turned forty, my father graduated from Nashotah House, was ordained a priest and, as the lingo has it, was called to be vicar of St. Mary's in Dousman, a seven-mile straight shot south on Highway 67 from downtown Oconomowoc.

The effect for me and my brother was what I see in hindsight as an artificially stable upbringing in Oconomowoc. But isn't all stability artificial? We moved to a house in town, at 400 South Silver Lake Street. Our neighbor, Mr. Wenck, had lived in the big house next door since the turn of the century. He had a barn at the end of his driveway, and an albino squirrel came and went through a hole in its roof. Mrs. Wenck was frail and nice and gave us gross blue candies that we had to accept out of politeness. Mr. Wenck wore overalls and spent most of his time sitting on a bench in back of his house, smoking a pipe. He hired me to cut his lawn with his manual mower, and when my friend Johnny Rabe, who lived two doors down on the other side, stopped by to shoot the breeze, Mr. Wenck told him, "Don't bother my man while he's workin'!" Johnny thought that line was really funny and repeated it many times.

A couple houses the other side of the Wencks lived the McGarveys, Irish Catholics with eleven kids. Their house was a dump, which bugged my dad. Relations were cool at the parental level, but one good thing was that, until the McGarveys got called in for dinner, we usually had enough kids for baseball or kick the can. Mr. McGarvey was a skilled mason and was always running for mayor against the incumbent, Florence Whalen. Mrs. Whalen and her husband Dick, who taught at the high school, lived on my *Milwaukee Journal* route, which never made me any money and was really cold in the winter but, so I'm told, built character. The Caseys were Whalen supporters.

On my American road trip I spent two weeks in Wisconsin, longer than any other place. One reason was topical: the still-recent capitol occupation and the state's political polarization. Another was geographic: it was on the way from Seattle to points east. But the main reason was personal: Wisconsin had been my home. Thus too it was available to me in a way that Missouri or Indiana would not have been. And Wisconsin is at once utterly distinctive and thoroughly representative: middle-class, middle-western America, writ medium-sized. And Oconomowoc is quintessential Wisconsin: so typical that it isn't typical anymore.

And that was part of what felt strange to me about Oconomowoc now, when I returned specifically looking for change: it really hadn't changed. In the seventies, the sign at the town limits said *Pop. 8,741.* After the 1980 census, that was updated to 9,909. Now it was 15,712. So it had grown, a bit. And where Summit School had been along Highway 67 on the way into town from the Interstate, where I had attended fourth through sixth grades, was now a strip mall. And Chuck's Supper Club on Silver Lake, where Bill Henning and I had been Junior Kiwanians for a month and where Elmer the elderly bartender had served us even though he figured, in my case correctly, that we were underage, was now called something else. And St. Jerome's, the Catholic church and school, had moved. And the Shorehaven nursing home had expanded. So, sure, Oconomowoc had changed. But really, it hadn't changed at all.

What was spooky was that it had to have taken real effort on Oconomowoc's part to not change. Change is normal; people, places, and things are supposed to change. I had changed. But then, I had left Oconomowoc. Feldschneider's, the family-owned grocery store and butcher walking distance from our house, where my mother kept a charge account she paid off monthly, was gone. But Winger's bar was still there, unchanged. The overgrown field between the end of Lowell Drive and the Olympia resort and its ski hill, where we had explored the basement of a ruined farmhouse and scrounged for vintage beer cans, was now an apartment complex. But the Pagenkopf Funeral Home was still there, and so was The Chocolate Factory, the ice cream place that now proudly boasted of having been in business since 1972, as if that were a long time ago. So was the Ben Franklin store that I had almost burned down. My mother was in the Ben Franklin shopping when the foam from the fire extinguisher I had been compelled to use came billowing out into the store from the stockroom, where I had failed to break down boxes sufficiently to push them into the furnace. "We have a new boy," the checkout woman explained to her. Mr. Johnson, the manager, explained to me: "Three strikes, and you're out." The fire was strike two, so I lucked out when Bill Henning got me a job washing dishes with him in the hospital kitchen. On my last day at Ben Franklin I ran into the owner and he said, "I guess retail's not your thing." No, Mr. Ray, retail was never gonna be my thing.

Some things in the now-vintage Whitman Park strip mall had changed. The Coast to Coast hardware store where Brewers infielder Don Money had signed my glove was no longer there. And one change for the better was that the bookstore, which had been a sorry little place called The Little Professor, was now bigger, better, renamed Books & Company, and clearly attentive to its role as a community institution. The owner, Lisa Baudoin, booked me to do a little event about my book on Haiti and, of the seven people who showed up, three were fellow OHS Class of '83 alums, and two were Mr. and Mrs. Whalen.

Jill, Jill, and Jamie were now middle-aged moms. The Whalens were nearly eighty but otherwise unchanged. Mrs. Whalen told me I was the best paperboy they had ever had. She must have meant it, because I was no longer a constituent and she had retired from politics. She said that when they moved down from Duluth fifty years earlier, she had told her husband, "This is the town I want to live in." Jill Worner, now Jill Riemann, was brainy and had played Lucy in Mr. Pasante's Cooney High production of *You're a Good Man, Charlie Brown*. She looked the part but was nice in real life. I thought I remembered that she had been my rival for top of the class, but she insisted that that had been Jenny Brown, who was also head cheerleader and girlfriend of the quarterback. Jill Redzinski, now Jill Radi, had moved to Waukesha and raised a daughter and a son. She and yet another Jill, Jill Schmitz, had worked with me and Bill in the hospital kitchen. One of the perks of that job was getting to ogle the Jills' rear ends in those white hospital uniforms.

I was there to talk about Haiti, but I emphasized that it had been through St. Mary's, just down the road, and the Episcopal Diocese of Milwaukee that I first went to Haiti; that those two trips as a teenager had exposed me to the outside world in a big way, but that embracing Haiti had not required rejecting Oconomowoc; that, even so, I had never come all the way home but had kept going, all the way to Pakistan. Now, I said, I wanted to find out what it might mean to see Wisconsin with the eyes of someone who had seen all that I had seen overseas. We talked about the Madison capitol occupation and how it had started because Governor Walker had tried to strip teachers and other state employees of their right to collective bargaining. "It was the public schools that were supposed to be bringing everyone together," remembered Mrs. Whalen, with a note of incredulous wistfulness. She also remembered: "Nobody ever asked me, when I ran for local office, 'Are you a Democrat or a Republican?' There's not a Democratic or a Republican way of plowing the streets or building the parks."

I noted how divided America and Wisconsin seemed to have become, but I stepped lightly because these were my old friends. "You just don't enter into the conversation, because it's just so painful," said Jill Radi. "The emotion's so high because you can't even listen." She remembered how united the country had seemed after September 11, 2001.

"Is that what it takes?" asked Jill. "And will we ever get there again?"

✳

A few days later I met Dr. Tom Jackson, retired from Aurora Health Care and now living near Oconomowoc and volunteering in a clinic at a church in Milwaukee. I wanted in particular to understand what the deal was with the huge new Aurora Summit hospital that now loomed on the Dousman side of the Dousman/Oconomowoc exit off I-94. Oconomowocians looked askance at the Summit hospital because they already had Oconomowoc Memorial Hospital, right next to the high school, where Bill and Jill and I had washed dishes.

"I think this is part of what's happening in health care all over the place," Dr. Jackson told me. "It's competing health systems. And even more so, it's competing health systems for people with money. As you're probably aware, it's interesting living out in Waukesha County and dealing with people's attitudes towards Milwaukee. Summit is a site to capture people with money around Waukesha for the Aurora Health Care System. The issue is that there isn't a need for that many hospital beds in that area. My impression is that both of those hospitals are sitting half empty. When Wilkinson Clinic joined Aurora, or when Aurora bought Wilkinson, however you want to put it, that created all kinds of issues for the health care system in Oconomowoc. One thing we heard from Wilkinson docs was that ProHealth, which owns Memorial, was not happy. I think that was one of the things that pushed Aurora to build Summit Hospital. And obviously Aurora's got a big advantage in terms of being right out on the freeway, versus Oconomowoc Memorial being in town and not visible. It reflects this consolidation of health care into big corporate entities."

"It's the services following the suburban money," I suggested.

"Exactly. And to do that, you have to build the big fancy facilities, to compete. Have you been in the Summit Hospital?"

"No."

"Just walk in the lobby and look at all the paneling. It's a beautiful facility. But it's three-fourths empty, and they haven't opened all the floors that were meant to be opened."

I told him that I remembered catching the Badger Bus to Madison next to a cornfield, where the hospital was now.

"That was that way until the hospital was built," he said. "That was still farmland. The other thing that happened around the time it opened was that the economy hit the skids. There were huge plans for that whole Pabst Farms area on the other side of the freeway. And now Columbia St. Mary's in Ozaukee County is suffering since Aurora opened that fancy hospital in Grafton. ProHealth is putting up a big building in New Berlin. They're all doing it. Some people would see Aurora as the villain. I think they're the biggest, so in some sense the villain, but they're not doing anything different than the other systems. All these systems are taking on a lot of debt, which adds to their costs, which drives the cost of health care up."

"One of the things that was really jarring to me when I came back to the States," I told him, "after thirteen years living overseas, was the commercialization of medicine."

He nodded. "The pharmaceutical ads."

"And the billboards all up and down the freeway, for the rival hospitals," I said. "It's cheesy and undignified."

"Yes, it is," he agreed.

＊

Someone told me anecdotally that Waukesha County was the third-most thoroughly Republican county in the United States, after two counties in Texas. That was a jarring piece of new information to try to incorporate into my sense of home. I had been away too long and taken too much for granted. So I went into my meeting with Cathy  Waller, the executive director of the Republican Party of Waukesha County, with mixed feelings. We met in a small room upstairs at the party office in a little strip mall somewhere in Waukesha. She let me take a picture of her smiling at a conference table, with a painting of a majestic-looking wild elephant on the wall behind her. She couldn't have been nicer to me.

She spoke warmly of Tommy Thompson, the former governor and Bush official who was now running for a Senate seat. "He was just so Wisconsin," she gushed, in the past tense. I wondered whether he might not be getting a little long in the tooth.

"He's seventy-one," she said.

"And he *wants* to be in the Senate?"

"Yes, yes. It's all about his knowledge in the health care field."

She confirmed proudly that Waukesha County was "the number one Republican county in the state of Wisconsin." I asked her about the capitol occupation. "You're in Madison, and they're just so aggressively verbal there," she complained. "My kids are in public schools. Their teacher doesn't know what I do for a living. I want her to be there for my daughters. We're here for the teachers, not for the unions." But teachers and schools had to show results, just like businesses. She had worked for the Kohl's department store chain, which started in Wisconsin. "It was my job, just like it's a teacher's job, to get them to turn things around. I think that's our biggest problem: we come from two different worlds."

So was it possible for people like her to find common ground with Madison liberals?

"I'm going to be honest: I don't know if we can. We're not going to get anywhere."

"But don't we need to get somewhere?"

"It's just going to take time to show that these things are working. The numbers are working. We're already in the plus. It just needs time." The teachers could have adequate health insurance, if only they wouldn't insist on being unionized. "If they chose to give up their union dues, the numbers pretty much even out."

I asked her about Scott Walker himself.

"They don't know the man that we know. He truly is good-intentioned and means so much." And Paul Ryan was "just an amazing person, an amazing wealth of information."

"Democrats and people like Paul Krugman would disagree with you," I said.

"But they're wrong."

"Do you think Ryan has helped Romney?"

"Yes. He can explain in layman's terms that this is going to work for them. To be honest, Ethan, whoever it was, they would have just gone crazy."

What about the widespread impression that the Republicans were a party only for white people?

"I think that's changing. That's definitely out there. I was at the national convention. They tried to bring out more minority speakers, like Marco Rubio. But yeah, we definitely have a lot of work to do in that area. And immigration, yeah, that's a huge issue. And Hispanics are so conservative. It's faith and family. I have two daughters, and one of them is dating a Hispanic guy."

Waukesha County had made the news for allegations of funny business in the counting of votes, as if Wisconsin were some kind of Third World country like Florida.

"There's absolutely nothing there," Cathy insisted. "She downloaded the votes, but somehow it just didn't get to our Waukesha County clerk. They caught it right away. But because it's Waukesha County, and they know we're the big gorilla in the state, they're going to try anything they can."

What about Republican attempts to tighten ID requirements for voting?

"That is one of the hugest arguments that's going on right now. There were two Dane County judges that blocked it." Dane County was code for liberal Madison. "And all it was was showing your driver's license."

"And you think it's not onerous to require people to show their driver's license?"

"No. We think we definitely need to do this."

"Why are you a Republican?" I asked her. "And what kind of America do you want to live in?"

"Honestly, I really want to tell you, it was working at Kohl's." She had also been influenced negatively, by high tax rates and by Bill Clinton and "everything that was going on with him, and the whole Monica Lewinsky situation. And I started listening to Rush Limbaugh, and he said, 'It's not enough just to vote. Get involved.' And I listen to the Tea Party people, and they say, 'Oh, you're just a Republican.' And I say, 'Hey, I was a Tea Party person long before you were!'"

So what about the Tea Party people, anyway?

"We welcome them in. We attend their rallies, and they come to ours. If it's fiscal issues, that's what we're about in Waukesha County."

I asked her about Romney's infamous comment insinuating that forty-seven percent of Americans were freeloaders.

"They need to understand that there's those of us who do pay taxes, and they don't contribute."

"Is Romney going to win?"

"Oh, I want to say yes. It's fifty-fifty and whoever gets the grassroots out. That's always the way it is, but it's true."

I thanked her for her time, took that picture of her, a cheerful, pleasant-looking blond woman under the elephant painting, and got up to leave.

"It feels like we're at each other's throats, and it doesn't feel good," I said as we shook hands.

"Yep," she agreed. "Definitely in the state of Wisconsin we are."

＊

Then I had a long lunch with Elisa Miller at a Mexican restaurant in the suburb of Menomonee Falls, also in Waukesha County. YMCA Camp Minikani, where I had been a camper and counselor, was near-by. So was the venerable Ernie Von Schledorn car dealership, famous for the catchy jingle in its TV commercials. Elisa was a former school-teacher in her thirties who had become a Democratic Party activist but was now feeling burned out. By choice she had done her political work here, in the Republican-dominated Fifth Congressional District.

"You have this white horseshoe of racist crap, and that was my area," she told me. "People were afraid to put yard signs in their yards. Just being a Democrat was very different out here. I remember telling my boss that my number one goal was to get people to put a yard sign in their yard, a bumper sticker, and protest. If all we do is ship people to Milwaukee because that's where the Democrats are, then we never shift our Fifth CD. I feel a Democrat in a Republican area has to be so much more informed than a Democrat in the Madison area, where liberals will eat their own because you're not liberal enough. Madison gets so wrapped up in the ideal that we forget the process, and we forget that not everybody is ready for radical change.

"I'm not a big fan of Republicans," she added. "They're arrogant. I've met some good ones in my day, but those are a different breed." As an example of a non-good Republican she cited Congressman Jim Sensenbrenner representing this very district, who had been around forever. "He's the one who said Michelle Obama had a big butt."

"Did he really say that publicly?" I asked.

"Yeah. If you google 'Jim Sensenbrenner large posterior Michelle Obama,' it'll come up. That's the kind of Republican we have around here."

I had found Elisa through the website of the campaign of state senate candidate Lori Compas, "an average person who thought that Scott Fitzgerald needed to be taken down," as Elisa described her. Fitzgerald was the Republican majority leader of the state senate and a close ally of Governor Scott Walker. "I could work on a multitude of political campaigns. But a lot of those aren't the Lori Compases. Lori Compas's campaign made Scott Fitzgerald spend $200,000 that he wouldn't have had to spend. That's why we have a 72-county strategy in Wisconsin. Almost like building a farm team, building a bench. So even if we don't win, we one, push our platform and two, force them to spend money."

I asked Elisa to tell me her own story.

"My brothers are all cops and teachers, and their wives are teachers," she said. "So I come from a family of public service. I come from a family where giving was the norm. I watched my dad as a pastor, and my mom as a pastor's wife, make service to the community a priority. We couldn't eat lunch until my dad was finished shaking hands with everyone in the receiving line. There were many nights when my dad would get a call from a police officer to transport a homeless person or give them a hot meal. Or a hospital visit to be with the family of a dying parishioner. So I always saw sacrifice, and giving to the community, as a priority. And I think that's why I gravitate to that. As much as it was a curse to be a pastor's kid, it was one of the greatest blessings."

I asked what her religion had to do with her politics.

"I affiliate as an ELCA Lutheran, but I really believe in some of the Buddhist teachings. My parents are very cool Christians. My brother voted for Obama in '08, but he's a very traditional Republican in the sense that these churches tell you what to think. It's the laziest way of living that I can think of. These churches prey on people who have addictions."

"He's Missouri Synod?" I guessed.

"He's Assembly of God," she said. "A.k.a. batshit crazy. When I went to his church, I could see why he believes what he believes politically too."

Elisa had been motivated to get involved in politics because "I would feel guilty that this is my country, and I didn't do what I could." As a teacher she had felt "like an enabler, like an alcoholic, but with the education system. You think the Mitt Romneys are selfish now? Wait until these CEOs hit twenty years from now. I never truly had hope until Obama ran. That was my first infusion of hope. Obama's people, especially in '08, were different."

Bluntly, I asked her: "Why don't I give a shit about him anymore, when in '08 I was so excited?"

"One is that Bush was so bad, and he was not Bush. But I like how he doesn't drink our Kool-Aid. I appreciated the creativity, the pragmatic part of it. And I don't think we as a people had the patience for the pragmatism. You don't show up to a gunfight with a knife. At some point he has to fight fire with fire, and change things from the inside out."

"Yeah, that's not a fault of him personally," I allowed. "It's a problem with society, with all of us."

"Yeah. And that's where I get jaded, you know?" She brought it back to the personal. She had gone through a difficult divorce, and "Obama just gave me hope that there was more to life." The economic crisis had been good for her: "I've been able to tame the American habits of consumption and over-indulgence. I've learned a lot from it. I was always the girl that was like, 'Oh, there's a new shampoo out? I'll try that.' But when you're unemployed, you use a bottle of shampoo until it's gone. When Walker said there's a one-week waiting period for unemployment, I know what that one week is like."

Losing in 2010, when she campaigned for Tom Barrett and Russell Feingold, had been difficult. "There are so many things that can trump hard work and ambition, and I had never experienced that. I'm trying not to be jaded in all of that. Trying not to lose faith in the candidate, trying not to lose faith in the process. There's nothing worse than a lame candidate. Tom Barrett. But even Feingold, who is awesome, is not the same Feingold who campaigned in front of his garage in Middleton."

In that year of the Tea Party, the Democratic office in Washington County had encountered what could be interpreted as a death threat. "Our field organizer was walking into the office in the morning, and a driver drove by in a truck and did like the shooting fingers. And then she just went in and was like, 'Whatever,' and went about her day. And it was a couple hours later that she left to use the restroom. She had to use a public restroom that was outside of the building and around a corner. When she returned, in front of the door was a bag of acorns, with a note that said something to the effect of, 'Obama better watch his back. There's fifty sharpshooters in the state, times that by fifty.' On the back was an invite to a recent Tea Party rally."

"Was it enough of a news item that people outside of Wisconsin might remember it?"

"I don't think so. Even Wisconsin didn't really pick it up. I think it was on the five o'clock news and never revisited. And only because our spokesperson, Graeme Zielinski, pushed it onto the news. I think it only got on like one news station. About a week after that, a volunteer was driving on a rural highway. So some traffic, but not a major highway. And she saw a children's play set with a noose hanging from it and a sign that said, 'Obama's Play Set.' By the time she told us and we said, 'Yeah, that's important, we better report that,' it had been pulled down. Within two days. This doesn't just affect Obama. This is domestic terrorism. Volunteers are like, 'You want me to knock on doors, when those crazies live out there?'"

Obama had been criticized for supporting Barrett during the June 2012 gubernatorial recall election with exactly one tweet.

"I think it was strategic," Elisa said. "He was being cautious. If people have such visceral hatred for Obama, does it really bring in the independent voters or only rally the base?"

"Which base?"

"It would have only appeased the strong Democrats. And you're right, it would have also rallied the anti-base to come out more. If Obama had stood behind Barrett 110 percent and Barrett would have lost, it would have been attributed to Obama. As much as we would have wanted him to come out more strong, he's really good at rope-a-dope politics."

"But the question is, when is he going to come back out of the corner?" I asked.

"Being a teacher, everybody was really upset that Obama didn't come out for the union," she said. "He didn't put on shoes, like he said he would."

"He said he was going to put on shoes?"

"He said he'd put on tennis shoes and walk the line with them. So I think he needs to own thirty percent, his lack of support. But at the end of the day, when people were so mad that he didn't come, I was like, 'I work for him, and I'm here.' He allowed his staff to collaborate. So his face wasn't here, but he allowed his resources to be used. But also, even the Democratic Party of Wisconsin didn't become the face of the movement. Because 37 or 38 percent of union members voted Republican, for Walker. Had this become a partisan movement, those 37 percent would have just gravitated back to their candidate. At the end of the day, this had to be about workers and their rights."

Wisconsin's toxic public atmosphere had affected her directly both as a political activist and as a teacher. "Hating teachers," she said. "Not just thinking a few are bad. I've never heard such horrible things. I've never seen such hatred. Every week I get harassed in my car. People will honk their horns and go, 'Fuck you.' And my stickers are Obama '08, Tom Barrett, Russ Feingold, and Jimi Hendrix: 'When the power of love overcomes the love of power, the world will know peace.' And I literally get harassed. One guy stuck his head out and said, 'Fuck you! Scott Walker!' Another guy pulled up and said, 'Are you okay?' And I'm thinking it's my gas cap or something. And I said, 'Yeah, I'm okay.' And he goes, 'Well, I don't think you're okay. I think you're the reason the country's going down the hole,' and whatever. I'm afraid. I actually am afraid of the world we live in. We're at a very pivotal moment. Whatever road we choose sets us up for decades."

✳

"I'm bothered that our society has gotten to a point where issues of importance are not really discussed," said Moshe. "There's a lot of gray in between that we ought to be able to talk about. I'm very disheartened that in dogmatic communities, their dogma dictates what their lifestyle ought to be. It's rare, even amongst friends, at a time when, this time of year, as a Jew I'm looking to find that spiritual space."

Moshe Katz was a real estate developer, a handsome fiftyish man, evidently in the prime of life. He carried himself with confidence and a bit of flair. I met him at the Comet Cafe downtown and at his office, and then he drove me around the city in his convertible.

"We need to share our stories," he said. "Last week my son, who's a junior in high school, had a parent-teachers night. The teacher's theme was, 'What is America?' It seemed like a nice enough teacher, nice enough class." Moshe had chosen to talk to the kids about the civil rights movement, and afterwards his son had asked him, "Why would you do that? Why wouldn't you talk about Israel?"

"Even to my own kid, I've become stereotyped," Moshe bemoaned. "'Dad's the Hebrew guy, Dad's the Israel guy.'" He had told the students: "This is our history. You need to know this."

"There's a wonderful line in our Passover meal that says, 'In every generation, every person has to see themselves as if they came out of Egypt,'" he told me. "I don't think I would have had that perspective if I hadn't had grandparents from another country. Parents who were first-generation. My mom's a teacher. And my dad was one of those that—thank God that he chose good obsessions. He chose art, he chose travel, he chose certain stuff that made our collective lives really enjoyable. Getting to travel, getting to see the world at a young age, counts for a lot. My dad and mom both grew up in Milwaukee. My grandparents all came from Russia and from Poland."

"Why?"

"On my mom's side of the family a good chunk of them were killed in the Holocaust. Literally the ones that got out survived, and those that didn't didn't."

When I told him I had grown up in Oconomowoc, he told me about the time he ran into a man who said to him, "Mr. Katz, where I come from we have no anti-Semitism."

"Where is this haven?" Moshe had asked the guy.

35

"I'm from Oconomowoc. We don't allow Jews out there."

"There's a side of Oconomowoc that is the wonderful beauty of America," Moshe said to me. "But then there's another whole side of it that's more than scary."

I had sought out Moshe because I wanted this book to include the voice of at least one staunchly pro-Israel American Jew. I got that and more. And I needed to find more to Moshe, because I needed to get beyond stereotypes and cant and entrenched positions. I had become pretty entrenched myself, because of something that had happened to a friend of mine. My friend Kathy Sheetz was in the flotilla sailing with aid supplies from Cyprus toward the Gaza Strip on May 31, 2010 when it was boarded in international waters by the Israeli Navy. Kathy was not one of the nine people killed in that incident, but she was imprisoned in Israel, her cell phone was confiscated, and for several days her family didn't know whether she was alive.

Moshe told me he had lived in Israel as a child. "I was seven years old in 1967," he said. He had been there during the Yom Kippur War and the massacre of Israeli Olympians in 1972. "Being a kid in that kind of setup was kind of weird." He remembered people painting their car headlights black and digging trenches. And he had returned to live in Israel as an adult, from 1984 to 1989. "To me it's just like, 'Should air be?'" he said. "To not have a Jewish place in the world is just silly. I believed in the dream that the greatest place a Jew can fulfill their destiny is Israel."

"Do you still believe that?"

"Ultimately yes, but realistically no. My being a plumber in Israel still has something to do with the country they're trying to build. But that doesn't mean American Jews can't live in America and live happy, fulfilled Jewish lives."

"Can an American Jew live a fulfilled American life?"

"Absolutely."

"Is there a contradiction between being fully Jewish and being fully American?"

"I think it's the opposite. There are some really powerful American lessons that are also powerful Jewish lessons."

He had taken his children to see the Nazi camps, and he had told them: "I want to take you to the camps, but I'm not going to go to the camps and then go play in Europe. If we're going to the camps, we're going to Israel."

"It was intense," he told me. "It was an incredibly powerful experience."

"Like me going to Haiti at sixteen."

"And you keep going back for more," he pointed out. "Too much teaching is, 'They tried to kill us, we won, let's eat.'"

"How do you counter that, as a parent?"

"There's so much more to Jewish life."

I asked him directly about my concern, as a citizen, that my country's foreign policy and domestic politics seemed skewed by an overriding priority in favor of Israel.

"The simplest answer is that we don't have a better ally in the Middle East," he said. "We're doing nothing to the Palestinians. Why has nobody absorbed the Palestinian people? We absorbed ourselves. And the same thing could be said of the Palestinians. At some point somebody has to take care of them, including themselves. I'm angry at Israel for one thing: in the 1970s, we should have built them a port. There are now Syrians coming into Israel. The Negev is now bordering a potentially horrifically hostile neighbor in the Sinai. There have been billions of dollars squandered by the leadership of the Palestinians. Land isn't the issue. Israel left Gaza. Why is the Palestinian question Israel's problem only, when it's at least Jordan's and a portion Egypt's? Give me a solution that gives me the right to exist."

"Maybe they don't want you to be their neighbor," I suggested.

"If that's really the case, there's really nothing to talk about."

Then he took me on a tour of what I thought of as Moshe's Milwaukee, starting with the Third Ward: south of I-794, west of Lake Michigan, east of the Milwaukee River. "It originally had a lot more older buildings, small factories, small businesses," Moshe said. "Principally an Italian community. There was a horrific fire down here, and it took out a whole lot of properties. There's been a terrific revitalization here. That's the good news. The bad news is that when you gentrify a neighborhood, that which you moved there for moves out. There's a lot of character still here, but it's in the buildings, not the people. A lot of that original charm of the neighborhood is not here anymore. This is where all the vendors were," he added, at the corner of Buffalo and Broadway.

"My dad's dad died when he was fourteen years old," he continued. "He left him a rooming house, a car, and a share in the family business. The first building they built was on Wells Street. My dad built the properties there when it was a nothing neighborhood, and left before it became a bad neighborhood. He was much more interested in the long hold. In a lot of cases, the properties that my dad died with were the properties that he built in the 1960s. That's it," he said, at Fifth and Cherry. "Where the chain-link fence is. This is where my grandfather's shop was. For a while I thought, 'Do I want to own this?'"

"Couldn't you build something on it?" I asked.

"You could, but there's nothing to be built here," he said. "As a real estate person, you must have a sense of smell."

He showed me the Golda Meir School, named for the great Israeli leader, born in Russia, raised in Milwaukee. "I think it's a wonderful statement that there's a Golda Meir School in Milwaukee. I also think it's wonderful that there's not one Jewish child in that school."

"She was a tough cookie," I remarked.

"She was," he agreed. "She was everything good and bad in the world. There were three neighborhoods that were consistently Jewish. One was the west side. The other is this area, Fourth and Cherry, and the other is Shorewood and Fox Point, the north shore suburbs." More recently Jews had moved further north, to Mequon and other affluent suburbs in Ozaukee County.

He pointed out mid-century apartment buildings at 2131, 2260 and 2233 Summit. "This is a building my dad built. These buildings already existed. And, at the time, all the rest of this street was like this. I managed these properties with my dad for twenty years. They changed the community by building these buildings in them. My dad really believed in providing fair, clean, nice housing, family priced, in a great location. And this is still a great location. These were built in the sixties, and here we are fifty years later."

"You're proud of that," I said.

"I'm proud of the fact that I've owned buildings. For a while our motto was, 'A Place for You to Call Home.' I love that I employ people.

The fact that a Jew has that kind of a relationship is important to me. If I can have a wonderful life, and send my kids to college, and drive around in a nice car, along the way I'd better be doing more than that."

"You're well situated, I gotta say," I said. I wouldn't have minded being so well situated.

"I am," he agreed. "This is gonna sound really, really corny, but I still believe in the American Dream."

He reminisced about a certain tenant. "When her mother died, the daughter sent us the ad that her mother had seen in the *Milwaukee Journal* for the apartment. She had seen the ad when the building was built. Weets was her name. She lived in the apartment when she was a child with her parents and her sister. And then she went off to school, and then she came back." Years later work had needed to be done on her apartment. "She literally moved across the hall. And we said, 'Weets, if you'd like to continue living in the other apartment, you can.' And she said, 'I think I'd like to go back home.'" Weets eventually succumbed to dementia, and her family moved her to a nearby nursing home. "And a couple times she got lost, and she wandered back to her old apartment. It was what she knew."

"Was she black?"

"No, she was white. My dad was the first person to rent to a black person on the east side, though. I got a lot of guff for hiring black managers."

I took a picture of Moshe in his leather jacket, standing in front of the building at 2518-2524 North Lake Drive, built in the 1920s. "We've owned it for years," he said. "As you can see, the name of my company is Atid, which means future."

"In Hebrew?" I guessed.

"In Hebrew. We have fun naming things. In a very simple way, I could make more money not having a business. I employ three full-time people, including paying for their insurance. If I just paid somebody else six percent to manage my properties, I'd make a lot more money. But there are other reasons you do things."

"You could be a slumlord."

"I could be a slumlord. I love the fact that I'm not. There's a really fine line between being a really nice guy and being a schnook, being taken."

"Can you identify that line when you're approaching it?"

"It's kinda like that stop light that you know you're not gonna make. Property management is a wonderful taste of the world. I have stories that could last forever." One tenant had been a recluse and died alone in her apartment. "It turned out she had like hundreds of thousands of dollars in various accounts." He had helped give it all away to charities. "I've now identified three or four bodies in my life. I had one because John didn't show up for his regular Thursday meal at George Webb. It's one of those smells, by the way. If you ever smell death, you don't ever want to smell it again. I was at a funeral the other day. A friend of mine's mother passed away. It was one of those times when I loved Milwaukee again."

As he dropped me off, Moshe reflected: "One of the recurring themes in the Jewish world was that for many, many years we were sitting on suitcases, was the saying. The suitcases were always packed. We could be somewhere for hundreds of years, and it was always temporary."

✳

"I studied up to twelfth grade in Mexico," Carlos told me. "But in Mexico, unfortunately, if your parents are poor, you have to make a decision: you either continue your education, or you work so you can eat. I decided to work so I could eat." In Cuernavaca, near Mexico City, he had worked as a gardener for foreigners. "When I came to the United States, it was with the idea of working and also continuing my studies, because I had heard this was a place where you could do that. I started working at Palermo's in 1999."

"Why Palermo's?" I asked. "Why Milwaukee?" Palermo's was a successful frozen pizza company, founded in Milwaukee by two brothers from an Italian immigrant family.

"I have a brother here. That's why I came here, because of my brother. He came two years before me, but for him it was only to work. In 2000 I enrolled at Journey House. They had an ESL program, and I also enrolled in a GED prep program. I was twenty-one then, and I had a lot of energy. I could work fourteen hours and still go to school. And then Journey House offered me a scholarship to do a computer class at Milwaukee Area Technical College. But it was just too hard to come home from work at four or five in the morning, go to class, and then go back to work. I did finish the computer class, but I was completely exhausted. I couldn't keep it up. I continued with my English classes, and I would continue for a few months until I found myself falling asleep in class, then I would drop out and return a few months later. I did that several times, because I'd just get to the point where I couldn't do it anymore. At one point an English teacher gave us an assignment to write about what we wanted to do on our vacations. A lot of people wrote about visiting their families, and doing various activities. I wrote, 'On my vacation I want to sleep.'

"I worked many years at Palermo's without ever complaining, and they really got to like me a lot. I was one of the people that they knew they could just demand whatever they wanted out of me, and I would comply and never complain, and I think that's one reason I was able to get a little more money. But there's a limit. Then in 2006 my girlfriend got pregnant, and all of a sudden I had a family. When she was pregnant, she would go for her checkups. We would have to go really early. One time I took her there and I actually passed out, I was so exhausted. The doctors and nurses gave me an apple. It took me twenty minutes just to get myself together. They thought it was funny because they thought I had passed out because I was there in the examining room. Maybe that had something to do with it, but all I can tell you is that my body was completely exhausted. I didn't say anything to them about how tired I was, because I was embarrassed. I just laughed with them. That's when I really started to realize that I just can't do this for the rest of my life." His girlfriend was also Mexican. "I met her at work, because that's where my life was," he said.

"Why are you on strike?" I asked Carlos, which is not his real name. He was speaking in Spanish, and a labor activist named Joe "Pepe" Oulahan was translating.

"To better our conditions at work. There were a lot of industrial accidents, and also general bad treatment of people. For the Latinos, it seemed like they demanded a whole lot more work out of us, and they

41

would raise their voices at us, and they had less consideration for us than for other workers, even though Latinos are 80 percent or more of the workforce." The company "used ICE"—Immigration and Customs Enforcement—"to separate the workers and to intimidate us. Twice in the past they've presented us with letters on Palermo's letterhead, talking about proof of being authorized to work in the United States. Then we would go to Voces de la Frontera, we made a petition, we went to Palermo's, and they let it go." Voces de la Frontera was a community organization on the South Side of Milwaukee. "They had caught on to the fact that the workers had started to organize. A few weeks before they presented us with letters talking about documentation, they put up posters warning us not to talk to anybody from outside. And they specifically mentioned nonprofit organizations and unions.

"Myself and all the strikers, our feeling is that as soon as they see that we're Hispanic, they think, 'Oh, good, we can take advantage of you.' Palermo's had always done that. If they needed twenty-one workers to work a line, they would use nineteen. If they needed eighteen, they would use seventeen. We were making 250,000 pizzas per day, and I think they were making 25 cents pure profit on every pizza."

"A little bit before the strike happened," added Pepe, "all of a sudden they came up to him and they started giving him all these extra people." Carlos was in charge of a group of workers in the warehouse. "The same thing happened in packing and on the production line. All of a sudden, they were getting all these extra people. And they had to train these people."

"I asked my manager why this was going on," said Carlos. "He said, to try to sound like a good person, 'Oh, we want you to rest more, to take it easy more.' We knew that wasn't true, because we had always worked with less than we needed. In the whole thirteen years I worked there, I never worked less than six days, and usually seven."

"How do you present this strike as something that should elicit the sympathy of Americans?" I asked.

"There are certain laws in the United States," he said. "And there are people who are using them for their own convenience. If Palermo's hired people without papers, they knew that they were doing it, and they were doing it so they could get a cheap workforce. For example, there was a packing and production supervisor. Whenever we would talk about our rights, he would say, 'What are you talking about? You guys don't have any rights.' The ugliest part of it is that he might have been born here, but he was Hispanic. He had started out as a mechanic, and then they made him a supervisor. He thought he was getting along really good with the company, and he didn't care about the workers. He would treat us really bad and humiliate us. In 2007, he tried to demand that they fire me. He was known as the man of production, the big shot of production. He got a lot of production, but the price was that it was as if he was carrying a whip. I don't know why, but the workers would always come to me with their complaints. I would listen to them and give them advice, and sometimes I would go with them to Human Resources. That's when this guy targeted me. He told the bosses, 'If you want me to keep up the production, either fire Carlos or get him on another shift.'

"That's something that happened to me, but I was also seeing what was happening to others. We started getting sick of the situation. There was a lot of abuse. There had to be some kind of solution. In terms of accidents, nothing happened to me, thank God. I'm okay. But there are a lot of people who hurt their fingers and hands. When somebody got hurt, they would push them to go right back to work, and they would try not to report it to anybody. I know a guy who hurt his back. There's a guy whose finger they put back on, but he can't move his finger."

"When did Voces become involved?"

"In 2008. It had to do with that supervisor. We figured out that if we got together and went to Voces de la Frontera with our complaints, Voces would have us sign a letter and Voces would go to the company. This was a road we could use."

"There's two issues here," Pepe asserted. "One is immigration. How many workers are undocumented? We don't know. But the truth is that we've been doing this for hundreds of years. Companies took advantage of this, and they still do, and Palermo's is one of them. But the real issue here is how we're treating human beings. There's things like this going on all over the country. But the idea that you can build a whole company that's very successful on the backs of people, and then toss them out and act as if you're the innocent party, that's b.s. And that's why this is such an important struggle, because it has all issues: it's got labor rights, it's got immigration. Don't tell me it's about one thing or another. It's about a whole bunch of things."

"I don't see them as evil, as rats," said Carlos. "But I do see them as being willing to take advantage of the situation. The owners, the two brothers, at one point hired a guy named Mike Walz. He has all the power. He tells the owners what to do. I heard one time that one of the owners wanted to buy a sports car, and Mike Walz told him not to do it, and he didn't do it. In my opinion, this guy is very ambitious and very greedy, and if they don't recognize that, that's going to be their demise." One thing Walz had done was to bring in temp workers to keep down wages and overtime. "So you could see that he was looking for even cheaper labor. There are always Judases out there. There are people that are working at Palermo's, that all they did was bring in different papers, and they let them stay because they weren't supportive of the strike. Since the strike started, I've gotten six calls from my manager asking me to come back. But I felt that would destroy everything we're trying to achieve."

"They act as if they've done these workers a big favor," said Pepe. "What's mixed up in there is that they come from an immigrant family. But this idea that they're doing people a big favor, it just turns my stomach. If you worked with a vendor that asked you to give them three pizzas for the price of one, you wouldn't do it. But you want much more than the standard from your workers. I don't want you to be my big daddy. I don't care how much prosperity you're bringing to Milwaukee, how many jobs you're creating, how tough the economy is. That's a wrong argument. You built your business on these people. So 'Adios amigos' isn't good enough."

"I had a manager who was a white guy," said Carlos. "He used to demand a lot from us. He would yell and swear at us, but he really liked the way I worked. So when the other supervisor demanded that they fire me, this white guy defended me. But he spoke to me privately and said, 'I don't know how much longer I can defend you. You shouldn't worry about the other workers. You put the meals on the plates in your house, and don't worry about the others.' I was the perfect slave. I did everything they asked me to do. The only thing that happened was that I saw what was happening to everyone around me, and that's what affected me the most. Sometimes I would stop doing that for two or three months, but a person can't change who they are."

Christine Neumann-Ortiz, the executive director of Voces de la Frontera, had briefed me and arranged this meeting. "Christine and a couple of others have suggested that this strike has national significance," I said. "Would you agree with that?"

"Absolutely, and for the reasons I told you," said Pepe. "It's workers organizing themselves. What I've loved about it is that it's homegrown, from the get-go. And I think unions should understand that the best way to organize workers is to let them organize themselves. They've been doing for themselves what a union would have loved to do for them. I think it's really representative of how the community and labor should be working together. And maybe labor should be taking some lessons."

"Through this whole thing we're suffering, but I don't feel the slightest bit bad," said Carlos. "It was my decision. When the owners do stuff for their own well-being, the society cheers them on. But when we do something for our own well-being, they tend to look at us as bad, as if we're doing something wrong. It's as simple as this: I have a five-year-old child. If he has a bag of cookies, I tell him he has to share them. It's like that. And these are adults; they should understand."

"If you don't go back to Palermo's, what will you do?"

"I won't die. I'll survive. I know this is a country of laws. But is it also a country of justice? I'm interested in finding out. A lot of things have happened to me in the last three months. On June 8, they fired me. On June 20, my daughter was born. In July I ended up in the emergency room with tonsillitis, and in August I had my tonsils out. At Palermo's I worked in the freezers. And this summer we were marching outside of Palermo's every day, and a lot of days it was over 100 degrees." He thought that might have been what caused his tonsillitis. Voces de la Frontera was helping with his hospital bill. "August 20 I started working for a temp agency. For thirteen years I paid into my insurance plan at Palermo's. I never used it. And after they cancelled it, I ended up going to the hospital."

"Welcome to America, buddy," remarked Pepe.

"Mine is not that bad of a story," said Carlos. "Some of my co-workers have gone through terrible things. I know one guy whose back is messed up, and I think it's going to be messed up for life. I'm lucky to have gotten out of that factory with my whole body in one piece."

I asked Pepe if he saw any connection between the Palermo's strike and the 2011 occupation of the capitol building in Madison, which had been led by unionized teachers.

"The connection that I see is the attack on labor, the attack on workers' rights," he said. "This thing that happened with Scott Walker didn't just happen yesterday. It's the result of decades of messaging and money. He made it so women can't file anymore for equal pay in the state. They have to go to the federal level. Their desired goal is a country where working people have no rights. They're pitting workers against each other. And I'm not sure that a lot of people who voted for Scott Walker understand that. I also think it's connected in the sense that you're seeing these home-grown efforts bursting on the scene. It's just showing up. It's like a science experiment. If you push a bunch of amoebas around long enough, one or two of them will look for a better place to hang out. There's new entities involved in this that didn't even exist before."

CHAPTER 2

Home Field

"How's your day goin'?" asked the teller at the bank in Lima, Ohio, where I was making a deposit. It was one of those little moments when I was reminded that, whereas I saw myself as being on some epic quest of discovery, many millions of other Americans were just going about their daily lives.

"Pretty good," I said. "I'm driving from Cincinnati to Detroit."

"And you came to *downtown* Lima to do this?" Interstate 75 ran several miles east of Lima.

"Well, I decided not to be in a hurry. I might not drive all the way to Detroit today. I might get a motel. The rain's kind of a drag."

"The rain is more than a drag!" she agreed, with gusto. "So, are you workin' in Detroit?"

"It's a longer story than that. I actually live in Seattle."

"That is a longer story. And a longer drive. Speakin' of rain!"

I did end up getting a motel room in Toledo. My world that day was lonesome and damp and dark, but it was good to have an evening alone with my books and thoughts. It happened to be my birthday. My friend Tom's couch was waiting for me any time in Redford Township just west of Detroit, but I wasn't quite ready to be back there. Tomorrow would be soon enough.

※

I had allowed just enough time to stay overnight in Cincinnati with Josh Kaufmann. Josh and I had roomed together for a week in 2004 at a weeklong workshop for microfinance practitioners in a village in

47

rural Haiti.[1] I felt grateful to Josh because, at a time when I was at a loose end in my life in London, he had tried to create a job for me in Indianapolis. It's funny how roads fork and you usually end up somewhere you didn't expect.

Josh had arranged for me to spend the morning visiting Mars Hill Academy, a "classical Christian" school outside Cincinnati where his father-in-law was the headmaster.

"I would say that we're countercultural," said Rick Santa, the school's director of advancement, who showed me around. "What we're doing is teaching a love of learning. It's the education that you and I would have gotten if we had been in school in 1850. We see ourselves as revitalizing the classical tradition in the United States."

Mrs. Liebing's second-graders sang for me catchy educational ditties, like this one:

Fifteen countries of Southwest Asia
Muslims, Christians, and Jews.

And this one:

I will obey, I will obey, I will obey
Never asking why-y-y
Never with a sigh-igh-igh ...

In young Mr. Stapleton's classroom the ninth graders stood and said: "Good morning, Mrs. Hall and guests." Then he led them in a Socratic-style exercise in biblical exegesis. This was prep for the 35-page papers on topics of their choosing that as seniors they would have to present publicly in front of fifty people and defend privately to a three-person committee.

"A lot of what's taught here is taught in light of the Scripture," enthused Rick, back in the hallway. "As a Christian father, it's exciting for me to have my kids realize that God made everything. We're really unique in that we're classical, but we're also unique in our Christianity. I have a love for learning. I just love to learn. So I want my kids to

---

1   Convened by Anne Hastings of Fonkoze (www.fonkoze.org), a fantastic organization and valuable institution in Haiti. I write about that workshop in my 2012 book *Bearing the Bruise: A Life Graced by Haiti*, pp. 159-62.

have a similar level of learning. For fun, my kids like to read. That's what they do for fun." Rick had a friend who was an enthusiast for computers and mobile devices. "He thinks we're crazy because we don't have students walking around with tablets. If you believe technology is the solution to all ills, this is the last place you'll ever want to come. It began as a group of local home-schooling parents, who decided they wanted to do better. We're very intentional. We're one of the few independent Christian schools in the state." That meant that Mars Hill took no money at all from the state or federal government, or from any church denomination. "As someone who comes from a Christian background, who loves to learn, and who has a little bit of a libertarian streak, it's like heaven."

I wondered how Rick squared his libertarian streak with making second-graders sing about obeying and never asking why, but I let that slide. I did ask him: "How do you handle potentially controversial scientific things, like global warming and evolution?"

"We discuss them," he said. "I don't see any inconsistency. I see that a God who can create the world can certainly cause human beings to evolve. Nobody says you have to believe in creation. Now, I'll tell you that, because we're a Christian school, most of our kids lean toward creation."

The headmaster, Mr. Wismer, was a retired Procter & Gamble executive and came across as a take-charge but benign and affable Rotary type. "I'm not an intellectual or an academic, but I know what works," he told me in his office. "We teach them to see God's creation and handiwork in every area. And kids understand that, because it's very intuitive."

I asked if they hoped for their graduates to influence the wider society.

"Yes, but through the back door," said Mr. Wismer. "I think our graduates will become lawyers and Supreme Court judges, and that's how we'll influence. That's how we're gonna be salt and light. We will not become a voting bloc. That's not what we're here for."

Mrs. Whalen, the former mayor of Oconomowoc, had reminded me that public schools had been supposed to bring us all together. Maybe the problem was that we didn't all want to be brought together.

I mentioned the confrontation in Wisconsin between the governor and the unionized teachers.

"The issue isn't the unions," insisted Mr. Wismer. "It's parenting and what's happening in the classroom. It's a process of discipleship, which is called life."

"Here's my vision," said Rick. "Twenty years from now we'll have Procter & Gamble coming to us and saying, 'We want your kids to intern with us.'"

"What about racial and class diversity?"

"Good question," said Mr. Wismer. "We have probably ten African-American students and ten Asian students."

"More than ten Asian students," said Rick. Students typically came from families with $75,000 annual income, and eighty percent of them made six figures. The founding families had made about half that. Nearly forty percent of current students got financial aid. "Most of that is needs-based."

"This is not flash and dash," concluded Mr. Wismer. "This is block and tackle. But the problem is, we're blocking and tackling against the culture, which wants flash and dash."

Josh saw me off over lunch at a nearby Skyline Chili. Josh was a guy like me: white, Midwestern, husky, sports-following, well traveled, literate. But we had come to virtual blows on Facebook just after the 2008 election, when I made some remark about Sarah Palin. "Funny, I never pegged you as a Democrat," he had written.

Skyline Chili is a Cincinnati institution and a good place to discuss weighty matters, because you can't take yourself too seriously while wearing the plastic bibs they provide to help you keep from spattering chili sauce and noodles on yourself. "As an individual," Josh said to me now across the booth, "I want to have God's heart as I understand it for people and for the world. And I think at one point in time you could sit down and have a conversation that was not incongruent with that desire. But I think we're so far apart now, that political discourse isn't about the best way to do something. It's more about being self-righteous: 'I'm better than you.' It plays out more virtually than anything. Because it's not as if, when you sit down with someone with an opposing point of view, you can't have a discussion. If you start out and your own pride is unchecked—'How can I outwit you?'—that isn't terribly productive. And it's ugly. Much of this is happening, initially, because we don't think we can talk to each other. We do it through surrogates. It's not me and Ethan having a conversation; it's the Tea Party and the teachers' union having a conversation."

"On this kind of reporting trip," I said by way of apology for writing more slowly than he spoke, "I have a compulsion to be as greedy as I can."

"Well, I'm always willing to pontificate," said Josh. "And if it's stylized, just make sure it's really stylized. Make sure I'm about fifty pounds thinner and really style-*ish*. What are you hoping to learn from this trip?"

"There are two ways to answer. As a writer, or as a citizen."

"I'm more interested in as a citizen."

"I hope to find that the American character is still intact."

"Maybe you're trying to say: Is there an America left? Is there anything collective that embodies us? I hate to say it, but I'm not sure that there is. What's left? We can't talk politically. We don't listen to live music anymore—it's all on our iPods." Josh and his wife Courtney lived in a diverse neighborhood that held block parties. "But we could easily not be intentional and not be a part of that." He cited theologian Tim Chester. Christian types like Josh had a way of pulling theologians I had never heard of out of their back pockets. "He says that the root of unbelief is not doubt, but pride. And the same goes politically. It's human nature to isolate, and to be unreconciled. I don't have to be humble to pontificate. I have to be humble to be your friend." He paused. "*That's* a winning quote."

"It sure is," I agreed.

"Just so you know, it's one-twenty."

"Yeah, I should go," I said regretfully. The driving was starting to take a toll. And, once I left a place and a friend behind, there was no saying when I would be back.

"You'll just have to dream of Graeder's ice cream."

"Tell Courtney I'll have it next time I'm in town."

"It'll be a good reason to come back. The other thing I would say is that the political process has a place in the Kingdom of God—*if* you look at politics as a way of addressing real problems. But I don't think we look at politics that way anymore. I'm interested in solving problems. I'm interested in God's heart being expressed. And in expressing my own heart, as I grow and mature. And that's Kaufmann with one F and two Ns. Did the Tigers clinch?"

"I don't know. But how 'bout those Reds?"

"Yeah. My two favorite teams are leading their respective central divisions."

"The NL Central is the most interesting division in baseball," I said with pride, since that was now the Brewers' division. "There are a lot of strong teams from year to year."

Josh consulted his smartphone. "Yeah, the Tigers clinched. And Cabrera's on the verge of winning the Triple Crown, for the first time since Yastrzemski. I'm just pulling for a Tigers-Reds World Series. I don't know if I could get tickets, but that would just be the most amazing thing."

✳

"All right," said Jeff the next day. "Brightmoor is a story, man, and this is the man who can tell it to you."

John O'Brien was a low-key, white-haired white man. Jeff Nelson was with him when I arrived at Scotty Simpson's Fish & Chips, on the corner of Fenkell and Dolphin streets in the Brightmoor neighborhood of northwest Detroit. Jeff was the pastor at Redford Aldersgate United Methodist Church in Redford Township, nearby across Telegraph Road. He was yet another tall, hefty white guy in early middle age. "Redford's history is in priding itself on being on the other side of Telegraph," he said. "It's fraught with blessing and with challenge."

"So Telegraph is like Eight Mile?" I asked.

"It is. It's the Eight Mile of the west." He turned to John. "Wouldn't you say?"

"It's even worse than Eight Mile," said John, "since the suburbs north of Eight Mile are significantly integrated."

"Western Wayne County is a very interesting place to be right now," said Jeff, "to see the reality of what I call the economic tsunami and the politics of race. The next town to the west, Livonia, has long been known as one of the whitest cities in America."

Twenty years earlier, Detroit had made such a big impression on me that I ended up feeling I had to leave. As with so many of my decisions and commitments, I hadn't understood what I was getting into then, until I was in too deep to emerge unscathed. One thing I had learned was that Detroit is the most American of American cities, where you can't avert your eyes unless you really work at it. Two decades later that truth hadn't changed, though a lot of other things had. "The neighborhood has," said John. "The restaurant hasn't changed at all. That's one of the things they take pride in. The cook is the owner."

I told them I had written about Haiti, and Jeff said he had been there. "You sit in the airport in Miami, and it's Haitians and Christians," he said. "You just don't know what agenda you're working out by going there. But you don't have to go to Haiti. All you have to do is come three miles down the road. In some ways, it's been harder to get my church to come three miles down the road than to go halfway around the world. You get involved in community work here, and you forget there's an election sometimes. We're all gonna wake up the next morning, no matter who gets elected, and have to go back to work. What do you think, John?"

"Oh, certainly," John agreed. "It's still remarkable that we've elected an African-American."

"It's okay in this context to have a political neutral zone," said Jeff. "As a preacher, you realize that you've got twenty minutes every week to speak grace and unity into that. But I figure my job every Sunday as a preacher is not to make things easier, but to make things more complex. Bein' a pastor, it beats the nice outta ya."

I mentioned the Clint Eastwood film *Gran Torino*. "Oh, that's not a Detroit movie," Jeff claimed. "It's a Wisconsin movie. We don't have a Hmong issue here. And the telling line, the line that tells you it wasn't written for Detroit, is where the kid says, 'I'm trying to get Lions tickets.' You don't have to try to get Lions tickets. You have to try to get Packers tickets."

"I was just in Wisconsin," I told them.

"Man, that state's got a story right now," said Jeff. "What a story that state has been. My brother's a public school teacher in Rhinelander. Wisconsin used to be known as the nice state. Whenever you had a character in a movie who was a naïve rube, he was always from Wisconsin. You were there when the state got unified again."

"Meaning what?"

"The blown call. All of a sudden, everyone was pro-labor."

With unionized NFL referees locked out by the league, a scab ref had cost the Packers a nationally televised Monday night game against the Seattle Seahawks on September 24. Both Paul Ryan and Scott Walker had called for the return of the real refs, and their political opponents were enjoying the irony.

This led to some discussion of football. Like the Badgers, the Packers in my youth had been underwhelming. As head coach in the seventies, the legendary quarterback Bart Starr had not exactly been the next Vince Lombardi. "He was kind of the Jimmy Carter of coaches," Jeff said. "He was too nice, too honest. He was perfect for Wisconsin, but he just wasn't perfect for football."

I asked Jeff how he had ended up in Detroit.

"I came here fifteen years ago for what was supposed to be a one-year experience," he said. "And Detroit rocked our world. I grew up in northern Wisconsin. I went to UW-Eau Claire. I got what I thought was a call to urban ministry, and then the Methodist Church sent me to be a youth pastor in Birmingham. That was my cross-cultural experience." Birmingham, in the far reaches of Oakland County, one of the wealthiest counties in the United States, the county north of the starkly defined city line at Eight Mile Road, was Michigan's byword for suburban affluence. "But that challenged my stereotypes of who rich people are. A lot of the problems that are out there in the city are hidden. There's an isolation in the affluent suburbs. If you don't think suburban housewives are isolated ..."

Jeff had ended up doing urban ministry in a different way, by bringing some of his Birmingham parishioners to Detroit. "People are very interested in working in the city, but they just didn't have anybody who could act as a tour guide. Are we solving all the problems of the inner city? Hardly. But these people are asking questions that they'd never asked before. People of suburban Detroit, people of conscience, are looking for a handle to hang onto. They don't want to see the city fall apart. You've got people who are saying, 'We're convinced we can't do it from afar.' One thing you learn, when you do this street ministry, is that underwear is gold. So

this church in Birmingham, this affluent church, became the underwear church. They were literally distributing thousands of pairs on the streets of Detroit every week. So I say the Kingdom of God looks like this: It looks like suburban housewives giving away gay men's underwear to black men in Detroit."

"Integration is effectively a good thing," said John. "We have to work together; we have to cooperate. We don't necessarily have to live together. The tough part is getting them invested in involving themselves with the community, rather than seeing themselves as white saviors. They don't necessarily see themselves as privileged by their whiteness."

"Are they privileged by their whiteness, even in the city of Detroit?"

"The decision to stay in the city is a decision of privilege."

"We always know that if things get tough, we can leave," said Jeff. "The schooling of your kids makes all of your politics complicated."

"There's a different dynamic in the city of Detroit," said John. "To be white is to be in the minority, and there are actually advantages to being black."

"So the resentments run in several directions," I said.

"It's the defining issue of this community," said Jeff.

"And it's an opportunity for us to rise above that," John asserted.

I asked how the national economic crisis was playing out in Michigan. Notwithstanding that I was driving around America, I tended to consider the invention of the automobile a good example of something that seemed like a good idea at the time, and I liked James Howard Kunstler's idea that the Obama administration should have made the bailout of General Motors contingent on converting its industrial capacity to manufacturing new rolling stock for a rebuilt national rail system.

"Those are real jobs that have been saved," said John. "The difficult reality, though, is that the infrastructure of the suppliers and the auto companies has moved out of Michigan, out of the country. So we've put a Band-Aid on a huge wound, but we haven't even begun to address the issue that we've exported our whole manufacturing infrastructure."

"I was in Birmingham in 2008 when the collapse began," said Jeff. "I can't even begin telling you about the fear that hit people in that community. A lot of middle-management people, the bailout meant something to them."

"So, did you buy your Honda before you moved to Michigan?"

"I bought it before I moved to Birmingham," he said. "When you're in the peace and justice community, you buy Hondas and Toyotas. They're more fuel efficient."

The bill came. "John and I got it," said Jeff.

"You sure?"

"Yeah. It wouldn't be a trip to Detroit if you had to buy your own lunch."

＊

We said goodbye to Jeff, then John gave me a driving tour of Brightmoor. "This far-west sector of Detroit grew as a community around 1910, 1915," he said. "It was a farming community up until that point. Henry Ford announced the five-dollar-a-day job, and the coal mines were getting mechanized, so thousands were following what we call the 'Hillbilly Highway' north." An individual developer named B.E. Taylor had bought and built on many of the lots in Brightmoor. "He built simple frame houses on wood foundations, and he didn't really provide any facilities. Four thousand homes got built in a short period. Oftentimes it was two rooms and a kitchen and a bedroom. Brightmoor thrived as this homogeneous monoculture." Most of its white working-class residents were around the same age, from similar backgrounds, attended the same churches, worked in the same auto factories. "That inbred monoculture thrived up until the 1960s or '70s. Then, what had been a middle-income community of homeowners became rental properties. Because people had good jobs, these poor-quality houses didn't immediately become a slum. But thirty or forty years later, when people without jobs moved in, it became a slum." Redford, on the other side of Telegraph, offered a contrast: "Even now, as it becomes integrated, it's staying owner-occupied. It's not rental properties."

"And that's a difference?"

"Yes. It's an important difference. You've got this whole wave of owner-occupiers that were the leaders of the community. But you've got churches moving out, because their congregations have moved. That so many white Catholics and Jews moved out of the city is really an embarrassment to those church communities. Instead of staying in the city and being part of the solution, they bought land and built new buildings in faraway suburbs. So you've got these very good church buildings that became available. So you've got the core city black churches moving out to northwest Detroit. And they've got something of a sense that they're moving out to a better neighborhood, but the reality is that the housing is not better. But an important part of that dynamic is this group of black pastors that are becoming important parts of the leadership in the community."

Through the 1980s and into the 1990s, white-dominated church agencies, Catholic groups as well as the United Way and the Salvation Army, had remained involved in Brightmoor. Then there was "an interesting series of collaborations going on through the nineties": an initiative called Paint the Town, demolition of derelict buildings, other projects that provided employment, "blitz builds" by Habitat for Humanity. Habitat was "an awful group to work with," said John. "They were just so patronizing. They came in with their four hundred volunteers, wondering why the community didn't come out to support them. And they raised money for Habitat, but they didn't do anything for the neighborhood."

"Just the other day in Cincinnati," I told him, "a lady was gushing to me about working with Habitat for Humanity in Haiti, and what a wonderful experience that was."

"Yeah, I can see how it would have been," he allowed. "From her perspective. What emerged was an integrated network of leadership, and the traditional white organizations chose not to participate. They accused us of trying to gentrify the community. And the guy from the mayor's office accused them of being poverty pimps. There was a moment where we wondered if, with the white organizations not participating …" He let his implied ellipsis speak for itself. "But the black pastors said, 'We've been working too long for this.'"

Much of what I was seeing, on both sides of many city streets in Brightmoor, was empty land. Some was being cultivated for vegetables, but much of it was reverting to grass and even woods. "Up until the eighties, there would have been houses on all these lots," said John. That had been the period when slumlords began neglecting the houses, crack cocaine was epidemic, and many houses were lost to fires caused by space heaters. "Most of these slumlords moved into selling houses, because these subprime mortgages allowed them to. As that whole subprime thing began to fall apart, it became more difficult for them to sell the properties, but they could refinance them. So they refinanced them far beyond what they were worth. And then they walked away from their mortgages. Most of this recent abandonment is because of that. The banks had no way to keep up with the rental businesses, so the properties ended up being vandalized and abandoned. It really calls into question how we handle homeownership in poor neighborhoods. Investment in low-income housing is always fraught with fraud and best intentions. What we should have been doing was moving towards something more like cooperatives or rental properties."

"Because the mortgages weren't sustainable?"

"Yes. And after the restrictions went away, people refinanced, and they were really susceptible to these subprime lenders. So there's a whole issue of sensitivity to the realities of low-income neighborhoods that we're still trying to get our heads around. We had this idea to bring in trailer homes, moving people into the neighborhood and then later building permanent houses for them. But in retelling the story of B.E. Taylor building on every other lot and what happened, we decided, 'Uh-uh, we won't go there.' Those trailers would be there forty years from now."

"Haiti comes to mind again," I said. "Temporary becomes permanent."

"Yeah," he agreed.

"A lot of this looks almost like forest," I said. "A lot of the trees we see maybe wouldn't have been here twenty or thirty years ago."

"Yes. Or they would have been a lot smaller. But it is part of this community's history that it was forest, two hundred years ago."

He showed me vegetable gardens that were clearly being attentively cultivated. "That organizing around the gardens ended up pushing out the criminal activity that was on this block. And the gardening idea kind of spread. This has become an important part of the discussion about urban gardening in Detroit. In contrast to some of the bigger corporate-sponsored gardens in other parts of the city, this has sort of gone on under the radar. There hasn't been a big debate about whether to do it or not or controlling land; they've just gone ahead and done it. This is the area that Jeff was alluding to, in that it's attracting some of the young white families that want to be part of the urban gardening effort. An odd dynamic. So, lots of fun stories." He pointed out beautiful, colorful murals on the exterior walls of some of the remaining houses. We stopped in front of the house at 15065 Lamphere. "This guy here that moved in is a real farmer," said John. "He's a real leader in the whole gardening effort."

"The murals are necessarily temporary," I pointed out.

"Yes. Though the intent is to remove the boards before the houses go down. There's been a real nice marriage between the public art and the gardening effort—the idea of trying to incorporate beauty into the neighborhood as we try to rehabilitate it. On the left here is one of the original houses that this B.E. Taylor built." The address was 15376 Lamphere. "We got some sort of historical designation for it, and the idea is to use it as a historical showcase. We were incorporating alternative energy into it, but the windmill and the solar panels were stolen."

"This is like a community center."

"Yes. The idea of the benches is that people can sit here and tell stories."

"I can see how you could develop the garden further."

"Well, most of the maintenance is done by the youth group from the church. So our ability to develop it is dependent on the energy of the youth."

"Are you a churchgoer?" I asked him.

"I am. The Catholic church in the community. It's the church I grew up in."

"So you've lived the history of this community."

"Well, a little bit further north, a more stable community. But this was always part of my background. And I've been working here now for twenty-three years."

"How do you feel about the bigger-scale urban farming projects?"

"Well, they're doing some favors for us by dealing with some of the political issues. We have a city that grew to the size it is only because of the anomalies of the auto industry. We're never going to need that much land again. If we had grown as a center of trade, or a port, we would probably have grown to a city of about 500,000, like Columbus or St. Louis. So we're effectively shrinking to the size that we would have been. So it's an effective use of land, that also provides some food for the local community. And it's attractive. It produces oxygen, it filters water, it does all of those appropriate things that responsible land use accomplishes. It doesn't have to be grandiose. And gardening doesn't have to be just a hodgepodge of peaches and pears. By designing it and putting some art in the middle of it, it becomes something more."

I wondered where Detroit would go from here.

"We don't need to set a land-use policy for the future, without knowing what land-use needs we'll have," said John. "What we can do is maintain the land in a responsible fashion. If we built unnecessary housing, unnecessary industrial parks, we're saddling the future with unnecessary problems. We had one developer come in using Ireland as an example. He was trying to convince us to set up an industrial park as a catalyst for a new housing development. He wanted to tear everything down and start over."

"Was that a good idea?"

"No. Look to Ireland for your answer."

"Poor Ireland," I agreed. "It's a pretty small place, and they've got all this junk and crap there now."

"Yeah, whereas their legacy was not having junk and crap." He smiled. "Historically they could blame all their problems on everybody else, and now they have only themselves to blame."

As we stood there talking in front of the showcase B.E. Taylor house with the garden and the benches, a young black woman walked past. "Hi," she said pleasantly.

"Hi," John and I both replied.

"It's beautiful!" she said.

John turned to me. "See what I'm saying?"

"I saw a bunch of cattails growing next to a house a couple blocks back," I told him.

"Yeah, historically this was a swampy area, feeding into the Rouge River."

He showed me the big new Samuel Gompers Elementary Middle School on Davison Street. "This is a new school. Three schools were closed and fed into this new school."

"Why were three schools closed and a new one built?"

"Good question. That's a fine piece of journalism to be written. But Gompers Elementary was a small school, but it was a good school partly because it was a small school. So they're hoping that by naming this one Gompers, it'll become a good school."

"What would a house that's liveable cost to buy in Brightmoor?"

"Since the subprime collapse, housing is again being bought up by investors interested in rental properties. And they're interested in paying about $10,000. So housing has pretty much lost its value again. It's kind of amazing that we were able to sell homes in the $80-90,000 range in this neighborhood."

He pointed out some new houses. "What's striking about those houses is that they're new but they're modest-sized," I said.

"Yes. So they don't overwhelm the neighborhood. And they give a sense that some of the older houses might be worth renovating. What's always frustrating is to have abandonment and burned-outs right across from new houses."

He wanted me to meet one particular community booster, a young black woman named Dawn Wilson. So we stopped at her house, one of the new ones, and I sat talking with her on her porch.

"Don't believe the hype," Dawn urged me. "We are coming together as a group of people who are compassionate and passionate about what we're doing in Brightmoor. Don't look at the abandonment. Don't look at the trash. What we are doing in Brightmoor is going to be something for the world to see. It's a process. It's a marathon, it's not a sprint. And

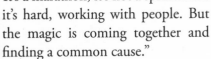

it's hard, working with people. But the magic is coming together and finding a common cause."

"Dawn is a veteran as well," John put in.

"I am," said Dawn. "I was in Wiesbaden, Germany. I was an accounting clerk. I didn't even know what Brightmoor was. I had no idea that it was the 'hood. And I thank God that He hid it from me. Because if He had not hid it from me, I woulda never moved here. My husband at the time didn't want to move here.

He said, 'This is Baby Saigon.' I told my husband, 'You gotta have a vision.' I had no idea of the initiatives that were coming. All I knew was it was a brand-new house, and all they wanted was $400 a month, and I wanted to be part of the change. Yeah, we've got our challenges."

"What are the challenges?"

"Our police chief was just suspended, for an extramarital affair, for thirty days. The same thing his predecessor was fired for." And there had been thirty murders in Detroit in the first twenty-eight days of September. "I spent my summers in Jackson, Mississippi with my grandmother, who was an amazing person. I am the only person on this block that does not want streetlights. Everyone else wants them."

"Why don't you want them?"

"Because it reminds me of the peaceful summers in my childhood. I almost said that there's been no drama since I moved in, but we did have one incident. A boy got shot down there on that corner. I saw him running, but I dint know that he was shot. I got the towels and held his wound. I'm a giver. I got five kids of my own, more than anybody else on this street, but everybody comes to me. I'm blessed to be a blesser. At thirteen I had already been pregnant. And it ain't me. It ain't me at all. It is nothing but the grace of God. I'm excited about my neighborhood. And we gotta be a part of the change. Nobody's coming to rescue us."

"The stories keep compounding and getting passed on," said John.

"It's layers and layers," said Dawn.

"What are your hopes for your children?" I asked her.

"For years I've been telling Dana, that's my oldest daughter, that she's gonna be the first African-American woman Supreme Court justice. But I just found out the other day that engineers walk out the door making $75,000. And that girl is really good at math. She made an interesting comment at the meeting last night. She said, 'What are you going to do about the 92 percent?'" Ninety-two percent of fourth graders and eighth graders were not reading or doing math at grade level.

I asked her about the election that was a month away.

"Obama all day. Romney's so outta touch."

"Do you see it as important that he's African-American?"

"Very! Can we get a brother a chance? That is one of the main reasons I support him. The other reason is that he just makes sense."

"Has he been a good president?"

"I think he's done the best he could with what was given to him."

"Thanks for taking so much time with me."

"Anything to put a brighter light on my 'hood."

Looming behind everything that was happening now in and to Detroit was the twenty-year rule of Coleman Young, the city's first black mayor, who had begun as a widely admired labor activist and ended up a highly polarizing figure. When I moved to Detroit in 1991, Young was still in office and a journalist named Ze'ev Chafets, who had grown up in far-suburban Pontiac before emigrating to Israel, had just made waves with a book called *Devil's Night and Other True Tales of Detroit*. Events had "conspired to leave the city uniquely impoverished, abandoned and militant," he had written.

> The bottom fell out of the auto industry, causing mass unemployment. The abundance of land beyond the municipal boundaries enabled suburbanites to create an alternative downtown in the suburb of Southfield. And the new mayor, Coleman Young, elected in 1973 ... was a militant former union man who consolidated power

by adopting a confrontational policy toward the city's suburban neighbors.

Detroit had, Chafets claimed,

> become not merely an American city that happens to have a black majority, but a black metropolis, the first major Third World city in the United States. The trappings are all there—showcase projects, black-fisted symbols, an external enemy and the cult of personality.

Devil's Night was highly provocative as well as slight, but it had touched a nerve. When I lived there Chafets was known around Detroit, not fondly, as "the guy who wrote that one book." And the book deepened, or at least articulated, the polarization. A retired dentist named Don Shapiro called Chafets's description of Young as an African dictator "extraordinarily perceptive." One of Young's showcase projects, the People Mover, "glides silently, like in some Ridley Scott movie set in a futuristic, apocalyptic world," he told me. "The cars go around silently, empty cars endlessly circling Detroit." I liked Don, but it didn't escape my notice that, although he had grown up in Detroit, we were talking on his deck in a gated neighborhood in a remote, mostly Jewish suburb. A black obstetrician in Southfield, by contrast, dismissed the book as "sensationalism" and "a bunch of crap." The problem was that they both had a point, but they weren't talking to each other.

Young "alienated a lot of people" from the start, a locally prominent black minister named Jim Holley, who was in Chafets's book, told me in 1991. "He has been promoting racism, to his advantage politically. When it got to the point where it really divided us, and we needed to work together, it was too late." Many black people defiantly sported I SUPPORT MAYOR YOUNG bumper stickers on their cars. A white singer I knew named Mike Ridley had a hit of sorts with a song to the tune of "Charlie Brown":

> Saw him on "Prime Time,"
> ABC
> Who said "motherfucker" on national TV?
> Mayor Young! Mayor Young!

Now, two more decades' worth of water had gone under the bridge. "The Coleman Young era really was an era, wasn't it?" I asked John O'Brien.

"Yes. Twenty years," he said. "He reinforced the polarization for his political base. But he really had a vision for the transformation of the city."

"Did he succeed?"

"In a way. But he was saddled by the collapse of the auto industry. And by the white flight, that unfortunately was reinforced by his rhetoric."

Part of what impressed me about John was that he knew the specific histories of specific houses and buildings. And there was a lot of history to know. At Burt and Finkell, just before he dropped me off back at Scotty Simpson's, he pointed out a multi-story brick building embossed GUARDIAN DETROIT BANK. "This is a building that we bought, and we were planning to renovate it for offices," he said. "But that's a pretty expensive proposition, so keeping it secure is our task for now."

"It was a bank," I observed.

"It was Edsel Ford's bank," he said. "Henry Ford invested in it. And during the Depression, Henry Ford pulled his money out, and it collapsed."

*

"This is huge for AFT Michigan," Rashida told me. "It could set a precedent, because Detroit is moving towards charter schools."

The friend who introduced me to her had piqued my interest by describing Rashida Tlaib as the first Muslim woman elected to the Michigan state legislature. Everyone I mentioned her to, in Detroit and later elsewhere, spoke glowingly of her. The more I learned about her, the more interesting she became. For starters, although she was Arab-American, she had grown up not in Arab-dominated Dearborn but in the city of Detroit. Her district in southwest Detroit was mostly

black and Hispanic. She had defeated a black woman in a primary challenge when her district was redrawn in a way that should have been to her disadvantage. "I have a huge immigrant community," she told me. Her district had twenty different ethnicities, and forty percent of its population was under the age of eighteen.

I met her in a coffee shop for what started out as a get-to-know-you interview and quickly turned into a little adventure in real-life politics. She was an attractive woman in her thirties, energetic, maybe a bit highly strung. A big issue in her district was relations between the community and a school called Cesar Chavez Academy. "It's one of the charter schools that have grown so quickly," she said. "I've heard parents really struggle with the safety of their kids. And they really feel that, by supporting the teachers, they're going to have an elevated voice."

An American Federation of Teachers organizer named Nate came into the coffee shop while we were talking. "And we really want to support the parents," he put in. Nate had a letter from Cesar Chavez Academy parents supporting teachers' demand to be represented by the AFT. The letter was the reason the staff at Rashida's district office nearby had redirected me here, and delivering it to Javier Garibay, regional vice president of the Leona Group, the for-profit company that ran the school, was her political errand for the morning.

"He knows our community, and I know he has a tremendous amount of respect for our community, but at the same time he has a job," Rashida told me on the way over in her SUV. "So I always come from that. I don't ever take anything personal. I really think that everyone wants to be able to make sure our kids get the best education possible, in a safe environment, a clean environment. I think Javier wants the same thing. However, they do have a business model approach that is not always focused on the best for the kids. I think they make $1.4 million off of our children. That's a lot of money. And for us in Michigan, basically a university authorizes the charter school to exist, and they appoint the board members, which is a political subdivision of the state. But when you talk to the board members of Cesar Chavez, who some of them are residents of mine, very much active in the community, they don't know what their responsibilities are. They're kind of just given an agenda and things that they have to vote on. It's more of an FYI kind of board meeting, rather than them deciding, 'I don't think we should do that; I think we should spend resources here.' Many parents are like, 'Where do I go with my complaints?' Traditionally we've always had a publicly elected school board, it's public information, people knew where the board meetings were, it was very transparent. Even though all those are required by law, you don't see that much engagement from the board with the residents. I think that's because elected school board members, because they're elected, they have to constantly be engaged with their residents and the voters, right? Where appointees, they just gotta, you know, stay out of trouble, so that they don't get un-appointed!" She laughed.

"And they're appointed by the state?"

"No, by the authorizers of the school. In this case, it's Saginaw Valley University that authorizes them. People are like, 'This is about choice!' You hear them say it all the time. But you're choosing a completely different system for how your kids are educated. Even the teachers. Everything is different. The culture's different. There's not a sense of, '*You*, school board, work for *us*, the parents.' It's more like, 'Us board members, we work for you, the management company.' It's starting to feel less and less like public education."

"And it is, officially, still public education, right?"

"Yes. Every single kid gets the allotment, they have to do 'count day,' things like that. They do the kind of process they have to do to see if they meet AYP, which is the proficiency exams to see where the kids are at in reading and math levels and things like that. But with this school, the Michigan Department of Education has said they're very concerned about how they're labeling some of the students. Some of them have been labeled a very odd way so they don't have to take the test. Things like that, so they keep their scores a little bit higher. From what I understand, an employee of the school, been there for years, started questioning that process. And she reported them to the Michigan Department of Education. And that started this movement that has begun, but now is gonna even get escalated as now this consultant is here and trying to intimidate the teachers. We have a principal at the high school that is violating all kinds of labor laws right now, and it's really sad that you can't really do anything about it other than file it, and there might be some sort of grievance or whatever, but nothing that would hold him accountable, like 'You're gonna lose your damn job.' Like '*You* are gonna lose your job, if you continue doing this to the teachers and the people that work for you.'"

"So he doesn't work in the same sense for the school board, in the way a traditional public school principal would."

"Exactly. He doesn't feel like his job is in jeopardy, because he's working for the management company, who doesn't want the school to be unionized."

"Who does the management company see as its own customers?"

"You tell me. These are business people. These are not educators. I have a charter school of a woman from the Middle East, who's a former teacher. And she just loves education. She's a perfectionist, she's a little bit hard on my parents, but she loves it. And her school's excelling, and she's actually become a model. But that's a very rare case of a charter school that's working. I have not seen that model anywhere else, in any of my charter schools. And it's frustrating. My Latino parents see Cesar Chavez: 'Oh, he's a great activist! He's wonderful. This school must be wonderful. Let me go down there and sign up my child.' You know?"

She parked at the school and banged her driver's side door as we got out. "So what's the union issue?" I asked her.

"The teachers want a voice. They want to be able to negotiate for resources for their children, for their classrooms. And the parents want them to be able to do that, because they're concerned about resources and the direction of bilingual education in the school. It's at a point where, organically, it's happening; the kids want more. The parents and teachers want more. They think they're being shortchanged."

"Are they being shortchanged because the company is keeping costs down?"

"Well, not keeping them in the loop. Nobody knows what's being spent. Even if you go to the board meetings, it's not very clear. Who's paying for the consulting? Is it my taxpayer dollars that are paying for this outside consultant to come in here and union-bust? How much money is being spent on bilingual education? How many of the kids that have been mislabeled didn't take an exam because you didn't want to not meet AYP? It's gotten to a point where the parents and the teachers believe, 'This is what we need. We need to be able to have a seat at the table, that we can decide what the direction of our kids' education will be.'"

"In Wisconsin, a big part of the issue was just the right to collective bargaining per se."

"Of course that's part of it. Collective bargaining, to me, opens up the door for better public safety, for better morale among teachers, and qualified teachers, and keeping the right teachers, and all those things that I think are important to a good education for our kids."

We walked in an entrance of the school, and Javier Garibay, the regional vice president, met us on a stair landing. "Who's this?" was the first thing he said.

"This is Ethan," said Rashida. "He's a friend of mine."

"We'll talk separately upstairs."

Much sooner than I expected Rashida emerged alone from the building, with smoke coming out of her ears. "I work for the parents!" she cried into her phone as she drove. "Parents elected me! You're appointed! You're not even elected! If the parents want it, then shit, it's a green light for me. Period! That's how it works for me! There's just a lot of contradiction. But let me tell you: they are pissed. They are pissed. They don't want a union, they don't care about labor laws, you guys better be prepared for a huge fight. But I wanna win this time, Nate. Please let me win. I mean, if there's any way I can get to the parents, the parent groups. I constantly say to the teachers, 'You guys don't have a parent group. You need to have a parent group.' You have to be invested in also engaging the parents. Not just 'Gimme your kid, gimme your money, and bye-bye.' They don't want the parents to say anything. It's like, 'Blah-blah-blah' in Spanish, and then hope to God they just forget about it. You better organize, and you better organize well, because this did not go well. He was pointing his finger at me and stuff. It was a volatile situation. Javier is huffin' and puffin', dude. And Ethan, who's like a friend of a friend, was just there by accident."

Back at the coffee shop I asked her sheepishly, "Was my presence unhelpful?"

"Oh no," she assured me. "He would have yelled at me regardless. How dare you even take Cesar Chavez's name and put it on this school, if you're gonna do this stuff? It's disgusting. Cesar Chavez would be turning over in his grave if he knew what was going on."

"What about contacting his family?" I suggested.

She brightened. "That's a great point!"

"Glad to help," I said. "I'm going to be in California later on my trip."

"You could deliver the letter for me!"

✳

"I'm as angry as I was on day one," said Keith.

"Every time I make a new entry, it's really draining," said Joanne, who was keeping a blog. "But I really wanted to record it, because so many of the details get lost."

I was meeting the Dalgleishes in their living room in suburban West Bloomfield. Jeff Nelson, the pastor I met in Brightmoor, had thought I should meet them; they belonged to his former church in Birmingham. "They're very interested in anyone who's interested in hearing their story," he had said. "They feel like their story kind of got lost."

"GM didn't even have enough guts to look us in the eye and deal with us," Keith was saying. "After all those years of being in business, they treated us as if we never existed. To this day, nobody from General Motors has ever contacted my dad and said, 'Thank you, see ya, screw you,' nothing."

"We were *the* Cadillac dealer of Detroit, the Motor City," said Joanne. "Right down the street from General Motors. All the mayors of Detroit, Martha Reeves, baseball players, all were our customers."

"We were the first Cadillac dealer in Detroit, and we were the last Cadillac dealer in Detroit," said Keith. "My dad, he's just a wealth of automotive history. The history is so rich. We're actually on the witness list for the Kwame trial." Kwame Kilpatrick was a former mayor of Detroit who had been forced to resign and was on trial on felony counts including mail fraud, wire fraud, and racketeering.

Dalgleish Cadillac had been forced to close, abruptly and by fiat, during the federal bailout of General Motors in 2009. "In the press, GM tried to make it look like they were good guys," said Keith. "But every single car that you see on a lot, that car is paid for. Not only that, but the parts. That whole story that GM was going to save money by closing dealers? Totally false. We had hundreds of thousands' worth of special tools. The day we closed we had about $80,000 in parts, and we sold those for about $5000. We probably had six or seven million in inventory. Just new-car inventory. That's important, because we'd paid for those cars. And who wants to buy a $50-60-70,000 car from a guy who's going out of business, unless they can steal it? Part of the wind-down, you had a choice: You could sign an agreement with General Motors that they would allow you to sell that inventory." If you didn't sign, you stayed attached to what was now dubbed the "old GM," and instantly by magic your inventory of new cars turned into used cars, because you could no longer offer factory incentives or warranties. "It would have been a total nightmare. I don't know if it's a good analogy, but it's like, 'Do you want me to shoot you in the head, or do you want me to shoot you in the stomach?' We really were a typical, true family business. We had employees that spent their entire careers with us. We had people that were with us from age twenty to age seventy. There's a certain celebrity that went with it. We told our employees the bad news within two days. In hindsight maybe we could have told them the first day, but we were in shock. Three things stick out in my mind. One was getting that letter. The other was telling our boys. They were sixteen and twenty—old enough. The third thing was we had 75 employees, and pulling them all together and telling them."

"And meanwhile around you, everyone is scared," said Joanne. "You didn't know if it was a bottomless pit, in terms of the economy."

"And we had employees who were with us for three generations," said Keith. "And ended up staying with us to the very end. Not one of them jumped ship."

"It's impressive that nobody jumped ship," I said.

"Thank you. I'll take that as a compliment. We really did feel that family connection. There were several of those employees who were in their early sixties, and they're still unemployed. And with all the dealers closing, there was a whole abundance of dealer-type employees. And we didn't hide it. We approached every politician in Detroit. Dave Bing, who was mayor at the time, he had bought cars from us for years. I got him on the phone, and he was all fired up: 'They can't do this. You guys are an icon.' I never heard from him again. I suspect that someone either at GM or in the federal government told him to mind his own business. We reached out to the city council, our representatives, and nobody lifted a finger. Ken Cockerell, who was president of the city council at the time, said: 'Well, what do you want me to do?' I was polite, and I bit my tongue, and I said, 'Well, you could use your voice.'"

"They were saying they were saving money by closing the dealerships," said Joanne. "Well, we were *making* them money."

"There was no savings by closing dealers," said Keith. "We were paying hundreds of thousands of dollars in property taxes, payroll taxes. We were immediately cut off from the factory. We were getting no new cars. And this is key, because this was at a time of year when new models were coming out. We didn't have any of that bait to help us get rid of our old products."

"So they killed us in the most painful way," said Joanne.

"That must have been a very painful period," I offered.

"It was," said Keith. "And it was all new ground for us. We were holding onto hope that some miracle would happen. Why it happened to us, we can only speculate."

"The answers to these questions are in the boardroom of General Motors," I suggested.

"The back rooms," Joanne corrected me.

"But a lot of those guys—as dumb as they are, GM isn't that dumb— a lot of those guys who were part of these decisions, they no longer work for General Motors," said Keith. "We had to go out with white paint and paint over the word 'Cadillac' on the awning, in order to get that wind-down money."

"That's demeaning," I said.

"It is," said Joanne. Some of their employees had put up a sign saying PLEASE SAVE OUR JOBS. "The Secret Service and the City of Detroit police department forced us to take it down."

"That auto task force," said Keith, "and I'm sorry to get political, but it is political, that auto task force that Obama put together, not one single member of it had any automotive experience."

"And they could only close so much through the unions," Joanne explained. "The UAW owns 20 percent of General Motors."

"Are you guys Republicans?" I asked.

"No," said Joanne, deadpan. Then she smiled to indicate that she had been joking, and that she knew that I knew the obvious answer. "Yes!"

"So the closing came, and that was a whole nother emotional period, that very last day," said Keith. Dalgleish Cadillac closed its doors on November 20, 2009. "It was a nice event, but really it was like a wake. It was a Friday, and we went back in on the Monday." Nearby Wayne State University bought the building and planned to renovate it. "They were very accommodating to us. They allowed us to stay in the building for several months. Our building was an Albert Kahn-designed building. We had been in the building for fifty-some years. February 19, 2010, when we actually walked out of the building for the last time, was another really tough day. It's funny how you remember these dates. They've actually called and invited us to the groundbreaking ceremony in a couple weeks."

"The first time we drove back into the city of Detroit, to go to a Tigers game, it was such a strange feeling," said Joanne. "Like we're not even part of it anymore. There's so many negative things that go on, but before, we felt like this is our team. But now we don't even feel like part of the team."

"We've been forgotten in this," said Keith. "The people that were unnecessarily sacrificed, we've been forgotten. It was really like a death. And not only did the killer get away with murder, but they're being propped up and glorified in the press."

"That's the way it felt to us, anyway," said Joanne. "We felt like it was a few of us standing on one side, against General Motors being backed up by the federal government."

Keith had heard from a guy inside GM about something another guy had reportedly told a meeting. "He was the head of marketing for Cadillac," he said. "And in front of a rather large group of personnel and outside advertisers, he made a statement that he wanted to start targeting soccer moms and stop targeting gangbangers. In the city of Detroit now there's two Chevy dealers, and that's it. You can read between those lines if you want."

"We feel they should have just let it play out," said Joanne. "And if we didn't survive because of the economy, then so be it."

"Michigan has pretty strict franchise laws," said Keith. "Once GM declared bankruptcy, all bets were off."

"I still don't get it, though," I said.

"I don't either," he admitted. "My future was in that place. My time was coming, so to speak."

"It was almost transition time!" said Joanne.

I asked if their sons would have taken over.

"My kids are too smart to be in the car business," said Keith. "Three years next month. It's hard to believe. There's two Cadillacs in our driveway, but we took those cars out of inventory that we already owned. But believe me, when I go to buy a car, it won't be a General Motors product. We'll mute the TV if a GM ad comes on. I can't watch."

＊

My friend Kate Conway picked me up at the Dalgleishes' house, and we drove back to her place in Ann Arbor. It was Kate who introduced me to several of the people in this chapter, and it was Kate who had burdened me, when I fled Detroit at the end of 1992, by saying, "Leave if you have to, but at some point you're going to have to turn back and face Detroit again." Those words carried authority, because she had grown up in the city, in a working-class Irish Catholic family. Her father died young, and her mother raised five kids on her own. Kate had still been living in the city with her own young family when I knew her twenty years earlier, in a relatively intact neighborhood near Seven Mile and Livernois in northwest Detroit, but as her kids approached school age they had moved to Ann Arbor. Her kids had grown up there and then moved away. Kate still worked in the city, managing the Henry Ford Health System's mobile clinic that gave medical care to students in public schools.

I told her about my meeting with the Dalgleishes. "Detroit doesn't do a very good job of holding onto its history," she remarked. This was something she and others said often, and it was such a statement of the obvious that I usually just nodded my head and mumbled agreement. There wasn't much else one could say. Then Kate said, "Kid Rock is gonna introduce Paul Ryan at a rally tomorrow."

"Oh, is he? I'm sorry to hear that."

"Oh yeah. He's a rabid Republican."

"What are Bob Seger's politics?" I wasn't sure I wanted to hear the answer, because I was a fan. Many white rockers from Michigan, like Ted Nugent and Alice Cooper, are very right-wing indeed.

"He lives in Harbor Springs," she said. "Lots and lots and lots of money. I mean, beaucoup bucks up there. I don't know. I don't hear about him being involved in that kind of thing."

"I'd like to think ..." I sighed.

"He's a graduate of Bridget's high school. Pioneer High School in Ann Arbor."

※

"It's a great job," Tom Derry told me. "I like bein' on my own all day. I get to walk around. It's nice to be able to walk outdoors in the fresh air."

Tom was another friend from my Detroit period in the early nineties. We were about the same age, and we had palled around together then. But whereas I was just embarking on my long career of never having a real job or much income, Tom had one of the most stable jobs anyone could hope for, as a mailman, and as a result he owned a Corvette. He let me drive it to Toledo the time we went down there together to see a Mud Hens game. We had also driven overnight, in Tom's van with our other friend "Baseball John" Miramonti, to Baltimore to see the Tigers play there, listening on the way to Tom's tapes of classic broadcasts by the team's Hall of Fame radio announcer, Ernie Harwell. Tom had been better than me over the years about staying in touch. He was a steadfast kind of guy. And when I walked around the side of his house to find him sitting on his back deck, it was as if I had never left. He was the same burly, baby-faced Tom Derry, now with a touch of gray at the temples, like a young actor playing an older man in a play.

"I did five years in Brightmoor, from 1985 to January 1990," he told me. "I watched the neighborhood deteriorate, people move out, houses burn down. Drugs were a real problem. Crack cocaine. But I personally never feared for my safety. No one ever bothered me. When I was about five years old I lived in Brightmoor for about a year, year and a half. So it was kind of interesting to walk down Virgil Street and remember. I remember delivering mail to my old house, that I lived in when I was five years old. But that house burned down a few years later, like so many houses in Brightmoor. But I remember going to St. Christine's Church, and I remember Scotty Simpson's Fish & Chips, and I remember the Irving Theater. It wasn't showing porno movies back then. I don't know if it's even still there anymore.

"I delivered mail with a guy named Bill Stack. He lived in Brightmoor in the fifties. He liked to draw. And I remember this picture that he drew, of an old lady at the corner of Fenkell and Westbrook. It was called 'Looking East at Westbrook.' Her name was Mrs. Blondia. You could see she's standing there on Fenkell, and the big building was right there, and you could clearly read the sign: 'GOOD PICTURES, POPULAR PRICES.' It made me think of the Brightmoor of old. I don't know how thriving it was, but this old lady had lived there for many years. Later she was murdered in her home. Someone came in and robbed her and killed her. And I believe she was about ninety years old. She lived on Blackstone Street, near Outer Drive. I delivered in Rosedale Park too. The ZIP code's 48223. And it was interesting to see how even though they were connected, in some ways they were like two different worlds. I remember bein' a kid, and my dream was to own a home in North Rosedale Park. Those homes were so beautiful."

"So, does this stuff count as stuff you don't want to talk about?" I asked him.

"Perhaps," he said. "But you go ahead and take your notes, and I'll think about it. It was low-income white people living in Brightmoor in the 1960s."

"And black people?"

"I was only five years old," he said. "I'm sure there must have been some. I don't remember that at all."

"Do you remember the riot?" The infamous July 1967 race riot, which had ended with the National Guard occupying the city.

"No. 'Cause I was way on the far west side of the city."

"Did you live in the city your whole childhood?"

"Yes. Most of the time was on Stout, north of Grand River. That's where I went to school: eight years at the Catholic school, Christ the King. And the school is still open. Most of those Catholic schools are closing, but Christ the King is still open. And I'm still friends with a lot of the people I went to grade school with, like the guy I was talkin'

to on the phone when you walked in. I have nothing but great memories of that neighborhood and Christ the King."

The things Tom remembered were examples of how recent was so much of Detroit's decay and loss, how much of the city now existed only in memory. But if flux is the real medium in which we all live, maybe Detroiters are more alive, or more alert, than many of the rest of us. Tom had bought his house in Redford Township after his mother died. "I was raised by my mother and my grandmother," he said. "My mom was a nurse, and my grandma was a teacher. Detroit Public Schools. I think she taught at Dixon Elementary School, on the west side. It might still be open. What I like about Redford is that it's very close to Detroit. My favorite places to go are all in the city."

"So why don't you live in Detroit anymore?"

"I moved out because my property taxes were way too high."

"How do you feel about the ways Detroit has changed since you were a kid?"

"It was disappointing to see everybody move out of my old neighborhood. But I guess it happens everywhere. It happens in all the big cities, so ..." He left the rest unsaid.

I knew a lot of it would have to remain unsaid, even now, maybe for the duration. I had hoped to say something new. But what? It had all been said. I didn't want to be world-weary or cynical or bitter, but sometimes it was hard.

"Let's talk about Tiger Stadium," I said.

"Okay."

"I don't know where to start," I admitted.

Detroit's baseball stadium, opened as Navin Field on the same day in 1912 as Boston's Fenway Park, expanded to its full capacity in the 1930s as Briggs Stadium, and renamed Tiger Stadium in 1961, had been replaced in 2000 and torn down in 2008, and a new stadium had been built to replace it at hundreds of millions of dollars in public expense. These were indisputable facts. It was the meaning of that history that was disputed. The very first thing I had learned on arriving in Detroit, way back in 1991, was that the disputed meaning ramified far beyond the foul lines of any baseball field. The meaning in dispute was about the uses of public money, the priorities of a society, the emotional and moral content of a city's history.

I visited Detroit in January 1991, and moved there that May, because I had heard about the very pointed battle being fought over whether Tiger Stadium, at that point one of only four remaining ballparks built during baseball's early-twentieth-century classic era, should be replaced. A few things about the stadium itself were very clear: It could be renovated thoroughly and elegantly to maximize revenue for the team owner, for a small fraction of the cost of a new stadium. It was steeped in sporting and civic and even national and world history. It was structurally sound. No other stadium like it would ever be built again. It had the closest seats to the field of any major league baseball stadium, especially in its upper deck. It had 11,000 four-dollar bleacher seats in the outfield. This last fact spoke volumes about a city whose story was all about the work and lives of working people.

The real dispute was about politics, which is to say about money and power. When an engineer with forty-seven years' experience declared the stadium structurally sound, Detroit mayor Coleman Young declared, "He doesn't know what the hell he's talking about." The fact that the engineer was white and the mayor was black shouldn't have mattered, perhaps, but it was certainly part of the context. When I asked square-jawed Detroit Tigers vice president Bill Haase, who kept a framed portrait of Ronald Reagan on the wall behind his desk, if the team benefited the local economy, he said, "I think you have to look at what governments do in order to entice other businesses to stay within their local area, in order to keep the economy flowing." In his office in the U.S. Capitol Building retired Tigers pitcher Jim Bunning, at the time Congressman and later Senator Jim Bunning, Republican of Kentucky, gave me a politician's dodge: "Tiger Stadium ought to be used until it can't be used anymore." Democratic state senator John Kelly, by contrast, said: "Every day they would play a baseball game in a new stadium, you would be taking seven police officers off the streets."

Over the eighteen months I lived there, I learned that to live in the city of Detroit was to live with a constant low-intensity anxiety and frustration. That emotional white noise was the residue of the city's history. And the city's history was intimately entwined with the history of the stadium.

In the 1930s, Tigers slugger Hank Greenberg, the first Jewish baseball star, who exercised by running up and down the stadium stairs, "gave every one of the Jewish people a feeling of acceptability, of normalcy," a man named Bert Gordon told me. "*He's* really one of the guys, so aren't *we* one of the guys *too*? One of *us* is one of *them*. Now *we're* like *them*." Bert's friend Max Lapides said that Greenberg hitting 58 home runs in 1938 was "like if Thor came down into Sweden. A lot of it took on almost mythical proportions." Their other friend, retired dentist Don Shapiro, told me:

> Hitler was wiping out the Jews in Europe, and you had Father Coughlin at the Shrine of the Little Flower going on the radio every Sunday, talking about international bankers, by which he meant international Jewish bankers. He was a dangerous political figure, with his anti-Semitism, right here in Detroit. And here was Hank

Greenberg, the idol of millions, and he didn't change his name. …
Everybody loved Hank Greenberg. Even the people who hated him
because he was Jewish admired him. He was a hero beyond heroes
to the Jewish community in Detroit.[2]

The Tigers of 1968, who won the World Series a year after the
watershed riot, "were a really exciting team," a fan named Randy
Westbrooks told me one night in the bleachers. "It didn't hurt that we
had a newspaper strike on that summer, so the media wasn't picking on
them, or beating up on them. You listened to the game on the radio,
and there was Ernie Harwell"—a major folk hero in Michigan—"and
they were winning. Everybody was listening to the game, and everybody had heroes. It was really a great summer." By the time of the
Tigers' next championship, a lot had changed. The abiding image from
the 1984 World Series was of Bubba Helms, a white teenager from
suburban Lincoln Park, standing beside a burning police car waving a
Tigers pennant. "I didn't do nothin'," Helms later told the *Detroit Free
Press*. "I just got my picture taken." But the Associated Press photo "got
wide usage in Europe and Asia," as an AP editor put it, and Detroit's
reputation was sealed. "In '84 when the Tigers won," said Randy Westbrooks, "people made a big deal about car burnings, and stuff that
happened downtown, that have happened in other cities since then,
but have not been publicized like in Detroit. They've never been here,
they don't know what we're about, and I just think that we've become
the whipping city of America. People in Detroit don't do anything any
worse than people in other cities."

"My fondest, earliest memories of the stadium sustain me even
today," Don Shapiro told me. "I lived in a small apartment on Twelfth
Street." Twelfth Street ran very near the stadium and had been renamed Rosa Parks Boulevard (and, like many other black Southerners,
Rosa Parks herself had come north to Detroit). "The streetcar tracks
ran right underneath my apartment window. It was a small apartment
for a whole family—six or seven of us packed into a three-bedroom.

---

2   The writer Roger Angell had profiled Gordon, Lapides, and Shapiro in a
wonderful 1973 *New Yorker* article, "Three for the Tigers." In 1991 I called *The New
Yorker*, got Angell on the phone, and asked him to introduce me to them, which he
gladly and graciously did.

I'd get up in the morning, play catch for a while. Around ten o'clock I'd get on the Trumbull streetcar." Tiger Stadium was famously situated at the corner of Michigan and Trumbull avenues. "I think the fare was a nickel at the time, and it would drop me off right in front of the stadium, on Trumbull. It must have taken about thirty-five minutes to get to the ballpark. My mother, of course, packed me the usual bologna sandwiches. This was the Depression; I couldn't afford to buy anything at the stadium." Don had lived for decades in West Bloomfield, within forty-five minutes' drive of his childhood home, but he had not been back. "Wouldn't it be something if my building was still there?" he wondered aloud.

It was: a three-story brick apartment building on the corner of Rosa Parks and Tuxedo. So was the warehouse across the street, still emblazoned, as Don remembered, CADILLAC STORAGE. But it was not a neighborhood to linger in, and the streetcar had long since succumbed to the insistent requirements of the car industry.

Marygrove College professor Frank Rashid, one of the leaders of the fight to save Tiger Stadium, had also voted with his feet, but his feet had voted to stay in the city. Frank remembered his childhood there in the fifties and sixties as "a microcosm, an urban experience. We had the influx of blacks. We had a Chinese family, a German family. I can't imagine a better childhood. Don't tell me it doesn't work. It worked. It was great, it was wonderful. What a way to learn from other people, and to get a sense of what could and what should be." Frank showed me his Lebanese family's grocery store, the only building still standing on its block, where he and his father had cowered during the 1967 riot amid scattered canned goods until their black customers arrived to escort them to safety.

From Detroit I learned that it matters who tells the story. During my year and a half living there I suffered the pleasures and pains of involvement, of caring, and I became friends with core members of the dedicated group called the Tiger Stadium Fan Club, who did, in fact, succeed in delaying the stadium's destruction. When Tigers president Bo Schembechler, the revered former University of Michigan football coach, insinuated that Fan Club members were "all politically motivated," a legal secretary named Eva Navarro told me: "It's insulting, because what he's saying is that nobody does anything for free. That there aren't people out there that care about something, that believe enough about something, that they're willing to take a stand and fight for it."

"In the Middle Ages all you had to say was 'The Church says,' or 'God says,' and that was it," said Frank Rashid. "Now, all you have to do is appeal to business. You can ask no questions further. It has its own theology. You can't say, 'Yes, but the poor are starving.' 'Yes,' they say, 'but we have to make a profit.'" Frank also told me: "I've gotten to where I really resent it when people tell me to keep up the fight. They're saying, 'We're not going to help you, but keep fucking up your life, because you have nothing to lose.'"

Then there was Tom Derry, mailman and uncompromising prophet of the Fan Club's message. "I don't see why we can't just say the truth," he said to me. "If it's the truth, we should say it." I liked Tom because he never accepted anyone else's definition of a term. When an expensive, unnecessary, overrated new stadium was built in Chicago and presumptuously named New Comiskey Park, Tom insisted on calling it "the new stadium in Chicago." "They say it's a ballpark, but it's not. It's a stadium," he insisted. "And it's not Comiskey Park. Comiskey Park was a ballpark."[3] When I told him I was disappointed that I had never seen a game at the real Comiskey before they tore it down, he corrected me: "You should be *mad*, because you can't see a game there *now*."

Along Tom's route in what he called a "scummy, white trash" Detroit suburb, there were many single mothers. "They're always happy to see me because I bring their welfare checks," he told me then. "The kids all run up to me and yell, 'Dad! Dad!' I bring 'em candy. I tell them, 'Look. You can call me Tom if you want, but *don't* call me Dad.'" Tom once asked me: "Why are you a writer? Because you couldn't be a major league baseball player. Same reason I'm a mailman. I was gonna be a Detroit cop. Am I ever glad the Post Office hired me."

---

3   Chicago White Sox owner Jerry Reinsdorf's people had approached Mary Frances Veeck, widow of the late great White Sox owner and baseball impresario Bill Veeck, to ask her blessing to name the new stadium Bill Veeck Park. It was after she said hell no that they named it New Comiskey Park. It has since been renamed U.S. Cellular Field.

Now, he asked me wistfully: "How many times, twenty-some years ago, would we talk like this, and we'd say, 'Oh, we're preachin' to the choir'?" Tom didn't come across as a leader-type personality or an institution-builder, but in fact he had initiated and maintained a couple of remarkable projects that mattered to a lot of other people. One was the annual Babe Ruth Birthday Party that he put on every February, at his house in the early years. "You were there," he reminded me. "I've got a picture of you. It's not real close up, but there's a bunch of people in it, like John and Judy Davids and the Burke sisters. And you can point and go, 'Yeah, that's Ethan Casey.'" The party had grown, and in recent years it had been held at Nemo's Bar on Michigan Avenue. So much time had now passed, and Tom had remained so steadfast, that the twenty-fifth annual Babe Ruth party at Nemo's in 2012 had attracted more than 700 people, and many commemorative t-shirts had been sold and buttons, hot dogs (714 of them, one for each Ruth homer), Babe Ruth cardboard masks, Baby Ruth candy bars, peanuts, boxes of Cracker Jack, and pieces of birthday cake given away. "I actually think about that party every day of the year," said Tom. "I put a ridiculous amount of work into it. That party means everything to me. The Grounds Crew has been a three-year passion, but the party has been goin' more than a quarter century."

"Can you spare one of the Babe Ruth party magnets?" I asked him.

"Oh, sure. Take this one. No, take this one."

Tom's other thing, the Navin Field Grounds Crew, was a group of volunteers who maintained Tiger Stadium's field in defiance of the city authorities. "You know the picture on my Facebook page, where I'm standin' next to my riding mower, and I'm holdin' the sign that says 'Babe Ruth Played Here'?" he said. "I believe that it's because of the history of the field that the city wants it gone."

I asked him how the Grounds Crew had started.

"Everybody would say, 'What a shame. Why didn't somebody do something?'" he answered. "And really, it's as simple as cuttin' the damn grass. After Ernie Harwell died, I heard that some people were remembering him by playing catch on the field where Tiger Stadium stood. This was May 2010. And I think that day, the seventh, I heard that. And I thought, 'Cool! I want to play catch on the field.' So I went down to the field on Sunday, May 9. It was Mother's Day. When I got to the field, I couldn't believe how tall the grass was and how bad the infield looked. It was completely covered with weeds. You could barely make out where the pitcher's mound was, and the weeds covered the base paths and the whole dirt infield. I played catch with my friends, and I took a few swings at home plate, but I wasn't that excited about it. I couldn't believe that the baseball field had gotten to that point. I figured I had a riding mower, and I could cut the grass, and I knew that some of my friends were big baseball fans, and I thought that they would probably want to come down and help out too."

"So that was the beginning of the Navin Field Grounds Crew?"

"Yes, although we didn't have a name for months. So I went home that night, and the first thing I did was I called Frank Rashid. I told him that the field looked terrible, and that I thought we should clean it up. I asked him if he thought it was a crazy idea, and Frank immediately said, 'Pick a day. Let's go down and do it.' And we decided to go down three days later. Wednesday, May 12, we went down to clean up the field for the first time." Tom had a knack for remembering dates. "There were over twenty-five of us there that day. Someone from the city walked out on the field and asked what we were doing there, and if we had permission to be there. Shorty after he left, the Detroit police came out to the field. They asked us if anybody there had made a complaint. We said no, and they left. Channel 4 was there too, and they did a very good story on us that night. So we continued pulling out the weeds and picking up garbage and cutting the grass. Some of the weeds were six or eight feet tall, and they went around the lot where the stands were. That was the biggest task, was cutting down those big weeds. I had to rent a brush hog for ten weeks to get rid of them. That was a bitch. That was the toughest part. I would go into that forest and just disappear. And the weird thing is that those particular weeds have not come back. Maybe two weeks later, I think it was a Tuesday evening, we were cleaning up the field, and some people were gonna play baseball. And the police drove right on the field, just as we were getting started. They told us that we were trespassing and to get off the field immediately, or we would be arrested."

"Were they nice about it?"

"No. They weren't real polite. So we left the field, and we were shocked. And we sat out there on Cochrane Street, talking about it." Cochrane Street was named for Tigers Hall of Fame catcher Mickey Cochrane. "We were in disbelief. Here we were, just a bunch of middle-aged people, armed with rakes and lawnmowers, tryin' to clean up the city."

"All white people?"

"That first cleanup? I can't remember. We have had black people help. But I don't remember that first day. So we sat out there on Cochrane, just chatting, in disbelief about how ridiculous the situation was. But the police were serious, because they sat in their car on Michigan Avenue, watching us, for a long time."

"Then what?"

"So we realized that it was obvious that somebody didn't want us cleaning up the baseball field. So I thought it would be best if we switched to Sunday mornings, when it would be lower-profile, when the city workers weren't around, so we might have a better chance to restore the field without being threatened by the city. And it seemed to work. They didn't bother us much after that. We still meet Sunday mornings at 10 a.m. The last time the police kicked us off the field was April 2011. That police officer was very friendly. He told us he did not want to kick us off the field, but he was instructed to."

"Was he white or black?"

"That one that came out in April 2011 was a white guy. But he told us we had to leave, and we left. And we came back a week later, and we had no problems. This year, 2012, April 20, was one hundred years since Navin Field opened, the same day as Fenway Park. We planned a little event at the field, to commemorate that historic occasion. We invited people to come on down to play baseball, and we grilled up hot dogs. And the city sent the police out to kick us off the field. Two officers showed up, they walked out on the field, and they told us they were instructed to remove us from the field, but they said there was no way they were gonna do it."

"So they just came to tell you that they weren't gonna kick you off?"

"Yes. And they told us, 'You guys are doin' a great job. Keep up the good work.' I believe that if it wasn't for our group, the field would be nothing but giant weeds, trees, garbage, and rats. Did I say garbage?"

"Yeah, you did."

"It would have turned into just an illegal dumping ground."

"What motivates you to do this?"

"Seeing how people have reacted. We get so much support about our group and what we're doin' there. And how cool it is that, because of our hard work, they can come on the field and play catch with their kids or their grandkids."

Tom had always taken an interest in my writing and travels. "Are you getting burned out yet, from this trip?" he asked me now. "You're meeting all these people and takin' notes, every frickin' day. And ninety percent of this stuff won't go in your book."

"Yeah, thanks for reminding me."

"This must seem trivial compared to what you've seen in Haiti and Pakistan."

"What do you mean by that?"

"You've traveled all over the world. After witnessing all that for all these years, I wonder if it might not seem so important to write about baseball anymore."

"But it's not really about baseball."

"True. It is about a lot more than baseball. Some people might think we're just a bunch of baseball historians and geeks. But it's about more than restoring a baseball diamond. It's about providing a green space in the city. We're providing a park that anyone can enjoy. Yeah, but it's obviously about the baseball diamond too. Even people who aren't baseball fans appreciate what we're doing. Because they know that otherwise, it would be just a giant garbage dump. It would be an eyesore. I like seeing the field used for other things besides baseball. And that's part of its history; it's always been that way. They had a boxing match there. The Detroit Lions played there. They had the concert under the stars in the 1930s."

"Eugene McCarthy spoke at an antiwar rally there in 1968," I reminded him.

"Nelson Mandela spoke there in 1990."

"The lady from the city said the site is not meant for baseball."

"Yes, she did. Sommer Woods. Obviously it was meant for baseball. The city can say it's not meant for baseball, but people show up every day to play baseball. That speaks for itself. Did you mention our Facebook page?"

"Let's," I said.

"People can follow us at Navin Field Grounds Crew. Keep up to date with our cleanup efforts and what's happening at the field. Not just people that come to the field, but things like that nice letter we got from the state rep." This was Rashida Tlaib, the same rep I had witnessed doing battle with the for-profit charter school company in her district. *Detroit News* reporter Terry Foster had published a front-page article on the Grounds Crew in July 2010. "That was probably the first article about what we were doing," said Tom. "He also has a popular radio show. We weren't yet calling ourselves the Navin Field Grounds Crew, although I was thinking about that name. I liked just being this unknown group that showed up, without permission, to clean up the lot. Nobody knew who we were, and I liked it that way."

"Why?"

"I liked just bein' anonymous. But then we started getting interview requests for radio and TV and newspapers. And we had discussion in a group about whether we wanted any media attention at all. But we thought maybe it could help our cause. And it has. And I tell you what, that last time when we got kicked off the field, in April 2011, that nice cop, he said, 'If you had the TV news out here, this woulda had a different outcome.' That kinda tipped us off. You know, it's kinda strange. Tiger Stadium was such a news story in the late eighties. And so much has happened since then, the Tigers have moved on, and the stadium has been torn down, but it's still a newsworthy story. I believe it's the most famous piece of real estate in the state of Michigan. So many baseball teams have left their stadiums in recent years, but this is the first time that a group of volunteers has decided to restore a baseball field that's been abandoned."

"You told me that you don't want to be a bitter old man," I said.

"I didn't go to Comerica Park at all for the first eight or nine years," he said. "But then I ran into some old friends that I grew up with, and they wanted to go to a Tigers game, and they said, 'You're not still boycotting, are you?' So I went to a few games at Comerica, just to hang out with my buddies. I'm not angry about the new stadium anymore."

"Are you glad the Tigers are in the playoffs this year?"

"It makes me happy that other people in the Detroit area are enjoying the team's success. I hope they do well. I hope they win the World Series. But I'm just not that much of a fan anymore. When they went on strike in '94 I took a trip with a friend of mine to London and Ireland, and I had such a great time that I decided that I'd spend my money traveling, rather than supporting major league baseball. Since then I've made another fifteen trips overseas. It's been a great experience. There's so many beautiful places in this world, and I want to see as much of it as I can. I love the way most European countries preserve their historic buildings. That was a lot of it right there. I thought, 'This is cool. They respect their history.'"

I begged his patience while I scribbled in my notebook.

"This is what you do, Ethan," he said. "You write. A fish swims, and this is what you do. That reminds me of a Babe Ruth story."

"Hold on a sec."

"Oh, this isn't something you're gonna want to put down. But when Jack Dunn was scouting for the Baltimore Orioles, and he saw Ruth pitching for St. Mary's, the school he was going to, and he said, 'Would you like to play baseball for money?' Ruth said, 'Does a fish like to swim? Does a squirrel like to climb trees?' And that's like you. Ruth played baseball; you write."

"Yeah, I'm the Babe Ruth of writing," I agreed.

The Tiger Stadium Fan Club had been founded in 1987 by a group of friends we called the Buddy's Pizza Five. "If they hadn't met that day at Buddy's Pizza, we wouldn't be here now," Tom reflected.

"That's right," I said.

"You'd already be in Pittsburgh."

I laughed. "Well, who knows where I'd be."

✳

The previous January I had been in town to speak at a Pakistani community fundraiser, and I had stayed then with Kate Conway. Kate's mom, whom I had known, had been avidly following the Tigers for ninety years. Kate's grandfather, James Conway, had been a grounds-keeper at the stadium. Kate had also been involved in the fight to save it, and it meant something to me that it was with her that I saw the empty lot for the first time.

Kate was living in Dearborn then, so we drove down Ford Road into the city. An outsider needed someone like her, with personal memories, to get the right kind of tour. Otherwise you either devolved into voyeurism, ogling the awesome scale of Detroit's ruination, or became complicit in the enforced collective aversion of eyes, because you didn't know what you weren't seeing. As Kate said about Tiger Stadium, "They had to get rid of it so that it would just sink into the background." Or, you saw Detroit only as what it now was: an impov-erished black city. It is that. But to dwell only on that obvious current fact, and the politics and racialized bitterness that go with it, is to skip over what brought it to this point, which is nothing less than the entire history of America in the twentieth century, in which we're all com-plicit. Detroiters, including white Detroiters like Kate and Tom who have lived the city's history and not left it behind, remember Detroit.

Kate and I had passed the Ford-Wyoming Drive-in. "I remember as a kid going there," she said. The drive-in was at the city line, where Ford became McGraw. "What I'm always struck by is how stark the difference is. It's like you can feel Detroit closing in on you."

"People think it's about Detroit, but really it's about America," I insisted. That was a truth I had taken away with me.

"That's what people don't understand," said Kate. "It could be like this anywhere. And it is, in many cities that don't have the bad rep. This is the Kronk Center, where boxers like Tommy Hearns and Joe Louis trained. And, as you can see, it's closed. And this is Grand Boulevard, which used to be the northern border of the city. It's called West Grand Boulevard because of all these grand houses." She showed me Northwestern High School and the empty twenty-story building next to it. "It's been like this I don't know how long. For years. So what I'm gonna do," she then said abruptly, "is go down to Michigan and Trumbull. Prepare yourself. Then we'll take Michigan downtown, then come back up."

And there it was. Or rather, there it wasn't.

"It's so ironic and weird that the only thing that's left is the flagpole," I said. There was even a big Stars and Stripes flying, in a big empty lot, behind a locked fence, in the middle of winter.

"Yeah. And why the flagpole? You know Catherine Darin died a few years ago? We scattered her ashes there." Catherine was a delightful and tough woman from Ireland who had come to Detroit in the forties as a war bride. She had been to more than five hundred Tigers games and had become the Tiger Stadium Fan Club's backbone. She and Tom Derry had been great friends. "It's just so depressing," said Kate. "It used to give me my bearings: 'Okay, there's the stadium. I know where I am.'"

Tom and I now left his living room, got in his big red pickup truck, and drove downtown. I drove, because Tom had recently fallen off a porch delivering the mail, and his leg was in a cast. Tom was sheepish about the bigness of his truck. "I know a lot of people think it's obscene, and it probably is," he said. "But I wouldn't be able to cut the grass at Michigan and Trumbull without it." As we exited off the Lodge Freeway onto the service drive, the familiar Brooks Lumber sign was visible from Rosa Parks Boulevard, behind the left field corner. But it shouldn't have been. "I hear there used to be a baseball stadium around here somewhere," I said sourly.

"Yeah, but there's still a flagpole," said Tom.

"It still pisses me off, Tom," I said. "You've had a lot more practice at not being angry."

"I think it's because I've gotten so involved in cleaning it up," he said.

Two decades earlier, in truth, I had been an outsider looking in, as I've been in so many places since then. Unlike the real core members of the Fan Club, I was not a Detroiter, not of Detroit. Where exactly I am of has been a chronic question in my life. If I had been completely of Wisconsin, I would have stayed there. But my feeling for what it meant to me to be a Wisconsinite had had a lot to do with my love of the Milwaukee Brewers, my baseball team. And it had been partly my loyalty to the Brewers that kept me at an emotional distance from the Tigers, and even from the stadium fight. The Brewers and Tigers were in the same highly competitive division, for one thing. Unlike Red Sox and Yankees fans, Detroiters were respectful because they were also

Midwesterners, but even they were bemused by the notion that I could care about the expansion Brewers as much as they had been caring about the Tigers since 1901.

So I know that I didn't make the most of my time in Detroit. For one thing, I didn't go to enough games during the two ball seasons I lived literally down the street from Tiger Stadium. I didn't really care if the Tigers won, because I was for the Brewers. But I met a lot of interesting people in and around Tiger Stadium. I saw the Brewers play the Tigers there, and friends told me how Brewers center fielder Stormin' Gorman Thomas had given the finger to bleacher fans who were riding him. Thomas was a folk hero in Milwaukee, and that story made me love and admire him all the more.

One night in the left field bleachers I had been introduced to John Sinclair: *the* John Sinclair who had been famously persecuted for possession of two joints, White Panther, manager of the MC5, and subject of the "Free John Sinclair" movement and the John Lennon song "John Sinclair" ("Won't you care for John Sinclair/In the stir for breathing air"). And United Auto Workers lawyer Bill Dow told me of finding himself standing at a Tiger Stadium urinal next to Alice Cooper. Bill had zipped up, offered his hand, and said, "Mr. Cooper, I'm Bill Dow, with the Tiger Stadium Fan Club." Baseball John Miramonti was a chronically out-of-work working man who knew a lot of Tigers and visiting ballplayers because he was famous as "the guy who sits in the right field bleachers," and the lower deck of bleachers in right field was at field level. John was on a first-name basis with George Brett, for example. And he liked telling the story of the time Kirk Gibson offered him a job. "I was sittin' out here in right field one day, really miserable and bummed out," he told me. "I was so quiet that day, and Gibby noticed it. He goes, 'What's wrong?' I go, 'Aw, I need a job.' He goes, 'Go up there and get a piece of paper, and write down your phone number.'" Gibson had hired John to cut his lawn.

And in the enormous upper-deck bleacher section in center field, at the unofficial annual Eugene V. Debs Memorial Kazoo Night on July 11, 1991, I had met Eugene McCarthy. The Kazoo Night organizers sent out hundreds of invitation letters every year to famous people, and McCarthy was the only indisputably famous person who ever actually showed up. I was there in the bleachers when an older gent in a light-blue windbreaker and gray slacks emerged from the tunnel, looking like somebody's uncle here to enjoy a ballgame. I contrived to be introduced and found myself chatting with him as we waited for the game to start. I asked what he thought of the Tigers' threat to leave town if they didn't get a new stadium.

"All these corporate guys do it," he replied. "They're like independent countries, ya know."

What about those player salaries?

"The whole thing of baseball players making three million dollars a year is"—he left a pause, for avuncular effect—"*un*believable. It's all a projection of television. It's like these damn television newscasters. Hell, they couldn't make a hundred thousand dollars a year as honest newspapermen. Eight million dollars for Dan Rather—what the hell? He couldn't even write a sentence, ya know. Any business or institution like baseball or television that exists because of a government monopoly ought to be subject to the salary schedule of the federal government."

I asked him about the 1968 Tiger Stadium rally against the Vietnam War, where he had been the main speaker. "It was a big rally," he remembered. "It didn't mean much in terms of the [presidential] campaign, because the Michigan delegation had been sewed up three years earlier. We let them know that they were being dishonest in not giving us any votes. We had a couple of big rallies. We had a big rally in Fenway Park, too. That was the only other ballpark. This was just about as big, probably thirty or forty thousand people."

A gray-haired white woman approached and sat on McCarthy's other side and introduced herself: "I'm Maryann Mahaffey." The universally respected then-president of the Detroit City Council was unabashedly starstruck. "This is the first time I've been this close to him," she gushed. "I want my picture!" I asked her about the stadium. Replacing it would be "ridiculous," she said. "It's a good stadium. And it's in good condition. I was on the Council when we did the deal that they would stay until 2008. And now they turn around and say, 'Well, it's not in that good condition.' And they want to use taxpayers' dollars. And we can't afford it!"

"It's just like the corporations," offered McCarthy. "They won't come to the state until you give 'em the capital and ..."

"The tax abatements, and all that stuff," said Mahaffey.

"The corporations, they're like separate countries now," said McCarthy, warming to his theme. "They have their own foreign policy, their own military policy, their own welfare programs. You've got to negotiate with them. They're not subject to the law."

I asked what he thought of Tom Monaghan, the infamous Ann Arbor-based owner of Domino's Pizza, who at the time was also the owner of the Tigers.

"He's one of those Irishmen that rocks on his heels. You ever know those Irishmen that do that? Look out for that guy."

A friend had told me that some people had voted against McCarthy in 1968 because they thought he was Senator Joseph McCarthy, Republican of Wisconsin, who had actually died in 1957.

"Well, I heard that too," said former Senator Eugene McCarthy, Democrat of Minnesota. "But we figured some people voted *for* me because they thought I was Joe McCarthy. So I guess it kinda evened out." The national anthem began. "We better stand up," he said to me with a wink and a nudge. "George Bush might be watchin'."

But my best memory of Tiger Stadium was of Tom Derry. One thing Tom did for the Fan Club was paint slogans on banners that people held up in the bleachers between innings. The standby, SAVE TIGER STADIUM, always drew cheers. Tom was always thinking up slogans. For the weekend series of September 28-29, 1991, he had something special planned.

The previous winter, team president Bo Schembechler had unceremoniously announced the termination of longtime radio announcer Ernie Harwell, effective at the end of the 1991 season. Ernie had loyally continued broadcasting, but this weekend would be his last Tigers home series. Tom painted two long banners: WE LOVE ERNIE HARWELL and BO FIRED ERNIE. BO MUST GO. On Saturday he and several others tried to hold up the second banner, but it was ripped out of their hands and confiscated by cops and security guards. "What you're doing is illegal," one of Tom's friends told a City of Detroit police officer.

"I know it's illegal, but we have to do it anyway," the cop replied.

At the Sunday game, they insisted that the banner be returned to them, Tiger Stadium being public property and it being a free country. As the seventh-inning stretch started and I watched through binoculars from the far corner of the bleachers in right-center, they unfurled WE LOVE ERNIE HARWELL. Then they let it drop to reveal BO FIRED ERNIE. BO MUST GO. The banner stayed up, and the entire crowded bleacher section sustained a chant of *BO MUST GO!* until play resumed.

✳

"Every weed out here bothers me," Tom was telling me now as we drove past Brooks Lumber along Trumbull in his big red pickup, behind right field. "It ticks me off. I don't know why. I don't feel that way about my own lawn, but this one I do."

We turned onto Michigan Avenue. "Geez, man," I said.

"Yeah, I know it's depressing, and it's a shame. But look at how well the grass is kept. Two years ago, the weeds were so tall you couldn't see anything."

"It really is beautiful, Tom."

We parked on Michigan Avenue, behind where the first-base side stands had been, and walked in through an unlocked gate. Where the first-base dugout had been, someone had set up a homemade wooden bench. "Yeah, to think that that's the pitcher's mound," said Tom. "Cy Young pitched there. Babe Ruth pitched there, Satchel Paige pitched there. Mark Fidrych. It's amazing to think that Ty Cobb stood right there, and Babe Ruth was on the mound pitching to him. When I was a kid my favorite Tiger was Norm Cash, who played first base. And it's so cool to stand there and think this is where Norm Cash played, and Hank Greenberg, and Gehrig."

"So this is the original dirt?" I asked him.

"Yeah, the dirt's the same. All we've added is a bit around home plate, where we have the erosion."

The turmoil and fan discontent caused by his hamhanded regime had forced Tom Monaghan to sell the Tigers, in 1992, to rival pizza baron Mike Ilitch. Ilitch had a much smoother and more effective PR machine—he was smart enough to rehire Ernie Harwell, for one thing, and let him retire with dignity—and leveraging his cordial relationships with city, county, and state officials and other business interests, he had forced through a deal for a new stadium, in a different part of downtown where he just happened to own real estate. He was less easy to hate than Monaghan, but that didn't make him a good guy.

"I wonder how Ilitch sleeps at night," I wondered.

"I'm guessin' he sleeps really well," said Tom. "'Cause he doesn't care! He doesn't give a shit."

Tom reminded me that the flagpole had been in play. "It was the tallest in-play obstacle in major-league history," he said. "And I believe the only reason they didn't take the flagpole to Comerica was that it was just too much work. But they took home plate, and I don't think that should have been allowed."

Behind the flagpole, on the other side of the freeway, the new Motor City Casino was visible.

"Casinos are bad," I remarked.

"Yeah, they are," he agreed. "Every time I take a picture, I try to take it with Brooks Lumber in the background, not the casino."

"But the casino's *right there*, behind center field."

"Yeah, and you can't keep it out of the picture, unless you Photo-Shop it or something. It's owned by Mrs. Ilitch. Sometimes I wonder if Mike Ilitch ever looks down from the upper floor, across the street, to watch the peasants working on the old ball grounds."

A writer named David Fleming had come to Michigan and Trumbull to write an article published in *ESPN: The Magazine* in April 2011. "He stood on the pitcher's mound, and he could barely make out the GM logo at the top of the Renaissance Center," said Tom. "And he thought about baseball, hot dogs, apple pie and Chevrolet. And he put that in his article, and someone at GM read it. And they contacted the city. They made an offer to maintain the field for free. And the city turned them down! People couldn't believe it. The city said it had major retail value, and here we are more than a year later, and nobody's making offers."

Half a dozen stalwarts constituted the core of the Navin Field Grounds Crew. "The guy who does the baselines, I've known since first grade," Tom told me. "Bob Blanchard. We used to play ball together. Over forty years later, we're still hangin' out. His nickname now is Baseline Bob." The others were Tim Meloche, a writer named Dave Mesrey, Joe Michnuk—"He worked in the clubhouse in '84 and rode in the parade with Sparky Anderson"—and Jerry Bagierek, who drove three hours from the town of Douglas on Lake Michigan to help out. "He's the guy who does the infield. That's the cool thing about comin' down here. The stadium's gone, but I've met people like Jerry, and so many others. The stands are gone, but the field remains. People come all the time. All the fuckin' time, people come out here. This is what it's all about. It's why we come out here. Whether the city likes it or not, it is a tourist attraction. This should be a city park that's the centerpiece of a rejuvenated Corktown."

As if to prove his point, while we were talking two middle-aged couples parked on Michigan, got out of their car, walked onto the field, and started taking pictures of the field and of each other. Tom always introduced himself to anyone who came and got names and pictures for the Facebook page. "I bring a piece of paper and a pen with me, along with my riding mower," he said. We introduced ourselves. The couples were Fred and Colby Moore and Dave and Nancy Denison from Traverse City, way up in the far north of the Lower Peninsula.

"I came down in '68," one of the men told us. "My grandfather took us down."

"Eleven thousand cheap seats," said Tom.

"That's good. Let the people see the game!"

"I'm so glad you're doing this. This is fantastic," said one of the women.

"This is special. This is very cool," said the other.

Tom encouraged me to run out to center field to experience the view and vibe from there, so I did. When I came back to the infield he said, "Did you feel Gorman Thomas out there?"

"Yeah," I said. "Gorman Thomas and Ty Cobb. Same center field."

"That Brewer team was loaded," said Tom admiringly. "What a lineup."

"Thank you," I said. It was nice that he had complimented my team, but what I was thanking him for was for bringing me here, and for maintaining the field.

"It's for those people who came out on the field. That's why we do it."

"So, will you put my picture on the Facebook page?" I asked him.

"You bet. 'Ethan Casey, writer, goin' around the country.'"

"I don't want to go."

"Yeah, but you've got the rest of the country to see."

✳

"I'm pissed," said Kate. "It was embarrassing."

It was now early evening, and it was my last day in Detroit. Kate had arranged to include me in a meeting at the St. Frances Cabrini Free Clinic in Corktown, just a few blocks from Michigan and Trumbull, but things had gone longer than planned with Tom, partly because of the rigmarole of getting him into and out of his truck, and back into the recliner in his living room back in Redford, with his leg in a cast, and I had been unwilling to rush our visit to the field. I had run myself a bit ragged with lots of driving back and forth around southeastern Michigan and even a side trip to Toronto, and I told myself I was doing the best I could considering that real life has no pause button. So I missed the meeting at the free clinic. I found Kate in front of the clinic on Porter Street across from Most Holy Trinity, Detroit's first English-speaking church built in 1834, in her car, about to leave without me. "This is more interesting than Tiger Stadium!" she said.

It was a strange thing to hear Kate say, considering how much she had cared about the stadium and the effort to save it. But I took her point: the stadium was gone now, and there was other important work that still needed to be done. She sighed, turned her engine off, and took me inside to meet Sister Mary Ellen Howard, the clinic's executive director. I had missed the window of opportunity for a real conversation, but we sat around Sister Mary Ellen's desk and chatted politely for a few minutes. "We're the oldest free clinic in the United States," she told me with some pride.

"So who do you report to, other than the Pope?"

"No, we bypass the Pope!"

"I lived in Detroit twenty years ago, and it made quite an impression on me," I told her, letting one inadequate sentence stand in for a very long story.

"Detroit gets ya," she agreed. "The young people who come here to work for a year all end up coming back."

Kate forgave me, and we went to Nemo's Bar on Michigan for a bite to eat and to say goodbye. She told me about a woman she had met at a conference in another city, who had felt at liberty to say something disdainful about Detroit, on the basis of having driven through once en route from Columbus to Buffalo. "I didn't have the presence of mind to say, 'How dare you say such a thing to me,'" Kate said.

I hugged her goodbye outside the bar and waved as she drove away. Kate was heading west, home to Ann Arbor, and I was heading east.

That was indeed the question Detroiters were entitled to ask: *How dare you?* I asked a version of it myself in July 2013, when I couldn't bring myself to read the *New York Times* coverage of the largest municipal bankruptcy in American history. *How dare you tell me what to think about Detroit?*, I thought. If you think for yourself, you don't need to read the *New York Times*. The same old tired cliches and recriminations were flying around the mediasphere, the Republican governor of Michigan was saying he didn't want the federal government to bail out the city, but plans were apparently still on track for some $283 million in public money to be spent on a new hockey arena for the Mike Ilitch-owned Red Wings. And I was remembering what Tigers fan Randy Westbrooks had said to me in 1991, as we sat in the Tiger Stadium bleachers: "They've never been here, they don't know what we're about, and I just think that we've become the whipping city of America."

CHAPTER 3

LEAVING HOME

I left the Midwest behind reluctantly. In Wisconsin and Michigan, I could rely on muscle memory. The next place that I could really call home would be my parents' house in Colorado Springs, and between here and there was a long road.

During my years overseas I had experienced a great deal of all the variety and adventure that the world has to offer a young person who's looking for those things, and I had learned a lot. But there had been a price. The day I found myself feeling lonely and bored in exotic Mandalay was the day it dawned on me that it might be possible to take the constant travel thing too far.

So it surely meant something that now, setting out to explore America, I had made a beeline for the Midwest. I had good reasons for having lingered in Wisconsin and Detroit, but I had a lot more of a large country still to see. As I drove south to Toledo on I-75, then east in darkness along the Ohio Turnpike to a motel near the Pennsylvania line, I was seeing this trip as a chapter in my life as a whole: a long story about coming home to places I was only passing through.

✹

"Maybe everybody from everywhere that's not a metropole has this sense," said Tim about ten days later. "But I always had a sense that the place that I was was representative of other places, of the country as a whole. It starts from this idea that Ohio looks like the rest of the country: the shape of the state looks like America. And then, pretty much everybody that's in America is in Ohio, one way or another. Not quite

99

the cowboys or the West Coast people, but the settlers, the Indians, the African Americans, the farmers, the city people. Pretty much all of the same white ethnic groups from the East Coast, right? It's all there. Suburbanization, we've got it. Big cities, we've got it. Countryside, we've got it. Rivers and lakes, we've got 'em. So when you come from that place, you have a sense that you actually know what America is like. Which is half right and half wrong. But then it's also internally differentiated. The cities have rivalries among themselves; the northeast and the southwest feel like, and really are, different places. The southeast and the southwest look at each other as backward. The northwest looks to Chicago, in a way that the rest of the state doesn't."

Tim had grown up in Centerville in the south Dayton suburbs, and he was amused to learn that I had briefly lived in the tiny town of Clarksville in Clinton County, very near his parents. I had happy memories of my interlude in that rustic corner of southwestern Ohio, of people I had known there, and of Cincinnati, where I had seen John Mellencamp in concert at Riverfront Coliseum in 1988. The moment in that concert that gave me a frisson I've never forgotten was when he sang "Minutes to Memories," from the *Scarecrow* album, a story song narrated by a young man riding a Greyhound bus from Virginia to Indiana, seated next to an old man who tells him his life story: "I worked my whole life in the steel mills near Gary/ And my father before me; I helped build this land." It very tangibly meant something, in that arena that evening, when Mellencamp sang the lines "Through the hills of Kentucky, across the Ohio River/ The old man kept talkin' about his life and his times." Ten thousand Midwesterners erupted in appreciation, and Mellencamp appreciated us back, waving without losing the beat as he sang the next lines: "He fell asleep with his head against the window/ He said, 'An honest man's pillow is his peace of mind.'"

"What's that part of Ohio like?" I asked Tim.

"The semi-idealized version of it that I have in my head is Northwest Territory, settlement, clearing," he said. "That part of Ohio was to a considerable degree settled by Quakers who were leaving behind slave colonies or the East Coast, for whatever reason. That yeoman imagery is what I have from childhood. The reality since then is that Cincinnati and Dayton are encroaching with their suburbs from both sides, as people fled those cities and as the agricultural land, not being zoned in any way, was, so to speak, unable to defend itself. So you have this sort of scatter-plot of, if you're a snob like me, unattractive houses in no relation with each other, and breaking up the landscape. And people who live in those places are very often living with the seventy-minute commute to Cincinnati, the sixty-minute commute to Dayton. And therefore they're reproducing that American lifestyle of thinking you're going to be happier if you're further away from the city, because you can afford a house, but in fact you spend all your life on the road. I'm no doubt exaggerating because I romanticize, but you're doubly uprooted, because you don't live in the city, and then you don't really live where you live either, because you spend all your time in the car. That has been a big change: that generic model of life, which is what we all have in common, because we spend a hell of a lot of time staring through the front windshields of our cars. That phenomenon of rush-hour deejays is what unites us."

The conversation took place at a lunch place down the street from Professor Timothy Snyder's office at Yale University, where he taught Central European history. In 2010 Snyder had published *Bloodlands*, a thorough and provocative tome about the lands of Central Europe caught between the murderous Hitler and Stalin regimes before, during, and after the Second World War. *Bloodlands* had been widely reviewed in the right places and had stirred up controversies, in which Snyder acquitted himself manfully. I had been impressed to see him, in Seattle, hold the attention of an au-ditorium full of people not his students for a full hour, entirely without visual aids or notes. All he did was stand there and talk about Central Europe. And I cherished and thanked him for *Thinking the Twentieth Century*, the book of conversations with the great thinker Tony Judt that Snyder had had the presence of mind to conceive and record in the months before Judt's death from Lou Gehrig's disease in August 2010. But it was because of two perceptive essays about the Midwest that he had published on the *New York Review of Books* blog that I had looked him up.[1] It was unusual and refreshing to read anything so respectful of provincial places in an East Coast publication.

"In Wilmington, as you know, there was one big employer," Tim said. "The courier company which was bought out by DHL. And then DHL shut down, and something like seven and a half thousand jobs went away more or less overnight. And that threw the entire local economy upside-down because, insofar as people had jobs, they worked for DHL, sorting and packing things up. So all of a sudden you have all this unemployment, and you have all sorts of people without health insurance, which is the incredibly depressing thing, which you don't really see from a distance, but you see up close. People getting sick, and then they have this Midwestern thing that, 'Well, I'm not that sick, I don't really need help.' Which really means, 'I can't really afford it.' So you have all these sad stories of people being ill in ways that you associate with the early twentieth century, or with some other country, but not with the United States. The other thing that's happened is that you need more and more land to make it in agriculture. So the individual who has a hundred acres can't possibly make it anymore. You have fewer and fewer farmers, farming more and more land, less and less of which they actually own themselves. So the identification of one family with one plot of land—it's not quite gone; there are still people like that, but relatively few."

"That was big news in the eighties, right?" I said. "You must have lived through it." Snyder was born in 1969, four years after me.

"No," he laughed. "Because my grandparents both got out of farming at exactly the right time. They did pretty well in the sixties and seventies, and then they retired, and then they had really long retirements. So yes, we were aware of it, and of course it was *the* story of life for people of the generation of my parents who didn't leave the countryside: that most of them weren't going to be able to stay. My parents

---

1 "As Ohio Goes: A Letter from Tea-Party Country," NYRblog, August 17, 2011, and "In the Land of No News," NYRblog, October 27, 2011.

had prepared to leave, and they had left. So it wasn't anything which touched us directly. But for that generation, people who are now in their seventies, it was a crisis, because people who hadn't planned any other sort of life often found themselves not really having any other chance, except for example working an unskilled job at a place like DHL. So now you have urban unemployment, you don't have anything else, you have plucky Wilmington, which is the county seat, with its one little bookstore held together by sheer existential courage and cafe snacks, but then you have urban blight. You have meth labs. The Wilmington paper used to be all local politics and 4-H prizes. Now it's all meth labs, with occasional violence. That's a pretty drastic change. Not that there wasn't crime in the seventies; I'm sure there was. But not every-issue-of-the-newspaper sort of crime."

"Could your family be seen as fairly typical of the area?"

"So typical that they're not typical anymore. My mother lives on property which has been in her family since 1806. That's so typical it's not really typical. The brick house that was built then still stands. That, again, is so typical it's not typical; those houses are all falling apart. You would want to think it's typical, but ..."

I told him about Oconomowoc and my recent visit to Wisconsin. "It helped me see it for what it is," I said. "As a real place, rather than as the Wisconsin of my idealized, Rockwellian childhood. I think that's the danger of having left and been away so long."

"Well, I tend to think that coming from places like that is helpful to people who end up being cosmopolitan, pluralist, liberal," he said. "Because if you grow up with, and you know intimately, and you care about, love, people whose views are, you know, typical Republican, red-state views, I think you have a better chance of understanding the virtues that can underlie those convictions, as opposed to just seeing them as mistakes. I think the way the Republican Party works is that it's sort of parasitical upon an idea of self-reliance. What it tells people is that they don't need anything. 'You men would be less than men if you needed things, and you mothers would be less than good mothers if you needed things. You don't need anything; you're independent, you're on your own. And the kinds of people that need anything, those are worse kinds of people.' And that's racialized, of course. But none of

103

that would work if there weren't people, perhaps more in the middle of the country than elsewhere, who really are astonishingly self-reliant. I like to think I'm a little bit more like that than many people on the East Coast are. But people in my immediate family are those things to an extent I can barely even perceive. So I take your point about de-romanticizing. And the county where my parents live has got to be one of the redder counties in Ohio."

"How can we honor or acknowledge the virtues of a place like Clinton County or Waukesha County, in a way that allows it to be part of the same America as northwest Detroit, where I just spent several days, or Miami, where I'm going to be a couple weeks from now, or Los Angeles? Is there room for all those communities in the same country?"

"It's an interesting question. If you had to rebuild America now, could it be done? These are all parts of one country now, but the sense of national identity depends precisely upon national institutions. Some of which are government, some of which are not. I'd say mobility is a kind of national institution. My life and your life are not really that atypical. That mobility creates a national identity, because you can be sentimental about where you grew up, you can hate it, you can rebel against it, whatever, but wherever you are now is something else, and that place where you're from then becomes a story that you tell those other people, who nod, or shake their heads, or don't care. So you're forced to try to find some common ground with people who don't have the same background. I tend to think that America has a genius for reproducing itself, which involves coming from one place, going to university in a second place, then working in a third place. So you don't ever have a good story. (Which is good. It's bad to have stories that make too much sense. Good stories are always good, but stories that make too much sense are always a little bit suspicious.) I think that makes national identity possible, because it forces these compromises. I also think it makes something like fascism impossible, because that sort of movement where you're really susceptible to rah-rah, colors, marching, and so on, basically are our university years. We get that out of our system with college football. And then we move on. So you continue to obsess about Ohio State football for the rest of your life, as members of my family certainly do. But you've moved on. You've gone somewhere else, where your obsession with Ohio State is relativized. Because wherever you've gone, there's some other college football team."

"The people you work with went to Michigan State."

"Exactly. So it's instantly relativized. It's very hard in this country, if you're educated anyway, to have a coherent story about where you're from: that sort of rootedness which is at the base of really dangerous, because internally consistent, right-wing politics. I think the game is to turn politics into a kind of sandbox, where you can pretend that it's all about you being the tough individual that you are. If the Republicans win, then they make the government do fewer things for you. If the government does fewer things for you, then it becomes self-fulfilling. If stuff doesn't work, therefore what good is the government?"

"By the time my book is published Romney or Obama will have won, and Ohio will have gone one way or the other. In that context, what's the importance of Ohio?"

"One thing is that the notion that was so popular in the nineties, namely that we're all going to be happy and rich, sitting at home on our computers, doing some kind of quasi-service job, is really nonsense. There are other places to see that besides Ohio. But Ohio's a pretty good case, because there are these moments where things shut down, and you're reminded of how dramatic it is for people who have certain sets of skills, not to be able to get work."

"Like DHL," I said.

"Yeah, DHL in Wilmington. Before that, lots of parts of GM, and Delco closed down in Dayton. Dayton used to be a major industrial city. It's where the automatic starter was invented; it's where the airplane was invented. I think the spark plug was invented there too. It still has Mead a little bit, and there's still a little bit of GM, but like a lot of places it's down to one big employer, and that big employer is actually the government: Wright-Patterson Air Force Base. In the seventies there was Wright-Pat, GM, AC-Delco, Mead, and then three or four other really big employers. And people you went to school with tended to work for one of those places, either on the factory floor or in management. The guy who wore the Izod shirt, his dad was a vice president of Mead, you know? You could fit in the local society, even in eighth grade, with the local economy. Now it's down to the Air Force base. And Dayton has really suffered as a result.

"Dayton kind of blew apart. When I was growing up there, it had fantastically high murder rates. The way you navigated it, as a kid from the suburbs, was with great care and a certain amount of knowledge of times and places. And it hasn't really made it back. Like a lot of big American cities. Ohio just has more cities like that than other places. Cleveland has made it back. Cincinnati's doing okay. Columbus is doing well. But the mid-tier, the Toledos, the Akrons, the Cantons, the Daytons, show how we do need manufacturing. Everywhere I've gone in America, the lesson seems to be confirmed that you want to have jobs for a certain kind of man. And it really is men that I'm concerned about. You want to have jobs that a certain kind of man can do with dignity, and actually support himself, if not the whole family. And with no manufacturing, you end up not having those jobs. We can delude ourselves, but if General Motors hadn't been bailed out, Ohio would be in a disastrous state right now. You can imagine the kind of Internet jobs that these guys would be doing. It's purely mythical, the notion that those guys would now be working as the tech support, call service guys—it just doesn't make any sense. The guys who were working manufacturing jobs, that were saved by the bailout, they would probably be unemployed now otherwise, and things would be much worse.

"The other thing is that the alienation of commutes makes people vote more Republican. Because they're not in any one place, the things that any one place has to offer them are less clear. The way the Democratic political logic works is, 'We set up the government so it offers you some stuff.' But if you're not really in any place, then you're not really perceiving the stuff the government's offering you. Which is ironic, because often it's offering you more, because the further you live away, the longer the water lines have to go and all that stuff. Right? But you don't feel it like you would feel it in a well-run city. It's the car more than anything else which creates the kind of weird American individualism. Because the car is where you feel like you can do everything, when in fact you can't really do anything. You're doing something exceptional, when you drive from Seattle. Most of the time when you're in your car, what are you doing? You're going to work. You're coming back from work. Can you drive where you want? No, because there's traffic. You're always driving in the same hours of the day, etcetera. So you think you're free. You think you're just about to be free: the lane's about to open up, or whatever. But in fact you're really just kind of contained. And I think that containment, and the alienation that goes with it, pushes people to the right. Ohio is more like that than it used to be. It's a bit of an exaggeration, but it's like the whole state has kind of become a suburb."

"And by the time you're in the exurbs of Cincinnati, you're halfway to Columbus," I said.

"That's true. By the time you get free, you are almost literally halfway to Columbus."

※

I woke up in that motel just off the Ohio Turnpike and got back on the road early, because I had a lunch date in Pittsburgh. From the booth in DeLuca's Diner in the Strip District as I waited for Bill Steigerwald to arrive, on the muted TV on the wall I watched disgraced Penn State assistant football coach Jerry Sandusky being led somewhere in handcuffs and a prison jumpsuit, over the caption SANDUSKY'S FATE. Bill had suggested DeLuca's. "It's a great place," he said when he arrived. "Every town should have a couple of places like this. On Saturdays there's a line out the door. I call it DeLuca's Paradox. It's the kind of place that every town would like to plan, but you can't plan. It's the kind of place that'll just happen, if the evil ones stay out of the way."

Bill had recently retired from a career in Pittsburgh newspapers. He had covered a visit by Hillary Clinton in 1995 to another Pittsburgh institution, Primanti Brothers, famous for putting french fries on its sandwiches. "My whole job for the day as a reporter was just to follow Hillary around and write something," he said. "She never touched the sandwich, by the way. And all the media were herded into a corner."

"Like a pen?"

"Yeah. It was kinda demeaning. Hillary's exactly my age, within two or three weeks. And she was a Goldwater girl. I always wondered where she went wrong."

Steigerwald was a libertarian, and not just in spirit but in name.

Libertarianism was a lifelong kick that he was on. "You're never gonna get along on everything with everyone," he said. "Or anyone, really." The other ism he believed in was journalism. "Newspapers are conservative in the worst sense of the word," he complained. "They did the same thing for a hundred years, and when the Internet came along they said, 'Fuck the Internet.'" He laughed at himself. "Here I am, a libertarian, worrying about the state of society. When you're a libertarian, you never run out of shit to moan about."

I confided in him, writer to writer, that I fretted about the topicality of driving around America during a presidential election. How historic would whatever happened to be happening while I happened to be traveling turn out to be?

"Steinbeck had that same issue," he said. "He traveled in the fall of '60, and he had the historic Kennedy-Nixon thing. If you read his original draft of *Travels with Charley*, he watched all of the debates, he commented on them. All of that was taken out. The only time the names Kennedy and Nixon appear is about page 170, where he gets into an argument with his Republican sisters."

I told him one thing I was doing was collecting predictions.

"It will not surprise me if Obama gets crushed," he offered. "This was long before the first Romney debate and everything else. In 2008 there were millions of Americans who said, 'He's a nice young man, he's got a nice family, he's black.' And he got students and young people energized, and that'll never happen again."

Bill Steigerwald had come to my attention when the *New York Times* ran an article about his claim that John Steinbeck had substantially falsified *Travels with Charley in Search of America*, his bestselling roadtrip book published in 1962, the same year Steinbeck was given the Nobel Prize. Bill wasn't blowing smoke, either. He had performed a mighty feat of reporting, doing legwork in libraries, at scholarly conferences, and at the National Steinbeck Center in Salinas, California, then meticulously retracing Steinbeck's route almost day by day exactly fifty years later and documenting it in his own book, *Dogging Steinbeck*. One thing I liked about him was that he wasn't intimidated by the reputations of famous people or the prestige of experts, including the group of academics he called the Steinbeck Studies Industrial

Complex. "If scholars aren't concerned about this, what are they scholaring about?" he had said to Charles McGrath of the *Times*. At the time we met, Penguin Books had just published a fiftieth anniversary edition of *Travels with Charley*, with a new introduction in which Steinbeck biographer Jay Parini had been forced to acknowledge Bill's discoveries but had neglected to mention him by name. "I sent Jay Parini, who's a big-shot professor at Middlebury College, a pissy email, and he sent me

something back that was so apologetic," Bill told me. "He said, 'I'm startled that I didn't credit you.' And I said, '*You're* startled?'"

He called *Travels with Charley* "really a sloppy book in so many ways." What was strange was that Steinbeck's original hand-written draft, which Steigerwald had taken the trouble to read at the Pierpont Morgan Library in New York City, contained a lot of interesting material that had been cut. Steinbeck had written about the exciting World Series, won for the Pirates over the Yankees in Game Seven by Bill Mazeroski's legendary ninth-inning home run, and about the Kennedy-Nixon election. "He talks about real people, real events, real places. It's the kind of writing that should be in newspapers and used to be, maybe. You end up with this book that's so weird."

. Fifty-eight years old in 1960, Steinbeck was tired and ill with heart disease, but also living the life of a literary lion in Manhattan and Sag Harbor, with vacations in Europe. "I'm a libertarian, so I'm gonna have a whole set of values that all those editors and other people in New York City don't have," said Bill. "New Yorkers often go out into the hinterland, and they go with all their baggage. They don't know what it's like here. They fly over us. Steinbeck had been living in New York long enough to think like a New Yorker. He was used to seeing wealthy, famous people—because that's what he was—and he had lost touch with the middle of America. Steinbeck went out there and saw all this stuff, and he didn't like it. In letters to his wife he calls people who live in mobile homes Martians and makes jokes about 'Take me to your leader.' In the book, he pulls those punches. He was the vaunted friend of the working man, and he goes out in the middle of America and complains about people being too materialistic. And I'm saying, 'Fuck you!' He had a terrible time writing it. Nobody said to him, 'Hey, John!' People were always after him to write it. He really had lost touch with America. He realized that he was out of touch, like most New Yorkers."

"At least he realized it," I said.

"He assigned himself basically an ambitious journalism project, as you would do, as I would do. And he wasn't long out of Maine before he was lonely, he was tired, his ass hurt, literally, as he said in a letter to his wife. And when you realize how fast he traveled and how much he was driving—I averaged 300 miles a day, and so did he, on lonely roads, two-lane roads, with all the truck traffic … It's kinda fun to be the guy who gets to babble."

"Well, keep babbling."

"Okay," he said happily. "Now, you can't go on US 10 across Montana, because they put the Interstate on it. So I sought out some old stretches of US 10. It's just been frozen in time. Buildings are there that were there when Steinbeck was there. I realized before I got out of New England that I was looking at the same crossroads, the same towns, the same buildings that Steinbeck saw. In 1960 three quarters of the people in America did not have a phone, and half of them had party lines. One dollar in 1960 is worth seven dollars today. When Steinbeck went through America, there were 180 million people. Now there are 310 million. I don't know where they all are. They're not on the Steinbeck Highway. In cities, I guess."

"My route is turning out to be mostly cities," I said.

"Well, you'll see a lot more change than I did."

"Did Steinbeck choose a rustic route on purpose?"

"Yes. And he liked water. He hugged the water. I can't believe that my life has been spent checking this stuff out. But I can tell you with assurance that he actually slept in his camper, under the stars, maybe once. The country's empty, anyway. It's big, it's rich, it's empty, it's prosperous, it's friendly. And mind you, I wasn't pokin' around in ghettos in Detroit and what have you. But even in the middle of the Great Recession, it's all those things. I have a combination of the Steinbeck stuff in my book, but also the America stuff. You know what the most white state is?"

"South Dakota?" I guessed. "North Dakota?"

"Further west."

"Wyoming?"

"Montana. There are four thousand black people in Montana, and a million people. There are more registered sex offenders in Butte, a city of thirty thousand, than there are black people."

Bill Steigerwald was unabashedly a man of the provinces, specifically of Pittsburgh. He remembered the steel mills. "Virtually all of that is gone now," he said. "When I came back in '89, there were trees growing out of the mill buildings, there were deer running around. Those mills gave those communities so much wealth. I didn't come by my anti-City Hall, anti-planning perspective early in life, but late, based on what I saw in Pittsburgh. I've always been annoyed at the national media. The national media tries to make every problem a national problem. It ain't." He had interviewed Jane Jacobs, the famous writer on urban theory, for the libertarian magazine *Reason*. "She was wonderful," he said. "I have pictures of her when she was a million years old, with a horn in her ear. She singlehandedly stopped Robert Moses and all those creeps in New York. She did some great writing about Pittsburgh." He had found her number by looking in the phone book in Toronto, where she was living. "This is what reporters are supposed to do," he pointed out. "That's why the Steinbeck thing was a natural for me. It's not like I'm Woodward and Bernstein. 'I'm writing a book, I'm gonna follow his route ... Oops!' Then I stood in those cornfields"—outside Alice, North Dakota, where Steinbeck claimed to have met a Shakespearean actor—and said, 'This is absurd.'"

"Honesty is a literary value," I suggested.

"If you read the real thing," he said, meaning the draft of *Travels with Charley*, "my argument is that it was a much more honest, and accurate, and true version of his trip. The editing was clearly designed to obfuscate the true nature of his trip. He was staying in these nice resorts with his wife. 'We decided that we would stay in some nicer resorts,' he wrote. Well, it wasn't for Charley's sake. Everything belies the *Charley* myth that he was roughing it. And it wasn't just a one-time thing. I would say ninety percent of the characters he says he met in that book, he never met. He certainly didn't meet 'em under those circumstances. Travel books don't work that way. You don't meet one all-American character after another. The young and the gullible read *Travels with Charley* and think it's what a road trip is like."

"Whose fault is it, Steinbeck's or his editor's?"

"Steinbeck is culpable, because he came home from a trip in search of a country that he didn't find and he didn't like very much. And he was forced to make up a nonfiction book. If you read the original manuscript, you would not be confused. It was the editing that created the myth. It was the editing that took his wife Elaine out, made Charley a more important character from beginning to end. The luxurious mode of travel was taken away by the editing. By the time the editing was done, the *Travels with Charley* myth was created and frozen in place, and it was able to fool people for fifty years. The sum of all those cuts, you would not walk away believing in the myth. There's outright lies in the book. I did an awful lot of stuff beforehand, so I'd know where I was going and what I was looking for. I did a whole lot of research, without any help from the scholars. He was gonna go to church every Sunday, he was gonna take pictures, he was gonna send dispatches from the road. He did none of that. And it all unraveled. I don't begrudge him staying in motels. What do I care? But it's this whole myth."

"You're obviously offended."

"Here's the thing. I'm used to being the outsider, the journalist who drops into somebody else's subculture, somebody else's world. So I dropped into the world of Steinbeck. I went to the Steinbeck Festival. And I suddenly realized that I knew more about this trip than any of those guys, because they didn't care. They treated me like I was just another Steinbeck nut, another guy who wanted to follow the route of *Travels with Charley*. But they didn't realize that I was gonna do it as a journalist. I didn't feel like I was given a lot of respect. It's kinda strange that the two Steinbeck scholars that I spent time trying to get a hold of were the two who showed up in the *New York Times*, dissing me."

"What's the essence of Steinbeck's offense?"

"His biggest offense was being willing to go along with the final product that was a poor reflection, and a dishonest reflection, and an inaccurate reflection, of his actual trip. And he had a lot of accomplices: his editors, his wife, the marketing people at Viking Press. It wasn't a conspiracy, but it was a whole bunch of people. They made it a book more about a man and his dog than a rich man and his wife. One reviewer, a scholar named Peter Lisca, rapped Steinbeck for the overdrawn characters, as though they were real people, never realizing that they were made up. People tell me that there's no victims. So what if Steinbeck did that? Well, I tell you what. Steinbeck's book sold for five dollars. That's thirty-five dollars in today's money. Viking, and then Penguin, made tens of millions of dollars in today's money selling a 'nonfiction' book that they said was true, and it wasn't. And if that's not consumer fraud, I don't know what is."

✳

I would have liked nothing better than to stay several days in Pittsburgh with Bill Steigerwald, but my momentum and prior commitments were pushing me east. A young journalist named Julia Hatmaker, a former student of a friend of mine in London, had learned about my trip and urged me to come to Harrisburg, the capital of Pennsylvania. So I got back in my car and drove another four tedious hours east along the turnpike.

"This is no longer the canary in the coalmine, but it's close, in terms of municipal finances," Julia's friend and colleague at the *Patriot-News*, Donald Gilliland, told me the next morning over breakfast at a diner downtown. "Two years ago, when things were really bad, there was a real fear that Harrisburg would be the first municipality to go under."

"In the country?"

"Yeah. We're no longer the first, but there's no question it's a failure. It's on life support at this point."

"Why?"

"In a nutshell, you have a mayor who's been in office for twenty years. And in the eighties he had advisers who introduced him to the concept of arbitrage. There comes a point in the early nineties where it's no longer a sleepy sewer and water authority; it becomes a bank.

The other problem was that the incinerator could not pay for itself. So toward the late nineties, you were having a major borrowing almost every year. It was going on to $100 million in debt."

"It's worse now," said Julia.

"It's much worse," said Donald. "It's $340 million. The things that are happening in Harrisburg apply statewide. We're not the only ones who are in this position. We're just in the spotlight. The total debt for Harrisburg and its various suburban entities, including the school district, is over $1.53 billion."

"And you have 50,000 people to pay it," said their other colleague, Eric Veronikis. "And one third of them are in poverty."

Harrisburg had no commuter tax, which was a problem because state employees worked there but tended to live in the suburbs, and state property in the city was tax exempt. So, in short, there was too much debt and too little revenue.

"Except for places like Bradford County, where there's lots of revenue because of fracking," said Donald.

I asked him to tell me more about fracking, the controversial practice of the hydraulic fracturing of rock for oil and gas, in Pennsylvania. "It's a big deal economically," he said. "They're all pro-fracking, and it's all because of the money. If they don't say Gilded Age explicitly, and some of them do, they talk about the late 1800s and the time when Pennsylvania's state legislature was arguably *the* most corrupt. There's no question that there's a lot of money getting pumped into rural parts of Pennsylvania that were poor." But Donald urged caution toward the documentary *Gasland*. "*Gasland* is enormously misleading," he said. "It conflates a lot of issues. Most of the environmental claims about fracking are at best speculative. The EPA did its own testing, and they came to the same conclusion as the state DEP. The EPA tests came back clear. The actual documented problem—and it's an issue—is migrating methane. We've had no issues with water contamination in Pennsylvania. There are some air quality issues."

"Do you feel like *Gasland* is propaganda?"

"Yes. That said, all the shit that the industry puts out to try to argue with *Gasland* is propaganda too." He recommended *The End of Country* by Seamus McGraw: "That book really captures what it's all about."

The City of Harrisburg's incinerator, said Eric, was "the big elephant in the room. If it wasn't for the incinerator, Harrisburg would actually be doing pretty well. So far all you're seeing is two tax increases on city residents, and the leveraging of city assets." The new taxes were a 0.8-percent real estate tax increase and a 2.5-percent school district tax. "We're talking about taxing poor people that are barely scraping by. It isn't possible. The other stakeholders haven't shown what they're going to bring in terms of assets."

And the state didn't seem to understand its responsibility. "It's their problem now, and they don't seem to get that. You took over this city. You can tax all you want, but how are you gonna get the tax revenue?"

"So is this an issue of class differences and local politics, or is it also ideological?" I asked.

"It's both. We're the heart of the region. You use it every day, and we're stuck with the problems."

Julia spent the rest of the morning showing me around. She and her parents had welcomed me effusively the evening before, when I arrived later than planned from Pittsburgh. *Later than planned*: that phrase could serve as an epigraph for my whole rushed but overstuffed road trip. Julia's parents were Southern, recently relocated, so they laid plenty of snacks and beer and conversation on me from the moment I arrived. It was great, and I didn't want to leave. Julia's dad was an executive with a trucking company. Julia herself was blonde and slim and exuded both positive aspirations and healthy self-confidence. She was twenty-three and still new to Harrisburg, but clearly she had been soaking up the town like a sponge.

"Hey, the Occupy people are still occupying," I said to her as we passed the state capitol building.

"Yes, they are," she said. "The same people have been there the whole time."

She showed me the Gamut children's theater, which was trying to move out of the city. "And this is the old *Patriot-News* building. It's for sale now. We're now on the West Shore, and we got a whole lot of crap for doing that." The West Shore was the suburbs.

"So what are your politics?" I asked her.

"I'm almost at the point where I think it's ridiculous to vote, because nothing's going to change," she said. "I think any time you want something to change, you have to do it yourself."

"Aren't you awfully young to be so pessimistic?"

"A lot of people tell me that."

She drove me through neighborhoods of neglected and ramshackle brownstones. "This is a lot like Detroit," I said. Except that there weren't brownstones in Detroit; but the neglect was familiar.

"Well, it shouldn't be," she said. "No place should be like Detroit."

"Detroit shouldn't be like Detroit," I said.

But Julia really wasn't pessimistic. She had the purposeful optimism of the young and competent. "There's still a lot to see in life, there's a lot of stories to tell," she said. "And maybe a story that I tell will make a difference to someone." She made a point of showing me the Amtrak station, "which is super ritzy. And then you go down to the Greyhound bus station"—directly below the Amtrak station—"and it's a completely different clientele. It makes me feel that you're lucky as long as you have a bed, and food, and people who love you. I don't know how you're doing this trip around America and not, like, crying all the time." And she took me to the Broad Street Market: "This is actually the oldest continuously operated farmer's market in America. You probably get that a lot of people have given up on Harrisburg, and I haven't yet. And part of it's because of things like Broad Street Market. I have too much faith in people to assume that they're going to fail."

Another good thing was that the Hershey's chocolate company had "just expanded a factory, which means a lot more jobs in this area." And, last but not least, Julia took me to The Midtown Scholar, a big and wonderful bookstore with a cafe attached whose owner Eric Papenfuse, like Richard Skorman of Poor Richard's in Colorado Springs, was using it to build a base for civic action and collaboration. Like Poor Richard's, it seemed to prove the point of the publishing guru Jason Epstein that independent bookstores can thrive in provincial cities with inexpensive real estate. (And, like Skorman, Papenfuse ran for mayor.) "I get really excited when I'm around books," Julia said. "This is where the movement is, where people are really trying to take hold of Harrisburg."

A related reason for coming to The Midtown Scholar was that Julia wanted me to meet her friend J. Bair, a young black hip-hop musician whose story she wanted me to hear. "There's so much more to the city," he told me as we sat on stools at a high table in the cafe. "People's perception of reality depends on what angle they're coming from. They can't relate to a lot of things that are going on here. But I have a saying: 'To not know is one thing, but to not want to know is another.' I think if people took the time to understand another person's situation, we'd all be better off."

J. Bair's full name was Jason. He was slim and athletic and handsome, a young man on the verge of coming fully into his adult identity and role. After this conversation I would be getting back on the road, an eight-hour heavy slog to north of Boston, arriving late at night. Hearing Jason's story was the last thing I had time for in Harrisburg, so I just sat there with my notebook open and asked him to tell it to me.

"Unfortunately, it's probably been close to the typical life of a young black male in this area," he said. "That leads to a lot of questions, and a lot of those questions can't be answered. You have a lot of frustration. As you get older you realize that, 'Hey, we don't have it so great.' It's  isolating. One thing about Harrisburg is, for the most part it's a minority city. But unlike other places, this place is surrounded completely by suburban white towns. So it makes for an interesting dynamic."

"Tell me more," I said.

"Well, even with high school sports. You've got basically an all-black team that comes out of this area. And all the other teams are not like that. One of the problems is, it stays like that."

"What do you write about?" I asked him.

"I write about pretty much my own experience. I was fortunate to be a knucklehead growing up. Got in trouble, got kicked out of school. My experience was a little different, because I was given an out. It was dead or jail, that was pretty much where I was headed."

J. Bair gave credit for the out he was given to a mentor named Rob

Golden, a black man who taught and coached basketball at a nearly all-white suburban school. "Rob's a huge influence on me," he said. "I don't know where I'd be without Rob. Seeing how he treats people and how he relates to people. Rob's a very interesting guy, very unique. Rob comes from an even more difficult situation than me. I couldn't be having this conversation with you, right now, if it wasn't for Rob. He's my go-to guy. If I had Phone a Friend, it would be Rob. His brother was a pastor at a church. The whole Golden family is amazing. He says this is probably one of the most racist areas in the country. Which is weird, because it's so close to New York and Philadelphia."

Rob had arranged for Jason to be enrolled at his school, Emmanuel Baptist Christian Academy in nearby Mechanicsburg.

"That changed my entire life. But it was totally unique. I may have been to the mall over there a couple of times, but you just didn't go there. It was like a whole nother world. It really felt like going to another state. There were no black teachers at all, except for Rob. All the students were white. Everybody's situation to me was pretty good. Everybody's mom and dad were together. I feel like that gave me more balance, for my writing. And it gave me more material. It opened my eyes to some things. Good and bad. I can remember a young lady who liked me, and her parents asked me to come to another part of the building, and basically threatened me if I had anything to do with their daughter." Another thing was "being around teachers that could absolutely not relate to you. And at three o'clock you came back to the inner city. You start realizing more and more that this is not the way it's supposed to be. People are just people."

He worried that there wasn't enough male leadership in Harrisburg's black community.

"Maybe you're the male leadership now," I suggested.

"It can be such a weight to bear sometimes," he said. "We don't have dialogue, enough conversations about it, and I think that would help. "

"Who are you trying to reach?"

"Particularly because of my experience in life, and because I've been around a lot of different people, I'm trying to reach anybody with an ear. We all pretty much want the same things. I think more people can relate to being honest. If you come from an honest place, there has to be somebody that can relate to it. Everybody has struggled in life. Everybody has experienced pain. I really feel it's for any and everybody, if they give it a listen. As you can tell, I have a lot to say. I just fell in love with the culture of hip-hop, and I love music."

"Do you feel you've already become the artist you want to be?"

"No, not even close. I don't think you ever really arrive. I don't think you ever really stop growing and learning. Sometimes you miss the mark."

"Do you read a lot?"

"Not as much as I want. My uncle challenged me to read a book a month. We have all these tools: smartphones and iPads. But we're just so busy, we don't read as much as we should."

"Tell me what Obama means to you."

"My mother passed a couple months after the 2008 election. I remember that feeling, the day after. What a lot of people don't get that are anti-Obama is what he represented. I know it's cliché, but he represented hope. I think if he had lost, it would have set us back as a society. I think it would have knocked the wind out of black America. I think it would have been a tailspin. I think it would have been like, 'It doesn't even matter now.' I don't think it was about the politics, for a lot of people. I remember that next day: there was such a sense of pride. Sometimes people just need to feel good. In my lifetime, I'll probably never see another one. But that one will be etched in the history book."

"What if he loses this time?"

"I think it would be difficult, but not like it was the last time. That was the one that counted."

"What about the people that hate him?"

"I think you gotta ask why. But there's a lot of good too. You've seen that bookstore, and that's great. Me and Rob talk about it all the time, and we're like we don't know how to feel about it. But overall, it's headin' in the right direction."

✳

"Everyone, introductions," said Bill Henning as we sat down. "This is my friend Ethan. We went to high school together. He lives in Seattle, he's driving across America."

I had arrived at Bill and Thomas's house in Salem, Massachusetts to find Marie Antoinette, in powdered wig, makeup, and gown, being served tea from a tray by a shirtless hunk, also in powdered wig, on the balcony above their front porch, and getting photographed by a young man wearing a black t-shirt and a backwards baseball cap. It turned out to be a photo shoot for an art exhibition called "Drag Queens of Domestic Desires," and my friends had been asked if their house could be used because it looked stately.

"Seattle? Great town!" said Marie Antoinette, who had taken off his

dress and wig but not his makeup. His real name was Alex. We were at the dining table, eating take-out burgers provided by Thomas. "I was just in Portland."

"Another great town," I allowed.

"I had major culture shock out there," said Alex.

"How's that?"

"I was in a strip club," he said. "And out there, they encourage you to touch when you tip. It took me forever to tip!"

It was Bill who had saved me from getting fired from the Ben Franklin store by getting me a job with him in the hospital kitchen. Bill had been the Eddie Haskell of the Casey family back in Oconomowoc, but that's unfair, because the original Eddie Haskell gave polite young men a bad name. I never got to know Bill's family because they lived outside of town, but the fact that we lived only a mile from the high school meant that Bill saw my family a lot. We played Risk on my front porch with Sean Sinitski, the town beatnik who went on to fulfill his ambition of being an actor. Sean was tall and skinny and kind of exotic-looking, so he was perfect for the title role in *Dracula: The Musical* our senior year. Bill and I also would walk through the woods at lunch hour to be fed by my grandmother in her little apartment at the Wilkinson Manor rent-controlled building for old folks. "Hello, Mrs. Casey. How are you today, Mrs. Casey?" Grandma Casey liked Bill. Everybody liked Bill.

Bill and I double-dated at our senior prom—he took Julie Petrosky, I took Nancy Debbink—and we stayed good friends, even as our lives took us in different directions. He went to UW-Whitewater to major in business, and from there to Chicago. I looked him up there at the end of 1992, when I was driving from Detroit to Colorado en route to California and Bangkok. Before I left Detroit we spoke on the phone. I told him about some of my adventures, and he filled me in on his life in Chicago. "... and that's when I met Thomas," he ended, with a tone and emphasis that made everything clear enough.

Thomas MacDonald was a suave and sociable black man from Bermuda, with a strong resemblance to Colin Powell. He claimed to have been mistaken for the general a few times. He and Bill had met while working together at Marshall Field's in Chicago. Thomas was a decade older than Bill, dressed well, and carried himself with the kind of air of dignity that only a mature gay black man can pull off, but there was a depth and wisdom to him that I saw for myself later, when he was working for Bermuda Tourism and we simultaneously discovered that London is a lonely place to be at a loose end. "London galvanized our friendship in its own right," he said. "Before London you were very much Bill's friend, that I liked. And that's why, at your wedding, I was so happy for you, having found this absolute jewel of a woman, knowing what you had been through."

Bill was understated, reliable, Midwestern, from a Wisconsin German farming family so typical it isn't typical anymore. You might suppose that Bill's mother might not have asked black gay Thomas to be a pallbearer at her husband's funeral, but if so you would be mistaken. "Bill and I have been the exception, in that both our families have been in our lives throughout our relationship," Thomas told me. "There's a sense of normalcy." Thomas had spent a lot more time in Oconomowoc over the years than I had. When I saw Jill Riemann for the first time in nearly thirty years at the little reading I did at Books & Company, she gushed about how he had charmed and entertained her kids. He and Bill had now been together more than twenty years. In March 2005, less than a year after Massachusetts became the first state to sanction gay marriage, they were married.

I had learned that, for all his dignified veneer, Thomas's interior was both deep and mushy, and that he liked to wax philosophical. "There's something to be said for belonging," he mused as we drove from Salem to Provincetown, the gay-dominated resort town on the tip of Cape Cod. "You and me and Bill in this car right now—this is right where we belong. I hate to think that thirty years from now this might be over. But tomorrow we'll be driving back on this road, and P-town will be in the past. But that's the way life is."

The conversation somehow turned to Anderson Cooper. "He's a 'silver daddy,' is what they call him in the gay world," said Bill.

"His mother's still alive," said Thomas, referring to Cooper's mother Gloria Vanderbilt, the artist, heiress, author and early developer·of designer blue jeans.

"She liked the tanning bed," said Bill.

"I think she was married to Anderson's father," said Thomas. "When she came to Marshall Field's to plump for her jeans, you would have thought Queen Elizabeth was coming." He told me about some special desk clocks, replicas of clocks that hang on the former Marshall Field's (now Macy's) building in Chicago, that had been given to visiting VIPs and later as rewards to employees. "Liz Taylor got one, and Cher got one," he remembered.

"And we got one," said Bill with a tinge of indulgent irony, because he knew well Thomas's knack for meeting famous people. ("It's not a knack," he told me. "He puts himself in the presence of famous people, and makes sure that it's documented in some way. And that's great. We could both be at the same event, there could be ten famous people in the room, I would meet none of them, and Thomas would meet all of them.")

Thomas had a question for me. "What is the sameness of America, and what is the stark difference of America, that you've seen thus far?" I told him it was a big question and that I would think about it. We passed a cop. "Oh no, oh no, oh no!" he cried. "Oh, I'm only going sixty-six. He's in the middle of a good donut. He just got down to the jelly."

"I find it hard to kiss people I don't know, male or female, full on the lips," reflected Bill.

"Well, I think that's diminished over the last few years," said Thomas. "Don't you think?"

"I think we're all on a continuum," said Bill. "There are very few people who are solely one or the other."

"Well, Ethan is solely one," said Thomas.

"I want to talk about gay marriage," I said.

"You take that one," said Thomas to Bill.

"Why me? You're the talker," said Bill. "I think that gay marriage is absolutely the way to go. It's something the whole United States should just embrace and get over. Marriage is a civil institution, not a religious one. And the religions keep trying to mix the two up."

"When you use the term 'same-sex marriage,'" said Thomas, "Bingo! People start thinking about penises and anuses. That's one of the problems in our puritanical culture. We need to talk about marriage equality. Marriage equality now offers hope and is able to help stem teenage suicide, or many, many years of suppression. We are probably saving many teenagers from jumping off a bridge or taking pills."

"But when Thomas is saying that, he's saying it in Massachusetts, where we exist in this silo," Bill pointed out. "He's not saying it in Montana. Even though we're in Massachusetts, there are still a lot of parents that don't get it."

"I just wanted to see what would happen," said Thomas, "if Mark Zuckerberg had announced, 'I'm getting engaged, and Mike and I ....'"

"Well, how about 'Karim and I?'" said Bill. "Or 'Tyrone and I'?"

Thomas had recently been asked to speak to a group from NAGLY, the Northshore Alliance for Gay & Lesbian Youth, consisting primarily of gay teenagers. "I said to them, I said, 'Okay, kids, close your eyes, kids, and imagine a world without Ellen DeGeneres, without *Will and Grace*, without Elton John, without George Michael, without Facebook, and imagine that twenty-three years ago I had to walk up to Bill and say hi.' And they looked at me as if I were from the Pleistocene Era."

"They probably can't actually imagine that," I imagined.

"Yeah," he agreed. "When I watch *Roots*, I can't really put myself in LeVar Burton's place. Now, if you ask me what it's like to be married to Bill Henning, just take what you and Jenny have, times ten. I'm the luckiest man in the world. You just feel undeserving."

"I'm gonna blush," said Bill.

We discussed the first presidential debate, the one where Obama barely showed up. "He understands what it's really like to be president," said Bill, excusing him. "You realize that you can't be idealistic about everything."

"Yeah, I saw all of that to some degree in his face, but it still doesn't excuse his performance," said Thomas. Thomas saw Obama's blackness in the context of political history. "You guys are too young, and I'm almost too young, but Kennedy coming to power as a Catholic—oh my God!" Then he waxed philosophical again: "These things are all contemporary stuff because we're the moths that are alive today. While we're in it, we can see all the tapestry of what's going on. Five hundred years from now, this'll be compressed into two sentences."

Massachusetts was in the midst of a close U.S. Senate race between Republican Senator Scott Brown, who had won the seat vacated by Ted Kennedy's death, and the Harvard Law School professor Elizabeth Warren. Bringing us back to the tapestry, I said: "Scott Brown just seems to be a pretty boy from Central Casting."

"Yeah. I hope she whips his ass good and proper," said Thomas with feeling.

"Unfortunately, it's tight," said Bill. "I hate to say it, but she almost comes across as too brainy."

"You guys were one of the first gay couples to be married in Massachusetts, right?"

"The law passed in 2004," said Bill. "And we didn't get married until 2005."

"That day, Ethan, was a magical day for me," said Thomas. "I was literally having an out-of-body. As I was standing there holding Bill's hand, doing our bit, at the same time I was up in the rafters looking down. And something caught my eye, and I turned to look, and it was Bill's sister holding her cell phone up so that Bill's mother back in Wisconsin could hear our vows."

"It's nice to visit our friends in other states and hear them ooh and ah that we have the real deal," said Bill. "They're envious."

"Bill and I were kind of mini celebrities on a cruise we were on," said Thomas. "Maybe it was the Med cruise in '08. They saw our gold wedding rings and asked where we were from, and when we said Salem, Massachusetts, they said, 'Oh my God, you guys are the real deal!'"

"And that's what brings it home again," said Bill, "because in Massachusetts it's almost a non-issue. And we think about that when we think about eventually leaving Massachusetts for retirement. Because there is no warm place in the United States that has gay marriage. Iowa doesn't count. We need a Florida, a California."

"And then the usual vacuous questions, like, 'What is that like?'" said Thomas.

"That is the question, isn't it?" Bill agreed. "'What is that like?'"

"Yeah. It's like, 'I've always been black.' But straight people in Massachusetts come right down to the individual. Fuck the big picture."

✳

"I saw Norman Mailer here once," Thomas told me. We were standing on Commercial Street in Provincetown, waiting for Bill to come out of a clothing shop. "He had two canes, and he was just walking down the street. And nobody even looked twice. Marlon Brando used to hang out here, back in the day. You know who comes here every year, is John Waters. He usually comes for the film festival. He's premiered a few films here. If I had had a picture of me and Norman Mailer, how iconic would that have been? But I didn't have my cell phone back then."

"Do you think he would have had his picture taken with you?" I asked.

He paused, a little ostentatiously, to think about it. "Yeah," he concluded. "Because he was just strolling down the street: 'Hi, hi.' People weren't lionizing him or rushing him. That's how I met Truman Capote, in New York, *many* years ago."

"Just walking down the street?"

"We were in front of the Plaza Hotel, Central Park South, me and my friend Michael, who was an actor. And I heard this voice"—he imitated the voice—"that could only be Truman Capote. He was with another gentleman, arm in arm, kind of like these two ladies right here. And I said, 'Mr. Capote, what a pleasure to meet you. I'm from Bermuda, and I'm visiting my friend Michael here in New York.' And he said, 'I'm going to Bermuda next month.' And so I started explaining what he should see and do while he was there. So he said he wouldn't be seeing and doing much, because he was working on something, and he would be ensconced. He said, 'I won't be entertaining anybody.' So I said, 'I'll give you a call when you're there, just to greet you. I won't impose on you.' And he said, 'You do that. I'd love that.'"

"That was the beginning of your career in Bermuda Tourism," I said.

"Unofficially, yes. But every Bermudian works for Bermuda Tourism. So a month later, on the date that he said he'd be there, I called the hotel, and I asked for Mr. Capote's room, and they put me through. He was very, very gracious, and we talked about nothing for about two minutes. And then we hung up the phone, and that was the end of that."

Bill came out of the clothing shop. "Oh, here's my credit card again," said Thomas. "What did you get?"

"Just underwear," said Bill.

"You were there, weren't you, when we saw Norman Mailer strolling down the street, with his two canes?"

"Yes."

"Was it right here where you saw Norman Mailer?" I asked.

"It was actually down there, where we smelled the hemp," said Thomas.

Over dinner that evening in a tasteful pub, he got mushy again. "You want to believe that there's a purpose of being here tomorrow. Because you want to be part of what tomorrow is going to bring."

"I don't expect us to come up with the answers here at this table," I assured him.

"I mean, your father's in that business. What does he say?"

"He's had a lot to say over the years."

Thomas paused and indicated the background music. "You hear Tina Turner? 'All we want is to get beyond Thunder Dome.' The answer's coming right out of that speaker."

✳

I had never given much thought to where exactly Bill fit in back in Oconomowoc; I was more concerned at the time with whether and where I did. Where he fit in was his lookout. But now I wanted to know.

"I don't wax too nostalgic about Oconomowoc," he told me during our drive back to Salem the next day. "Because there was a distinct difference between my growing up in Ixonia and being from Oconomowoc. In high school I still felt like an outsider, even after becoming involved in some activities. I think all kids who were from the country, and not the town, probably felt that way. My real connection to Oconomowoc was that my grandmother lived in Oconomowoc, and my mother was raised in Oconomowoc."

"I felt like an outsider too," I confessed.

"Yeah, I would imagine you would," said Bill. "It's like how Thomas and I felt when we came to Massachusetts. They really know how to make you feel like an outsider. It's down to an art form. I haven't gone back for reunions. I think I went for the first one, and that was it." Our thirty-year high school reunion was to be held the next summer, and neither of us was planning to be there. "Oconomowoc has an inflated sense of what it is. They still parlay their historical role as a vacation place for the rich from Milwaukee. And it's really not that anymore."

"What made you feel that difference?" I asked him.

"It was because you weren't part of the crowd that came from the town. I'll use [So-and-so] as an example." So-and-so's father was a doctor, and they lived in a big house on a lake. So-and-so's mother was a housewife, and I liked her because, if we were sitting around her dining table playing Dungeons & Dragons when she came home from the grocery store, she always made a big point of fussing over us and giving us snacks. My mom was great, but she wasn't that kind of mom. "I was never going to be great friends with [So-and-so]," Bill continued. "You were never going to be included in that crowd. It was fine to be an acquaintance, and you could be included if it was convenient, but you were never going to be great friends."

Wisconsin was on my mind during this political season, not least because of vice presidential candidate Paul Ryan. I considered the guy an embarrassment not only to my home state but also to my nominal ethnicity. One of those Irishmen that rocks on his heels, as Eugene McCarthy would say.

"He kinda looks like Eddie Munster grown up," was Bill's comment.

"What does Wisconsin mean to you?" I asked him.

"Really just the place I was born and raised. Other people place it on me. They say, 'You're a cheesehead.' So I laugh and say, 'Yeah, I'm a cheesehead.' I'm proud that it tends to be independent to a great degree, that I come from a state that's not red."

"Were you always going to leave Wisconsin?"

"These difficult questions! Um, I didn't realize that I was going to leave Wisconsin until I got to college and began to realize that I was gay, and I realized that I couldn't live in a small city. And part of that was that I didn't want my family to be impacted by my being gay. You can be swallowed up in a big city if you're gay. You can't do that in a small town."

"So Chicago was the nearest big city."

"I guess it could have been Milwaukee or Madison. But those felt too close. Chicago was a bit farther away. But it was also job opportunities. For Marshall Field's to come to campus, and to get an interview, was a big deal. So for all of those reasons, Chicago made sense."

We were in heavy Boston traffic now. "This is why I'm glad I'm not going to be on the planet fifty years from now, when this is the new normal," grumbled Thomas at the wheel.

"Don't worry, Thomas," I said. "We'll run out of oil before that happens."

"Yeah, it'll be my horse and his horse."

"That's why we're going to go electric," said Bill.

"We'll be the first gay Amish," said Thomas.

"I would say that I am proud of the fact that Wisconsin is prominent in the news, and that it's helped to open this debate," Bill went on.

"Which debate?"

"I'm thinking specifically of the union debate with Walker. The governor tried to do something, and the people didn't just sit back and take it. They fought back. And even though they didn't win, they did what they could within the system. And unfortunately it's led to other states trying the same thing around the country, because they think it's all right to do that sort of thing."

"Part of what I picked up in Wisconsin was that Barrett was a completely lame and useless candidate," I said. Barrett was the Milwaukee mayor who had lost twice to Walker.

"Oh really?" said Bill. "Because I can't talk about that with my family. I would call and ask them what's going on, and they'd say, 'Oh, we're not following it, we're not really interested in that.' My family isn't political at all. It's frustrating when you're outside, and you're calling them, and they're *right there*. And I wonder, if I had stayed in Wisconsin, if I would have been the same way. But I think that if you're gay you become political, because you realize that the only way we're going to make progress as gay people is through politics. Once you cross over, and you become politically minded, and your family isn't, it's one more thing that separates you. Because that's what you want to talk about. You call back, and you're like, 'Oh my God! You're in the middle of a firestorm, and you don't know it!'" After a short silence he added, "What else do you want to talk about, Ethan?"

"I want to talk about Romney."

"Oh. Bastard! It was okay to have Romney as a Republican governor, because you knew that the Democratic legislature was going to protect against him doing something stupid, or putting forward too much of his agenda. Massachusetts people like to think that they want a balance. Every once in a while they throw a Republican into the mix, because they can say, 'Oh, we've got balance.' That's why I think the Scott Brown thing happened. But we should be embarrassed now that we let it happen, because it was the stepping-stone Romney was looking for. I think most people are just embarrassed by him now. There was a clip on TV this morning, where he was debating Shannon O'Brien, who was the Democratic candidate that ran against him for governor, and he was saying, 'I will absolutely protect the right of a woman to choose.' Such a concrete example of how he just blows with the wind."

I also wanted Bill's views, as a banker, on the banking crisis. He now worked as a small-business lender at a local bank in downtown Salem. "We're small peanuts compared to the big banks," he told me.

"Part of the current economic problem is people not being able to get loans, because banks are scared to lend," he said back in Salem that evening. "So the government has tried to encourage banks to lend. Banks aren't altruistic. They want to help, but they still have to do that within a framework that allows them to make profit. So there's this tug. They want to lend, but it's hard to do that in a way that you know you're going to get paid back. And fortunately there are still the community banks, who are very focused on really trying to get money in the hands of their community. And they are not the ones that caused the problem. The big banks caused the problem, and they're the ones least likely to get money in the hands of small businesses."

"Are you willing to name some of the big banks by name?"

"Sure. Any of the big ones. Bank of America, Chase, Wells Fargo. They'll have a lending division that's supposed to focus on giving small business loans. But in order to keep control, the box is small. And if you don't fit in that box, you don't get your loan. They keep the lending criteria really narrow, because they don't want to take a risk on the loans at the edges that might go bad. Even though if they do a $100,000 loan and it goes bad, for them it's a drop in the bucket, whereas if I give a $100,000 loan and it goes bad, it's a bigger hit to a small bank's bottom line. But I'll take the risk and give the loan, because it's a business in my community. Not all the time, but I'm going to give that business more leeway to prove that they can repay the loan. Small banks go into a loan saying, 'How can we do this loan?' Whereas it *feels* as if the big banks go in saying, 'How can we *not* do this loan?'

"And I speak from some authority, in that I worked for a large bank for the first two years of my lending career, and I've worked for successively smaller banks since. And I see the difference. The regulatory environment for banks is hard enough, but it's going to get worse. And I'm not going to say Dodd-Frank is bad, but it is going to cause banks more compliance headaches than they had before, and monitoring for compliance is a cost. Enough added regulations are being layered onto the small banks because of what the big banks did, and small banks can least afford the additional cost. It's sad for small business, and I agree that it's one of the things that's going to help bring the economy back. It's a chicken-and-egg thing, because they don't want to invest in borrowing money. They don't want to get themselves in the position of not knowing if they can pay the money back."

❋

On my way out of New England I showed my trip-in-progress slide show at the Renaissance School in Springfield, in central Massachusetts. Afterwards I was eager to get out of town, but one of the students buttonholed me and got special permission from the principal to spend the afternoon showing me around. The student's name was Jesse Lederman, and he kind of swept me off my feet.

"This is a bonus," I told him. "I thought I was just going to speak at a high school and then skip town."

"Well, we can't let you leave without seeing Springfield."

As we drove around in his cluttered car, Jesse told me: "We're called the 'city of firsts'. Cars were invented here. Guns were invented here. Smith & Wesson is still based here. Innovations in manufacturing were the city's forte. Beautiful neighborhoods for the most part. Up until the seventies, the schools were nationally acclaimed. But the neighborhoods deteriorated and, for a long time, Springfield was known as a poor city. But it wasn't known as a dangerous city until probably the early 2000s. The Mafia, in addition to controlling the local government, controlled the gangs. Gangs distributed the drugs, and the Mafia controlled the gangs. A lot of people didn't really mind the Mafia. But the education system was deteriorating, the management of the city was deteriorating. And, especially under Romney, there was no oversight of Springfield and western Massachusetts in general. There was no support from the state. By 2002, Springfield was just completely bankrupt."

Like Detroit, and like Seattle for that matter, Springfield was a city of neighborhoods. "There's seventeen neighborhoods in Springfield, and every single one of them is unique," said Jesse.

"You're a real enthusiast for Springfield, I gotta say." I was amazed that someone seventeen years old could know so much history.

"I love Springfield. Every neighborhood in Springfield thinks it's the best, including the worst. And now that they have representation by ward, they each have their own city councilor. Our city councilor is called E. Henry Twiggs. If you google him, you'll find out why he's awesome." Jesse made me stand on a corner on Bay Street and look in both directions. "This is the Mason-Dixon Line of Springfield," he said. Bay and Oldhill were on one side of Bay Street, and on the other was a neighborhood called McKnight. "McKnight is the oldest intact Victorian neighborhood in the United States. McKnight is so interesting, because McKnight is so representative of Springfield. McKnight was the first planned development. The McKnight brothers bought all the land and sold plots to rich people. There's no talk about how to create a good neighborhood. It's all about how to look like a good neighborhood, and how to draw middle-class white people. The other subculture of the neighborhood was the elderly black people who had owned the houses and lived here since the fifties. That's the way Springfield is. There's these whole groups of people that basically want to pretend that the poor people that live right next to them don't exist."

"So they really don't interact?"

"No. They haven't interacted for a long time. But now there are groups that are coming out and saying that if we don't interact, we're not going to change anything."

Driving along Bay Street, he said: "Look around you. Now wait five seconds."

"I just see a parking lot," I said.

"Wait another five seconds." On both sides were four-story brick buildings.

"Is this the projects?"

"No. This is subsidized housing, though. This is one of the worst neighborhoods in the city." We turned left around a corner. "And this is Merriam-Webster's headquarters. That's just the way Springfield is, because it's so historic."

"I get their Word of the Day by email," I told him.

"It's probably sent out from that building."

"How did you become so hip to all this?"

"I have absolutely no idea. I don't come from a political family. My dad was a social worker; my mom works for Baystate." Baystate was a hospital and health care system based in Springfield. "My parents bought our house for $78,000. It was a crack house, it was fucked up, they fixed it up, and before the housing bubble burst it was appraised at $199,000. Being white, and coming from a middle-class background, but from, as Elizabeth Warren likes to say, 'the ragged edge of the middle class,' that feeling that you're one step away from being poor, that at any minute you could be pushed into a completely different social setting than you're used to, I felt that I could represent that middle-class white view, but also the opposite. We were organizing a public safety forum, and I was all ready to go door knocking in the projects. And a lot of the white people who were with me were like, 'What do you mean we're going door knocking in the projects?' And I thought of course—they're part of the community. And the projects are a great place to door-knock, because you totally bring out Democratic voters. And we door-knocked, and it was great, and what happened was that we ended up talking to a lot of nice older black ladies."

Then Jesse took me to see the Springfield Armory Museum. "This is another example of Springfield's claim to fame, which was also its downfall." The armory had been commissioned by George Washington. "And when it closed after World War II, it was part of the downfall of the manufacturing. Now it's a museum."

"Like the breweries in Milwaukee," I said. "Why Springfield?"

"It was the cross-roads of America at the time. It was very easy to get things to and from Springfield."

Jesse was eager to introduce me to his friends at an organization called Arise for Social Justice, so we stopped by their storefront office. "They're respected by social jus-

tice institutions and feared by politicians, so they're good," he said. "They're definitely a force." A woman he introduced me to named Ellen Graves described Arise as "a poor persons' rights organization and the voice of the homeless."

"Arise was one of the backbones for the tent city," Ellen told me, "where people put up tents because the shelters were being closed. The city's been pissed off at us about homelessness since we had the tent city, eight or ten years ago. It went on the bishop's front lawn. This was a new bishop—the old bishop had left in disgrace for molesting—and we figured he didn't want to make any more enemies, and it was a really great lawn. We do not have enough shelters in the city at all. We used to have a soup kitchen and a food pantry. Arise is involved in a lot of stuff. The police officers think they have the right to just beat people up. We have a lot of problems with 'driving while black.' They hide behind the badge. There's that blue network, where they're never going to tell on each other. This is what we're fighting, as well as the housing issues. We're part of No One Leaves, a movement against housing foreclosures. A year ago we did a big stand-out against Bank of America. And last Friday we did a big eviction blockade. We were all standing there, waiting to be arrested. Somehow Senator Kerry's office got involved. And the fact that we were all there, and there were TV cameras, brought more pressure, and the bank said they would start negotiating with the family. Aurora Bank in Colorado. And that's part of the problem, because no one knows who they're dealing with. It's not like the little bank down the street."

"This is a national subject," I said.

"It is," she agreed. "It's a national disaster."

"Sometimes it takes months and months to figure out who owns the mortgage and who holds the title," said Ellen's colleague Liz Bewsee. "And of course with all the robo-signing that was going on ..."

"When I hear about robo-signing I think about Florida and California," I said.

"Springfield has the biggest number in Massachusetts," said Ellen.

"How bad are things in Massachusetts?"

"In foreclosures, or in general?" asked Liz. "One of the biggest things we deal with is family homelessness. Earlier this year they started making it harder and harder for families to get into shelters. This is a cash cow that the motels really don't want to do away with." The cost for a family to stay in a motel for a month could be $3,000, whereas in a shelter it would be more like $1,500. "We've been working with so many families in the last couple of weeks. You don't want to tell people that they have to lie, but sometimes they have to lie. And it's not getting any better."

"And look at the houses they could fix up and people could be living in," said Ellen. "They also took the benches out of the park, because the homeless people sit on them. But no one deserves to be homeless. No one deserves to be beat up by the police." In the winter of 2003, two homeless men had frozen to death within two weeks. "And I knew both of the guys. Larry Dunham and Darryl Cooper."

Jesse also introduced me to 27-year-old Reuben Santiago, a paid staff member and vice president of Arise. "Before I got involved with Arise, I was homeless for a year and a half," Reuben told me. "I was in the shelter, in the rescue mission. It was tough. They only gave me one thin blanket. I was kind of skeptical of Arise at first, but there were a lot of positive individuals that helped me. I was couch surfing." Reuben was now also involved with MOCHA, the Men of Color Health Awareness program at the YMCA, and in mentoring other young men. And he was assistant manager at a rooming house in return for reduced rent, and a certified nursing assistant. "I'm trying to get myself in at Baystate," he said. "That is my dream. My mom died of lung cancer on August 24, and that inspired me."

"How do you feel about the job market?" I asked him.

"Since this recession hit, it's no jobs. There's jobs, but not good jobs. I actually want to be in a hospital setting. I love helping out the community."

As Jesse and I got back in his car he said, "Are these the coolest people in the world, or what?"

"You seem a lot more plugged in to what's going on at street level than I was when I was seventeen," I told him. "And you seem like you're in it for the long haul."

"I hope so," he said. "This is one of the community gardens. There are five throughout the city."

The gardens were a project of a group called Gardening the Community. "They farm these local plots, and they sell the produce at the local farmers' markets. And those markets are geared towards lower-income people."

"This is like what I saw in Detroit."

"Mostly the land is donated. They're trying to get more land."

Jesse dropped me off at my car in the Renaissance School parking lot. "Things just change so fast here," he said. "Springfield is so weird. They're probably going to build a giant resort casino downtown. I can't tell you what the city will be like in five years."

✳

All I managed to do in New York City was catch up with my friend Taimoor Shahid. Taimoor was a wonderfully literate and intelligent young Pakistani writer who had won a Fulbright scholarship to do a graduate program in South Asian Studies at Columbia University. A mutual friend had introduced us in early 2011 when I was in Pakistan, and Taimoor had put me up for a couple of nights in Karachi. I took the train in to Harlem from White Plains, walked crosstown in the rain, and spent a couple of hours walking around with Taimoor. I asked him how things were going.

"When I come here, I have to operate as a brown person," he said.

"What does it mean to operate as a brown person in America?"

"Even in New York, which is a very cosmopolitan city, when you're walking in a subway and you walk past that ad, you're bound to feel that you are brown and Muslim, in a way that you don't feel back home." The ad, purchased by a group called the American Freedom Defense Initiative, had run on New York subway platforms the previous month. It read:

IN ANY WAR
BETWEEN THE
CIVILIZED MAN
AND THE SAVAGE,
SUPPORT THE
CIVILIZED MAN.

SUPPORT ISRAEL
DEFEAT JIHAD

"You feel that your identity is being glossed by these categories that are being created by other people, and not you," said Taimoor. "It becomes: 'Oh. This is what I am here. This is how I'm perceived here. I should keep this in mind.' I can't get away from this category that makes me feel that I don't belong in this place. If you're speaking in support of Muslims too much, you don't know what kind of person you'll be perceived as being. You have to tone it down."

I asked how his studies were going.

"I'm in Edward Said's department," he said. The famous Columbia literature professor, left-wing gadfly, and author of *Orientalism*. "My academic project is looking at how Persian cosmopolitan literary culture shapes vernacular literary culture in northern India. Actually, coming to this department made me a very political person, in a way in which I was not before. I have come to realize that they are not distinct categories. The literary is very, very political. I've become more political in the sense that, fine, you can have a historical understanding of the world, but which side are you on? It's an ethical choice that you have to make."

"So what are you going to do with that?"

"I don't know. I don't have an articulated position. But it is not with this current system, this liberal, capitalist democracy. I don't want to write from a position of disdainful scorn that this liberal position carries in Pakistan. In order to engage with people like Pervez Hoodbhoy, or Nadeem Paracha, or Najam Sethi"—big-shot Pakistani liberals—"you need to engage them in the sense of saying, 'For God's sake, understand history.'"

We passed a lady walking five dogs.

"You know how there are people in New York City who are professional dog walkers?" I said.

"Yes, I learned that from watching Woody Allen movies. I'd like to think that there is some space that is beyond political space. But it is very difficult to find that."

"Would you say that you realize that to a greater extent than when you and I first met in Karachi?"

"Yes. My project is important and relevant only because it is a political project. Otherwise it would be like, 'Get a life, dude!' History is not about the past. History is about the present. It is through these narratives of and about history that you create the present. If you want to take a very broad-brush example, it would be this idea that Muslims have always been extremists and that Islam is an inherently intolerant religion. That is a narrative of history that is created and used to support present political concerns. It is a foil for the present understanding of Islam and the Muslim world. That is why, if somebody like me is studying the interaction between the Persianate and the Indic world, it is not only about that world."

Like any pair of Manhattanites, we fretted about the futility of it all while drinking coffee.

"We should realize our limitations as human beings, that we cannot change the world," Taimoor said. "However, that realization should not deter us from doing whatever we can. It is a very difficult and a very mature realization. If you think it's a horrible movie and millions of people are watching it, and your article will only be read by a hundred people, you should still write the article. And be okay with the fact that God is playing an elaborate joke."

We left the coffee shop, and I went along with him to one of those unofficially obligatory departmental get-togethers that people in grad programs at universities have to go to. There was wine and pizza. As we stood around, Taimoor introduced me to various colleagues. He described me to one of them, an Indian woman, as a travel writer.

"Travel is a genre that's difficult to write without romanticizing or fetishizing," she remarked.

I stood there waiting for her to say something more. The longer the pause became, the more I felt accused. Then my allergy to academic leftism kicked in, and I made my excuses and my escape.

*

"How did we end up here?" asked Katie, age 14, as the Burhop family was getting ready to leave the house for shopping and soccer. It was Sunday, and I was headed separately to Princeton, where I had a thing that afternoon.

"We lived in Queens," Katie's mother Annmarie told her, "and my father, your grandfather, wanted to get out of New York City. He worked for the Veterans Administration, so he asked for a transfer. So they transferred him to Little Rock, Arkansas. Which was a big culture shock. We were there for a year. My dad was very happy, the rest of us not so much. So he got transferred here, which was a good compromise. It was far enough from New York, but still close enough to be near family."

"Here" was the western Philadelphia suburb of Havertown. Jerry Burhop had graduated from Oconomowoc High School a year ahead of me and ended up here. We hadn't been close in high school, but as adults we had stayed friendly and in touch. I had met Jerry's family here nearly a decade earlier, when Katie and Emma were little and I was still living in England and came to the East Coast on work.

"How many miles have you put on your car?" Annmarie asked me.

"About nine thousand so far."

"Did you buy a new Prius?"

"No, that's a rental. Enterprise has a good long-term program that makes it easy. It's called the Month or More Program."

"That's great," said Jerry. "That way you don't have to worry about mileage."

"Or maintenance, or selling it afterwards, or anything," I said. "Some people suggested that I get sponsorship. But what if the Enterprise company turned out to be big Tea Party donors or something?"

"They are family owned," he reflected. "Have you thought about the irony of driving a foreign car around America? You couldn't have got a Chevy Volt?"

Jerry was squat and balding and a thoroughgoing family man. I saw him as everything I wasn't: stable, civic-minded, a productive member of society. He made his living as a financial advisor.

"Sometimes I think I got into this work by accident," he told me over lunch. We had driven to the restaurant from his office in his spiffy sports car, which he joked Annmarie had let him buy to satisfy his need for a mid-life crisis. I couldn't tell you what make it was, because sports cars don't interest me. Jerry had gotten his bachelor's degree from UW-Madison in agricultural journalism. "So you were gonna be a farm reporter," I guessed.

"Well, no, I was not going to be Les Nesman," he laughed. "I was focused on advertising. My first job out of college, I became a licensed broker and tried to build a clientele at a brokerage firm. I did that for less than a year. I think I got licensed in May '88 and, if you remember, October of '87 was Black Monday. The firm was not the most ethical. I couldn't sell what they were selling. And I'm not a real salesman. The job market in that time was actually not that bad." So he did management training and ran a rental car office in Appleton, Wisconsin, hometown of Joe McCarthy. "Great town," said Jerry. "But there's only so much going on there. It was one of those nowhere-to-go-but-up scenarios." So he took a transfer to Philadelphia, then became a district manager in New Jersey. "The rental car thing was paying the bills pretty well," he said. But when the Budget franchise changed hands, he was laid off. "So I took a finance course and hooked into the whole finance thing."

"The economy the last five years has been—what?" I asked him. "What adjective would you use?"

"'Turbulent' is a good one," he said. "I think most people would say we're still in a recession at this point. We're clawing our way out. And clawing our way out is a good way of describing how we're going to emerge from this recession. It's going to take time."

"How does this affect your clients' investments?"

"Well, the market is probably the best indicator of the economy. So trying to predict the market based on economic indicators doesn't work."

"Because it's backwards?"

"It's totally backwards. But we try to do it anyways, in our business. Keeping people in an investment, and keeping them in the market, in an appropriate portfolio, is one of the ways we add value for our clients. Sometimes we're more counselors than we are investment analysts. The market makes a correction, or something happens in the economy, people get emotional about their money, and they call up and they want to pull out their money, and that's usually the worst time to do it. Successful investing is all about discipline. A lot of it is hand-holding and explaining to them that the market is somewhat separate from the economy, in that it predicts the economy, rather than vice versa. The market has already priced in the election."

"Huh?"

"The market is really good at pricing in things before they actually happen. We see a little market turbulence in the second quarter of this year. That, I think, was the market trying to figure out what was going to happen in the election."

"What did it figure out?"

"That's the trick," he said. "It doesn't tell you. The market has it figured out, but it isn't telling us. Historically, even with crucial elections, the market doesn't move dramatically after an election. It moves before. And we don't see it in real time. Now, what the market hasn't figured out is the fiscal cliff."

"What's the fiscal cliff?"

He gave me an incredulous look. "You've been living under a rock, economically speaking."

He explained the fiscal cliff to me: that Bush-era tax cuts were due to expire, and cuts in government spending were due to kick in, both on January 1. "These two things are going to be the exact opposite of what should be done," he said. "If they don't do anything, unemployment for a lot of people gets cut off. If they don't do anything, taxes go up. There's other things, but those are the two big things."

"So obviously it matters a lot who wins the election," I said.

"I think it matters more what happens in Congress in the lame-duck session. The fact that it's going to be a lame-duck session helps, because you're going to have senators and representatives who don't have to worry about being reelected. They can do the right thing."

"Who are you going to vote for?"

"Most likely Obama. I'm eighty percent there. There's some aspects of Mitt Romney that are attractive, but I don't think he gets it. He doesn't have the kind of track record that I'd like to see. His business background is appealing, but government is not business. That's the conflict."

"Some people say he's a predator," I said. "That he chews up companies and spits them out."

"That's just part of market efficiency."

"So you don't see Romney as some evil predator?"

"From what he did at Bain Capital, no."

"Do you think the right thing was done with General Motors?"

"That's almost a coin toss."

"People I've talked to in Michigan say they really appreciate what did happen, because it saved a lot of jobs."

"If the economy had been fine, you wouldn't have seen a bailout," said Jerry. "GM would have been allowed to go into bankruptcy. People say, 'Was the bailout the right thing to do?' I think it was the right thing to do *at that time*."

I asked what he thought of Paul Ryan.

"I didn't know a lot about him initially," he said. "Some of my initial impressions, some of the legislation that he was involved in, I thought was creative. But being a guy with creative ideas, I would have expected him to be a little more compromising. But it was like, 'Here's my creative idea. If you don't like it, too bad.'"

"How do you feel about him being from Wisconsin?"

"It's the home team, you know? I've never been able to figure Wisconsin out politically. As you dig deeper into what's going on in his district, he's got the GM plant in Janesville. That shut down. What was he doing to prevent that? The only thing I've heard from him about that was that it was Obama's fault. But Obama wasn't elected until after it was shut down. This campaign is a pick-your-scapegoat approach to politics."

"I've always had the impression that you're a pretty liberal guy," I said, maybe a little plaintively.

"Pretty much," he said. "I don't remember the last time I voted for a Republican."

"But you're considering it this time."

"Like I said, I'm eighty percent Obama. I have a hard time casting a vote unless I consider both sides."

"Don't you feel a responsibility to vote Democratic to balance out your brother?" That elicited a giggle from Jerry, which turned into a chortle and then into a guffaw. Jerry's brother Ed had been good friends with my brother Aaron, and still was. It all started on the first day of seventh grade, when our mom packed Aaron a tomato sandwich in his lunchbox, and the juice from the tomatoes made the bread all soggy and gross, and Ed took pity on Aaron and gave him half of his sandwich. But Ed was one of those right-wing blowhards who snipe at the rest of us on Facebook and call anyone who disagrees with them a moron. The exasperating irony was that the Burhops' mother was Mexican-American, so Ed had enjoyed the benefits of preferential financial aid for minority students.

"It's interesting," said Jerry. "I coined the phrase 'pick-your-scapegoat politics' in an email to my brother. Do I, as an individual, living in my suburban community, see recession? I don't see a recession unless I look for it. My demographic sector is okay. I have to look for the recession. But Ed claimed to me in an email that there's no one going hungry in America. I volunteer in a food bank. About three or four times a year we go, and part of what they do is, they have a video to raise awareness. They'll interview people who use the food bank and need it. And that number has grown. But part of the problem is that if you don't see people that need help, it's very easy to say, 'They're lazy' or 'It's their own fault.'"

"So it becomes us against them," I said.

"Well, not so much us versus them, but that we don't see them. So then it becomes about 'my tax dollars.' It's about *something* that's taking my tax dollars. Not even *someone*. Fifty percent of high school-educated black men are unemployed."

"You know a lot of these sta-tistics because it's part of your work," I guessed.

"Yeah. On the unemployment website they show statistics for different demographics, and it's very eye-opening. If you have a white male with a high school education it's better, but it's still like thirty percent. I think part of the reason we're not seeing any more of these Tea Party demonstrations is that half the people who were in those demonstrations are unemployed."

As I had done with Bill Henning, I put Jerry on the spot about Oconomowoc.

"I don't care how aware you are of the world around you, your hometown is always filtered through the rose-colored glasses of childhood," he said. "If you had a good childhood, you've got good glasses. I didn't realize how little I had as a child, until I grew up."

"So how do you remember Oconomowoc?"

"Great place to grow up as a kid. Safe. You could ride your bike anywhere. You had a lake; you could ride your bike to go swim. You didn't have to worry about the bad things of the world coming in. They didn't."

"We played kick the can until it got dark at nine o'clock in the summer," I remembered.

"Yeah. Even after dark. You played football in somebody's yard, you went down to the park to play baseball. I put so many miles on my bike. That's probably why I still like to ride my bike. But somewhere along the way in high school, I came to realize the socioeconomic structure of Oconomowoc. You talk about the haves and the have-nots. In Oconomowoc it was the haves and the have-lots. We didn't see poverty. We were lucky if we saw people of color. And they were fine too."

"That's why they were in Oconomowoc." If there were any. I never saw any, unless you counted Jerry and Ed.

"Yeah. It trickles down to the point where it affects how your classmates treat you. They had a boat and they could go water skiing every weekend. I had to ride my bike down to the lake to go swimming. And I guess that kind of taints my memory of Oconomowoc."

"Your dad worked at the Carnation plant?"

"Yeah. Blue-collar factory worker. General maintenance."

"Was it hard for you to adapt to being on the East Coast?" Annmarie was very New York City, very Italian, and very attached and devoted to her family.

"Not really, no," he admitted. "My wife asked me that several times, and my response was, 'People are the same everywhere, just different.' I was already displaced when I came out here, before I met her. What's the difference?"

I had lunch with Annmarie separately the next day, on my way out of town. From their house in Havertown the drive became more and more autumnally idyllic the deeper I went into the woodsy upscale suburbs where she was a public school teacher. I picked her up at her school, and we went to the quaint little downtown nearby and had sandwiches at the kind of place where ladies do lunch.

"This is what's called the Main Line," she told me.

"I've heard of the Main Line."

"So most of our clients out here are wealthy."

I knew about the Main Line, the ritzy communities along the old Pennsylvania Railroad commuter line, from my friend Lenny Miller. Lenny and his father, Len Sr., had for many years been among the only black team owners in NASCAR and other car-racing circuits. They were fascinating people, with stories galore. They had hired me to edit Len Sr.'s autobiography, *Silent Thunder: Breaking through Cultural, Racial, and Class Barriers in Motorsports* ("A revealing story that is a winner"— Paul Newman). Len Sr.'s whole car thing had started right here on the Main Line, where his parents worked as household servants and he learned to customize cars from a white guy named Butch Clapsaddle.

"What's it like these days to be a public school teacher?" I asked Annmarie.

"It's incredibly challenging," she said. "It's not just working with kids anymore. It's also working with politicians. Somehow, in the past ten years, public school teachers have become the bad guys and the fall guys. One of the biggest frustrations for me is that I can't remember when we had a Secretary of Education who actually worked in the classroom. How do you measure success as a teacher? It's not easily quantifiable. There's always kids who achieve and kids who struggle. And there are always parents who are involved and parents who are not involved. In our society we set out to educate all our children. That is necessary, and it's a noble pursuit. However, it's not easy. That includes all our poor children, and all our special needs children. And when you look at other countries, they don't educate all their children. So it's not apples to apples. A lot of teachers have to fight to earn a decent wage. So now it's like, 'That's taxpayer money, and I'm your client, and you work for me.' And that's rich and poor."

"And that's more prevalent than it was twenty years ago?"

"Yeah. There's more animosity toward my profession than there ever was before."

"You must have been paying attention to the Wisconsin stuff, Walker and the capitol occupation."

"Oh, yeah. There's so much beyond the teacher's control, for test scores. When you look at what businesses and employers say they want in graduates, they're saying teamwork, problem solving, creative solutions, innovative thinking, people skills to work in a global world. How do you measure those things on a standardized test? You don't. Administrators' hands are tied, in that they have to go by the standardized tests."

"My mom got out just in time," I reflected.

✳

From lunch with Annmarie I drove south. I spent a night in Delaware, where I gave a little talk at the university, then drove the length of that state and the Eastern Shore of Maryland, crossed the Bay Bridge, passed Annapolis, got sucked onto the canyon-like Beltway with its tall, ominous sound barriers. I had spent my adult life avoiding other people's rat races, and driving around D.C. did nothing to dissuade me of the wisdom of that course. The exit signs for famous suburbs loomed over me: Silver Spring, Bethesda, Falls Church. Was I ever glad I didn't live here. I had, though, long ago between adventures.

In the spring of 1990 I had been living in Berkeley, enjoying my life in California and my painless and scenic half-hour bus commute to the Transbay Terminal in downtown San Francisco. At The Information Store on Second Street I wore a tie and took orders from librarians at East Coast pharmaceutical manufacturers for photocopies or, if it was extra-urgent, faxes of scientific papers published in journals held at the UC-Berkeley and UCSF libraries. I would write down the order and put it in a tray, then a runner would take it and hurry over and back on his motorcycle to beat the FedEx deadline. Talk about a doomed business model. My clients were mostly middle-aged women at corporate campuses in New Jersey, and they enjoyed chatting with me because I was a fine young man. My hours skewed early because of the time difference; I got to the office as early as seven-thirty and home by four-thirty or five. On October 17, 1989, that meant that I was already back in my room in Berkeley, walking toward my television to turn on the pre-game show before Game 3 of the World Series, at 5:04 p.m. when the big Loma Prieta earthquake hit. There was no more splendid sight in urban America than the morning sun hitting the San Francisco skyline as the bus emerged from the tunnel on Yerba Buena Island on the Bay Bridge, especially early in the morning in winter. My commute always made me think of that song "Lights," by Journey. Why I ever left the Bay Area, I don't know.

Except that I do know: my brother Aaron invited me to join him on a foreign adventure. In May and June 1990, as the Berlin Wall was crumbling, we rode the U-bahn to the Friedrichstrasse station in East Berlin and the train from there to Prague, then around in a circle through Bratislava, Vienna, Budapest, Debrecen, Krakow, Warsaw, and Gdansk. By the time we returned to East Berlin, border controls had been dropped within the long-divided city. The five-week jaunt ended for me in an idyllic moment alone in a beer tent in Leipzig, sipping a stein ordered from a bosomy waitress like a St. Pauli Girl logo come to life, listening to oompah music and enjoying the surreal sensation of having come home to Milwaukee in an alternate universe.

And at the end of that trip, with no job to go back to in San Francisco, I moved to D.C. because my brother was living there. I would walk to my temp jobs on K Street down Connecticut Avenue from where I was living near the National Zoo, over the Taft Bridge, past the Free Tibet protesters outside the Chinese Embassy, along the sidewalk where an elderly lady named Kitty walked her fat little wiry gray fifteen-year-old dog every morning, and across Dupont Circle. Like my bus ride from Berkeley to San Francisco, that walk was a great way to start the day. But if San Francisco couldn't hold me, D.C. certainly wasn't going to. And, as it turned out, Detroit couldn't hold me either. Neither could Bangkok, Lahore, or London. Only Seattle could do that.

✳

"I told my parents that if Obama wins, there's gonna be riots," said Lenny Miller. "There's gonna be lawsuits, recounts, all that."

"If you were President of the United States, would you be more vocal than he is?" I asked him.

"Oh, I would. I'm Morehouse College. He's Harvard."

After this lunch just outside the Beltway, I would be heading south into the bowels of Virginia. Lenny lived near Dulles Airport because he was a pilot for United Airlines, and we were meeting at Legal Sea Foods in the Galleria in Tysons Corner. My gig editing his father's book about breaking the NASCAR color barrier had turned into a real and enduring friendship. Lenny and his dad were two of the most interesting and enterprising people I had ever known, and Lenny had a talent and penchant for playing angles and connecting his friends to each other in productive ways. He had read Richard Branson's book *Losing My Virginity*, so he called that sort of thing a "Branson move" or "pulling a Branson." Lenny prided himself on his Branson moves.

"For any black leader, including now the President of the United States, the saying in the educated black community is that you have to be twice as good in order to get half as much," he told me. "You have to be almost perfect in order to be respected a hundred percent, and that's impossible for anyone to do. You're not allowed to make mistakes. You're not allowed to be on a learning curve. Where a white person—you take Sarah Palin, who's educated but she's rough around the edges, and her husband's blue-collar, she's accepted. She's more accepted than Obama. She became a celebrity, and she knew how to ride that wave. She rode it all the way to the bank. Alaska attracts a lot of white, lower-information people, 'cause it's the Last Frontier. I think he's just up against a lot of blue-collar racism. And that makes up a lot of America. People that booed Michelle Obama and Dr. Jill Biden at Homestead Speedway an hour south of Miami, back in November 2011. You can YouTube that."

I asked him who he thought was going to win.

"I think he'll win. It's gonna be close. It's gonna come down to those swing states: Ohio, Wisconsin, Virginia. Either way, it's gonna be close."

"And you're gonna be watching it for three days."

"That's right." Lenny had long since made a point of requesting his flight schedule for November, so he could be home for three days around Election Day.

"What's the historical meaning of Obama's presidency?"

"That he made the effort of trying to make everybody work together."

"What about his blackness?"

"Yeah, that's huge. He'll stand out compared with other presidents."

"Were you surprised when the backlash happened?"

"I'm not surprised, no. Any time a black person is in a leadership position, especially if he's commanding white people, you're always gonna have backlash."

My road trip made Lenny nostalgic for the big cross-country jaunt he had made in 1978, as a teenager, with his mother and sister. "We started out in Philadelphia on Greyhound," he remembered. "Then Ohio, Missouri, Amarillo, Texas. Across the Southwest: Albuquerque, Grand Canyon, L.A. We went to Disneyland. Then Vegas, Salt Lake, Yellowstone, Bismarck, North Dakota, Chicago, and back to Philadelphia."

"What was Bismarck like?"

"Nothin' there. In Bismarck we stayed in a Holiday Inn with an indoor pool, and the only attraction was Clyde the Bear. Some bear named Clyde. Months later, the vice president of Greyhound was fired because they lost so much money on those discounted tickets. And most of the Greyhound stations were kinda rough. And in those days, people rode it. That was an eye-opener. You grow up on the East Coast, you think every place is like where you are." He had been interested, for example, to learn that people in Oklahoma said *sack* and *pop* instead of *bag* and *soda*. "And after that trip, I said I would always live on the East Coast or the West Coast, never in the middle of the United States."

"That was your takeaway from that trip?"

"Yeah. I had my eyes set on L.A., but I never made it. And if you remember from my father's book, it was in September 1978 that Tommy Thompson was killed at Trenton Speedway. Two weeks after that trip." (This Tommy Thompson was not the governor of Wisconsin, but a black driver for Miller Racing Group.)

"Your father didn't go on that trip because of work?"

"Yeah, he was running a business. My mother was a schoolteacher, so she had summers off. She always gave me and my sister very productive summers. It was an eye-opener. It was my first time in the middle section of the country. It was a lot different than I imagined. And a lot of sparsely populated areas. But very picturesque. I remember the news stations. If you're in the middle of Ohio or Missouri, in a motel, and you turn on the news, it was almost like you were watching a college TV station. Not that it wasn't important, just that it wasn't as big or grand as you had in the Northeast. I also, at that age, couldn't imagine living that far away from the coastline."

"You didn't go through the South," I pointed out.

"It was good. I'm glad I did it. I accumulated a lot of states at a young age. The only two states I haven't knocked off, and it's starting to worry me a little bit, are Mississippi and Arkansas. I don't want to go through my life without going to all fifty states."

CHAPTER 4

DOWN HOME

I wasn't in the Northeast anymore. The Midwest was far behind me. I was now in the South. Unlike Lenny Miller, whom I had left behind in Tysons Corner, I felt more at home away from the coast. In some ways the South is another country, but as I wound south and west along the Blue Ridge Parkway, I felt happy to be back in the hinterlands.

The hinterlands were the parts of America where, way back when, my family had found homes. My mother's family was German on her father's side, from Omaha by way of somewhere in Kansas and, before that, apparently somewhere in Switzerland. Mind you, that's only one branch of all the Romingers chronicled in the tome titled *The Romingers Roam*. My grandparents left Omaha for Houston and then Dallas, and that's a long story in itself. My grandmother was one or another breed of Irish. Her sister Lois married a Bozell and their son, L. Brent Bozell, became William F. Buckley Jr.'s sidekick and brother-in-law. Brent and his wife Tish, Buckley's sister, were very nice people, but they were extremely right-wing and super-Catholic and believed in some wacky stuff. My grandmother basked, as my father put it, in the Buckley connection.

My grandmother's other sister, Polly, went to Chicago. She was a cool lady. She had been in high school plays in Omaha with Henry Fonda. She married a rich guy from Kentucky named Dick, who died young and left her comfortable. She filled her time buying antique doodads and contraptions to fill her big apartment in Evanston and interviewing people even older than herself for the Illinois State Historical Society. She was prim and brisk. You had the sense that she had a lot of back-story, like Aunt Augusta in Graham Greene's novel *Travels with*

My Aunt. She kept a series of Scottish terriers, which she walked with a leash in one hand and a cattle prod in the other against muggers. She had her groceries delivered by taxi, which struck me as very big-city and sophisticated. My weekend visits to Polly were among my earliest solo adventures: riding the Amtrak alone at age ten or eleven south from Milwaukee, the conductor calling out, "Sturtevant, Glenview, and Chi-*cah*-go!" Polly would pick me up at either the quaint suburban station in Glenview or the enormous, magnificent Union Station in downtown Chicago. Chicago sure was a big city. One exotic thing about Chicago was that it had different TV stations than Milwaukee, but Polly didn't let me watch TV. Instead she showed me her old stereoscope, and her collection of novelty canes that held things like really long, thin swords or whiskey flasks or that doubled as .22 rifles, and old photos and clippings and invitations pasted in the family album she kept. She didn't go to church, which was kind of outré. She took me to fancy restaurants. At one of those she got a piece of food down the wrong way, and the waiter brought her a glass of water and fussed over her, and when she was fine and he went away, she said to me, "What a nice young boy. Such a nice young boy. (You know he's gay.) But *such* a nice young boy." Polly was very cool.

My father's family was thoroughly Southern and obscure and had no famous connections whatsoever, unless you count Mighty Casey, who is a fictional character, or Preacher Casy in *The Grapes of Wrath* (ditto), or my grandmother's claim that she had known Bonnie Parker as a customer when she was a teller at the Greenville Avenue Bank in Dallas. "All the ladies said Bonnie would have turned out just fine," she said, "if she hadn't got mixed up with that *darn* Clyde." But that's probably fictional too, though I like to think it's not. Grandma Casey was born Wanda McAllister in Quitman, seat of Wood County in East Texas. The other famous connection, come to think of it, is that the actress Cissy Spacek also grew up in Quitman.

Grandma Casey helped raise me and Aaron in Oconomowoc, and her stories of her own and my father's childhoods imparted my sense of Texas and of family on the Casey side. I wouldn't have gotten that from my father, because he was busy running away from Texas. She alleged that he had been scouted by the Kansas City Athletics. When

I went to him for corroboration, he allowed that there might have been a scout in the stands at some point looking in his general direction, but added: "Your grandmother is living in a dream world." In her stories my father was a fine young man, pretty much perfect as far as she was concerned, a paragon impossible to live up to, who got up very early every day before school to deliver the *Dallas Morning News*, and his black customers always paid him on time, but the rich white ones didn't. That kind of thing bugged my grandmother. Lots of things bugged her. She loved Franklin Roosevelt. She was big on fairness and right and wrong, and she never let anyone off the hook. "You know darn well that's just plain wrong, Ethan Casey," she said, often. "And I'm agin it." Her hairdo and cat's-eye glasses gave her a strong resemblance to any one of tens of millions of Chinese peasants, and we called her polyester pantsuits her Mao suit. When we teased her she said, "You Casey men are always tormentin' me." One time at the grocery store the checkout girl said, "You have an accent. Where are you from?" She shook her finger in the girl's face and expostulated, "Now, listen here, young lady. Ever'body has an accent. *You* have a *Wisconsin* accent. *Ah* have a *Texas* accent."

She told stories of her father, Hugh Hunter McAllister, who was a farmer and local worthy in Quitman, of her brother Bob and sister Ruby and her older brothers Sid and Hilliard, of standing in the rain at her mother's funeral on her sixth birthday, of going to live for a while after that with her Aunt Nig and Uncle Slick, of her stepmother Miss Ruby. The McAllisters of Wood County were Scotch-Irish, with some Welsh in there somewhere on her mother's side. Hard to get much more down-home Southern. She said they had come to Texas sometime in the nineteenth century on a boat from Alabama. Wanda McAllister went to Dallas as a young woman and met Lester Casey, from Waco. They always lingered on Sundays at the Greenville Avenue Christian Church until he saw every last little old lady safely onto the streetcar. "Those ladies thought Lester Casey hung the moon," she said. He died of a heart attack in September 1958 at age 51, three weeks before my father's twenty-first birthday. My father once told me that she nagged him to death.

Lester Casey's mother, the original Grandmother Casey, was a Dupree from Louisiana. It was from that nugget, plus the fact that the Casey side was Southern and Protestant, not Catholic as Caseys would normally be, that I imagined a usable family history that began with a proto-Casey debarking during the potato famine not at New York but at New Orleans, then making his way to Texas and deciding that, way out there, beyond the Pope's ambit of surveillance, there was no need for him to be Catholic anymore. When I put this hypothesis to my dad, he was less skeptical than simply uninterested. "You know," he said, "if I really wanted to, I could do a whole lot of research, and I could probably find the first Casey who came over from Ireland. But you know what? I don't care."

✳

"As luck would have it," George told me when I called him from the road to suggest lunch, "we have a preliminary hearing in a murder trial tomorrow afternoon. This guy beat his landlord's skull in with a baseball bat and then set the house on fire. So he's a real charming fella. It's nothin' grandiose—your basic probable cause hearing. This is a case of a murder that took place up in Marietta, South Carolina. Not to be confused with the suburb of Atlanta. In this case, Gregory McCarson is charged with the murder of Robert Neloms. There was a fire reported at the house, and the fire department found Neloms's body inside. And an investigation revealed that he had blunt force trauma to the head. The defendant has an alias of Crazy Horse. The victim has an alias of Lightning. It's hard to keep track of what people's real names are."

George Campbell was an interesting young man I had met a few days earlier in Greenville, South Carolina, a prosecuting attorney in the Greenville County solicitor's office. I had to backtrack to the Research Triangle area of North Carolina because of commitments I had made there, and now I was on my way back down.

Greenville had charmed me my first time through. I had planned the Southern leg of my trip around it because two women I had met in Haiti lived there. Jackie Williams was a classic, and very classy, Southern-style little old lady who now spent most of her time in Haiti and ran the craft center and gift shop and gave English lessons in

Cange, the extraordinary manmade oasis associated with Partners in Health and Dr. Paul Farmer. Jackie's late husband had designed the impressive running water system for Cange, and Jackie now was a revered elder there. She described herself as "a Republican in South Carolina, and a Communist in Haiti." She preferred Cange to Greenville because she felt useful there. "I want to go out with my boots on," she said. Right now Jackie was in Haiti, unfortunately for me.

But Jackie's friend Ghislayne Warne was in town, and I was staying with her. Ghislayne was in her sixties and ran an important new agricultural project near Cange called Zanmi Agrikol: Agricultural Friends or Partners in Agriculture. She and her husband Charles were Australians who had lived in Greenville long enough to have become fully enmeshed in the town's civic and social fabric. "Greenville is a very welcoming community," she told me. "It's by far the most giving community that we've ever lived in." She came from a farming background in Australia, could be alternately rugged or elegant to suit the occasion and, strangely, remembered having come through Greenville as a young woman, long before she had any idea she would settle there. "I came here with my father, who was in the textile business, on my way to school in Paris," she said. "He was in the wool trade. Life is very strange. And of all the things that I have to offer, it all came together in Haiti."

Ghislayne introduced me to her neighbor Betty, whose family had owned the *Greenville News* for decades before selling it to the Gannett chain in 1995. "We sold at the top of the market," Betty said. "It broke my heart at the time. But that money has stayed in Greenville, and it would have evaporated otherwise. And we wouldn't have been able to save the employees, the way newspapers have gone."

Betty had deep roots in Greenville. "We were backcountry," she told me. "We were not Old South. They looked down on us as rednecks." Greenville, she said, "started as a trading post with the Indians. In the 1890s, Northern textiles started coming down from New England, because of cheap labor. And hardscrabble farmers. The only way they could survive was to come down from the farms in the hills and work in the mills. This is red dirt land."

"Were the workers in the mills white or black or both?" I asked.

"They were all white. And some child labor. The mills then spun off to Third World countries, and Greenville was left with no industry. It was going down in the eighties. Greenville really reinvented itself with some foreign industry coming in, like Michelin." The town's civic savior was a Jewish immigrant, Mayor Max Heller. "Every time he said 'America,' he filled up with tears," said Betty. "He came here from Austria in '37, before they started gassing the Jews. He had a vision for Greenville as a European village that was pedestrian-friendly."

"Once Max got that going, the whole vision of Greenville started to change," Ghislayne interjected. "Conservation of green trails and everything else. There's a huge awareness of our surroundings. What has helped with the development of downtown is this extraordinary park. It's the largest natural urban waterfall in the United States. Our garden club clawed that park back from kudzu chaos. It's being used at all times of day and night." Greenville also had South Carolina's Governor's School for Arts and  Sciences: creative writing, performing arts, music, dance. "It draws kids from all over the state. The lead in *Porgy and Bess* on Broadway graduated from the Governor's School."

"All three of my children lived in Atlanta for twenty years," said Betty. "They all wanted to live in a big city. And one by one, they came back."

＊

"Greenville's come a long way, and I hope it continues," George said when we met for lunch downtown. A friend of his named Drew happened to be there, and George introduced us: "Drew is one of the region's most renowned organic farmers."

"Man, I got butternut squash all over the place," said Drew.

"I'm a closet tree-hugger," George confided to me. "Don't tell anybody—it'll ruin my reputation. I'm not against development, I'm against urban crawl. South Carolinians and Southerners are actually very close to China and Asian culture," he added as we turned to our menus, "because we're the only other ones who eat rice and worship our ancestors."

"You obviously didn't make that one up," I said.

"Nope," he admitted. "I got it from my father, and I don't know where he got it."

George was twenty-nine years old, an ambitious and articulate young man busy making his way and, at every step, in every conversation, doing his best to square his positions with his positioning. He loved talking politics, and he collected bits of wisdom to live and build

 a career by, like what his boss, Walt Wilkins, had told him: "You can always tell a man's character by the way he treats his subordinates." At the dinner party at Ghislayne's house where we met, he intrigued me by addressing the woeful state of the Episcopal Church, which was personal to me because my father was a bruised survivor of its internecine wars, from a candidly illiberal point of view. "It's sad, any time you get any organization that falls apart like that," said George. "It was such a bullshit move on the liberals' part to reframe the debate around homosexuality. From, I think, a rational conservative's point of view, you've replaced the faith given to the saints with a worship of eros."

I fancied George a future governor of South Carolina. He demurred but clearly kept that option open. His tall, beautiful, and intelligent wife, Marquin, urged me not to encourage him. Marquin was an artist who kept a studio in a shopping center on Augusta Road called Vino & Van Gogh, where she sold her paintings and held classes for local women and children. George was blond and handsome and had a *je ne sais quoi* that made you want to be in his company and wish him well. He had a precocious gravitas and a deep voice that would stand him in good stead as he got older. My thinking was that if a place like South Carolina had to be governed by a Republican, it could do worse than George.

Wrapping up lunch, we headed separately to the courthouse for the hearing, because my car was crammed full, including the passenger seat. George cut a stylish figure striding through downtown Greenville with a fedora on his head.

"We have an average of twelve to fourteen thousand felonies every year," he told me in his office.

"In this town?"

"In this county."

"That sounds like a lot of felonies."

"I'm sure Seattle has at least as many."

"Who's committing all these felonies?"

"I'm on a first-name basis with a lot of 'em."

With a little time to kill, he shared with me his views on national life. "Marquin was in a design class up in New York," he said, "and somebody asked her who she was gonna vote for, or what folks were thinking down in Savannah. And she said, 'I'm goin' to vote for John McCain.' And you woulda thought she said, 'I think we should let the Chinese annex New York City.'" He saw no good reason that the American world must revolve around New York and/or Washington, D.C. "Potomac Fever is real. Every man should have to return to live in the world he created, without the perks and benefits of public office. And that's why I'm a big fan of term limits." The character needed in national leaders was exemplified by none other than George Washington: "When you have that much power sitting in your lap, and you're at the top of your game, and you let go. That's a man of honor right there."

"Does the American system have what it takes to self-correct at this point?" I asked him.

"Yep, it does," he assured me. "The system does. The question is whether the people do."

"Do the people?"

"I grew up a child of Reagan. And, regardless of policy differences, it was a time of optimism, that the American people have what it takes. As long as that's what drives us, freedom and independence and self-reliance, that spirit of 'I am going to create my own destiny'—as long as that's the overriding movement, we'll always be fine."

"Who was the greatest founding father?"

"Washington, for the reason I described, no question."

"Not Jefferson?"

"No. Jefferson was a cool dude. He was weird. But none of this would have been possible if not for Washington. It's kind of like in business, nothing happens until someone sells something. In politics, nothing happens until somebody gives up power."

George left to prepare, and I walked upstairs to Courtroom One. Seated inside the door was a squat uniformed black man. George later told me his name was Sergeant Anderson. "You a friend of this one?" he asked me, nodding toward George.

"Yeah," I said.

"Poor you." He shook his head.

"Well, somebody's got to be his friend," I said.

"You known him long?"

"No, just met him."

"He's a good fella," said Sergeant Anderson. "He's got a style about him. That's what I like about him."

The hearing began with George questioning a deputy sheriff on the witness stand. McCarson, the tattooed and shaven-headed defendant, sat silently in an orange jumpsuit on the right side beside his court-appointed defense lawyer, a black woman. I sat in the back row on the left, the only spectator.

"... But he goes on to tell us that he had permission to have the truck, which dudn't make a whole lotta sense," said the deputy, who was tall and had a buzz cut. Then he described the victim: "He was extremely burnt ... and he had massive blunt force trauma to the head."

"When you say blunt force trauma, what does that mean?" asked George.

"He was beaten to death. The arson investigators were unable to determine the cause of the fire."

"Their finding was that this was not an accident," said George.

"Correct," said the deputy.

The black woman defense lawyer stood up for cross-examination.

"You said the defendant showed up covered in water, sweat, and mud, or water, sweat, and blood?" she asked.

"Both," he said.

She then went back to questioning the deputy about the witnesses he had interviewed, in particular a family McCarson had visited shortly after the alleged murder. "And where did my client tell these people he had been?" she asked him.

"He said he robbed a—he used a racial slur—and that he got a bunch of money in the truck," answered the deputy.

"What exactly did he say?"

The deputy left a very short but discernible pause, then said: "That he robbed a nigger, and he had a bunch of money in the truck, and that he wanted them to go with him to a titty bar in Atlanta."

"A what bar in Atlanta?"

"A titty bar in Atlanta, a strip bar. That's a direct quote."

"And the reason you charged Mr. McCarson with murder is?"

"Well, I guess we can start over," said the deputy. "Prior to the call from the neighbors reporting the fire, they looked outside and saw the truck running with the lights on. There was DNA evidence and McCarson's prints on the vehicle. We know that he had been in an argument with the deceased, prior to the death. We know the deceased died of blunt force trauma to the head, and McCarson had a metal bat covered with ash in his fire pit. So I think that that's sufficient. So we charged him."

"The state moves that this case be bound over for presentation to the grand jury," said George. The judge agreed, and the case continued on its way through the legal system. George introduced the deputy to me as Eric Whaley. Eric nodded toward the defendant in the orange jumpsuit and said to me, sotto voce, "Boy, he does not like me."

"I bet he doesn't," I said.

George and Eric invited me to tag along with them to poke around the scene of the crime. I could hardly believe my writerly good fortune; I felt as if I had parachuted into a John Grisham novel.

"We're gonna check out Marietta," George told his paralegal, Connie.

"All right. Y'all be careful," said Connie.

"I have to do these murders and such just to stay sane," said George as we rode out of town in Eric's official car. I sat in the front passenger seat, and George was sitting in the back. "Otherwise it's just a bunch of donuts and computer screens. But there's nothin' I like better than bustin' a scam artist or a corrupt government official. (I say that in jest, cuz I don't like sendin' anybody to jail.)"

"You gonna be around a little bit?" Eric was saying into his cell phone. "I'm gonna take the solicitor up to Marietta and show him McCarson's happy spot." Eric was one of six investigators in the county sheriff's office. "Just a regular old normal deputy sheriff," he told me.

"Is this normal?" I asked.

"Yep," he said. "Daily."

"Do you ever get tired of all the trashy doings?"

"Absolutely. It kinda wears on you. Twenty-five years. Twenty-six years now."

Eric had grown up in West Virginia. His dream, now a firm intention, was to retire to Wyoming and spend a lot of time hunting and fishing. "Now we're in the modern age of everybody you talk to has a cell phone, a video recorder, and a camera, all in one device," he said. "So you have to approach everything you say as if 'I'm on *Cops* right now.'"

I told him about a man I knew, the father of a friend, who had been a cop on the BART rail system in the Bay Area during the Vietnam-era student unrest in Berkeley. On one occasion he had been on the verge of giving a protester the particular authorized kind of karate chop to the neck that he was trained to do, when he noticed a TV camera aimed at him and thought better of it. Eric nodded with understanding. You had to talk and act tough, though, he said. "Cuz if you don't speak to 'em in a way that they understand, they think you're weak. Why are you writing all this down? I just noticed."

I explained to him that I was writing a book.

"I love to read," he said. "I can't spell for shit, he can attest to that, but I love to read."

"Does my long hair mean that I count as a hippie or something in the South?" I asked them.

"Naw, you're all right," said Eric. "You'd fit right in in Asheville."

"Do you remember that guy who burned his baby up in the crib?" George asked Eric from the back seat.

"I do," said Eric.

"That was the only time I ever saw pure evil in a man's eyes," said George, with a little dollop of drama. "At the point when it came to a guilty plea, he said there was some teenage blonde-haired girl in his head that told him to do it. See that little tin building up there? That's where we tried all the cockfighters."

The burned-out house was in a woodsy area some miles outside and uphill from Greenville, with a small barn and trailers and other wooden houses nearby. Downhill to its right was a kind of separate terrace of land shielded by trees.

"Okay, this is where the camper sat," said Eric.

"Is that the house?" George asked.

"Yeah." We went in the little house and walked around gingerly amid the ashes. "Watch those cracks in the floor where the fire department vented it," Eric warned.

"Smells like ..." said George.

"Chicken?" said Eric.

"Yeah."

"That's burnt flesh."

"Seriously."

"Naw, I'm just kiddin'."

"You can tell people have been in here messin' around," commented George.

"Strippin' out the metal," said Eric.

"Mm-hmm," said George. "At least they saved that poor dog that was locked up in the barn."

"They start to run together," Eric admitted. "We've had quite a few of these cases in the past couple of months."

There wasn't much more to see, so after a few minutes we got back in Eric's car and drove back into town.

"The most professional lawyers won't ever call the cop a liar, unless he really is a liar and they can prove it," George reflected. "A lot of times it would be easier for us to just charge someone and get it in the system. But we'll work on it for weeks and weeks and ask, 'Can we really prove it?' Even if we know the guy did it. It's all about the money. It's not about the bad-assedness, so to speak. They run a ton of drugs. And they diversify into arms trafficking and prostitution. Like any other business, it's about diversifying risk." He recalled one bunch he had busted: "They were driving around the Southeast stealing used restaurant grease. And then they drive it over the mountains into Tennessee, where they get a tax credit from the federal government for makin' biodiesel."

"They say a lot of drugs go up and down I-95," I said, as if I were knowledgeable about such things.

"Uh-huh," he affirmed. "Drugs go north and east. Money goes south and west."

As we neared town, we pulled up behind a pickup truck with a sticker in the rear window of the cab, with the letters "KKK" in the colors and style of the Confederate flag. Eric noted down the truck's license plate number. He shook his head.

"You gotta have brass balls to ride around Greenville, South Carolina with a KKK sticker on your car," he said. "You've had an interesting life," he added to me.

"Yeah, I wouldn't trade it," I said, and I guess I meant it. I told him a few anecdotes of interesting people I had met in Asia, like Aung San Suu Kyi at her house in Rangoon during a brief period in the mid-1990s when she was between house arrests, and Benazir Bhutto's maverick brother Murtaza, whom I met at the same famous family house in Karachi where he was gunned down eighteen months later.

"Your life makes ours look pretty dull," said Eric.

His life didn't sound dull at all to me. "The difference is that in your work you get to know one place intimately," I said. "I know a lot of places, but not nearly as well."

"I can drive down the street," he mused, "and say to myself, 'I had a dead body in that house, I had a murder in that house ...' That's why I want to move."

It was now late afternoon. Before getting back on the road, I spent a little more time with George in his office. I told him I would be staying that night with friends in suburban Atlanta.

"Atlanta has finally overbuilt itself," he declared. "And it doesn't have a transit system that's worth a damn."

I asked him how he would go about fixing the American health care system.

"Why should I be in the same risk pool as someone with Type 2 diabetes?" he said. "You've got this gimmick where your employer can pay for your insurance tax-free. Well, why not just let individuals pay for their own insurance on an open market? You've got a very simple equation, which is access times quality equals cost. And there's no way around that in the health care market. The point is, you have to create somewhere for them to go that isn't the most expensive thing you can think of. What we did was take the worst parts of the system and made them mandatory and universal."

"How do you feel about Obama?"

"In what way?" he asked. "Because 'feel' is an interesting question. I look at Barack Obama, and I strongly disagree with almost all of his policies, for various reasons. I do feel I can find a lot of common ground with him on education, though. Because I'm a big believer in public education. But I don't trust him. I don't buy into the whole Red-baiting scheme that he's a Manchurian candidate. But his worldview is one where you can't get something without taking something away from somebody else."

"That sounds like what conservatives would say about any liberal president," I said.

"Yes," he said. "You've got more people ridin' the wagon than we've got pullin' it."

He had a problem with the welfare system: he felt too many people just showed up to click on the website to show that they were looking for work. "I would say you show up and click, *then* you go sweep the sidewalk." To illustrate, he told a story:

"This guy, he and his daughter—or his daughter, basically—had figured out this title loan scam. In South Carolina, you're able to print out a form on the Internet, fill it out, and take it in to the DMV. You forge the lender's name, and normally it's a company, so you just write down somethin' scribbly. And they wouldn't check whether the loan has been paid off. So then when you submit that form, you can also request a duplicate title, which is clear and shows no liens. So they take that clear title to the next shop down the street and get a new loan on the car. He had racked up thirty-some thousand dollars on a 1984 or '87 Ford or Chevy van. His daughter was clearly the mastermind behind the whole thing, cuz this guy could barely read. So his defense attorney brought him in the conference room, and I said, 'Okay, what happened?' So we talked about it, and it was obvious he was not smart enough to come up with this type of a scheme. He was a nice guy, simple guy. So I said to him, 'It's clear to me that you're not the mastermind. But do you have a job, or any way to pay some of this money back?' And he paused, and said, 'Well'—I thought he was gonna say, 'Yeah, there's this thing I can do to pay it back.' But he said, 'Well, I'm kinda enjoyin' unemployment right now.' That's the hardest part about this whole job, is people who don't want to help themselves."

"White or black?" I asked him.

"This particular guy was a black guy. But this goes across all racial, ethnic, and religious spectrums. We all want to help people," he opined. "Whether you're on the left or the right, you want to do what's best for people and for society. But when the rubber meets the road, what happens? You can't just throw money at the problem. It takes more effort than that."

"Who's going to win the election?"

"I think Romney's going to win," he said. "That's my call. It's a dead heat. But the president hasn't been able to punch through. It's like a ceiling he's hit that he hasn't been able to hit through. Had it been Romney that hadn't been able to punch through, that would be one thing. But for the incumbent President of the United States to hit that kind of ceiling, I think that's a real problem for his campaign. But a week is a long time in politics. A lot can happen in a week."

"It could be an interesting week," I said.

"Yeah," he agreed. "We've got the hurricane goin' on, we've got the Benghazi thing goin' on, we've got a jobs report comin' out on Friday. Yeah, it's crazy. This is one of the weirdest election cycles I've ever seen. I try to stay out of the echo chamber, but I knew Romney had done well when Rachel Maddow said it was a draw. I think history will look back on this presidency, whether it ends this time or in four, and say, 'What a tragedy that this was the first great chance to elect a black president and unite the country, and fix some of the things that are wrong.'"

"Are the two teams even on the same playing field?"

"I don't know. You've got crazy people like Todd Akin in Missouri running for the Republican ticket, and then you've got people like Nancy Pelosi, who I think is completely off her rocker on the left. So, do you think Obama's gonna be able to pull it out?"

"I don't know," I said. "I think it's a tossup. It shouldn't be a tossup."

"Yeah," he said. "The American people oughta know what they want."

"That's poignant," I said. "Because they don't."

"Cuz they're scared," said George. "They don't know where the world is going. They don't know where we're going as a country. I think it's a crisis of self-confidence, if you want my unlettered, unprofessional, unsubstantiated guesswork. Do the American people still believe in themselves?"

"Is there any hope for America?" I asked.

"Absolutely. We have a system that works. The question is whether the people want it to work."

I asked him to tell me about his own background.

"My uncle had a boating accident and became a quadriplegic the summer before I was born," he said. "And my grandfather's business had gone bankrupt in the 1980 recession. So all we had was disability and Medicaid. He had most of the monument business in north Florida and south Georgia. And then, thanks to our buddy Peanut Carter, and Paul Volcker's harsh but necessary correction with the high interest rates, he went broke. The policies of the mid- to late seventies really hurt him economically. And my uncle never got to go to college because of it. My grandfather was the first Republican elected in Georgia since Reconstruction. And both my granddads were staunch supporters of integration, at a time when it was not popular. He'd say that he threw away too much money on politics, that he grew his business too fast. It wasn't Carter's fault that he went out of business. His philosophy was that you have to own your flaws. That that's the only way you grow. You gotta work on weakness."

"He was a believer in self-reliance?"

"Oh, absolutely. If he had bootstraps he'd pull himself up by those. But he just pulled himself up by the hair on his legs. When he was twelve years old he had a paper route, stocked shelves at Woolworth's, and trapped rabbits to sell the pelts."

His phone rang and he took the call. "I'm just wrapping up a meeting," he told the caller.

"I gotta get to Atlanta," I said.

"No worries. But that's something that, both granddads, if I find a common thread, it's 'Just go out and help somebody.' Kindness is the cheapest and pays the biggest dividends of any investment. Because it's so infectious."

"It's a blessing to me to be able to share other people's stories," I said. I'm sure it sounded corny, but I meant it.

"We're growing to the point where nobody really knows who anybody else is," said George. "You don't look at the world the way I do. You've got to take an interest in people, and find out who they are, if you want to have a conversation with them. Because we live in the Tower of Babel."

As we left the building together he said, "I just hope I come out of whatever ends up goin' in your book alive, without bein' excoriated." And he offered some advice about Macon, where I would be headed after Atlanta. "Check out my buddy Homey Joe. He's a crackhead who lives downtown. Used to walk us home from the bars." And he recommended a coffee shop there called The Joshua Cup. "It's a Christian gig, but they're pretty nice."

"Some Christians are nice," I allowed.

"Fill up before you cross into Georgia. Higher gas taxes there."

*

I hired an assistant to help me plan and execute my route and meetings, a young guy in suburban Chicago with a marketing degree named Brian Seredynski. Just as I was arriving in the neighborhood of the family I would be staying with in Macon, Brian called me to discuss forward planning. So I stopped in the empty parking lot of a bank— empty, that is, except for a sheriff's car that I didn't really bother to notice—and called him back. After I had been on the phone about half an hour, pacing back and forth in the parking lot, a middle-aged uniformed deputy, complete with paunch, strolled out of the bank.

"Hi!" he said. "What are you doin'?"

"Oh, hi," I said. "I was on my way somewhere, and I got a phone call, so I decided to stop here before I got there, to finish my call."

"Where you goin'?"

"I'm going to my friends' house, on Such-and-such Circle." I didn't mention that my friends were Pakistani.

"Why don't you just go there first, and then have your phone call?"

"Well," I explained, "once I get there I'll have to socialize with the people there, so I thought I'd better finish my phone call first."

"That your car?" He was looking at my Washington State license plate.

"Yes, it is."

"You suspicious, man."

"Brian, I gotta go," I said into my phone. I turned to the deputy. "I guess I can see why," I admitted. "Because of my license plates. You really think I'm suspicious?"

"Yeah."

I started to explain: "I'm a writer. I'm driving around America, I'm writing a book about driving around America. I'm sorry I look suspicious. I saw your car and kind of figured maybe it was a sheriff's office."

"Naw, it's a bank," said the deputy. "We're just providin' s'curity. You written other books?"

"Yeah. I'm a journalist. I've written a book about Haiti, for example." I didn't mention that I had also written two books about Pakistan.

"Haiti, huh?"

"Yeah, the earthquake and all."

"They got thangs sorted out there yet?"

"No, it's still a mess. But people are doing what they can to pick up the pieces."

"How 'bout New York now? You oughta be writin' 'bout that."

"I was just there, about a week before the storm hit."

"Hope you don't get nothin' like that to write about here."

"Yeah, I hope not," I agreed, and it was apparent that I was off the hook.

"You got a card?"

I didn't, but I wrote down my name and website address in his notepad.

"Yeah," he said conversationally, "they just tole me there was some gah out here. I'll look out fer yer book." With that he went back inside the bank, and I called Brian back to finish our call.

✳

"Have you been to Georgia before?" Aamer asked me a few minutes later, at his house.

"Only very briefly to Atlanta." I didn't like remembering that visit years earlier; it had been in weird and unhappy obligatory circumstances, trapped with people I didn't like very much in a chintzy McMansion, somewhere way out in the godforsaken exurbs.

"Atlanta is more urban," said Aamer. "Macon is basically an old Southern town that's not very vibrant. The median income for Bibb County is $15,000. There is a lot of what you would call old money, but the city of Macon itself is at least fifty percent of African-American population. Some of them are very poor, and some of them are okay."

Aamer's elderly father greeted me with a hug. He told me he had been reading my book *Alive and Well in Pakistan*, and that he had been making notes. For example, my mention of *Tata Durbar* on page 207 should be *Data Darbar*. He had written what he considered the correct transliteration in the margin. "If I find any more errors, I will bring them to your notice," he said in a jocular vein.

"This is my mother," said Aamer.

"As-salamu alaykum," she said to me.

"Wa alaykumu s-salām," I replied.

"I am his mother, and she is my daughter-in-law," said Aamer's mother, indicating Aamer's wife, Aniqa. "I read your book, and I know several of the people that you mention, specially Naveed Shahzad."

"Mrs. Shahzad was my boss," I said.

"She was a student at Kinnaird College, and she was the head of the dramatics society. She was the daughter of Justice Rehman. She was Naveed Rehman."

"She was an actress," I remembered.

"Yes, a very talented one. She married some fellow from the Shahzad family who was not as talented as she was," she added, laughing.

I had come to know Pakistani communities all around the United States rather well. Pakistani-Americans had their versions of the issues any immigrant community faces: a first generation establishing a toe-hold and founding ethnic and religious institutions; their children balancing the demands of the old country's ways with the exigencies of getting on in America; tensions and accommodations between the generations and between the community and the wider society. But that normal stuff was complicated for Pakistanis in America now by the tense relationship between their countries of origin and adoption.

An irony was that their community was dominated by affluent physicians and engineers, and it was hard to imagine a squarer or more law-abiding bunch than most of the Pakistani-Americans I got to know. Dr. Aamer Shabbir of Macon, Georgia, for example, was a cardiologist, and he was very square, though with an impish gleam in his eye. He was bald and very middle-aged, though he was two years younger than

me. The Pakistani doctors of America generally lived in big new houses on cul de sacs, sometimes in very big McMansions in gated communities, and sent their kids to places like Harvard, Princeton, and Cornell. With their ambi-tion and smarts and good  breeding and manners and attentive and supportive, not to say pushy, parents and extended families, it was easy to imagine such young peo-ple becoming American leaders in various fields. The problem was that they didn't tend to go into various fields; they tended to go into medi-cine. I thought it might behoove them to broaden their vistas, but I learned that saying so could be considered impolite. When I spoke to a dinner at the annual convention of the Association of Physicians of Pakistani Descent of North America (APPNA) in Washington, D.C. in 2008, I used a line that I thought was funny: "Please don't make all your children become doctors." Some of the doctors did laugh, but the fierce, tiny lady who had invited me told me pointedly afterwards: "I minded that."

As both striving immigrants and observant Muslims, Pakistani-Americans also tended to be straight arrows and very family values-oriented. Thus most of them had voted Republican until 2001, when abruptly most of them began supporting Democrats. "I was a Republican for fifteen years," a Pakistani in North Carolina confessed to me. "After 9/11, a man called me up and said, 'You used to come to all the meetings. Why don't you anymore?' I said, 'Firstly, your party has equated my religion with terrorism. And secondly your party, which used to be compassionate, has been taken over by the extreme right wing.'"

Thus, on my way through Boston, I had found myself invited to a fundraiser in Lexington for Congressman John Tierney, Democrat of Massachusetts, at the home of a citizen named Tahir Chaudhry. In the q-and-a following a buffet-style Pakistani dinner and Tierney's good stump speech, several audience members spoke of issues of special concern to their community. A woman spoke of "guilt by association—that's something we're all living with." And a man named Javed asked: "All of us over here, we hate the Taliban, we hate these evil guys. But aren't we doing more damage by doing these drone attacks?"

Tierney replied that he had asked the Obama administration about drone attacks in Pakistan. "The target is important," he said. "The decision making is important. I think there's a role for drones. I don't think there's a constant role." The relevant congressional committee "should be very much involved, not told about it after the incident. Is it right, or are you killing people that you shouldn't be killing?" And there was the political damage: drone attacks were "turning people against us. And I think at some point it has to get more transparent too."

On the general matter of running America, Tierney claimed that Republicans "don't want to make it work. In essence they're at war with their own government." He offered what he called a "reading assignment": *It's Even Worse Than It Looks* by Thomas Mann and Norman Ornstein. "These majority Republicans passed sixty-one bills. That's one-fourth of the bills that the do-nothing Congress passed that Truman complained about. Things will not get completely better until the Republican Party gets rid of this extreme element and gets back to where it used to be. If you just repeal the Affordable Care Act and you don't put anything else in its place, you're going to see a lot of havoc out there, and a lot of people are going to be suffering."

An older man brought a rousing round of applause by saying: "I want everybody in this room to know that the Congressman voted against the Iraq war." Then someone asked Tierney: "What are your thoughts on this war with Iran that people are pushing for?"

"We did a war gaming scenario of how things would play out," he replied, "and it wasn't too attractive to a lot of people. There's time for negotiations to work. I don't want the Iranian people to suffer with the sanctions. But I tell you, I like the sanctions a whole lot better than the bombing scenario. If we don't have the sanctions, Netanyahu surely is going to go in there and bomb."

I had been standing throughout at the back of the room, chatting with Tierney's aide, a young woman named Maria. "Is he going to win?" I asked her.

"I *think* so," said Maria. (He did.)

And in Cary, North Carolina, I had met Nadeem Iqbal, a Pakistani who had come to the Research Triangle as a student and stayed and raised two daughters there. Nadeem was an engineer and claimed to have prototyped a tablet computer. "A lot of my friends saw it. I made the drawing in May of 2006, when Israel was bombing the Palestinians. And I made my presentation, and out of 42 CTOs, CEOs, and technologists, only two came. I still have my elevator pitch recording, and I still have my full recording. One of them saw it, and he said, 'It is too far in the future.' And I said, 'We cannot wait. Two years from now the market will be flooded with these devices.' iPad was not invented then."

The first evening I was in Cary, the local community had held a dinner for me at a Pakistani restaurant. "That shows that there is a genuine concern among Pakistanis about Pakistan," said Nadeem. "And about America. Because we are in both boats, and we cannot get out of either boat."

Nadeem had lived in North Carolina for thirty years and was one of the first members of the area's Pakistani community. "I came on the 17th of August 1982, in Raleigh, for NC State, with one suitcase and $700 in my pocket," he told me. "One of my friends was here already, Dr. Bader Abid. He started a Pakistani Students Association, with three

Pakistani students. I was the fourth Pakistani student." One thing that bothered Nadeem was that, whereas Jewish students celebrated Hanukkah, there was no comparable commemoration of the Muslim festival Eid. So he had helped organize an Eid celebration at NC State in the mid-1980s. Many years later, on Thanksgiving 2006, Nadeem had a friend over to his house and he asked: "What about starting an Eid festival?" His friend said sure, the local Pakistani association could do it, they could probably get a hundred or so people.

"I'm not talking about that," Nadeem rejoined. "I want to do it on a Muslim-wide basis." He formed a committee of eight people. "Out of eight, six ran away. Most religious people, they think that Eid is only for Muslims. They believe in it, actually. I never went into argument with them; there is no need. On the other hand, there are modern people who don't want to have anything to do with religion. I got punched from both sides. Like a punching bag. At parties I was stopped and asked why I'm doing this, I'll go to hell. I hope I don't. We did it in 2007, and twenty-two hundred people showed up. We ran out of parking spaces. It was good, but it was a lot of hard work. I had to get electric permit, space permit, food permit, parking for the handicapped. We ended up spending something like $1500 just for the permits. So this was a learning curve for me. The whole idea was to listen to other people before you tell your story. And the main motive was that we live in America, we need to celebrate our religious festivals in this new environment, and we have to add that flavoring. We are celebrating it as an American holiday event. And when the manager of the town parks and recreation department, Lyman Collins, looked at it, he said, 'Approved!' He said, 'Number one, nobody else brought me a two-page proposal for any event. Number two, the thing that caught my eye was celebrating Eid as an American holiday event. And three, what took you so long?'"

In 2009, Nadeem succeeded in getting Democratic Congressman David Price to attend. "He did not know much about Muslims, so we had to give him some information about Eid," said Nadeem. "And he gave a wonderful speech. The mayor did not show up. The council members were very reluctant to come. People are afraid of the unknown, basically. Once they see that they are not going to be harmed in their public position, they come. Their opponents can use it against them, so I tried to make it easy on them, that this is strictly a celebration. Politics is strictly prohibited."

"Are you a supporter of Congressman Price?" I asked him.

"I supported him, yes. First of all because he changed his position on Pakistan, after visiting Pakistan."

"Is he going to win his election this time?"

"I think he will. He has a difficult time, because of the new boundaries of his district."

"Why is this kind of work important?"

"I think that my children and their children are going to live in this country, and they should be treated fairly. But the only way it can happen is for them and us to become part of the greater fabric. I'm not talking about assimilation, but about being able to participate in American society on an equal basis, without fear or compulsion. In 1980s it was *haraam* to vote. And now they are having political meetings in the mosque. So things are changing, slowly. We just had a meeting with the candidates gathering. But it took them many years to convince the mosque to have this gathering. And many of the candidates told me they never knew of the existence of the mosque, and they were living maybe three blocks away. Doing religious stuff is important from the religious point of view and the social point of view, but getting involved in the larger society is equally important."

*

"In this house lives a neurologist," Aamer told me as we drove out of his neighborhood on the way to an evening potluck at the Islamic Center of Middle Georgia. "He is also from Pakistan. Over here in this house is the man who actually brought us to Macon. We had a kind of parting of the ways, but he might be there tonight. He's also a cardiologist. In that house over there lives another doctor. He's from India."

As we left the subdivision and turned onto the road, he said, "One thing that you cannot help remarking on here is the number of churches. Just on this road there are five or six."

"That's how you know you're in the South," I said.

"Most of them are Baptist," he said. "Some of them are Methodist."

Robins Air Force Base was an important presence around Macon, and we were headed toward its neck of the woods. "This area is mostly where we work," said Aamer.

"So are you based at the Air Force base, or do you have a private practice?"

"We have a private practice."

"Do people here eat a lot of Krispy Kreme donuts and barbecue pork sandwiches, and that's why they need cardiologists?"

"Actually, all over the country they need cardiologists," he averred. "It's mostly because the population is aging."

The Islamic center was a converted warehouse in what felt like the middle of nowhere. The black imam wore a burgundy fez and greeted me effusively in his office. "Here is my card," he said. "I grew up in Guinea." He pointed to a world map on the wall. "Then I studied in Saudi Arabia." He pointed again. "Four hours' difference. Then I went to Malaysia. Four hours' difference." He pointed again, laughing. "Then I went to Japan, then I came to the United States."

Potlucks always made me think of what my dad liked to say at St. Mary's, back home in Wisconsin: "... and if everybody brings Jell-o salad, we'll just eat Jell-o salad!" I helped myself and sat down next to a young Syrian man. I wondered what life was like for Muslims in these parts. "And the local people aren't ..."

"Redneck?"

I laughed. "I'm sure some of them are."

"Of course some of them are," said a Bangladeshi man sitting to my left.

"Actually," said the Syrian, "because of the base, they are used to the foreigners. My wife wears the scarf. All the wives wear the scarf. My wife never told me that she had any problem. We get the respect, actually."

In the car on the way back, Aamer said to me: "It's not a very glamorous place, Macon. But we don't need a lot of city life. But you do need a certain critical mass. There are enough Muslims here that we can support each other."

Aamer had bounced around America a fair bit over the two decades or so he had been here. "We lived in Green Bay for a year," he told me. "Our eldest likes animals. So they asked her if she preferred the Packers or the Bears, so she said the Bears."

"Yeah, that was a mistake," I said.

He laughed. "Anyway, she survived. When you live in an area, it has an effect on you, and you have an effect on your neighborhood. Toledo, Ohio has a large Polish-American population. When I was training over there, I was nicknamed Aamerski. So when I came here, they got me a Georgia Bulldogs hat. They wanted to teach me how to cheer for the Bulldogs. So these are little things that you acquire."

"So do you cheer for the Bulldogs?"

"I don't even know football. I don't know how the game is played. My partner, Dr. Saeed, he's the tall fellow who was there, he has people over for the Super Bowl. Every year he invites people over to his place. He orders Pakistani food and arranges a get-together on Super Bowl Sunday. So now I know some of the rules, like what a touchdown is."

Growing up in Pakistan around the same time I was growing up in Wisconsin, Aamer had been exposed to American culture of a sort. "We watched *The Six Million Dollar Man*. I remember in elementary school, we used to imitate the sounds and everything. I came here primarily because I didn't want to be left behind. I figured that was the best country you could live in, the United States of America, so I came here. I probably should have been a scientist. I had a little chemistry lab when I was in high school, at home. I would mix up chemicals. But we had a tradition of medicine in the family, and we just made the most of it. But I think it was curiosity more than anything that brought me here. But I think that for my kids, the opportunities are much more. The change that used to take ten years now happens in one year. They have a chance to be at the cutting edge, much more than me. By the time they are my age, the landscape of this country will be very different. Out of 250 or 300, I think that close to one hundred of my classmates are practicing in America. All of us had a common problem, which was how to overcome the two-year rule."

The two-year rule required holders of Aamer's kind of visa to return to their home countries for a minimum of two years, but you could get around it by committing to practicing medicine in an underserved area in the United States, which is how Aamer had found himself in Natchez, Mississippi. "There had not been a properly trained cardiologist in that community of 25,000," he said. Someone introduced him to a man nearby in Louisiana named Tim Westmoreland, who promised to help him set up a practice. "This fellow was more of an entrepreneur than an employer," said Aamer. "He was not very straight, but also creative. He used a gummint grant to set up medical offices in rural areas of Louisiana. After I got there I realized that his income guarantee was only on paper, and I was to fend for myself.

"In Vidalia, Louisiana, I was looking for an office. I was looking at this building. It used to be a real estate office, and I wanted to rent it and upgrade it. The owner of that building, he was about eighty years old. One of his sons put us in touch with his wife, who was about forty years old. I heard from other sources later on that he was friends of a former governor of Louisiana, and they used to run a brothel. In the Mississippi River there are these things called 'blue holes': these swirly things that if something falls in, you cannot recover it. Someone told me that they used to dump bodies in blue holes. But I saw him in a weakened, debilitated state, and the guy eventually died. The other cardiologist in that area was Dr. Mal Morgan, who has now passed. Do you know a movie called *Patch Adams*?"

"I've heard of it," I said. "I haven't seen it."

"He used to behave like Patch Adams. I was told that he used to be called Malpractice Morgan. In that context I was able to do well, because the contrast was so much. People didn't care who I was; they just wanted to be taken care of. After a year or so of being there I was invited to something that was strange to me, and that was the Confederate Pageant. They actually dress up in Confederate uniforms, with swords, and they do waltzes and all that. We realized that besides us the only person that was not white over there was the security guard. There's a place in Pakistan called Sialkot."

"Where the soccer balls are made," I said.

"Yes," said Aamer. "That's also where they manufacture Confederate uniforms. I was listening to NPR the other day, and I heard that."

"Like the ones they wear at the Confederate Pageant."

"Yes. They were probably made in Sialkot. I thought that would be an entertaining piece for your book."

A few weeks after the World Trade Center attack, Aamer had been approached by one of his patients. "He told me that if anybody gave me any trouble, he would come over to my place and bring his shotgun with him. I was not aware that the danger was so much. I said, 'Is it really that bad?' And he said, 'You don't know.' I don't know if he was demented, or if he knew what was going on. I was surprised to hear that from him, but at the same time, I felt better."

"He was a white guy?"

"Yes. He was probably in his mid-seventies at that time."

Not all the problems Aamer had encountered were specifically to do with his being Muslim or Pakistani, though; some were simply because he was foreign. "In Memphis, Tennessee, when I was accepted there, one day I was in an elevator and the program director was with two other residents," he told me. "And it was me and I think the Guatemalan doctor, and he said, 'Here come the carpetbaggers.' But you know, we should not just gripe and gripe. We have been successful over here. I would say that once here, this is how I want to identify myself: as a Muslim, as an American, and then as a person of Pakistani origin. We wish Pakistan well, but it's not my home anymore. If we were that secure and that well established over there, we would not be coming here anyway."

Aamer was eager to talk, and all I had to do was listen. "This is the part of Macon that used to be thriving," he told me, heading west on Eisenhower Parkway. "Relatively newer stores, etcetera. But there has been a lot of flight from this part of Macon. We went for the goat slaughter to Fort Valley," he went on. "In some ways, Georgia is a lot like Pakistan. My parents, they felt that Fort Valley was so much like Punjab, with the cotton crop ready to be picked, and the general terrain. I showed them the pivots, the irrigation system. They felt that that was so much like Punjab. There were a couple of guys over there, they cut up our goats and cut them into little pieces and so on. And they actually run a deer processing plant. A lot of people around here eat deer. I think we slaughtered thirty-five or forty goats that day. There is a Muslim family in Fort Valley. I think they have a few convenience stores, etcetera. But I think they wanted to cater to the needs of the community. A lot of times if you own a convenience store, you have to sell liquor and lottery tickets, etcetera, and they wanted to move away from that. So they bought the goats and sold them to us."

"And they slaughtered them?"

"Well, I slaughtered a goat, because it's the head of the family that does that. But they arranged for these white guys to skin the goats and cut them into smaller pieces, take out the intestines, etcetera. And one of them said, 'Are you a doctor?' He told me that I had treated his father for a heart condition. He said, 'I never thought I would see a heart doctor in this place.'"

On my last day in Macon, Aamer drove me to pick up my car at the Firestone dealer on Eisenhower, where I had left it for scheduled maintenance, then we said a fond goodbye and I got right onto the same I-75 I had driven earlier in the other direction, from Cincinnati to Toledo and Detroit. I was in a hurry to get to Orlando, where some other Pakistani friends were holding a dinner party for me that evening. I had misjudged the distance, wishfully supposing it would take about five hours, whereas it turned out to take seven. I think I thought Orlando was nearer the state line than it is. I got there on time, but I had to keep my foot down. George Campbell in Greenville had recommended a different route, on older and less trafficked highways through Thomasville, where his family had lived. I couldn't take him up on the suggestion because, as I had occasion to reflect again throughout this long day, the United States of America is a really big country. I-75 in Georgia was flat

and straight and tedious, but tawdrily fascinating for its forest of obviously unregulated billboards. Most people who drive it must be on their way to Florida. The dominant themes of the billboards, not necessarily in order, were: 1) visit our strip club, just down the road; 2) accept Jesus Christ as your personal Lord and Savior, or else you'll go to hell; 3) stop Obama

from turning America into a totalitarian socialist regime. A couple that
I managed to scribble down were:

We the People
2012
STOP OBAMA

OBAMA ISN'T WORKING
47 million Americans
on food stamps

In Lake Park, Georgia I made a quick stop at a cinderblock Florida
Information Center and then at the convenience store across the road,
to stretch my legs and get an energy bar. All the driving was giving me
leg cramps, and by this point I had stopped even pretending to myself
that I was taking care of my health. Looking around in the brightly lit
store amid the shelves of crap for sale, I overheard a snatch of conversation between two truckers:

"Ya gotta go upstairs to go to the bathroom?!?"

"Yup."

"Dang."

So I found the stairs and the restroom, and then I got back in my
car and soon was in Florida.

＊

My purpose in Orlando was to see the Teen Xpress mobile clinic in
action. Teen Xpress had been recommended to me by Dr. Elliott
Attisha, the pediatrician on HANK (Health Alliance for Neighborhood
Kids), the equivalent mobile clinic in Detroit. HANK was adminis-
tered for the Henry Ford Health System by my friend Kate Conway.
HANK was a 38-foot Winnebago RV customized with examining
rooms and medical equipment, which parked most weekdays at a different public school in the city. Both clinics were affiliated with the
Children's Health Fund, a national organization of affiliated mobile
clinics around the country.

Elliott had been born in Detroit, in a Chaldean or Iraqi Christian family that moved when he was small to the suburb of Royal Oak. He was in his early forties but youthful, earnest, and enthusiastic.

"I worked in private practice for nine years, and I was in suburbia," he told me. "I felt more like a machine than a pediatrician. I was making a ton of money. I was making more than a pediatrician should make, if you ask me. I wanted to slow down, spend more time with my family. I started to think, 'What do I want to do with my life?' I'm twice as happy now, making half the money. It's very rewarding work, and I'm just really glad I found it. I trained in Detroit, and then I went out in the suburbs. So coming back to Detroit is like coming full circle. Unless you come into the city, you don't know what these kids are going through."

"Pediatricians are all the same," said Kate. "They're the best kind of doctors to work with."

"We're out trying to fix other countries," said Elliott. "Why don't we do something at home first? We know that kids that are in poverty have a good chance of staying in poverty. So if we know that, why don't we do something about it? We had one child who came in to one of the clinic's sites. He's a 13-year-old boy who weighs about sixty or seventy pounds." The boy had an underdeveloped left arm, scoliosis, and asthma. Detroit had twice the percentage of children with asthma as the national average, and many inhaler and other prescriptions went unfilled because twenty-five to thirty percent of HANK's patients lacked access to a car. Elliott himself had asthma, so his concern was also personal. "We have ten-, eleven-, twelve-year-old kids, sometimes down to nine, self-managing their asthma. If we can't get the parents into our office to educate them, how can we get their kids' asthma under control? And you can't blame the parents; they're trying to work, they're trying to make ends meet."

Elliott was developing a simplified, color-coded inhaler for kids, but even such a simple innovation was not simple to implement. "If you have an action plan that's green-yellow-red, why not color all the preventative inhalers green? Why not color all the reliever inhalers yellow? The feedback I got was that the pharmaceutical companies are going to prevent you from going forward with this, because it's their branding. I feel like the pharmaceuticals are really getting in the way of treating asthma for kids. All we're doing is confusing the kids." He was suggesting a compromise, with green or yellow on the top half of the inhaler and the company's branding on the bottom. "We're also working on putting a nurse in all of the schools, so that when we get there we can be a lot more efficient."

"How are you going to be able to fund that?" I asked.

"That's a good question," he said.

"That's my job," said Kate.

"It's shocking that you don't have nurses in schools."

"Where they cut first is in those services that are not measured on the state tests," said Kate. "And the nurses are the first ones to go."

"I don't want to minimize what we do, but I still feel like we're a Band-Aid," said Elliott.

"What you're trying to do is rebuild a medical system from the ground up," I suggested.

"Yes, in a way," Elliott agreed.

Most of the money for the Children's Health Fund came from donations through the TV show *American Idol,* and the singer Paul Simon had become an advocate and put on star-studded concerts to support it. Kate and Elliott and their colleagues from other cities had just attended one such concert as part of a conference in New York.

"Good for Paul Simon," I said.

"Yeah, he's my new hero," said Kate.

"He said, 'If there's one reason for my fame, it's to bring attention to this,'" said Elliott. "Kate, of course, is our administrator, and without her this doesn't happen."

"You do catch the bug," said Kate. "I know I've found my home, in terms of my work."

"I'm really glad Kate is there. She doesn't settle. It's nice to have someone in your corner."

"If you go in our clinic, it's nice," said Kate. "My idea is that these kids have enough junk in their lives." She had once refused the use of a janitor's closet. "I said, 'We will not work in this space. We need a clinic.'"

I didn't get to see HANK in action in Detroit because of timing, but Elliott eagerly introduced me to mobile clinic colleagues in several other cities.

✳

"Many Florida schools don't have a well-integrated health structure," Dr. Veenod (Vinny) Chulani told me on the Teen Xpress mobile clinic, parked outside Maynard Evans High School on Silver Star Road in Orlando. "In Florida, many schools don't even have a nurse. We don't do a lot of sick visits; we do high-level primary care. We're trying to give a smaller client base a higher level of care. We're trying to get the teens to buy into having a primary care provider." A prime criterion of students' eligibility for access to Teen Xpress was lack of access to health insurance. "Right now the uninsured is going down, because a lot of families are signing up for food stamps, and when they do that they get Medicaid," said Eileen Navarro, the clinic's nurse practitioner. "But they don't know how to navigate the system."

"We can't recreate a whole system," said Vinny. "We're trying to connect them to the system, rather than become a substitute system. We found ourselves to be ineffective at best in terms of higher-level needs." The clinic chose schools to work with, seeking out particularly ones whose students were underperforming academically. "It becomes a bit of a challenge getting buy-in," he admitted. "But in truth, school is a place to learn. School is not a place to get health care. But it becomes the window of opportunity."

"We did have a principal once that told us to leave the campus because of this reason," said Eileen. "But then you end up with kids sitting in the office waiting for their parents to pick them up. They're not learning anyway."

"Part of it is making the case," said Vinny, the pediatrician. "These are schools in high-need communities."

Teen Xpress was attached to Arnold Palmer Hospital, and it had evolved into a full mobile clinic from an initial grant to do HIV testing. The Children's Health Fund was its biggest funder. "My salary is all grant-funded," said Eileen. "We have to sustain every year. It's always strategic. They're always looking for ways to move things around."

I had some familiarity with Miami's Little Haiti neighborhood, but I knew little about Haitians in Orlando except that there must be some here. "Our sense of the Haitian community is that there's a bit of a concentration in this neighborhood around here, Pine Hills," Vinny told me. There was a Haitian consulate nearby on Colonial Drive. "There's also a smaller population in Paramour. There's an issue of health literacy. First, there's a language issue. When they first come to the U.S. and try to access health care, they need brokers. Not only because of language, but also because the health care system isn't easy to access." Medical residents from Arnold Palmer Hospital went on a Creole-language radio show on Saturdays and Sundays to share health care information. "Haitians are still kind of reverent of doctors and the health care system. They wear their Sunday best. When you ask about health history, they're not very forthcoming. That's kind of your dirty laundry."

"You have a lot of different caregivers," said Eileen. "There are a lot of disconnected caregivers."

"How do you try to get around that?" I asked.

"Well, recently I'm trying to work with the school social workers. I find that avenue is going to be a good avenue to get in."

Andre Minott, a non-Haitian black man who was on the mobile clinic staff, told me about a home visit he had made. "I went to the home maybe five minutes early, so I sat out in the parking lot," he said. "And the dad comes out and says, 'What are you doing here?' Just because we are providing a service doesn't mean all the family members welcome that service. So you have to be mindful of your circumstances. The neighborhoods are not too great. Some of the houses are extremely dirty. And you have to be mindful too, because you're going into their space. Some are uneducated on the system, especially if they're Haitian. They get confused, and they feel like we're INS or we're going to report them."

Another staff member was Stew, a likeable fellow who had emigrated from Zimbabwe. "We're finding a lot of Haitians that have to wait five years," he told me. "Also, because of the earthquake and the flooding, they were given what's called temporary protected status, which means they can live here without fear of deportation, but at least in Florida it means they're ineligible for Medicaid, food stamps, or any other sort of programs."

I didn't understand the part about waiting five years. Vinny explained that, because of the Deficit Reduction Act of 2005, "Even if you're in the U.S. legally, and even if you're on the path to citizenship, you're not eligible for Medicaid for the first five years."

"Do you see any of this in political terms?" I asked.

"When I think of trickle-down," said Vinny, "and I look at this population, I wonder how much of this is going to trickle down to them. When you look at Florida's elected officials who are minority, like Mel Martinez and Marco Rubio, their narrative is 'up by the boot-straps'. Forgetting how the odds are stacked against them."

"Both of those examples are Cuban and Republican," I pointed out.

"Yeah," he said, and I felt he let his knowing facial expression say the rest.

A lot of Haitian teenagers lived in turbulent domestic situations and even found themselves kicked out of the house. "They're stuck," said Eileen. "So they end up homeless sometimes, or living in a hotel."

"You see them filling a lot of positions where there's not a lot of social mobility," said Vinny. Many Haitians worked at Orlando's theme parks. "I would say that ninety percent of the kids we work with, whose parents are employed, are employed at Disney or one of the parks," said Stew.

Unlike Elliott Attisha and his staff in Detroit, the Teen Xpress staff stressed that they tried not to become what they called a "medical home" for the teens they served.

"Why don't you want to be their medical home?" I asked.

"Well, these kids will eventually graduate," said Vinny. "Some of them will drop out. And if we say we're going to be your medical home, after they graduate they're going to be as disconnected from medical care as before."

"We're like, 'We can't be your medical home,'" said Eileen. "Well, we are their medical home. They trust us, they know us, and we're ac-cessible. I guess because of the time and everything that's happened with us, it's made me help them see the reality of it, and not mommy them so much. It's just that they're missing so much TLC in their life.

There are just so many barriers that eventually we were just like, 'You know what the best thing is for some of these kids? For them to turn eighteen.'"

Dr. Lisa Gwynn, the pediatrician at the affiliated mobile clinic in Miami, echoed Elliott Attisha in Detroit: "I live in Fort Lauderdale, in a very nice area. It's two extremes. This hasn't been my passion all my life. I worked nine years in private practice. Since I've been here for about two years, you can't help but become more passionate about the issues. I've gotten of an age where I'm like, if we don't do it, who will?" The Miami mobile clinic served many communities, from Mexican farmworkers in Homestead to Argentinean hospitality workers in Miami Beach. The day I met Lisa, the clinic was parked behind the Center for Haitian Studies on Second Avenue in Little Haiti, because it was a Tuesday. "This community center gives a gift every year to the mobile clinic, a financial gift," she said. "It's a win-win for both of us. They're happy with us, and we're happy to be here. Basically it's checkups for the kids, immunizations, a dental van, vision checks. It's comprehensive. We really give these people everything that they need."

"Is it adequate?"

"If you ask the pediatrician in me, I would say no. And access to specialty care is a real challenge. No specialist wants to see a patient for free. But for many of the kids here, this is it. And also there are public health implications to taking care of these kids. The patients really trust us. For our patient population, trust is a matter of, 'Are they gonna tell on me? Am I gonna be deported?' They won't come to the doctor if they think they're gonna be deported. The Haitian population is really, really difficult. Because they don't have the literacy level to understand the consequences of not dealing with their health care needs."

"I've seen this in Haiti," I said.

"Yeah! It's an extension of Haiti. You never really know what you're gonna get when the day starts. Miami-Dade County is a very unique population. There are a lot of immigrants—and fresh. It carries some political implications that we choose not to get involved with, because a lot of people come here on tourist visas and choose not to go back. So they're uninsurable. We try to serve the people who fall through the cracks."

"That's never going to change, I suppose," I suggested.

"Well, not unless they change immigration policy," she said. "To me it's a human issue. It shouldn't be political."

"Of course, to say it shouldn't be political is political," I said.

"Yes," she agreed. "You can't get away from that."

Language was a big issue for both clinics. Lisa Gwynn had been born and raised in Miami and spoke Spanish, but not Creole. "I cannot communicate at all. That's a frustration," she told me. Teen Xpress in Orlando had no Creole-speaking staff member. "It would help us a lot is if we had a staff person who could speak Creole," said Eileen. "I feel like it might get better when some of the younger Haitian kids go to college and can come back and be bilingual." In Miami the clinic's mental health counselor, a Cuban woman named Gladys, told me, "The children went through the earthquake in their country. So we have children with PTSD. We have programs here that specifically work with those children. We try to send them to those programs in the community. Plus, the translators help us understand. Guy has been great, because he's Haitian and he understands the issues."

Dr. Guy Thélémaque was an elderly Haitian doctor who served as interpreter. "Not only interpreter, but I help them with the cultural part," he told me. "Not only the language, but the content is important. What is important for them to know is how to formulate the questions, to have the answer. Because there are culturally big differences."

"What are the differences?"

"You can formulate your question very straight, and you can get a straight answer. But with Haitians you must go around. And you must also understand what they are saying. I don't do a just literal translation. I formulate a question in a way that they understand, and then I translate their answer."

"Can you give me an example?"

"Today, for example, an American doc asked, 'How safe do you feel at home?' And the mom of the kid answered, 'Oh, not safe at all,' in English. Because she speak half English. But this is not safety, this is comfort."

"Dr. Gwynn told me she thinks of you as the chief marketing officer of the clinic," I told him.

"Yes, because when I do something, I want it to go up! I want it to be healthy, and make it positive. The mobile clinic is not enough known. They don't know. Even when I go out and tell them about it, and I give them flyers, they are like, 'Really?'"

"Do you enjoy this work?"

"Of course."

"Why?"

"It's an easy way of being helpful. It's a way that I can contribute to the welfare of the human beings. Not only Haitians. But I can be more productive with Haitians and Latin."

On the Teen Xpress in Orlando I ended up spending quite a bit of time with the mental health counselor, Susie Raskin, and through her with two Haitian teenage girls who agreed to talk to me. Susie had grown up in South Florida but had lived in Orlando since 1995. "We have a lot of students who are from Haiti, or their parents are from Haiti," she said. "So we've learned a lot."

"I'm interested in Florida as an extension of the Haitian world," I told her.

"Yeah, it's like that in places," she said. "I see more females than males. They're generally very polite and kind, and sometimes a bit wary. They're very dedicated to learning. I see a lot of females that are open to counseling, but the males can be like, 'No way, lady.' Often what I see with our teen females is that they're with Dad and the stepmom." Their mothers often stayed back in Haiti. "I think they go through a lot of cultural struggles. What often ends up happening is a lot of family discord. The girls report a lot of depression. There's a lot of 'targeted racism.' This is a primarily African-American school, but there's a big difference between African-Americans and the kids that are Haitians. They get called names. A lot of the kids just try to get under the radar. I feel for them, because it just seems like the families are fragmented. A lot of times it's like, 'I want to talk to my mom, but I don't have enough money to buy a calling card. I haven't talked to my mom in six months.' The ones who have only been here a year or two, they're just like a deer in headlights. But I feel like they don't have many people giving them credit for hanging in there. This is a rough school for anybody."

"Are there any white kids in this school?"

"Not very many."

"So what prompted you to want to be a counselor in the first place?"

"I think it's a matter of when you grow up with chaos, and you want to recapitulate. I thought this was a way to learn about myself and these crazy people that I grew up with, and maybe do some good along the way. I grew up in a suburb in Fort Lauderdale, so most of what I saw was if we happened to be downtown, or what we saw on the news, or what my parents, who were pretty conservative, had to say. My parents grew up in Philadelphia, and they came to Fort Lauderdale because of the cold. We were zoned for schools that were not very good, so my parents put us in Christian school. And it was very much like 'We're Christian.' Talk about a bubble!"

"It's possible to grow up Anglo in Florida and be oblivious?"

"Oh yeah. There's something to be said for people and their bubbles."

"So coming to Orlando coincided with leaving your bubble?"

"I think it was more becoming an adult."

"You wanted to be exposed?"

"Yeah. I figured if I was going to be a counselor, I should do it right. And I think being open to the fact that I didn't know anything. And then, going to grad school was what really did it. That's when I realized that a homeless person is not just a bum; there's a story there. You do have an option: you can be open, or you can be closed. And I think just being in South Florida. You may not be positively aware, but at least you're aware. A lot of people just prefer to stay where it's safe."

✳

"I came here in December 2010, and after that I didn't go back," the first Haitian girl told me, sitting with Susie in her tiny office on the Teen Xpress.

"Why did you come here?"

"My dad wanted us to get a better education. In Haiti it was pretty expensive."

"So your dad lives here with you?"

"No, he's in La Gonâve." The long, barren, largely roadless island in the Bay of Port-au-Prince. "My mom and dad kinda trust me to pick my own guardian. It's kinda on me." Her father was from La Gonâve, and her mother was from the city of Cap Haïtien on Haiti's north coast.

"Why did you come to Orlando and not Miami?"

"I came because my godmom was living here."

"What's school like for you?"

"It's a challenge. But now it's a everyday activity. I feel like it's my house. When I first came here, they look at me different. The way those youths are, that's not the way I am. They all into having boyfriends and girlfriends. If I study, they say I'm a nerd."

"Do they feel uncomfortable because you do better in school than they do?"

"Yes. Mostly I get A's. I tell my teacher, 'Don't say my name, don't say my grade.' They look at me bad for not being bad. They say they can turn you like them. I'm like, 'No, 'cause I got my head screwed on my shoulders.'"

"Why do you think your head is screwed on your shoulders so well?"

"First, because of how my parents raised me. Second, it's because of me livin' in this state, without my parents."

"Where were you when the earthquake happened?"

"I was in Haiti."

"In La Gonâve?"

"In St. Marc."

"Can you tell me what it was like?"

"I didn't really know what it felt like. I was watchin' TV and I was like, 'Mom, why are you shakin' the bed?' She was like, 'I'm not.'"

"So your house was damaged?"

"Mm-mm. But my brother's studio was. Half of it fell down. It could have fallen on him." Her brother was a singer, and he had been recording in the studio when the earthquake hit.

"But it didn't fall on him?"

"No."

Neighbors had told the girl's family that they had to sleep outside that night, but she didn't understand why.

"Do you talk to your parents often?"

"Not often, but pretty much to satisfy us. The situation. We can't do anything about it. We have to deal with it. That was his dream, for us all to be in the States."

"Would your parents like to live in the States?"

"They came here before I was born."

"You have two more years in high school?" She was a 17-year-old sophomore because she had been held back one year. She would be 18, going on 19, when she graduated.

"Yeah."

"What do you want to do after that?"

"I have two big options. First I want to be a pediatrician, after that a detective."

"Did you speak English before you came?"

"Mm-hmm. From YWAM." Youth with a Mission was an international church organization active in Haiti. She thought she recognized me. "Were you in St. Marc, in YWAM?"

"I've been to St. Marc," I said. I had never been with YWAM, though.

"I saw you there."

She seemed to take some comfort or pleasure from thinking she recognized me, so I let her think she did.

"People look at me and say, 'You don't look Haitian,' she said. "I'm like, 'Uh, I am.' Most of the kids from Haiti don't want to admit that they're Haitian."

"Why do you think that is?" asked Susie.

"Some of the kids say bad things about Haiti."

"You get all A's?" I asked.

"My GPA used to be 3.8. And my report card just came out, and it was 3.1. I don't know if it's because I got stress, or what. The reason why it kinda hard is I gotta be my own self parent. It's like I'm doing the parent's work, and revise it to myself as the kid. Kids that have a mom and dad, they should be thankful for that."

"Do you miss your mom and dad?"

"Oh yes. That's a big yes, in a green marker."

"When do you think you'll see your mom and dad again?"

"Probably when I get through high school and have a career."

"Is there anything else you'd like to say to me, that you think people who are not Haitian should hear?"

190

"What I think is, first, try to put theyself in the same position as the Haitian. Because I hear Americans first of all saying bad about the Haitians. Second, they take advantage of Haitians. Even though it's hard for you to understand what the poor are going through, try to understand."

On a hunch I asked her, "Do you have an opinion about the presidential election?"

"According to what I just said, I would say Obama," she said, with a glance at Susie. "The most point is, why would you choose somebody who's already rich, that don't have a clue about what it like for the poor? And again, you already rich. What's the point of you wanting so bad to be president?"

Susie was beaming proudly. "Well, we'll see tomorrow night," she said.

"Yeah, I'll be in front of the TV," I said.

"It gotta be fair for everybody. That's the way I see it."

"Thank you."

"You did good, girl," said Susie.

"I just like talking."

The second Haitian girl was a 16-year-old whose older sister worked at Disney World. This girl had been in Orlando almost six years, since well before the earthquake.

"Why did you come here?" I asked her.

"I don't really know, but when my dad died in Haiti, he made my auntie promise to bring us here, then she did."

"Do you enjoy school?"

"Sometimes."

"How did you do on your report card?"

"I had a D because I missed six days of school."

"What do you do after school?"

"After school I do wrestling."

"Do the American kids treat you well?"

"Sometimes they don't, but sometimes they do. They make fun of your clothes or the accent that you have. Sometimes I wanna skip school, but I don't, because that's not a good idea."

I asked her what work her sister did at Disney World.

"Serving people food and cleaning," she said.

"Does she like her job?"

"I guess so. She don't really have a choice."

"Does she work full-time?"

"No. She only work part-time. She pick up shift."

"Have you been to Disney World?"

"I have been there once."

"When?"

"I think last year."

"Why did you go there?"

"We went there just to have fun."

"To ride the roller-coasters?"

"Mm-hmm."

"Was it fun?"

"Yes. It was the best day!"

"What's your favorite subject in school?"

"I would say writing, but I'm not good at it."

"What do you like about writing?"

"That's what I do when I'm at home. I get out my pen and I write about my feelings."

"What kinds of things do you write about?"

"My mom passing away, my dad, my grandma, my sister."

"What do you want to do after you graduate?"

"I was going to do police officer for the kids."

I didn't follow everything that she said next, but the gist seemed to be that the police had arrested her and put her in jail because her aunt claimed falsely that she had beaten up a girl who was pregnant.

"One time, my aunt is so evil. She brought us here, but she say her bill too much. My aunt would just buy food, but she wouldn't leave none in the house for us. She brought us here, but she regret it for some reason. We don't know why. We been through hell in that house." The girl and her sister had lied to the police because they feared being separated. "But we didn't tell them the truth, because we think they gonna make us separate, so we say we weren't in the house. We just didn't want them to take us away and be separate, so we just lied. So since that day, I just don't think the police do their job. I think they should listen to kids more."

"You would have to go to police school," I said.

"Yes," she agreed. "And if I can't be a police officer, I'll just go be a nurse. I'll go help people in Haiti. That's how my mom died."

"What do you mean?"

"She had tuberculosis, and I think that if they had more nurses and doctors in Haiti, she would still be here."

"Did you have to stay overnight in jail?"

"I stayed in jail for three days. No food or drink, or nothing."

"They didn't give you food?"

"They did give me food, but I didn't like that kind of food, and it just looked nasty."

"Is there anything you would like them to know or to understand?"

"It's really interesting to meet new people that come to different places. Because at the end of the day, everybody going through difficult times. Teenagers, adults, everybody."

"I hope you get to be a police officer, so you can do the job well for other kids," I said.

"Me too."

"If you don't get to be a police officer, will you be happy to be a nurse?"

"Yes, I will. I would like to go back to Haiti and help people."

CHAPTER 5

FAR FROM HOME

Back in Provincetown, Bill Henning and Thomas MacDonald had introduced me to their friend Shawn Nightingale. Shawn owned a chain of stores and a strip mall in Florida, and he had been living in that state in 2000, so I had to ask him about that year's presidential election.

"It was like a really, really bad movie of the week," he told me. "Starring Valerie Bertinelli as Katherine Harris. I was thinking, 'All this, but of course Gore's going to win.' And then the political machine, the juggernaut—it was like being punched in the gut. And Gore was weak in the fight. And that's when I started thinking that we were going to lose. How can you let a mechanical error, and all the proof of the uncounted votes, and the snowbirds, and all that, determine a presidential election? It definitely took away my belief in our system as being practically flawless."

But the weird thing, Shawn said, was how oblivious most people had seemed, even in Florida. "Besides the local coverage, which was all you heard, you wouldn't know. None of my clients knew, and they couldn't have cared less. It was talked about on the street a lot, but a lot of it was, 'How could this have happened?' And 'How could this have happened in our country?' You know what I wanted to do? I wanted to go there and have a gymnasium full of ballots, and count every fuckin' ballot. It took away our democracy, as far as I'm concerned."

On Election Day 2000 I myself had been in Port-au-Prince, which kind of drove home to me the point about the way the election went down. Haitians were surprised, and a bit amused, not that that sort of thing was happening, but only that it now was happening in the United States. I hadn't been paying much attention to the U.S. election campaign that autumn, because I had other things on my mind, and I assumed that the differences weren't very great and the stakes weren't very high. It turned out I was wrong about that.

In Haiti again just after the 2004 election, I interviewed a political prisoner, a prominent Haitian priest named Father Gerard Jean-Juste, who claimed he had been arrested to keep him from traveling to Miami to help mobilize Haitian-Americans there to vote for John Kerry. Way back when, most Americans might have dismissed such a claim as a paranoid delusion. I have no idea whether Father Jean-Juste's claim was true or not. But after *Bush v. Gore*, after chads, after the shenanigans of Florida Secretary of State Katherine Harris, how could one be sure it wasn't?

I spent a lot of time in the second half of 2004 flying back and forth between Miami and Port-au-Prince. Big events were going down in Haiti that year, and it's a long story but I also was kind of desperately trying to relocate myself to Miami from suburban London. I wanted to return to live in the States, I had nowhere in particular in the States to return to, and I figured why not Miami. One thing that bugged me about England was the highly vertical and exquisitely self-referential intricacy of its social caste system. An outsider, and especially, I felt, an American, who doesn't drink the English system's Kool-Aid will eventually find himself chewed up and spit out by it. It's nothing personal; it's just that England's delicate national digestive system doesn't know what to do with you. Paul Theroux got it right when he wrote that, when he finally left after twenty years, he realized that all that time the English had just been waiting for him to leave.

And part of the appeal of Miami was that it was not at all like that. It had a totem pole, to be sure, with, roughly speaking, Cubans at the top, white Anglos second, and Haitians at the bottom. But in between was a multitude of national groups from all around Latin America, shady characters, revolutionaries, realtors and other con men, retirees, crackers, and Jews and other Northern transplants. Carl Hiaasen captures its weirdness well in his murder mysteries, perhaps slightly exaggerated for effect. So does Russell Banks, on a more downbeat note, in his novel *Continental Drift*. In short, South Florida was an undeniably interesting place, the shortcomings of its barren intellectual life and trashy philistine culture and real estate rapacity notwithstanding. Whoever you were, nobody was going to tell you that you couldn't or shouldn't just show up, rent an apartment or buy a condo, pick up a used car and some flip-flops somewhere, and, you know, welcome to Florida. Unless you were an illegal immigrant or, like the novelist Edwidge Danticat's 81-year-old Haitian pastor uncle, a hapless old man who made the mistake, in his confusion while fleeing violence in his Port-au-Prince neighborhood, of asking for political asylum. In that case, you might find yourself thrown into the Krome Detention Center. But that's another story, told painfully well by Danticat in her memoir *Brother, I'm Dying*. Fortunately for me, that's not part of my own experience.

I had been coming to, or at least through, Miami en route to Haiti for thirty years, but only in 2004 had I started getting to know it. And I still felt as if I had only started. Miami also was a moving target, which was part of what made it fascinating. Whenever I came to town I stayed with my cousin Cindy Haralson and her husband Paul. They had been very good to me in 2004, letting me come and go with pretty much no questions asked, taking me out to dinner, plying me with conversation and (Paul's doing) cognac and cigars. Paul and I became good buddies. He was a lawyer with his share of local business and political connections, so I trusted him when he told me, about a job I was interested in applying for, "I wouldn't hire you, because you don't speak Spanish." I would and could learn Spanish, but somehow the separate fact that Burger King was headquartered in Miami kind of tipped me off that it wasn't a town where I could make much of a living.

In Miami I felt I was always on the outside looking in, though in a different way than in London. Miami was worlds within worlds, scatterlings from upheavals and showdowns throughout the Western Hemisphere, and not even people who lived there and spoke Spanish could keep track of them all. "I think Miami is very divided," said Anai Cuadra, a Nicaraguan clinical psychologist I met when I visited the mobile clinic at the Center for Haitian Studies. "There are certain neighborhoods that are known for one country that lives there. Really things have changed. When I first came in '84, mostly it was Cubans and Nicaraguans." Hurricane Mitch in 1998 had brought Hondurans and Salvadorans to Miami; Colombians came fleeing drug violence in their country; Venezuelans came if they opposed or disliked the leftist president Hugo Chavez. "More Haitians came since the earthquake," said Anai. "The Haitians, there are periods of time when they came. The other groups, they don't have power." She meant other than Cuban. "They're not represented, they're not councilmen. The other groups don't bother with that. They want to establish themselves in professions or business."

"Miami is very appealing, because just the cultural atmosphere here is very different," said Anai's colleague Sharlet Anderson, who was half Korean and had grown up in Alabama. "I wanted this specifically. In Atlanta it's not as varied, or at least it's not perceived as as varied. Here, the traditional majority people have much more of an interface with the minorities. In Atlanta, it's easier for them to maintain white privilege. Miami is always swirling."

"Ethnic minorities are so different across the United States," Anai remarked. "I went to D.C., which was another world. Then I went to L.A., which was *another* world."

I asked Anai and Sharlet about the election—this year's election, that is.

"The Republicans have to awaken about this multiculturalism stuff, and this immigration stuff," said Anai. "You gonna stay out of the White House for a long time."

"Even if I hadn't been voting Democratic my whole life, I would have, because I think that's the principle that we need in this country going forward," said Sharlet.

On Election Night 2012, Paul and Cindy and I went out to dinner in Miami Beach, then went back to watch the returns at their house. Two nights later, I drove a ways up Interstate 95 to attend a rehearsal of the South Florida Jubilee Chorus, an all-women's singing group that my friend Ginny Vaidhyanathan and her daughter Mehala belonged to. Ginny was a white American who had vowed to herself as a girl that she was going to marry a foreigner. She and her Indian scientist husband had reared their three children in Buffalo, then retired to a high-rise condo building in Avenida north of Miami. Mehala had been a math teacher at a local college, known to her students as "Ms. V." Mehala's brother, Siva, was my original connection to the family. Siva was a professor of media studies at the University of Virginia and author of books with titles like *Copyrights and Copywrongs* and *The Googlization of Everything*. Mehala proudly told me that Siva's next planned project would be a thorough journal article about the U.S. Supreme Court's controversial *Citizens United* ruling.

"To have a secular group singing this really American music—this is the American stuff," Ginny gushed at Applebee's after rehearsal. "Music just gets the funk out." Their group had recently auditioned to sing the national anthem at a Dolphins game, and had secured the coveted Thanksgiving Day game gig. "We just blew 'em away," she said. "We were their number one choice, which is why we got the Thanksgiving weekend. We have red sequined outfits that we'll be wearing."

"I assume there's going to be a video?" I said.

"I hope there will be! I'm especially proud to sing the national anthem this year. It was just such a relief Tuesday night. It wasn't a celebration, it was just a relief. I was just so happy to see Romney just get run over this time. I tell you what: we voted down *Citizens United* in this election. And I will sing the national anthem with more pride and joy than I have in a long time."

"We were two of the people that delivered those annoying pre-election weekend phone calls," said Mehala.

"Florida is an unwieldy state," I proposed to the table.

"It should be two or three states," Mehala agreed.

"Or possibly two or three countries," said their friend Viv.

"I really appreciate you coming for this," said Ginny. "If we show up in your book, fine, if we don't we don't, but a little bribe never hurt."

✳

I was out late with Ginny and Mehala but up the next morning in time for lunch with Edwidge Danticat at the Buena Vista Deli in Little Haiti. Edwidge had a long-established and well-deserved reputation as a fine and sensitive writer and chronicler of life in Haiti, ever since the publication of her first novel *Breath, Eyes, Memory* in 1994 when she was twenty-five years old. But it was *Brother, I'm Dying* (2007), a work of personal nonfiction both beautifully composed and fearless in several senses, that had cemented my own admiration for her.

Her husband, Fedo Boyer, was with her. Getting to meet Fedo was a bonus, and he seemed like both a jolly and an intelligent fellow. "Is this for an assignment?" he asked me.

"I just felt like writing a book," I said.

"And you felt like driving around America," said Edwidge. "Well, we're honored that you spent Election Night in Miami."

"I thought I might witness some more chads or something," I said.

We started talking about life in the United States in general and Florida in particular, and Fedo told a story about a Frenchman he knew. "He moved to Tampa, started a business, and had some American friends working for him," he said, "and every now and then he would go hunting. One time we were having a conversation with him and he said, 'I didn't know you guys came from a country that was so racist.' I asked him what he was talking about. And he said, 'I go hunting with these white guys, and I'm surprised by some of the stuff that they tell me.'"

"Places like Miami and L.A. and New York are so diverse that nobody's in the majority," I said. "Everybody has to deal with everybody else."

"It's a kind of bubble, because you think every place is like that," said Edwidge.

"But it's not," I assured her.

"So eventually they're gonna become like that," Fedo insisted. "Because if you look at the map of Florida a long time ago, what would be called the I-4 corridor didn't have that many Hispanics, but now it's flooded with Hispanics of all kinds."

"I think Middle American white people ..." I began. I'm not sure what I meant to say next, but it got the conversation rolling.

"They're worried," said Edwidge. "My gosh, you can see how worried they are in the news. This whole conversation about the 'demographics,' like people on Fox, they're terrified. There's this sort of panic, that I almost feel like it's gonna lead to some kind of violence. I'm really concerned."

"You watch Fox?"

"I have to watch a little," she said. "You have to know what people are thinking."

"It's terrifying!" said Fedo.

"They also say that the panic that Karl Rove was having on Fox the other night really had to do with the promises that he made," said Edwidge. "And all that money that he took from these people, that he didn't deliver on. It's amazing that the will of the people overcame all that, especially in Miami. People were just standing in that line, no matter what they did to discourage it. People were motivated to overcome these obstacles that they put in their way with the money, with the politics, with the driver's licenses."

"Yeah, I didn't think that Florida had the guts for it," said Fedo.

"And it seemed like Obama wasn't stepping up, either, like the enthusiasm wasn't really there," I said. "But in the end it was."

"Part of it was these attempts to disenfranchise people who were voting at one a.m. Wednesday morning," Edwidge said. "I think they said the last vote was cast at five a.m. on Wednesday morning. That's why they're still counting. You should have seen these lines. And this is the basic thing you want the world to have, right? They're always telling the Haitians ..."

"Well, they can't really tell the Haitians anything anymore," I ventured. "Part of the working premise of my book is that the U.S. is not distinct or different from Haiti or Pakistan or any other Third World country. It's subject to all the same human nature and political bullying and whatever. White people out in Middle America don't perceive that, or maybe they're beginning to perceive it. With the economic crisis and all the political stuff we've been going through, they're beginning to. As one of them, part of my job is to take this message to them."

"Because you've seen the other side," said Edwidge.

"Right, and guess what, folks. We're not so different from Haiti, but that's okay."

"Because that's the first thing that people always say," Edwidge said. "Like in Katrina, what did you hear? 'This is not Haiti,' or 'This is not Africa.' And even people who are standing in gas lines, they're saying, 'This is not a Third World country. This is America.'"

"Just by shouting that loudly and often, you can sort of make it not be like that," I said.

"Yeah," she said, "but I think they shout it like that because it's the greatest shame to be this other thing, to be this Third World country. Even now, Greece is the Third World country of our nightmares."

"Right. 'This is not Greece.'"

"But this is where everybody's headed."

"And Americans have to get okay with that, I think," I said.

"I think it's very hard for them to get okay with that," Edwidge said. "The American exceptionalism has been going on so long."

"What does it mean to you to be an American?" I asked her.

"Well, I feel like I don't know Middle America that well. Because I've always lived in these urban centers, and we were always told that Middle America is sort of the norm, that 'We want to talk to Middle America.' But what it means to me to be an American has always been hyphenated and diverse, because I've always lived in these melting-pot cities. When I first came to New York, I went to Brooklyn and so, to me, that was America: people speaking Spanish, people speaking Russian, Korean. You have your Haitian groceries at the Korean store. So that, to me, was America: this place where all different kinds of people meet, and sometimes people who are enemies elsewhere can be friends there. Like Haitians and Dominicans might not get along on the island, but in America, in Brooklyn, they're neighbors. I just felt like America was this place that brought all these different kinds of people to the same block."

"It's not like that in the town I grew up in, in Wisconsin," I told her.

"I think that's what we're talking about, these different Americas," she said. "Because a child coming like I did to Brooklyn is very different than one that goes somewhere in the Midwest and is the only black child in their class."

"You could still be Haitian in Brooklyn."

"Yeah. And you can actually be in this family, this first generation family, like two of my siblings. They were born in America, and two of us were born in Haiti."

"How do you feel being an adult in Miami, versus being a child in Brooklyn?"

"Miami is practically in Latin America so it's totally different, you know. When they talk about the rest of Florida being conservative, it's very hard for me to address. I've seen a little bit of it, but Miami's super diverse, so if you've left from Haiti, you certainly haven't left the sort of climate that you're used to. A lot of things are different, but it's not such a hard landing. That's why I think a lot of people, even adults who are still leaving these different Latin American countries, a lot of them settle here. My daughter goes to a school, for example, where you have the native Miami, but you also have a lot of diversity. You have Creole-speaking kids, you have Spanish-speaking kids, and you have the second-generation kids, too, or first-generation. I think places like Miami, they tend to be an extension of where the different roots come from."

"Have you ever driven up I-75 to Georgia?" I asked her.

"No, I haven't. Am I missing something?"

"My brother lives in Georgia," said Fedo.

"Yes, we have," Edwidge corrected herself. "Because Fedo has a brother who lives in Georgia. It was at night, you drove, that's why I don't remember."

"Well, I drove from Macon down to Orlando in one go, like seven hours. First of all, there are tons of billboards, billboards galore."

"Election-related?"

"A lot of them are 'Stop Obama.' That's the phrase."

"There's some here."

"Those are Zionist, whereas the ones up in Georgia are racist," I said. "Almost blatantly racist. They have him with a Hitler mustache."

"That stuff exists, part of the undercurrent," she said.

"If you ask people on the East Coast and the West Coast, some people in the middle, you would find what an American is," suggested Fedo. "The formula would probably be different in every place, so you would probably say at the end, 'To be an American is to be five or six of these menu items.'"

"I think Middle America has had a huge seismic shift this week," said Edwidge. "Because I think the first time Obama was elected, it's like, it's history, but this time it's a different choice, and all this con-versation about 'the country's changing,' not just the nut cases. I think there's gonna be an internal examination of their place."

"Is this ultimately going to have a positive result?"

"In some cases, I think it'll be positive. Even on the fringe of Middle America, you have a lot of mixed marriages. You have brown babies, so I think reasonable people are aware of this. I think that in the mid-dle there'll be this conversation about, 'So what is America? Are we like Brazil now?' I think a lot of people would have had a shocking revelation this week. You see it in the things in the states, with the homosexual marriages. For a lot of people, it's like, 'No,' and they're not the extremists but a lot of people in Middle America. Their kids do go to school with Muslim kids. Like my daughter. I said to her, I haven't seen So-and-so's daddy.' And she said, 'Well, maybe she has two mommies.' She's three."

"Have you ever thought about setting a novel in the U.S.?" I asked her.

"*The Dew Breaker* was partly set there but, no, I haven't, not completely with American characters."

"You're not up for that, not ready?"

"Not yet."

"You must speak at colleges in places like Indiana and Tennessee."

"Yeah, sometimes. The last place I went was Denison University in Ohio, and it's very strange, because they have this little gallery, they have Haitian art, and you know that these kids would've never encountered this if the school hadn't wanted it. Often that's their first exposure to Haiti, the things they do around the visit."

"So what do you say? How do you communicate with kids like that?"

"Well, lucky for me, you're not just coming at them blind; they read one of the books and they research. So, usually, they just have the initial exposure with the school, but I have to say they don't have as ignorant questions as before. Maybe ten years ago, people would say things like, 'Do they even know how to read in Haiti?' But they're often shocked that I speak the way I do. They all say, 'Oh, I was expecting someone with a big accent,' or something like that. And one woman once said to me, 'We were expecting a Haitian accent, and you have a Brooklyn accent.'"

"Maybe she meant that as a compliment," I said. "Do you think the earthquake has changed Middle America's impression or awareness of Haiti?"

"I think it's sad that most of Middle America's exposures to Haiti are through disasters. If I go to a small town, people will say, 'Oh, yes, we have a mission in Haiti,' or 'The church has a school or an orphanage in Haiti.' That's often their exposure. Nobody says, 'Oh, I was on a great vacation.' But you can talk on different registers with people if they feel like I know this experience of being Haitian, but I also know what it's like to grow up in America. And, more and more, there are a

lot of people who share that experience from different countries. There are a lot of kids who are the first ones in their family going to college, and you see less and less outright culture clash, and more adapting. It's more like, 'How do I balance these new things here?'"

"This gets back to the election and the seismic shift that you suggest we've just been through."

"It feels like less of an emotional choice this time, you know?"

"In a good way?"

"In a very good way. And what is this saying about who we are as Americans? When I was a kid I would watch Ronald Reagan, and you know when they say, 'My fellow Americans' on the news, like if you're watching those speeches, they always begin with, 'My fellow Americans.' And I would always wonder, 'Do they mean me?' At some point I thought they were really speaking to a specific group of people, like they're not necessarily speaking to me. So I used to think that I'm sort of eavesdropping on this intimate conversation between the president and his fellow Americans. I didn't think that meant, like, everybody who lives in the country. 'My fellow Americans.' I don't even know if they say it anymore. Call your book *My Fellow Americans*."

"Does Obama say that?"

"I don't think he does. I think that was a Reagan thing."

"Yeah, it was definitely part of Reagan's shtick," I agreed. "He didn't invent that phrase, but he rode it to death."

"Yeah. And I remember when I was in college, I went to study abroad, and I came back and I heard again, 'My fellow Americans.' And I thought, 'When is that going to mean me?'"

"I haven't heard it in so long, I don't know how I would react to it," said Fedo.

Fedo spoke of the reactions he got, as a Haitian living in Florida, when he returned to Haiti.

"We go there and we go like, 'We're Haitian, we speak Creole,'" he said. "And they go, 'You're not from here.' 'Yeah, I'm from here. You know I was born in the south.'" He meant the south of Haiti, in the city of Les Cayes. "There's just something different. They really want you to admit that you're not from there at all. I was born in *aux Cayes*, best city in Haiti. You can ride your bike on the streets."

"You have to compete with the motos now," said Edwidge.

"When I was a kid, we'd just go on bikes," said Fedo.

"That's a nice part of Haiti," Edwidge said.

"I loved *aux Cayes* when I was a kid," Fedo went on. "I say this to my friends: I only learned that Haiti was poor when I came to this country, because when we lived in *aux Cayes*, we had all the things that a suburb has. We used to go to school on bikes, everybody trusted everybody, some kid's father was picking up from school and everybody would jump in the back of the truck, because we didn't have to think about it twice." He sounded like my high school friend Jerry Burhop, reminiscing about Oconomowoc. "We had two soccer teams, we had everything. We had the superstars. We used to record albums and stuff like that. Some of my best memories are from growing up. It doesn't matter what changes or how good it gets here or whatever, it seems the best memories are from growing up in *aux Cayes*, in a small town."

Edwidge and Fedo had been in Haiti recently. "We saw so much construction," she said with distaste.

"Is there a good side to that?" I said. "You're not willing to say that?"

"Maybe there's a good side. But there's the other side. It's like the whole factory thing." The so-called international community and big outside institutions like the World Bank were always trying to lay low-paying factory jobs assembling things like t-shirts and baseballs on Haitians, whose heritage was in peasant agriculture and whose history had taught them a deep-seated suspicion of white foreigners.

"How do you feel about the improvement of the national roads, the repaving?"

"The road to *aux Cayes*, I understand that was long in the making, right?"

"We don't know what Sandy has done to it," said Fedo. "It's not so much the damage; it's the time that it takes to repair it."

"Tell me about Sandy," I said. Hurricane Sandy had hit Haiti.

"We got hit by it on both ends," said Edwidge. "In New York, my mother's house had a bit of damage. It's not a big deal compared to what some are suffering. In Haiti, right now, I think we're going to feel the aftereffects of Sandy very strongly. From what I've been reading, it's just been flooded."

"Middle America notices when it happens in New York, doesn't really notice when it happens in Haiti?"

"I think they notice. But even when someone is writing about what a church has done, a Middle American church, they write, 'Well, take care of your own.' You know, like when some white people adopt a baby from Haiti, it's like, 'Why don't you adopt one in America?' I don't think it's that people don't notice, but in this time that we're living in now, I think people do have donor fatigue when it comes to Haiti. After the earthquake, and then we had these unfortunate situations where so much of the money was misused. Things are very bad here even without storms for a lot of people. I do think, in terms of disasters, people feel like, 'My ten dollars that I texted solved the problem, leave me alone.' And you also have to see that through the lens of all these problems people here are having. And we've seen here, in this community, people who, when they lose their jobs, like if a certain kind of person, man or woman, loses his or her job here, not only are they in trouble, but the family they're supporting in Haiti is in trouble. And I do think, the way the economy is, people just have less and less to give. I don't think it's so much that they don't care about Haiti. It's like Haiti's not their problem. Also, on some level, we have to get to a point where we take care of ourselves, and I'm not comfortable with the model of always having to have a bowl out. So I can't put that on others, that you must give."

"I wanted to touch a little bit on Florida politics, or the communities in and around Miami," I said. "Venezuelans here are anti-Chavez; they're sort of like the new Cubans. Is that right?"

"I'm sure there are some who are for Chavez, but a lot of them are very anti-Chavez," she said. "They're here because of Chavez."

"Just like the Cubans are here because of Castro?"

"But the Venezuelans here, a lot of them have money, so they're powerful people."

"Are the Cubans always going to be dominant in Miami?"

"I don't even think they're dominant anymore," she said. "You have some younger Cubans who are very different from their predecessors. Cuba is not as big a preoccupation for them. I mean, it makes sense, but they're really looking to politics here. They're not as hardline. They're happy to go back and see Cuba and come back."

"But they're not obsessed with Castro in the same way?"

"Not the same way that their parents and grandparents were."

"Is there ever going to be a substantial Haitian political factor in Miami?"

"Well, we think there is. Not on the national level, but Miami, for a long time, was the only place in the United States where you had Haitian elected officials. The mayor of North Miami is Haitian."

"Will there be any congressmen?"

"I think there'll be a congressman or woman sometime, definitely. People want to have political power but, unlike the Cuban community, we don't have this huge amount of money. And maybe the numbers are not there yet. Especially on issues that we care about, we have a vocal community, but we don't really have a powerful community. I volunteered the day of the election to do translation, so I was at this poll where sometimes people would come in, and all they said, these old Haitian ladies, they said, 'I want to vote for Obama, and I want to vote against abortion. Show me where those things are.' The people were really proud; they vote a lot."

"So are you known around Miami and Little Haiti as Edwidge Danticat the distinguished novelist, or are you known as just Edwidge, the community lady?"

"No, it's not like that. And I prefer it to be like that, just in the community."

"Do Haitians read your books?"

"Yeah, some of them do."

"When Haitians in Florida read your novels, what do they have to say?"

"Some of them like them, some of them don't, but I think a lot of them, like me, have sort of experienced both worlds through their parents. I feel like I'm speaking to them."

"Speaking for them?"

"Not for them, to them. I don't speak for anybody."

✻

My friend Pete Sabo had flown to Miami to drive with me as far as Houston, and after lunch we drove up I-95 and camped at Jonathan Dickinson State Park, named for a seventeenth-century Quaker merchant who had been shipwrecked nearby. Our conversation with Edwidge and Fedo had left me reflecting on how all Americans except Native Americans, not only recent immigrants in Miami, are in a sense shipwrecked or stranded in this country. Pete, for example, was an American because of a choice that had been forced on his grandfather.

Pete's grandfather, an immigrant from Slovakia, had supported his wife and three children with a job in a boiler factory in New York during the Great Depression. His boss had a relative who wanted to sell a house, and the boss somehow learned that Pete's grandfather was laying aside money to move back to Slovakia. So he called him into his office and bullied him into spending the money he was saving on a down payment on the house. Pete's grandfather felt he couldn't risk losing his job, so he bought the house and never made it back to Slovakia. And I had just been reading a passage near the end of *American Odyssey*, Robert Conot's authoritative history of Detroit, that summed up a string of similar stories:

> The exhaustion of the Cornish mines and fisheries drove the Lenticks to Michigan's northern Peninsula, and when the mines there began to give out they migrated to Detroit. The Cavanaghs were forced to flee Ireland, and two generations later Sylvester Cavanagh correctly perceived that prospects were brighter in industrial Detroit than on his family's farm. William Norveth, who was made redundant by the overpopulation of Hungary and the American mechanization of agriculture, was sucked into the maws of the industrial machine. Black Bear's ancestors were deprived of their lands by the white men's guns. Odie Stallings would have starved in a Virginia economy in which he had no means of support. Wallace

Mirow was expelled by a land that revolted at its rape. The Jansens became immigrants when the herring was fished out of the Baltic and the trees of Sweden's more accessible forests were felled.[1]

I had been asked to speak that Sunday at a rally organized by the Pakistani community in Orlando in support of Malala Yousufzai, the teenager in the Swat Valley who, a month earlier, had gained international notoriety after being shot in the head by the local Taliban for her vocal advocacy of girls' education. "She is not only a brave girl," the imam of the Islamic Society of Central Florida told the rally, "but she is one of those very people who are going to change the outlook of people toward Islam.  Malala Yousufzai is fighting Taliban, she is fighting terrorism. Malala Day is being celebrated all over the world. And this gave me great pleasure, because Malala is going to revolutionize this *umma*. The time has come that we as Muslims should stand for woman education, so if we do so I believe that the destiny of Islam will change for the good."

My friend Dr. Rubina Inayat spoke of "the Pakistan that the world has failed to recognize lately." And another woman, Maryam Tabrez, said: "I think she is a true inspiration, not just for Pakistan, but for everyone all over the world."

As we walked around on our little march, which was covered by an Orlando TV station, I fell in with Dr. Deeba Ahmad, who turned out to be a board member of the Orange County Democratic Party. I told her that in Detroit I had met and been impressed by Rashida Tlaib, the first Muslim woman elected to the Michigan state legislature. "I went

---

1 On the facing page (p. 856) in Conot's book published in 1974 is this prescient nugget: "The unorganized, subeconomic latecomers will be required to make good on the commitments that members of the organized economy were able to exact at a more affluent time. If the overtaxed lower income population of the city continues to grow, and the economic base is not expanded, Detroit is on a collision course with fiscal disaster."

to the DNC convention in Charlotte, and I met her at the Muslim caucus," Deeba told me. "We have a Muslim caucus now that's close to a hundred people. She was sitting at my table. And I said, 'Oh my God! You're exactly the kind of person we're looking for!' I wish we had more like her, who are vibrant, fearless, gregarious." And Deeba reflected on her own role in U.S. politics: "I'm extremely honored to be able to do this for my country. I was born in Pakistan, but my parents were not. They were born in India. And a few generations before that, they were from Afghanistan. And before that, maybe they came from Iran and Uzbekistan. I've been here for twenty-six years. Maybe seventy-five years from now someone will say, 'My great-grandmother came from Pakistan.'"

Also at the rally I met Rachel and Shahab Sehgal, a middle-aged couple who made their living selling health insurance. They were a talkative and interesting pair, and I prevailed on them to sit with me for an hour and educate me about Obama's health care reform. Shahab had grown up in Britain, Rachel in Kansas.

"There's a misconception about how health care was sold to the American people as a national health service as in Europe, and it is nothing like that," Shahab said. "What health care reform essentially was was to regulate the insurance companies, not to convert your insurance plan into a national health system. And that is a big difference. A national health system is when the government actually is controlling the health insurance. You are getting your health insurance through the government, similar to an HMO. When you go to an HMO plan, the doctors have a fiduciary responsibility as well as a medical responsibility, so they're controlling the dollars as well as your health care. Whereas health insurance is nothing like that. Health insurance is: the doctor is just supposed to take care of you, irrespective of the fiduciary responsibility.

"So Obama introduced certain steps. By 2014, all adults will be covered for pre-existing conditions. He also secured all these wellness cares and an unlimited cap on insurance. If you recall Christopher Reeve, Superman, he had a million-dollar policy. He burned that up within ten months, and then he had to get charity or whatever. But one of the most fundamental elements of health care reform is to replace group health insurance, where most small businesses are paying between $1,500 and $2,000 or $3,000 a month in health care insurance. If you are a healthy man and you go to the gym four times a week and you have a healthy diet, and your neighbor is a woman of childbearing age, and another neighbor eats greasy food and doesn't work out, you'll be paying for their health costs. That's how it works now. What Obama is saying is: 'Hang on a minute, we want to change that. We want to give the best rates to people who have a healthy lifestyle.'"

"It's kind of like saying, 'You pay for your own car insurance because you're a safe driver,'" explained Rachel. "You don't go around running red lights or running into people. You pay for your own home insurance when you own a home. Why can't you pay for your own health insurance? People think it's great that someone else is paying for their health insurance, but it's not. You're being gouged, and you don't even know it."

"Another good thing that Obama did," said Shahab, "which no other president has ever done, what has never been done in this country, is that he introduced what is known as PCIP, the pre-existing insurance plan. He said, 'If you have been declined insurance because of a pre-existing condition, if you are uninsurable, then you will get a policy very similar to what the House and the Senate have.' Any client who's had cancer or a triple bypass or is typically uninsurable, we show them the PCIP web page, which is from the U.S. Department of Health and Human Services. We tell them, 'This is the premium, and actually it's cheaper than what we're selling.' But we don't get a commission. We do that as a courtesy and say, 'This is what you can have.' But some of our clients say, 'Well, what is this? If it's from Obama, we don't want it. We don't want anything to do with that man.' It is unbelievable! Until July 31st, 2010, the PCIP didn't exist. The guy's a saint. And you've got these frickin' redneck clients who have got cancer, and they will not take Obama's plan."

"Americans don't understand their insurance," Rachel said. "You can't explain something to someone unless you sit down like this and have a long conversation."

"How did the two of you meet?" I asked.

"You want to hear something funny?" said Rachel. "He was born in Kenya. I'm from Kansas. I thought we were the only ones. I'm not kidding you. Obama started out doing international relations, and that's actually what our son started out doing overseas. It's just kinda weird."

"I'd better keep an eye on your son."

"Do you want the truth?" asked Shahab.

"Yeah."

"Okay. I came over here because I was doing some work—I was a consultant—and we went to Los Angeles. It was during the Reagan era, and while I was here, I met Rachel. Rachel worked at Bob's Big

Boy. The assignment I was working on was involved with the technical aspects of Libya, and just when I had a nice job, a nice paycheck and everything, and just when I did my training in California, I was being shipped out to Libya. But just then Reagan bumped Libya, and then he banned all scientific projects to Libya. So I was given the pink slip. She was a waitress, and I used to talk to everybody, as you can probably believe."

"Yeah, I can believe that."

"I can hardly get a word in edgewise," said Rachel.

"This was twenty-six years ago," said Shahab. "And she said to the people I was with, 'Why is he quiet? He's usually talking.' And they said, 'Oh, he's going back to England.' After we ate, she said, 'Is there anything else I can do for you?' I says, 'Yeah, you can marry me.' So three days later we got married in Vegas."

"He says three days," Rachel said. "It wasn't three days, it was more than three days. We got married on January 3rd. It was three days before that?"

"Oh, it was a couple of weeks."

"It was more than a couple of weeks. It was more like a couple of months."

"No it wasn't. I only came to America in December."

"No, no, no. It was a couple of months."

"It was soon," I said.

"Yeah," said Shahab.

"Twenty-six years later, you're still married with three kids," I said. "Congrats. That's a great story."

"Yin and yang," said Rachel.

"It's thanks to Reagan," I observed.

"We have three wonderful kids as a result," said Shahab.

"All forward-thinking, I hope," said Rachel. "We used to be Republicans, you know. We saw the Democrats as leeches, whatever. And in 2007 and 2008, with all the stuff going on in Iraq, when we were really questioning the Republicans, our oldest son was still seventeen. He comes home and I said, 'I still don't know who I'm gonna vote for.' He said, 'You're gonna vote for Barack Obama.' I'm like, 'But he's black. He's not gonna win.'"

"She's not a racist," Shahab assured me.

"No, I just knew that he was not gonna win," she said. "I like to vote for somebody that I think might win. And he goes, 'You're gonna vote for him because I can't vote, okay? All the kids at the high school, they all want Barack Obama. You should see them, Mom.'"

"Yeah, we were going to vote for Romney in 2008," said Shahab. "We went and met Romney. We were actually going to vote for Romney. That evening we spoke to him and I said, 'What are you doing about Muslims? They're getting treated badly.' He said, 'Yeah, I'll take care of it.' We were going Romney, but he didn't get the nomination. Then after that, we went with Obama."

"So what does it mean for health care and for America that Obama won reelection?"

"It's gonna get better for a great majority of people," said Rachel. "It can't be repealed now."

"Even the GOP said it's here to stay," said Shahab. "Even if Romney had gotten in, it would not have been repealed. I was never scared of it being repealed."

"How important an achievement is it?"

"It's as important as Social Security that Roosevelt introduced. You don't see the measure of it. The real impact of it will take twenty years."

"I can give you my take on this thing," said Rachel. "Just something to think about. In 2001 a lot of people remember 9/11, but what they don't remember is Enron. And Enron was so evil. They were so evil that the people at the top got taken away, like they should've, but what people don't realize is that people who actually did the really bad stuff, they didn't; they went to work on Wall Street. So if you look at what's happened from 2002 until now, the price of health insurance has skyrocketed so much in that short amount of time, it's unbelievable. Group policies, group plans, they've just gone so high. It's taken away people's yearly raises, that's what it's done. It's taken that away, so there's no money left to give them a raise because of their insurance, and people don't understand. That's how I think it's all come about: because of Enron, in a very sly way."

"I think I'm going to have a chance to interview Sherron Watkins," I told them.

"Oh, that will be interesting," said Rachel.

"Who's that?" said Shahab.

"The whistleblower," Rachel told him.

"She was the Enron VP who brought it all out," I said. "She lives in Houston."

By the time Pete and I left Orlando it was late afternoon. We were due in New Orleans the next evening, so we drove as far as we could through the belly of Florida and along the panhandle. We couldn't find a campground, so we just drove onto a side road and pitched our tent in the woods. Driving through Port St. Joe the next day I saw these signs in front of churches:

Need a sign to go
to church? This is it

Don't give up. Moses was
once a basket case!

And we also started seeing signs like this one:

BP CLAIMS
Monday-Saturday 9am-6pm
850-653-4968

✻

"This here was a really big mall," said Todd McDonald, driving us the next day around New Orleans East. "And, as you can see, it's no longer there." On Reed Boulevard, he told us: "All of these houses probably had eight feet of water or more. If you dig five feet underground, you're hittin' water. The problem was that the water just sat for two-three weeks."

Todd's father, Alden McDonald, was the CEO of Liberty Bank and Trust, the third-largest African American-owed bank in the United States, and we had come to the bank's building so I could interview him. Todd was in his early thirties and had attended a graduate business program at Northwestern University with a good friend of mine, a Pakistani immigrant named Fawad Butt.

"We were the first building back after the storm, because there was no electricity in the area," Todd said. "Literally, at night, we were the only building with the lights on. It took us a year to get the elevators, because they had that much backlog in demand. They had a ton of power outages. So you could have a regular day like this, and go home and no power. And they probably had something like seventy percent out, so you just kinda went home after work."

"How many floors in your building?" I asked.

"Six, and we're on the sixth floor. So a lot of the employees that couldn't, or didn't feel like walking up, they just kinda stayed in Baton Rouge." Baton Rouge was where the bank had decamped to "after the storm," as New Orleans people tend to say, demarcating their lives with reference to Hurricane Katrina. "And you know we had a Six Flags here, and that's vacant. New Orleans is mostly hospitality, so it's a lot of hourly wage."

"What you have is hospitality and oil?"

"Yeah. And then with the medical piece, hopefully that'll make us a hub. So three industries are better than two."

New Orleans had a large Vietnamese community, some of whom lived around here, but they weren't Liberty Bank customers. "It's hard to get into that community, because they're very close-knit," Todd said. "And they do a lot of financing themselves. You can see how they have their own self-contained market. They're in the community, but I never hung out with them on the weekend or anything."

I wondered how New Orleans was experiencing the aftermath of the housing bubble.

"I generally feel we're going to feel a shock in real estate in this area," said Todd. "And then BP comes along, has the oil spill, they inject a lot of money into Louisiana. People are just kinda surviving off this insurance and recovery funds, and I feel we're going to get a shock, a late wave with the real estate bubble."

"So you're still in the bubble?"

"I'll see a house with two thousand square feet, selling at $200 a square foot, and it's not even near downtown or a nice part of the city. And you go anywhere else in the country, and it's $80 a square foot. People are coming into New Orleans without really knowing the market, so they're buying. And we may pass through it, hopefully so. But I'm cautious."

"That strip mall that we just passed, that's all boarded up, that's for sale. Is that ever since the storm?"

"Yeah," he said.

"And that kind of sight is normal?"

"Yeah. Actually, the movie theater over there, that my dad and his friend owned, never reopened. And over there is the Regional Transit Authority—never reopened."

"We opened our bank in 1972," Todd's father told me back in his office. "We're forty years old this week. If you take a look at the lack of financial services that were available during slavery to the African American in the United States, you begin to understand some of the history as to why we lack wealth. Prior to 1966, there were no African Americans in the banking industry in the state of Louisiana, other than janitor positions. Which means that the African American community did not have access to financing of any kind other than finance companies, where interest rates were much higher than normal."

"Pawn shops?"

"Yes. So if you take a look at why we came into existence: Number one, to perhaps afford a population access to financing at reasonable rates when it previously was not available to them. If you take a look at the sixties and you take a look at today, 2012, barely two generations of turnover of real estate, African Americans not only here but throughout the United States actually purchased real estate from the white population when the white population was buying a second or third house and moving out of the community. Which meant the African American population bought it at a higher level given the previous equity. And if you take a look at that whole system, we've only had the opportunity to turn the real estate from our family members twice, whereas other populations had the opportunity to turn the real estate several times.

"The 2008 economic crisis was a setback for a lot of individuals who now have homes that are upside down in market value. How long will it take for those homeowners to gain value again? The recovery of that is going to be very, very important. And I think this election is really going to go down in history and, at some point, people will realize that what Obama did in his first term because of the economic crisis, he tried to change not only the thinking of people, but the understanding of where our economy was heading. It was too far to the wealthy side. The wealthy continued to make the rules in favor of their preferences. And it's not bad to make money, don't get me wrong, but there was becoming an imbalance as to the amount of wealth in America and how lopsided it was, and the middle class having an opportunity to really live the American dream like a lot of people talk about."

"Does Obama really understand that?" I asked. I wasn't sure.

"I think he does, from this point of view: Number one, the crisis that he inherited was much more serious than the general public is aware of. I just happen to be on a committee in Washington that identified the crisis by accident. We were dealing with the under-banked and the unbanked. Sheila Bair was the FDIC chairman at the time, and she had a passion for the unbanked and under-banked. My other son had an experience that I brought up to the committee. I'd been in banking all these years, and I don't consider myself to be a smart guy but an average guy, and I could never understand how people could buy a house with no money down and with income levels that did not support a mortgage. It just blew me away. To make a long story short, my son was finishing his residency and on his way to Houston to do a fellowship. His fellowship was going to pay him $55,000 a year, unmarried, one income, and he was purchasing a townhouse for $380,000 because Mom and Dad were going to help. Or that was the game plan, and we were going to finance it. But when he was looking at acquiring the property, a number of brokers prequalified him and approved him for a loan: a one hundred percent loan for $380,000."

"Without you?"

"Right, without us. They didn't even know that we were in the picture. Based on $55,000 a year."

"What year was that?"

"That was either late 2006 or 2007, because it was about a year before the public knew about the crisis. And the day before the closing, the broker came back and said, 'Uh, we need for you to sign one more piece of paper,' stating that he was making $155,000. It was undocumented income. Somebody had falsified some paperwork. When we talked about that in our committee meeting, other people knew about what were called 'resets,' where you got a two-percent mortgage in an environment where it was normally five, or whatever the number was, and it would reset years later, so they would put you in a mortgage at an interest rate that you could halfway make if you didn't have falsified reference numbers. The government agencies who were part of this committee went back in their records to look at how many resets were out there, and when those resets were going to expire, and they got to see much more than what they wanted to see, and they knew it was going to be a crisis, a housing crisis. So Obama had that to deal with, unexpectedly, and I don't know how old you are, but I'm sure you've had some student loans."

"I've been very fortunate so, no, I haven't," I told him. "I'm forty-seven years old. I went to the University of Wisconsin as an in-state student, and in the mid-eighties when I was there, it was $700 a semester tuition."

"Well, somebody in accounting thought they should exempt student loans from bankruptcy," he said. "Now the right thing to do is pay it back, don't get me wrong, but there's no out for the whole student loan problem. Obama's plan was to find a different way of having people work student loans off, working in government or giving hours back in teaching, or whatever, which would have been a great piece, but he was unable to do that because of some of the seriousness of the whole financial world, and he was trying to balance how much he would give back to society and so he elected not to go that route. The housing piece is not solved yet, and what he was attempting to do when the debacle came about was to find different ways of having people stay in their homes. I think he's going to work on that in the second term."

"This election could have gone the other way," I said. "It was very close, or it seemed very close."

"Right," he agreed.

"What would have been the ramifications if it had gone the other way?"

"You would have gotten more of the typical Republican platform, which was leaning toward business. The tax breaks that businesses get, in my opinion, are not really good for the country. When you take a look at the tax breaks that businesses got for shipping jobs overseas—I mean, when do you stop that? Let's take a look at the steel industry back in the sixties, when we began making automobiles and automobile parts abroad, when we moved those jobs out of the U.S. We basically shifted our work force to other countries. When do we bring that balance back? When Obama came into office, no one was paying attention to the employment piece. You know what happened in 2008? The same thing that happened to us in 2005 in Katrina. We had an opportunity to downsize because of the event. We didn't hire as many people back. We didn't do a lot of the things we did pre-Katrina, post-Katrina."

"When you say 'we,' you mean Liberty Bank?"

"Yes. The year after Katrina was our most profitable year in the history of our bank."

"Because of the downsizing?"

"Yes, because of a lack of expenses that we should have made the adjustments for anyway. Now, I give you that example to tell you about how, in 2008, our country had an opportunity to restructure its work force and its jobs. It had a reason to lay people off and to downsize and to rebalance their balance sheets for survival. Some made it, some didn't. In 2008 we not only had the upside down in the housing values, we had a serious adjustment in workforce in jobs that a lot of companies eliminated because of the crisis. Two thousand eight was an opportunity for the workforce to adjust, so unemployment will be high for a period of time and gradually come down as we find new jobs for our economy."

"What industries are those new jobs going to be in?"

"Technology, medical industry. Because why? We are redesigning the whole medical industry. Everything's going to medical records, so we've got to retrain."

"But we can't run a whole country just on people giving each other medical care," I objected.

"No, no, no. That's one, I said. You asked. I mean, I don't have the answer either."

"I'm looking for the full answer, though," I said. "What does it mean to you that Obama is African American?"

"Of course, we're all proud that we have an opportunity to see something like this happen. Will it ever happen again? I don't think so. I think this whole thing was a fluke, but everybody was very happy to see it, and it gives us a lot of hope because racism is very much alive, and you can actually see it in the election. You could see people voting against their own benefits. I mean, if people would just sit and think about what the hell it is they were voting for."

"Are the Republicans chastened at this point?"

"That's a good question. I have not seen anything that will cause them to change. I think some leadership is going to have to rise on that side to get people to begin looking at what's best for the country, as opposed to what's best for the party. Everyone has to realize that we have to get the budget in line, no two ways about it, but we have to do it together. The bipartisan committee came up with some recommendations that the Obama administration put together, and the Republican Party rejected. Now, Alan Simpson, who was not only a well-known but a well-respected Republican, was co-chair of it, and I knew Alan from some past relationships, and we've talked about his work privately. He's terribly upset for his party, terribly upset. Well respected, staunch Republican, and he could not believe the pushback he got from his party. So we have a lot of things to worry about, we have a lot of things we have to fix, and at what point does the leadership of this country come to the forefront and say enough is enough? Let's begin looking at this so we can fix the problem. We can fix the problem. If you take a look at Louisiana, we have an asshole governor who, because of party politics, is refusing programs from Washington. The state of Louisiana has opted out of the medical reform piece, so the federal government will have the medical system here if he doesn't change his mind. Maybe we can change his mind, now that the election is over. He refused Medicaid money. It's a three-to-one match. Why would you refuse it? For every dollar you spend, the federal government gives you three dollars. I don't understand it. We have laid off many, many, many people in the medical field. We've closed all of the mental health hospitals here. We have no mental health care available, because of politics."

"He was on the shortlist for Romney's running mate but didn't make it," I reminded him.

"Thank God! Well, Obama would have won much easier if he was on it."

Todd had told me that there soon would be a new wave of consolidation in the weakened sector of African American-owned community banks, but that Liberty Bank was one of the stronger ones.

"How will you use your relatively strong position?" I asked Todd's father, the CEO. "Are there things that you can do with that to make the situation better?"

"Well, we try, and we participate on the national level. We have good relationships with people in Congress, people in the banking industry. We've put forth some solutions for people to stay in their homes, policy changes that the government can make to prevent foreclosures. We got the information to the White House twice. I spoke to a White House person three weeks ago, and he asked me to send it again. We sent it to Treasury, and everybody's running so scared with the Republicans blasting them for giving money away and doing crazy things, nobody's got the balls now to put it on the table."

"The president just won another mandate for another four years," I said. "Does he have the balls?"

"I think so. He's got nothing to lose."

221

"Tell me about your own experience after Katrina."

"It was a hell of an experience. It's an experience that will test an individual and an individual's ability for survival, both personally and in business. All of this was underwater. Everything you're looking at. Anywheres from six to ten feet."

"All the way over to the other side of the freeway? Those houses?"

"Yeah. Everything you're looking at. You walk around this building, and everything you see all the way to downtown was underwater. I had to get back here by boat. This area did not have basic services for a year so, literally, we left on a Sunday with two pair of short pants, four pair of underwear, and we've done this many times before, so you come back afterwards and restart your life but, this time, everything was gone. All the clothes, everything that you had in life that you were saving. My scrapbook was gone and photographs, paintings, everything! And things you thought you couldn't live without, all of a sudden you didn't have anymore, and you had to start all over again.

"And the business, because everything we had was mostly on the first floor. We had some of our computer systems on the third floor in this building, and our whole operations center was on the first floor of the building. We were about to move the operations center before the storm. We had about three months to go. All of our records, all of our files, all the history of the accounts: all of it was underwater, ruined. So we couldn't run our computer system, because all of the infrastructure was gone. We had no telephone communication, no cell phone communication, no Internet communication, and all of that was done from here. Nobody would even think that your infrastructure would go away just with flooding. Some of the highways that we used, phones, etcetera all went out, so we had to start from ground zero overnight.

"And on top of an operational issue, on top of regulatory issues, we had a marketing issue. Because you had to convince your customer base that everything was fine, while you're tryin' to rebuild this baby. So we literally operated the bank for a week without any records, and I made the decision that when people came in to get money, just give it to them. Write it down. We were writing it down in a spiral notebook to count the money they took out. People came in, and we would let our customers know that if you need money, we'll make you a loan, because we knew most people lost their automobiles, they didn't have a place to live, and if you can remember how expensive it is to set up a house. If you're going from having everything you need to needing to buy everything again, and most people who bank with us, most people we know, live from payday to payday. That's America. So, even if you rented a place, you had to buy a mattress, box spring, towels, sheets, pots and pans, groceries, socks, shoes, clothing, toothbrush, cleaning supplies."

"You were here at the time?"

"No, we left the Sunday before the storm. I wasn't going to leave, but my family forced me to leave. I would have been one that they would have had to rescue. I had some people stay here, and what we normally do is put a couple of ice chests in place and water and sodas and food, canned goods, blow-up beds, lanterns. But you normally ride it out for a couple of days until the power comes back. The town is used to the power going out and being out for a while, so we know how to live through that. I was operating out of Baton Rouge. In other words, that's what our disaster plan was: for people to report to our Baton Rouge location. So I came in from Atlanta to Baton Rouge the day after the storm. The storm was on a Monday. I went to Baton Rouge— no, I stayed in Atlanta on Tuesday and had a friend of mine who was running a bank in Atlanta to help me think through this, because I was looking at TV like everybody else, and I knew that we were without everything, and I had to get this bank going."

He saw me out from his office and took a few minutes to show me around the sixth floor. "See those two buildings there? Vacant since Katrina. That building over there used to be AT & T's operations center. Vacant since Katrina. Everything that you see was underwater." He didn't mean in the mortgage sense. "This here was a shopping mall, that they tore down. All of this was underwater, all the way to the skyline."

"Is this ever going to come back?" I asked him.

"Nope," he said bluntly. "I don't think so. That's my opinion. But everybody's optimistic."

"Is it okay to be optimistic?"

He smiled. "Sure. I just won't waste my time bein' optimistic. See that building way out in the background? All of that was underwater."

✳

Coming up earlier in the elevator, Ra'shaud Haines, a young vice president of Liberty Bank and former classmate of Todd McDonald's at Morehouse College, the elite historically black college in Atlanta, had told me that he had returned home to Ohio before the election to canvas for Obama. Now I buttonholed Ra'shaud in his office and asked him to tell me more.

"I was born and raised in Akron, Ohio," he said. "It all kinda started in the Kerry election. In the Kerry election I was workin' in Cleveland.

 Todd and I are fraternity brothers. One of my other fraternity brothers from Morehouse is an attorney in D.C., and he's been a poll watcher for the last three campaigns. He stayed with my family in Akron, so it's kinda been an every-four-years kinda thing for us. We did the same thing in 2008, went up there and actually still voted there. This past time my friend called me up again, and he said he was going back out to Ohio and asked if I was gonna come up, could he stay at the house. So I said okay. So I go up there. I'm a big political nerd inside. I wake up watching MSNBC and CNN and kinda flip around. So I'm in this exciting battleground state, and this time we were deep in the trenches. I went up there on Friday. Saturday I did canvassing in Akron. Akron is largely Democratic, it's an old tire town, so the big focus is gettin' out the vote. So I went out there, did four hours. You want to know how the process went?"

"I want my book to be readable ten years from now, so too much of the inside baseball will be lost," I told him. "But I want some details, and I want some color."

"Okay, plenty of that. I went to the local campaign office. They partner me with a girl, a young lady that lived in the project around the block. It's right near where I used to live at. It was me, her, and I picked up my brother who's twenty and my nephew I was babysitting. My nephew's five, and I figured I didn't know how it was gonna go canvassing, so I figured you couldn't be too mean to somebody with a five-year-old. So from there they give you a neighborhood and you walk the neighborhoods, you knock on the door, basically tell them where the voting places are. It was a big push on Saturday for early voting, to get people out to do the early voting and just avoid the lines and avoid any kind of craziness afterward. I'm not sure how they got the list, but most of them were at least Democrat-leaning. Probably the most interesting people I met that day were two ninety-year-old women: one ninety years old, one eighty-eight, both of them huge Obama supporters. The first lady I actually spoke to was eighty-three and a white woman, big Obama supporter. I don't know what I had in my head but, you know, that's not what you think of as being the typical demographic for it. She said she had voted already. We had a good little five-minute conversation. The second one was a ninety-year-old white woman, and the neighborhood I was in was probably a swing neighborhood. It was literally Obama yard sign in one yard, and two doors down there'd be a Romney one, and so on and so forth."

"Was it mixed racially, too?"

"Not really, that neighborhood. I would say the neighborhood I was in the first day was probably seventy to eighty percent white. This is probably less than a mile from where I live at, so I know the neighborhood pretty well. It's near a high school. My sister went to that high school. It's predominantly white working class. The second white woman I talked to, she came to the door, she was like, 'Save your conversation.' And I'm thinkin', okay, this has got to be a bad one. She said, 'Save your conversation, I'm voting for Obama, Obama's my boy.' This is exactly what she said: 'Obama's my boy.' And she looks across the street at a Romney sign, and she says, 'I just wanna go kick that guy's ass 'cause he put that Romney sign in there.' I'm not a big social media person, but I think I actually tweeted that. So that was day one.

"That night I was supposed to meet up with a friend. He actually got a precinct of his own in Cleveland, so he was workin' in Cleveland and managin' that one up there, so we were supposed to meet for a drink in Cleveland. Cleveland's about forty minutes away from Akron. He said he had a meeting at eight o'clock, so I get up there at nine o'clock. He's like, 'Well, the meeting's runnin' over a little bit.' So I thought I'll go grab a drink, but he's like, 'Come on in for a second. We've got a couple things we gotta do to wrap up.' This was a hub of the different people that go out and do what I was doin' that day. So I end up goin' in there, and they're doing data entry. You had to type in whether they were home or whether they were not home, if they voted, those kinda things, so they would update the list the next day so you don't knock on the same people's doors that have already voted or whatnot. So where I thought I was goin' there for a drink, it turned out three hours of inputtin' data, because it had to be done by midnight in order to be updated for the next day's list. That was Saturday. Sunday I went back to Cleveland and canvassed. This time was in an all-black neighborhood and it was in East Cleveland, which is probably one of the harder-hit economic areas in the state. So whereas the first day people were kind of leaning Obama, this one was hardcore Obama. But that challenge was more getting people out to actually vote. We were in low-income apartments. We're in some neighborhoods that I wouldn't go on a normal basis, but everybody was so supportive. I had my mom's minivan, had posters on there, Obama bills. We're rollin' around. I did two shifts there. Worked from about 8:30 to 7:30, just hittin' the streets.

"This is Sunday before Tuesday. And the cool thing was that Cleveland is in Cuyahoga County. Everybody talked about Cuyahoga County so much. The lines were very long, so on Friday they had a barbecue and I think Stevie Wonder was there, or somebody was there; it was a big performer. Saturday they had a barbecue, so that gave you a little extra somethin' when you went to the door, you know, because you ran into people who said, 'I'm big Obama but, you know, I might not have a ride.' That was the other thing. A lot of people didn't have transportation, so we were settin' up transportation for people that didn't have rides. And then just kinda gettin' people motivated to go out there besides givin' the usual spiel about why you should vote and why you should vote Democratic. You were tryin' to get people literally outta the door to the polls. On Tuesday, I sat at the poll or rode by the poll just to see. I took some pictures. There were still lines out there, and people were just really camped out there to vote."

"So was that a more intense experience for you than either '04 or '08 was?"

"It was definitely more intense than '04. Oh-eight it was different. Oh-eight, I wasn't on the ground as much. I went to a couple of the rallies. I did canvas the day before, because the day before you go around and you hang up door knockers and things like that, and people were voting, but you felt just a little better in 2008 because there was history. People were really excited. Goin' into 2012, I was a little bit more worried because, you know, he was already president. All the newness had kinda worn out, so I didn't know if people were gonna be as intense in gettin' it out. But I was much more in the trenches this time, and it was just really encouraging to see people just as excited as they were before, and for maybe different reasons this time, but it wasn't necessarily because it was going to be the first black person to be president. And that didn't even come up too much. It was more of talkin' about what he's done and that kind of things. It was different. In 2008, you felt you were a part of history a little bit more. Two thousand twelve, you felt really nervous and you really were fightin' a lot harder, because things were tightenin' at that point."

"Ohio was the state everybody was watching," I said. "How nervous were you going into Election Day about Ohio?"

"You know, I was nervous. Ohio's a weird state, because you have Cuyahoga County, you have Summit County where I'm from, and you have Columbus and a few other major urban areas, but, like I said, I was born and raised in Ohio and there's parts of Ohio I've never been to. Western Ohio is, you know, it might as well be kind of, you know, Kentucky. It's very rural. I've only been out there one time. So I was nervous up until I flew back on Tuesday, and I stayed at home because I didn't wanna be out, you know, if the worst case happened."

"So why was it important to reelect Obama?" I asked Ra'shaud.

"I think you need at least eight years to allow the vision to go all the way through," he said. "I'm a banker, so I'm pretty pragmatic. There's not really too many sexy arguments. He looks like me, so that helps. It's relatable but, on top of that, if he hadn't of gotten elected and somebody else did, then you kinda start over. You lose any momentum from where you're at before. So I thought it was important to have that consistency for that next four years, so that you at least have a chance for another two years to get something done before, you know, elections start all over again. On a policy standpoint, bein' I'm kinda right smack dab in the middle of the middle class, the tax arguments don't really bother me that much. If it changes one or two percent, it's not gonna bother me much. As far as the health care bill, that was very important to me because I have a lot of friends and family that aren't as fortunate, and I think it just makes good business sense to have everybody that can get insurance. I feel like he cares a little more than his opponent did and, on top of that, the fact that he has student loans: his story is a lot more like my story and people's stories that I know. Not just a black person's story, but he had actual student loans up until very recently and, unless you have those kind of experiences, I don't feel like you can relate to the issues that I have."

"How long have you lived in New Orleans?"

"I moved here in April of 2005, right before Hurricane Katrina."

"Tell me a little of your Katrina experience."

"I moved here four months before Hurricane Katrina, and this was my first hurricane. I don't know if you've ever been a part of a hurricane, but it's a very eerie experience. It goes through these different stages. The Friday before, we were at work, and it was a regular work day. We went out for drinks that Friday and kind of watched the hurricane. They had these watch parties and, to me, it looked very scary with this big mass coming at you. It was coming toward Miami, so everybody was joking about it hitting the MTV awards or something like that. Nobody that was from here seemed very concerned so, you know, I wasn't very concerned if they weren't. Then as we got to, I wanna say, the Saturday before, Todd called me and said, 'We're thinkin' about leavin'.' So I'm like, 'Should I be worried?' So I packed four days' worth of clothes. We're just gonna shoot to Atlanta for a few days while the storm passes over, and I actually parked my truck here on that roof over there, and we rolled out to Atlanta."

"By road?"

"Yeah, we drove. I drove with Todd. Me and him were in a car. His parents and, I think, grandparents were followin' us. So we head out, and just all of a sudden we hit traffic. There's no gas anywhere, and the city is kinda clearin' out, so you get kinda nervous, because I've never seen like an evacuation really happening. So there's no gas. We drive, and we're actually running out of gas. We have to go get gas, lose the parents at some point, and it ends up taking us about sixteen hours to get to Atlanta, where it's usually about eight hours. So we were just sittin' in traffic and all that time things goin' through your head, you know, 'What's goin' on?' I didn't have as much invested here. I mean, I had an apartment which I was plannin' on stayin' at because it was one of those refurbished warehouse kind of things. It was very sturdy, it had been here a hundred years. It was a can company, American Can Company. I wasn't even really plannin' on leavin' but, anyway, we get to Atlanta and kinda hang out, watch the storm come and the first day, you know, we dodged a bullet, because it kinda passed over, didn't really hit very much. So we're preppin' to go back, move back down, just havin' a regular day, went to the campus of my school, kinda hung out with friends, and then that night you start seein' the flooding comin' in. There's kind of a sense of denial, because you see it but they're showin' the same scenes so you're kinda, 'Well, maybe just one little area was hit,' and then it kinda sunk in that the whole city was underwater and nobody really knew what was what. You couldn't tell whether it was your neighborhood.

"So then I ended up goin' back to Ohio and really thinkin' about what I was gonna do period, because I wasn't totally invested in Liberty Bank. You know, I had an apartment, but it wasn't a really big deal, and I'm thinkin', 'Am I gonna try to get my old job back, or do I need to find a new job?' So I'm kinda in my own little mini crisis and try to figure out what to do, 'cause I moved down here, not against my parents, but I worked at a larger bank in Ohio, so to them it didn't make sense to move down to New Orleans, 'cause I had a good job up there. I probably was on a track to do fairly well, and so I'm thinkin' I'm gonna try to figure that out. But I get a call from my manager here, and the bank had relocated to Baton Rouge, so they called me back in and said they had housing and all that. So I said, all right, I'm gonna try to finish what I started, go back down. So we go back to Baton Rouge, and it was real weird. I go from, you know, I had my own apartment, a nice little thing, and then we're in this house, Mr. McDonald's friend or somethin' let them use it, so it's me, Todd, Mr. McDonald and his wife and the grandparents, the in-laws. And it's a small house, so I'm sleepin' on one couch, Todd is sleepin' on another couch, and then they have the bedrooms over there. So it's just surreal, and that was for about a month, sleepin' there, sharin' one bathroom."

"You thought you had a job and an apartment and then you ended up ..."

"Yeah, in our command center. I don't know if you talked to Mr. McDonald about that, but it was like one branch, and everybody was in this branch with like a table stretched, and I'm doin' like entries. And that might not mean much, but that's not what I came to do. Accounting, you know, real menial kinda stuff, not what I really came to work for. I had a degree, and I was already leavin' a big bank to come to a smaller bank, and so now I'm doin' even smaller things: takin' customer service calls. So that went on for a while, and it was just so crowded all the time. It's just amazing that Todd and I are even friends still, because me, Todd and my boss, Matt, were in an office smaller than this for a couple of months, and then we'd go home and it'd be me and Todd on couches side by side. We moved back in here in probably March or April of 2006, so it was about six or eight months in Baton Rouge. There was a time when I was in Baton Rouge longer than I was in New Orleans. So we moved back to this building, which is weird in itself, because this is probably the slowest area to come back, so this building was literally the only thing around. There's no food places, there's nothing really here. We just had this office, but it was still a step up."

I asked Ra'shaud to tell me more about his parents' attitude to his taking the job in New Orleans.

"My mom has a small business up in Ohio," he said. "My dad is a bus driver. So their whole thing is stability, you know? My grandfather worked at his job for forty or fifty years. So if you get a good job, they don't understand why you'd leave it. And all my family was there. I don't really have any family down here, and Todd was my only real friend down here, so I just, kinda to them, went off on a limb to come down."

"Did your parents go to Ohio from the South, or was it their parents?"

"Their parents. My mom moved from Alabama when she was prob-ably four or five, and my grandmother is from Alabama."

"So your parents were like, 'Why would you move to the South?' Is that part of it?"

"That was part of it, too. You know, the South is racist. New Orleans is racist, too, but it's not like the Mississippi, Alabama kind of racist. But yeah, I think that was part of it. But, you know, I'm the oldest and they kinda wanted me around, too."

"So why did you move down here? What's important about work-ing at Liberty Bank?"

"Well, Liberty Bank is a piece of it. New Orleans is one of those places that kinda wraps you in. I had come to visit a number of times. I ironically came down here for stories. Like I said, I thought I'd get more experiences down here. It was just completely different from the Midwest. Cleveland and Ohio, it's just dark. I tell people it is literally dark for about five months of the year, and I was goin' to work and it was dark, and comin' home and it was dark. It was cold. So I moved down here for all those wrong reasons, and I really liked Liberty Bank in that it's a minority bank. I had a relationship with Mr. McDonald. He was kind of a business mentor. I felt like I had an opportunity to grow and that I wouldn't necessarily be cuffed into doin' anything, where you kinda get cuffed into different things at a larger bank. So from a business standpoint, it was a gamble. I mean, I came to a smaller market, a smaller kind of thing, but there's a small group, so I figured if you do well you can move up pretty quickly here. So that's what hooked me on Liberty. Then once I started it, I felt like I needed to finish, even though I was only here for four months. So that's what compelled me to come back."

"And seven years later, you're still here."

"Yeah, still here."

"Have you moved up?"

"I moved up a little bit. Never as much as you want, but I've done pretty well. I've got a house, I can go to Ohio for a few days and can afford to pay for it, so no complaints."

"What does Morehouse mean to you?" My friend Lenny Miller, the

United Airlines pilot who lived near Dulles Airport and had owned NASCAR teams with his father, was a Morehouse grad, and very much into it.

"Morehouse was the best decision that I made in my life," said Ra'shaud. "I met Todd there, I met a lot of other amazing people. I've been to a bunch of weddings; I still keep in touch. I've been to homecoming. This year was the first year that I missed, and I'm getting married in April, so I'm kinda broke, and I was going to Ohio the next weekend. So homecoming was three weeks ago, a week before Ohio, and I had to buy one or the other of the tickets, so I went with the Ohio one."

"Maybe next year you can take your wife to homecoming."

"Next year I'm gonna take her to homecoming, yeah. Actually last year, this was the coolest thing: me, Todd and another friend, James, who had just gotten married, we all brought our fiancées in at the same time, just so everybody could meet and run around. So the experiences you have there can't be recreated. It's kinda like a fraternity. I graduated almost ten years ago, and I can have not seen you for three years, and we can pick right up and talk. I have those experiences all the time, and there's always somebody, somewhere, on the business side. Todd, for instance, with this bank. I would never have ended up here without having known Todd, and I know Todd well. So, yeah, it's hard to explain everything. Up until I was a senior in high school, you couldn't have told me I wasn't going to Ohio State. I was a big Ohio State football fan, and my mom graduated from Ohio State. It's an hour away. I just thought that's where I was goin'. And then I went on one visit to Morehouse and changed my whole life."

"Would you say Morehouse is about developing African American leadership?"

"Yeah, absolutely. And it's more about developing the full person. Dress is important, traveling is important, reading is important. So I developed that culture. And you take it for granted a little bit when you're eighteen, nineteen, twenty years old, but you see those ideals that you have and then above that, I now have people that—you know, you're in this friendly competition all the time. You don't wanna be that guy that's not bein' successful. So if Todd is doin' a business and Todd is doin' a million different things, it's hard to keep up with him, but you can't be that guy that's workin' at the grocery store or whatever. I have four or five other friends that are attorneys, doctors ..."

"You keep tabs on one another."

"Yeah. People keep you accountable, and you can't get too full of yourself either, so it allows you to stay humble, so they breathe that kind of competition, but it's not that I will pull you down. Todd, if he has something that would interest me, he would, without question, give it to me."

"I think Ohio State would have been the same kind of experience that the University of Wisconsin was for me, which is, 'Welcome, here's your number, good luck.'"

"Yeah, exactly."

"Ohio State has like sixty thousand students."

"It's a city in and of itself," said Ra'shaud, "and a lot of great people come from there and do great things. But, you know, it would have been different. You wouldn't have been interviewing me right now. We wouldn't be talkin' about this."

✳

Todd also wanted me to meet Tyrone Williams, who did landscaping for the bank and the family and had a story to tell about surviving Katrina. Tyrone was a middle-aged black man who spoke unselfconsciously in that mesmerizing Cajun accent.

"Katrina just messed up a lot of people," he told me in a conference room in the same building. "I stayed here for Katrina, and I felt it wasn't gonna be that bad. And some people left and some people stayed, and they say the people that was poor stayed, but there are people that I know for a fact have money and stayed. So they got caught up like everybody else. They was living like everybody else, poor, had to get it how you live. You know, it was just a bad thing. I saw dead bodies floatin' in the water. I saw snakes, alligators. I done saw it all. I even had some neighbors, friends, people that went to jail and did bad things, but they didn't serve their time and just helped people out. You know, it was just a lot of people came together and just started helpin' people out that day. It was a storm, and all of a sudden the water came through, and I don't know how high it was, but it was higher than the stop sign. You know how you go to a corner and they have a stop sign? You couldn't see no stop sign. So I'm walkin' down the street. I'm standin' at 9708 Hammond Street. That's out in the east. That's right across from Resurrection Church, a nice Catholic church, and I stood home and I saw this water, it just kept risin' so I had to leave my house, and I jumped everybody's fence in my neighborhood and just kept my body to the wall because they had swimmin' pools and I don't know how to swim but by me cuttin' through everybody's yard in the subdivision, I knowed who had swimmin' pools and who didn't have swimmin' pools and my neighbor, he pulled me in his house. I stayed in his house for three or four days. He had a two-story house, and I stayed with him and his mama, and the water just kept risin' and I'm walkin' down the street in people's backyards just like that's how high the water was, up to here. I was swallowin' some of it."

"Up to your chin?"

"Yeah. Up to my face, and I was scared. I was really scared that day, and my neighbor pulled me in his house. So when I got in my neighbor's house, I'm right here and they had a snake right here. It was a black snake with a yellow stripe on his back. The snake was right here, but the water around the snake is high, so I got more scared because I never come across no snake before and, like I said, they had snakes in the water, alligators, and I was just blessed and lucky to make it."

"So how did you make it?"

"They came and got us with a helicopter, I'd say about the third day."

"From your neighbor's house?"

"From my neighbor's house. About the third day they came and got us with a helicopter, and they took his mama 'cause she was up in age. That's what he was workin' on first, gettin' the elderly to safe ground. Then they came back and picked us up maybe about a day or two after that and I saw so many dead bodies, and I looted. I mean I ain't looted for no jewelry, I looted for food, 'cause everything was out. You know we had to get it how we lived, you know it was hard. So when I did come back to New Orleans, it was pitch dark, and I mean pitch dark. It was like a scary movie. I was with Mr. Wiltz, Ed Wiltz, and he took me in. I stayed with him for like at least three months, 'cause I was at the Astrodome. That's when they brought everybody into the Astrodome in Houston. I was getting lazy, sluggish, and somethin' told me to just go outside and get some fresh air, and when I went outside and took ten steps, he was in my face, and he started cryin', and he took me with him. And I stayed with him for like maybe three to four months, and we was back and forth to New Orleans, checkin' up on property and checkin' up on the way things was goin', and it was like it was hit with a bomb. It was like everything was shut down, everything was just pitch dark. You know, it was a scary feeling."

"Did you grow up in New Orleans?"

"Yes sir, I growed up in Cross Canal in the Ninth Ward."

"Were you living in the Ninth Ward when Katrina hit?"

"No, when Katrina hit, I was standin' in the east right here in Hammond."

"And your family before you, were they always from New Orleans?"

"They was raised and born in New Orleans. Like I said, me and my friends was comin' back to check up on things, you know, to see how everybody's property was. And one day I just asked them to see if Mr. Wiltz would drive by my grandfather's house, so he said all right. So when we got to my grandfather's house, they had an ambulance. They took the body out already. My grandfather and his son, he's dead from Katrina. He didn't want to leave for nothin'. Older people is stubborn. So when we did get to the house, the ambulance was there, but they already took him out of the house, but I didn't know that was my grandfather and my uncle."

"How long after the storm was that?"

"That was maybe a week after the Katrina. About a week, about a week and a half, something like that, 'cause we had to wait for the water to go down, 'cause the water sat for a long period of time, and when they did come get me in a helicopter, everywhere I turned my head, there was nothin' but water, nothin' but water."

"How did Katrina change your life?"

"Oh, Katrina changed my life. I respect things now more than I ever did before, because life is too short. You know, I was respectin' things then, but this was a wakeup call for me and, I guess, for a lot of other people, too, and like I say, people helped people out that day. It was a miserable feeling. And when everything was over with, the following or next day, it was like nothin' ever happened. It was a pretty, shiny day. Birds was flyin' like nothin' ever happened."

"How do you feel about the way the government and the rest of the country responded to the hurricane?"

"Well, I'm gonna be honest with ya. I just feel like they did a good job but nobody trained for nothin' like this here, and that's why I say I can't put the blame on this person, I can't put the blame on that person. Nobody was expectin' nothin' like this here, but we learned our lesson, and I'm quite sure other people, they see what we went through. You know, some people figured we was thugs because they heard on TV that New Orleans is the capital of killin'. And everybody's not like that, but that's how we got judged. I don't care whether you're a millionaire or poor. Area code 504, that's just how it was. You know they treated us good the first few days, but after that, they was like different."

"Different?"

"Different attitudes. They didn't trust us. Like I say, I was in Houston, and I didn't stay long because I was in the Astrodome, but I went to New Iberia, and I stayed in New Iberia for about a month and a half with Mr. Ed Wiltz. And they treated us nice the first week, everybody, but when we couldn't go back home, it was like, you know, they turned their back on us."

"Why?"

"Because they figured area code 504 from New Orleans, they figured everybody is killers and murderers and thieves, and everybody's not like that. And, as I say, they had a lot of people that I know that went to jail, drug addicts, crackheads, but that day everybody helped everybody out. When I say everybody helped everybody out, I'm talking like the older people. They was stealin' boats to get people to high ground, and they was goin' back to get other people, you know, to do the same thing. Some people made it and some people I haven't saw yet and I don't know if they moved and are staying where they stayed at. I don't know if they couldn't make it or what. A lot of people died in Katrina 'cause they couldn't get out of the attic."

"So there are people that you don't know whether they made it or not."

"Right, people that I know, I don't know if they made it or not. I don't see everybody, and Katrina's been five-six years now, seven years.

And you feel you'd see somebody. I still see some of my friends, but a lot of people I don't see no more. A lot of people moved, and that's where they're stayin' at."

"So who was Ed Wiltz?"

"Mr. Wiltz, he's like a big brother to me and a daddy to me. He took care of me, him and his wife."

"Are they black or white?"

"They black, and they stayed. I know from my heart, Mr. Wiltz got money like Todd McDonald's dad, like they have. Like I say, I know a lot of people that have money and stayed, but they put on the news all the poor people that couldn't get out, you know what I mean? 'Cause Katrina hit on the twenty-eighth, and a lot of people get their checks on the first and the third, so I guess they were waitin' on their checks. Some of them, they couldn't afford to leave, but they coulda had a better system of pickin' people up, but they say they want everybody to get out, meet us at this spot here so they'll have buses for y'all, but nobody feelin' it's gonna be that bad."

"So you choose not to blame anybody in particular?"

"No, from my heart, I can't, I really can't. You know, when they was blamin' people like the mayor. I don't care who was the mayor, they couldn't handle it themselves."

"What about the governor and the president?"

"Well, the governor could have moved a little faster but, like I say, the president could've moved faster but nobody too much care about people down here in New Orleans. I don't know if because we have a big ratio of blacks, but it took them a long time to respond to us and that's why a lot of lootin' was happenin', because people had to survive: to eat, you know. They had a family. I saw ladies walkin' down the street with no shirt on, just a bra. I saw kids with no clothes on, just walkin' down the street with no clothes on."

"You make your living from the landscaping."

"Yes sir."

"And you run it as a business, right?"

"Yes sir."

"How long did it take you to get your business back up and running?"

"Well, Mr. Ed Wiltz, I was tellin' you, we stayed in New Iberia and he had this big contract in Baton Rouge. They got one in Baton Rouge and they got one in New Orleans. So what I did, I was still workin' with him and the money I did make with him, I couldn't touch it because he was holdin' it for me to get my tools back to get me back started, and when I did get back started, I bought one lawnmower, one weedeater, and one blower and, as I made money, I was just buildin' my tools back up. I was buildin' my tools as I made money."

"Your room and board was taken care of during that time?"

"Yeah, he took care of me like I was his son. I didn't have to pay for nothin', I didn't have to come up with no kind of gas money, and he spent a lot on gas 'cause he got a truck and take a lot of diesel, and I didn't have to come out of my pocket for nothin'. And a check I did get from FEMA, it was like $2,500, I didn't even cash that. He didn't want me to cash that."

"Why not?"

"Because he wanted me to get my tools back when I do get back here and get back to work. So I had money to buy me some tools."

"Your business is taking care of people's houses and yards and stuff, right?"

"Right."

"But a lot of those yards must have been wiped out by the flood."

"Yeah, I had subdivisions. I lost two subdivisions. They came back but when they came back, the same people who had the house before, they moved. They didn't worry about comin' back. So the people who bought the houses, they was young people, so they cut their own grass, so right now I have a lot of commercial contracts. I just thank the Lord I was able to bounce back after all the stuff I've been through."

"Do you mind if I ask how old you are?"

"I'm forty-five."

"Do you have a family?"

"No, I'm single. No kids."

"So at least you had only yourself to worry about at the time of Katrina."

"Right. Like I say, I'm forty-five years old. I can't read. I can't read a lick, but I know how to make money. I know how to survive. Didn't rob nobody to survive. A lotta people figure like a person can't read, they're illiterate, the only thing they got to do is rob people to survive, and I can't do that. I guess I can work every day, seven days a week sometimes, and I tell people sometimes I can't do this, I can't do that, and I just tell 'em to put it in your mind, in your brain that way, because if I can't even read what's on that book right there, how can I make all this money?"

"Well, how can you make all that money?"

"I have a secretary, manages everything for me. I have a secretary. She's the best thing in my life. Like I say, I been cuttin' grass for a long period of time, and I get paid on the first of the month. By the sixteenth, I was dead broke. Ain't doin' no drugs, just ta-kin' out four hundred here, three hundred there, and before you know it, that money goes. So, about four years ago, she took it over. Well, Todd Mc-Donald's daddy took it over. Said, 'Tyrone, you're spending too  much money. You got nice contracts, you got to have something to fall back on when you get older.' And right now I'm seein' more money than I ever saw in my life. My own money, and I thank the Lord every day because of the predicament I'm in, sayin' that I don't know how to read. I know how to survive, and I know how to make money, and I know how to talk to money when it really comes down to it."

Tyrone wanted me and Pete to meet his secretary, so he took us to a lower floor of the building to introduce us.

"Mr. McDonald's a good man, I think," I said to him in the elevator on the way down.

"Oh yeah, he solid," he agreed. "He solid. One thing about Mr. McDonald, he like helpin' people out. But you gotta help yourself too."

Tyrone's secretary was named Diane Cooper, and she had the same

Cajun accent. Diane was the executive assistant to Mr. Burns of the Burns Management Group, and she kept Tyrone's books on the side.

"This is my friend, my lifeline," Tyrone said.

"What's better than having money in the bank?" Diane asked rhetorically.

"Yeah, it's a good feeling wakin' up in the morning and know you got money," said Tyrone.

"I wish you good luck with your book," Diane said to me. "Yours might be the only one I read. It's heartfelt memoirs that I can't really look at on a hard copy. Maybe some people can, but I can't. Two thousand five was a hard year. And since that year, I tell myself that I'm never ever again evacuating. But you were blessed. In some way, you were blessed from that devastation, if you survived it. Even if Katrina was very difficult, I don't complain about Katrina. Because Katrina was gonna happen anyway, and I survived it. To come back and have whatever financial assistance that I did get was a blessing. I used to love hurricanes when I was a child. I used to ride around and see the after-effects. Now you an adult, and that's no fun. After Katrina I came in here every day, and I came to work every day. And it was a desolate area around here. All the little eateries are gone. Used to be a wing shack across the street. The scenic route became the horror route. You used to see the after-effects of Katrina. You still do. The East is still Katrina-town. People tryin' to get back to the way it used to be. Which it will never be."

Diane had a lot more to say in the same vein. Eventually, and reluctantly, we took our leave.

"You didn't know when you introduced us to her that we'd end up staying so long," I said to Tyrone.

He laughed. "That's the way she is, though."

✳

Then we went downtown to City Hall to meet Ann Duplessis, who also worked for Liberty Bank and who had served two four-year terms as Louisiana state senator for the district including the Lower Ninth Ward. She now worked as Deputy Chief Administrative Officer of the City of New Orleans.

"I've spent the last eight years as a leader and a state senator," she told me. "And during the eight years, unfortunately, I had to experience Katrina, a brand new legislator, really trying to understand the ropes. I represented Eastern New Orleans and the Lower Ninth Ward, which was the most heavily devastated. I mean, the Lower Ninth Ward was wiped off the map, so there were a lot of things that we had to address and a lot of issues. This was a population of about 120,000 people that I represented, and the powers that be didn't see fit at one point for that population to come back at all. So we had a lot of things that we had to deal with, had to battle with, had to fight for. So it was not a very good time, and there were challenges.

"Katrina messed up a lot of people. I, for instance, was out of my home for two years. I'd lost everything. I mean, literally. I went home, and my husband's a strong, strong, strong person, and when the storm came in, I think it came in at fifteen feet, it went down to ten, and it settled at four. So it wiped out everything. My husband went home to survey, and he came back in tears. I've never seen him cry like that. I mean, he literally came back in tears. We were blessed, though, because I have a two-story, and the day before we left to go to Baton Rouge, I decided to take all my pictures, everything that was somewhat important to me, and put it in the attic. And the water got to the second level, but not to the attic. So we were blessed that we didn't lose pictures, we didn't lose a lot of important stuff, and we had everything that really mattered, and that was my family in my little two-bedroom, one-bath apartment in Baton Rouge. But we were not able to rebuild for two years, and we went through some of the same financial struggles, you know."

"Meanwhile, during all this, you're also an elected official," I said.

"And I still work for the bank, and I had to help Mr. McDonald. We were in Baton Rouge, and I had to work long hours trying to bring the bank back. Most people had begun to have like two or three families living in one house. Well, I had, at one point, fourteen people living in my two-bedroom apartment. It allowed for a bonding that you can never imagine. And you'll hear this: people now want to live together. It's like, 'We've got a big enough house, why don't you come here and live with us now.' It was hard for me, but it was fun in some instances where we slept on the floor. I have three daughters."

"How old were they?"

"My youngest is sixteen, so she was nine. My middle daughter is twenty-five. She didn't know a storm hit because she was already at LSU in a dorm so it's like, 'I came to Baton Rouge to get away from you guys.' I was like, 'Really?' And then my oldest daughter who's twenty-eight was twentyish. The oldest one was at Xavier University, the youngest one was at school in Metairie, and I wanted them away from this, I didn't want them to see this. I don't think journalism is a bad word, because my sister's a Middle Eastern foreign journalist. She started her career with the *Picayune* and then NPR and then Knight Ridder, and she worked with the World Institute of Peace in Prague for five years, and she's done most of her work in the Middle East and in other countries. She was in Prague at the time, so I sent my girls to Prague. Which was a great experience, but a horrible one, because every night they called and cried. They loved being with their aunt and her family, but my baby was nine years old, and I had to send my baby away so that I could take care of others, and that was hard. Think about this: If you look at what you have on and you had to buy everything you have on all over again, how much would you spend?"

"A hundred dollars?" I guesstimated.

"Okay, a hundred dollars. I had a family of five. Most people left for the weekend. I had two pairs of jeans, I had a t-shirt, pair of pajamas. My kids, same thing. We had maybe two outfits apiece. So now, you have to buy everything for a family of five."

"Did you really expect to be gone two or three days and then be back?"

"Yeah, a weekend. We've done this before."

"You did not expect what happened."

"No, not at all. I knew that it was going to be bad because as a senator, I got the calls. 'Senator, have you left yet? We need you to get out of New Orleans.' So I knew that it was serious, but what caused the devastation in the Lower Ninth Ward was a barge. It went over the top, went straight through the barrier. Those were things that shouldn't have happened. Walmart made a killin', because we had to buy everything all over again for a family of five. Not only that, most people who weren't blessed enough to have a place had to live in a hotel, buy food. You know, you had no place to cook. You had to buy food for a family of five: food, pay the hotel, pay your other expenses at home, credit cards and this and that with no income coming in and so, when you got a check from the insurance company, it's like, 'Okay, we can survive now a little bit.' Now that was the majority. Yeah, there were people that abused it, but I don't believe it to be as widespread as the world wanted to make it appear."

"Why did the world want to make it appear that way?"

"You know what, I don't know. I think that the world saw a lot of money being pumped into this community. They saw a lot of confusion. They got hold of a few stories of fraud and abuse and they ran away with it. The majority of people here are poverty level. In New Orleans, our main industry was the service industry. So, guess what, those aren't $200,000-a-year jobs. They were not able to pull themselves back on their own savings account."

"Maybe they didn't have a savings account."

"Not maybe. No one had a savings account. I didn't have a savings account that could support two lives. The good that came out of it is I think people are more tolerant of others. It created a sense of community among races, ages, everything."

"Is that sense of community real, and did it last?"

"It was real. I'm afraid we're losin' it, and it's unfortunate. I don't want to say we're losin' it, but there's the threat of losin' it, I think, just because of these last four years of a Democrat president and the last year of campaigning and elections, and just undertones and all of the above, that has started a divide again, which is so unfortunate."

"That divide is there nationally."

"Yes, but in the Southern states, it's more pronounced."

"And even the shared experience of Katrina hasn't been able to overcome that?"

"People forget, and time heals all wounds. People forget."

"How has that reemerging divide expressed itself here in Louisiana?"

"I would like to think it's not more a racial divide but more status, and there's a belief that people, regardless of their racial makeup, can pull themselves out without assistance. Well, I can't a hundred percent buy into that, because if you've grown up in a world that you've not seen or been taught or been given a road map on how to pull yourself up, or how to do better, your belief is in the world that you see every day. If you don't, at a point, identify some mechanism or some relief to people, regardless of their racial whatever, what will happen is you will create savages. And I say that meaning that a person is going to survive, one way or the other, and if we make it harder for them to survive, then that impacts all of us."

"They're still going to do whatever they have to do," I said.

"My dad was a Baptist minister," she told me. "He was a cab driver. Worked every day, was a wonderful, wonderful person. My mother was a schoolteacher. We were poor, but I didn't know it. I grew up watching my dad, in an era when Baptist ministers didn't get a salary. They got an anniversary offering once a year, but my dad paid the church's bills. They would sit at the dining room table. They would pay the household bills, make sure that all the expenses were done, and then he'd pull out the church's bills and talk to my mom and say, 'Do you think we can pay the church's electric bill? Because we're a little short.' If they had enough money left over, then he'd pull out some of the church members' bills and say, you know, 'Sister Sue couldn't buy her medicine, and she asked the church to help. I think we can give her twenty dollars for her medicine.'

"So that's what I saw, right? This is a person who had a tremendous, tremendous heart, and he went to his cab one day. During that time, the cab drivers used to park in front of the Winn-Dixies and wait for the little old people to come out, and he'd haul them to home with their little groceries. And this particular day, doin' his normal thing, two guys who were attempting to rob the Winn-Dixie were thrown out of the Winn-Dixie. No one told him, they got in the back of my dad's car, and they made him drive off, and he was shot seven times, and he had like ten dollars in his pocket. So, unfortunately, he crossed the path of two young people who didn't have an opportunity, right? And they killed him. I believe that people should work hard and that we shouldn't give away anything, but I do believe that, as a society, we all have an obligation, if we want to survive as well, to ensure that everyone has the right opportunity. Now everybody's not gonna be saved, I get it. Everybody ain't gonna do right even if they get opportunity, I get it. But that's not black and white, and that's why for me it's critical that we don't lose that and that the people that are elected, and the decision makers, are those people who understand that, right?"

"In telling your father's story, there's a political subtext to it," I pointed out. "It's unavoidably political. I think you took some care to narrate it in an ostensibly non-political kind of way, but we all understand that it is, inevitably, political. What you're laying out is a political argument for why we should have this kind of society, rather than that kind of society."

"Right," she said. "An inclusive society."

"There's this ideological element that, if anybody—you or President Obama or anybody else—would tell the story or make the argument that you just made, their answer would be, 'That's socialism.' Isn't that what a lot of people say?"

"Yes," she agreed.

"How do you respond to people coming from that place? There must be a lot of them here in Louisiana."

"I sometimes couch it with a question," she said. "What is the alternative if we don't create a society that, at a minimum, allows for honest opportunities for engagement? Engagement in educational issues and jobs, real jobs. One thing I do is, before I debate anyone, I almost become the expert of the issue. So if they're just parroting or mimicking something they've heard, and they can't understand or they can't tell me what actually is the reason they feel like that, I ask, 'How do you believe whatever it is you're talking about is really going to impact society? Just tell me.' And if they can't, then it forces them to start to self-reflect. Now, they may not, but they will probably not be as vocal in the future."

"Because you don't let them off the hook."

"No, I don't. But I help them understand that if they're gonna have a position about something, they really oughta understand that position. I am blessed to have friends, black friends, white friends, very rich friends, very poor friends, who say stupid stuff. I love Google. I mean, go and just read the newspaper. No, don't read the newspaper. Because the media will tell you what you're supposed to believe, and people really believe that when they hear something, it must be real. And okay, some of it is, but I always try to couch it with a question. When there's opposition, if someone can seriously talk to me in an intelligent fashion and have an inkling, I'm like, 'You know what? Okay, you might even change my perspective.' But typically that helps them understand that the world isn't really flat, that perhaps their views are based on what they've been told to think."

"So now that President Obama has won reelection, where is America headed?"

"You know what? I am encouraged. I really am. I saw a news story either yesterday or this morning that talked about who voted for Obama and what that looked like, and who voted for Romney and what that looked like. And how you could see the marked difference in the campaign, in the parties. When you saw Obama's campaign stuff, you saw like a melting pot, a gumbo of people, all kinda people, really. When you saw Romney's campaign stuff, you saw all big fat white men. I'm sorry, I shouldn't have said that. You saw a certain kind of person, right? That newscast talked kinda negatively about the lack of diversity in the party and what the party has to do to really be now a party that truly understands the voters, and who the real voters are, and the up-and-coming voters, the young folk and Latinos and women. I thought I was gonna fall out of my chair when in the debate he talked about …"

"Binders full of women?" I guessed.

"I said, 'No he didn't. Did you hear the same thing I heard? Tell me you are a little bit disturbed.' And they go, 'All right, all right, all right.' So I think I'm encouraged, because this now allows for some of the people who had opinions that were formed because someone else told them are now starting to say, 'You know what, I don't know if I really want to be a part of this hate.' You know, the more stories I hear of people who are doin' just cuckoo stuff because Obama won. Like the lady who ran over her husband."

"I haven't heard that."

"You didn't hear that this morning? This lady was so upset that Obama won, she and her husband got into an argument or something, and she ran over him."

"In a car?"

"In a car. He's in the hospital tellin' his story."

"Was her husband for Obama?"

"I don't know. They didn't say in the story. Oh, I know what it was. He didn't vote, and she blamed him for want of a vote for Romney. So they got into an argument about it."

"Where was this?"

"I can't remember. You know, you're drinkin' your coffee and puttin' on your makeup. It was on this morning's news. So, again, I encourage stories like that so people can start to say, 'I don't wanna be a part of this.' My daughter, my baby, she's sixteen, is at Country Day. I don't know if you know Country Day. Country Day is a very private high school, upscale, very private, and it was difficult for her during this time because, unfortunately, some kids were coming to school saying the same things that they heard. And she's an extremely smart child. So she's a leader in the school, and she's one of the ones that everybody looks up to and, you know, president of the school, her class, and all of the above. I said, 'Listen, here's what you do: You don't get into a debate, and fortunately this will pass, and you don't ruin friendships over issues that neither you nor them understand. But you ask, 'Why do you hate Obama so much?' And if they answer, 'My momma said so' or 'My daddy said so,' you ask them the same question: 'Really? So everybody your momma or your daddy hates, you're gonna hate in life?' So she's used that a couple of times and she says, 'Ma, that worked, it really worked. It stopped the debate.' People don't wanna look like they don't understand what they're saying, especially when you do it in front of other people. It's kinda reverse bullying, right? So this one guy came and said something about, 'I hate Obama because he's gonna cause my grandmother not to have medical treatment.' And she says, 'And how much money does your family have? You live in a two-million-dollar home, and your grandmother will go without medical care?'"

"I have a couple more questions," I said.

"I talk a lot," she admitted cheerfully.

"People who talk a lot are my bread and butter," I assured her. "Hurricane Sandy has just happened. Apparently, in some ways not as big a catastrophe as Katrina, and in other ways, probably as expensive or more in economic terms."

"Right."

"Do you have any perspective, as a survivor of Hurricane Katrina, to offer to the post-Sandy situation?"

"I guess the bright side is that there is a playbook now that they can use in dealing with post-disaster recovery efforts," she said. "Now, you still gotta go through it. Personally and individually, people are gonna have to cope with the individual losses and what that means to them, and every single one has its own DNA. So there is no one-size-fits-all. Every disaster causes each family their own unique set of issues, that nobody can deal with but you. One might say, 'Oh, they should have planned, they should have saved money, they should have, they should have.' But when we talk about socialism and support and just being human, there's always gonna be an aspect of using those who have, to help those who don't have. So as it relates to the victims of Sandy, I'm glad that the federal government has reacted a lot better. You just make sure that the support systems are in place in a global sense, and each family is gonna have to figure it out for themselves, but it's a lot easier with help."

"Is there any sense in which the response to Sandy was better because it was in New York, or is that unfair?"

"The world had never experienced this, Katrina, never! And so fast, right? So we were the learning ground. We've written the script now; we've written the playbook on the basics. You know, certain cell phones you couldn't use. Little things like just dealing with the human capital that you have. That's critical in any plan. If you worked for me and you were a critical person and I'm gonna do all I have to do to plan and make sure that you're taken care of, okay, the first thing you're gonna do is: 'I have children. What are we gonna do about them?' That's what you saw with the police department. The police department did a fabulous job ensuring that the police had a place to stay, had food to eat. But their families—my husband was a police officer at the time. He was a sergeant, and you had people who were caregivers for elderly and, literally, there was no allowance, in many cases, for them, because this happened just like this." She snapped her fingers. "For them to be able to make sure that their elderly grandparents or parents were safe somewhere, there was no accommodation for that. 'Where am I gonna bring them?' The storm hit that Monday. Saturday, actually, my husband was on vacation. We were home. He called and said, 'Listen, are there any commands for us to stay?' And his supervisor said, 'No, we've not gotten anything. You're on vacation.' He said, 'Well, I'm gonna get my family to Baton Rouge.' He says, 'We'll call you if there's anything.' Well, the storm came so rapidly on Monday, but when the levees broke was when all hell broke loose. It happened so fast that there was no way to plan for the stuff that you don't even think about. 'What do I do with my family? How do I make sure that they're fine, and then I can protect and serve everybody else.' I don't know why I said all that," she added. "We were going somewhere with all of that."

"It's all great stuff," I said to encourage her.

"It's just reflecting back on all the stuff that we had to deal with. We had so many of our employees who ended up in the shelters. We had to go looking for folk. Like I said, I had fourteen-plus people in my apartment, and we had nobody to answer the phones for the bank. So I went home late one evening and I said, 'All right, I want everybody, one at a time, to say, "Liberty Bank and Trust, how may I help you?" And if you sound okay, you're comin' to work with me tomorrow.' I literally took five or six people with me. I needed people. I needed bodies. They just had to speak well. If you can answer a phone in a tone that you don't scare the person on the other end, then I'm good. You got a job."

"Have you seen Spike Lee's documentary, *When the Levees Broke?*"

"I did not see that one. I know that there were a couple of my friends in that one. I think he did not speak well of our education reform in that one, so I didn't see it. Are you familiar with Ben Lemoine?"

"No."

"He was a reporter who did a lot of stories on crime, and he completed two years ago a documentary called *The Experiment*, which is absolutely—you gotta see it. It's award-winning, and it talked about the tie between education and school reform, and he goes through the whole evolution of what happened pre- and post-Katrina in education, and he follows three families, three kids who went from a failing environment, from the Ninth Ward, to choices. He's very focused on choice, parental choice, and how and where to educate my kid. It's awesome."

"We haven't talked specifically much about the Ninth Ward," I said. "At the time, you were representing the Ninth Ward, and that's historic, really. The Ninth Ward is what everybody hears. What can you say about the experiences of your constituents at that time?"

"The people in the Ninth Ward were very, very territorial with their community, regardless of economic status. You had a tie to the Ninth Ward. People who lived there and were raised there, it was generational. I mean, you just like never left. And the homes were all generational homes. And contrary to popular belief, I think like seventy-five percent of the people who lived in the Ninth Ward owned their homes. But here was the issue, the problem: They were generational homes, which meant that people just lived there. They never opened succession. Your great, great, great, great grandmother probably built the home, and families just lived there. So there may not have been a mortgage; they may not have been able to afford insurance. So the issue with why it's been very difficult for those families to rebuild, to come back, was not that there was a threat. Because remember the reason that they flooded was because the barge broke through the levee and the whole river just came over. But the formula we used to determine how much money you get was based on actual value and, if you didn't have any flood insurance, you were then penalized for not having flood insurance. So they deducted money. At a minimum to rebuild, you had to spend $150,000, when they were only giving you what the home was valued at last appraisal, and that's fifty or sixty thousand.

"So lots of people had no choice but to sell their properties, and they couldn't come back. A lot of them were elderly, so they were on fixed income. So my office spent an enormous amount of time, and I was really grateful to have a legislative assistant at the time whose heart was just broken with every single call. We got thousands of calls, and she spent hours, hours that I couldn't pay her for, on her own time, receiving calls. So we kinda started forcing some of the rule changes, but it was harder because you had elderly, and these were a lot of elderly people who had nobody, so a lot of people died. A lot of elderly people died just out of sadness. The only thing they ever had in their life, gone with no hope of getting it back, and you had a system where they just didn't understand. It was, 'Why won't they listen to what we really need?' And I'm one legislator. My constituents in the Lower Ninth Ward were either unemployed or elderly, very few middle class, so it just literally broke my heart daily. I went through, on a daily basis, emotional swings like this. I realized early on that the Ninth Ward was never gonna be back the way people wanted it back. They wanted their old Ninth Ward: better, but their old Ninth Ward. I recognized that there would be gentrification, and it had to happen. You're not gonna bring those elderly back in and, seven years later, they're not gonna be back. And during that time you had a community where people were fighting each other, in a sense that there were opportunities for investors to come in, but that was a community that did not trust outsiders. They didn't trust politicians at all, because they've always been lied to."

"Did they trust you?"

"They should have, but they had no choice, because I was the only thing there to help them. I don't want to say it like that. I wasn't the only one there. There were a number of good people who were elected officials that were very passionate about the community and felt the same things that I felt. But unless you're able to, I mean, 'We love you and we know you really care, but unless you're able to help me get back in my house, really, really get back in my house, and like it was before, I mean, what good are you to me?' And that was the most hurtful, because you could never tell people the number of hours and the emotional ups and downs that you went through. And then I began to see the gentrification. I began to see the change. I'll never forget the Lower Ninth Ward, of course, and Holy Cross, were predominantly African American, and I'd go to community meetings. Every weekend I'd go to a different meeting. We'd have planning meetings a lot, and I'd see African American faces. Well, one meeting I went to, I looked and it was, 'Okay, who stole my people? Where are my people?' It had totally changed. People started buying, people who were not even from Louisiana. People were coming in. You know, the 'I want to come in and be part of the rebuild' people. And now I'm looking at these young, white faces and I'm like, 'Where did you people come from? Where are my people? What have you done with them?' But I realized right then and there that the Ninth Ward will never be the same. It will never be like it was, and it shouldn't."

"What happened to the people who left and couldn't come back?"

"Again, they were elderly. A lot of them died. A lot of them moved in with relatives away."

"Away like Atlanta or Houston?"

"Away like Atlanta, Houston, wherever. Not many of the elderly came back. Some of the unemployed came back. 'Okay, so I'm either gonna fill the streets there or live under the bridge.' It is slowly taking root. You've had some efforts like the Make It Right Foundation who tried to build homes and tried to create programs to help people who had some means to come back, but it will be a long time before we will know what that community will eventually look like. I don't see it ever going back to the way it was."

CHAPTER 6

MISSING HOME

"Ethan's my wife's cousin," Paul explained. "So we're friendly, and Ethan's spent a lot of time down in Miami with us. And I wanted to tag along on part of this journey, but it just didn't work out in my schedule. And I knew he was gonna be in Texas. And I went to UT as well—I know you're a Longhorn too. So I kinda set this whole thing up with my wife's family, goin' to the TCU game ..."

"Thursday," said Sherron.

"... and renting a house in Austin. And somehow it all came together."

"No one's from Austin, but y'all are doin' the game and Thanksgiving in Austin?"

"Yeah."

"Fu-un!"

"And my wife is flying from Seattle for the long weekend," I said. "I haven't seen her in two months. I've been driving around America."

"And she's a Longhorn also, but doesn't care about the game," said Paul. "So I glommed onto this part of the trip, just to spend a little time with Ethan. We've been running kinda crazy, but it was fun."

"Galveston was fun," I said.

"If you can get the book about the 1900 storm," said Sherron, "the one that's ages old, it's really interesting. It's like *A Day in September*, or something?[1] They knew a storm had crossed Cuba, but it was basically like a Katrina. It gathered steam in the Caribbean. And the two weather guys went on to start the National Weather Stuff, you know?

---

1   She must have meant *Weekend in September* by John Edward Weems, Texas A & M University Press, 1957.

But Galveston was really the port, it was where all the activity was. It was really established. And Houston was barely a pipe dream. And the storm killed eight thousand people. It was the largest natural disaster in U.S. history. My grandparents would tell stories of their parents, who just took the bodies out to sea, dumped 'em at sea."

"They had to burn a bunch of 'em too," said Paul, who had read a more recent book. "It was really horrific."

"And some of 'em came floating back," said Sherron. "It was a huge storm, so it did like Sandy did. Once the surge comes up and knocks down some houses, you now have huge timbers coming with the water, so it just knocks down everything. But one of the weathermen guys was in a house, and he kinda knew the way a house would float away. So he actually went to the corner, when the storm was coming, with two kids in hand, and as the house got lifted, that was the corner that went up. He knew it would go up. Or something. But it changed the nature of Galveston; it never came back. And Houston became the port city."

I had heard Sherron Watkins, former vice president of Houston-based Enron Corporation, speak nine months earlier at the annual two-day National Character and Leadership Symposium at the U.S. Air Force Academy in Colorado Springs, where I had also been an invited speaker. She spoke often to students and other audiences about the chain of events set off by her August 2001 memo to Enron CEO Kenneth Lay, which ignited one of the largest and most notorious business scandals in American history. She and fellow so-called whistle-blowers Cynthia Cooper of WorldCom and Coleen Rowly of the FBI were *Time* magazine's "People of the Year" for 2002.

The biggest name at the Air Force Academy symposium, Ross Perot, had leaned heavily on folksy charm and flattery of military person-nel, but otherwise the symposium was excellent. During Perot's speech the girl cadet who was one of my volunteer escorts for the two days whispered to me, "He's so cute!" I had to explain to her who he was, though. Sherron's speech had been in the same large auditorium as Perot's, but at eight-thirty in the morning, and the hall was not full. She gave quite a speech, though, and afterwards I asked the symposium organizers for her contact details.

She had suggested breakfast at this coffee shop near Rice University in Houston. She was the most normal-looking Texas-type middle-aged white lady you could imagine.

The Enron scandal "did change my life forever," she told me and Paul. "I'll never work in corporate America again. And I don't know if I'll ever hold another real job." For one thing, just meeting co-workers in the hallway could be awkward. "They don't know why, but somehow you make them feel uncomfortable. And it might just be that you did something that they know they wouldn't have had the courage to do. It could have more evil intent: they know that they're kinda pushin' the edge of the envelope, or whatever. But part of it becomes, 'Well, some people say that she just did all that to get attention, and she loves the media, and her star is losing its shine, so maybe she'll just use our institution to come up with something else.' They can use whatever excuse. It only takes one person to have a boogieman scare tactic. But it's not like I'm clamorin' to get back into corporate America."

And she was doing just fine as an in-demand public speaker. "I'm at conferences and get to meet all kinds of incredible people. Raymond Baker, I met at a conference. He worked for one of the oil companies in Nigeria for most of his career, and he wrote *Capitalism's Achilles Heel*. You know, Nigeria is a mess. All these oil companies are in there, and sure, they've been doin' everything legally, and payin' their share of royalties to the government, but they've been paying to a corrupt government! So there's no improvement, hospitals, schools. His point is, this is the resource of the country, that would allow it to expand and grow. Yet what responsibility do you have, when you're takin' that resource and payin' the royalty to a corrupt government? And it's not just Nigeria."

She preferred to fly Southwest Airlines, which meant that she had to make some inconvenient connections, so she got a lot of reading done. "I ended up reading the *Hunger Games* 'trology,' or however you say that, which is a young teen book. And it's very simplistic writing. Some of it's just ridiculous: 'The wild blueberries squished flavor in her mouth.' A bit too much."

"But super-popular with that teen crowd," offered Paul.

"But the concept of it is very interesting," said Sherron. "Did y'all see the movie or anything?"

"No," I said.

"Just generally know about it," said Paul.

"Well, it's a future population. There used to be thirteen districts, but District Thirteen rebelled and was dusted, by some nucular mishap or something. The heroine is from the coal-producing states, Appalachian district. But there's farming and agriculture, there's seafood, there's some that are making the toys, you know, the high-end retail kind of stuff. And every year there's two tributes from each district that go to the capital, which is around the Denver area, and they do these games to the death, with just one person surviving. But if you survive you're in a great house; you live great for the rest of your life.

"And the districts are always starving, just barely makin' it. So you're following two people to these games. And they're just shocked: 'Do they not know we're starving?' And in the capital they've got, you know, orange and yellow eyelashes, and it's all the latest fashion. So you go from gray drab to looks like fashion week in New York. And they all just live glued to the set, and they bet on who's gonna win, and they get sponsors. It's like *Survivor*. Well, I couldn't help wondering, when I was reading it, 'Wow. This is so much the rest of the world and the United States.' We're not thinkin' about the folks in Haiti livin' in those little tents, or in Nigeria. And why not? Because 'Who's going to stay alive on *Lost*, and what's happening on *Survivor*?' How much Facebook is about *The Voice*, or *American Idol*, or who's voting for who? We're kept entertained, and not in the know. So eventually the books evolve to where some of the folks in the capital are trying to help these district folks. But it's got some parallels that are kinda scary."

"I had just heard about the fighting to the death part, and I thought, 'That's gross; I don't want to read those books,'" I said.

"Well, it is alarming," Sherron said. "But what kind of message is it sending? I think it sends a good one. That we're not paying attention to what's out there in the rest of the world."

"When I heard you speak, you had a pretty powerful story and message to bring to people like those Air Force cadets, and you hit on it pretty unsparingly," I told her.

"Well, the 2000s—Enron, WorldCom, HealthSouth, many other collapses, then you had self-dealing with the mutual funds," she said. "You had all this stuff. Really culminating with Lehman, Bear Stearns collapse, Merrill Lynch collapse. The whole Wall Street fiasco. There is a root cause to the problem, and I don't know why we don't just fix it. It has an easy fix. I'm gonna get technical here, but this is really the problem: You've heard how J.P. Morgan said to his fellow robber barons, 'Hey, we shouldn't make more than twenty times the average factory worker.' And there was no SEC, hardly any regulation, but all of his peer group said, 'Hey, J.P., you're probably right.' And for the most part CEOs made, on average, twenty times the average hourly factory worker. In 1970 it was still somethin' like twenty-seven. In 1980 it was forty-two times. In 1990, it was eighty-five times. So in the country we started to get alarmed that CEOs were making such large amounts. So in 1993 we passed a law that CEO salaries above a million dollars could not be deducted on corporate tax returns. Because they were concerned about that eighty-five factor.

"That had horrible unintended consequences. Horrible law. What happened was, CEOs were making two million, three million, four million a year. So their non-performance-based pay went down to, like, nine hundred and ninety-five thousand a year, and the difference was made up in stock options. Well, let's just say you're making three million, and I've gotta pay you one million, but now I've gotta make up the difference. Well, those stock options have to be priced at today's stock price. Meaning if your stock is trading at twenty-five dollars a share, I've got to price those stock options at twenty-five, not twenty, not fifteen, because they have horrible tax consequences to you and the corporation. So they're priced at twenty-five, and you're hoping they're gonna rise to twenty-eight, twenty-nine, thirty, thirty-two. But you use very normal growth and risk factors.

"But to give you two million dollars' worth of stock options today, for this past year's performance, I'm really giving you more like six million dollars' worth. Because there's the time value of money, the fact that you're gonna have to see the stock price increase, you're gonna have to stay alive, keep working, all this stuff. So year one, you get your million dollars in cash and six million in stock options. Year two, same thing. Year three, six or eight more million in stock options. And the issue there becomes, you don't want any kind of blip down. You want the stock price to keep goin' up. And if you can get the stock price to double, to fifty or sixty, that eighteen million in stock options is worth a hundred and twenty-seven million to you. It's amazing how much it's worth to you. And so as an executive you really start focusing on the stock price. Not necessarily consciously, but it's there in the back of your mind, 'cause so much of your compensation's based on it.

"Well then, there are problems to stock options that are just focused on the C class: chief executive, chief financial officer. It's better if it's company-wide stock options. I started at Enron in '93, and we had employee stock ownership plans. Well, they quickly stopped that. By '94, it was stock options. Well then, by the late nineties—'96, '97, '98—I'd be goin' '*What?!?*' I was getting so much in stock options. And it's because, you know, *this* guy was getting so much. By the time you pyramid it down to the lower guys, we were still getting a lot. So you were always talking about these stock options that were gonna be vested. 'Do you still have your thirty-dollar tranche?' 'Oh yeah, I haven't sold yet.' So now you have your whole employee base not wantin' to see the stock price go down. And it has this impact of, if there's gonna be manipulation, if there's gonna be swinging for the fences, you're all in. Sorry to use the Petraeus thing, but all the employees are all in, because it means so much to 'em personally. We all made so much money. I mean, I'm in a house in this nice neighborhood from sellin' stock options.

"When you sell stock options, it blows through your W-2 like ordinary income. So I had years where my W-2 was five-six times my annual base pay, because I had sold so many stock options, like to buy the house. If you look at Bear Stearns' remuneration table, they have like a February year-end, or a January 31 year-end, and they kinda went bankrupt and got rescued by Chase a month later. Same with Enron. You look at remuneration, and it's the same, or greater, than the total earnings of the company. Enron made a billion its last year of operation, in 2000, and our remuneration was about that. You don't pay that in cash; it's in the stock market. Employees exercise stock options, and it flows through all those tax tables as if you paid cash to the employee."

I was more or less following all of this. "But especially in its last year in existence, that's not real money," I said.

"Well, it's real cash, but it came out of the marketplace."

"So if there's investors who are buying stock at eight," said Paul, "and the employees are sucking that money out from the market ..."

"Yeah," said Sherron. "You're buying the stock from the company at forty, the same day you're selling it to the market at eighty. And that profit went through the W-2 statement like it was salary. And that doesn't happen. Companies don't pay their total earnings out. So it's coming from the market. The long story short of that is that by the year 2000, CEOs in this country made five hundred and thirty-one times the average hourly worker. And that did not diminish in the 2000s. In 2010 it was a similar number. The closest other country is Brazil, and it's like fifty-two. Great Britain is forty-five. Canada and Europe is twenty, and Japan is ten."

"Yeah, but how do you unplug this, now that everybody has this expectation of stock options?" asked Paul.

"Well, that's really the root cause of Lehman Brothers," said Sherron. "And when Enron first collapsed, Congress looked at stock options. And the business community gets the Business Roundtable and the U.S. Chamber of Commerce beatin' down on Congress like crazy: 'Don't touch stock options.' Well, Paul Volcker, before he was in Obama's inner circle, had the wisest solution. You probably won't hear him say it anymore, but you can find where he suggested it: Repeal that '93 law, and pay executives whatever they're worth. If they're worth fifteen million a year, pay 'em fifteen million, and let it be deductible. And for the C class executives, no stock options, no stock credits. Just cash only."

"It's more transparent that way," said Paul.

"It's more transparent. Then, all of a sudden they start listening to their risk managers. Because now they want the job for fifteen years, not just five or six. Look at Stan O'Neil. Chuck Prince. There was a revolving door of CEOs that made legacy wealth. Their great-grandchildren will still be livin' off the wealth they made. But yet their companies had to be bailed out or went bankrupt. So something's wrong with that picture. And if you look at Matthew Lee, from Lehman Brothers, Dick Bowen at Citibank, there's plenty of whistleblowers within the financial community. But they were no longer being listened to. Paul Moore, with HBOS in Britain, was let go. There were plenty of risk managers that were telling this doom, but they got canned."

"Post-2001, pre-2008?" I asked.

"Yes. But with Dick Bowen, Congress went through the rejected SOX complaints to try to find whistleblowers, about the 2008 mess." (The Sarbanes-Oxley Act of 2002, or SOX, stiffened standards for the boards, management, and accounting firms of public companies in the U.S., compelling top management to certify the accuracy of financial information and setting severe penalties for fraudulent financial activity.) "So they looked for rejected SOX complaints for Citibank, Chase, Lehman. That's how they found these guys!"

"Wow," I said.

"They were there," said Paul.

"Yep. And so the CEO will listen to his risk manager when he's not makin' legacy wealth by swingin' for the fences. Or basically betting red on the roulette table. If it comes up red in the first year, 'Great!' Makes lotsa money. Red the second year, great! Third year, fourth year, it's black: 'Oh, the company's bankrupt, so long.'"

"But these options also create the culture that no one wants to step forward," said Paul.

"Our stock price had gone up with the tech boom because we had Enron Broadband," said Sherron. "And when the tech bust happened, and prices started to go down: 'Oh, great. Look at those sixty-dollar stock options we got in February. What good are *they* gonna do us? They're now sellin' at forty. *When* are we gonna see sixty again? Might as well kiss that tranche of options goodbye.' I mean, that's *all* the talk. The focus is the stock price, the stock price, the stock price. Which is a horrible focus!"

"So if you step forward, now you're screwin' with someone's livelihood," said Paul. "Now they're saying, 'Don't you say a word. If you step forward, you're ruining my ability to pay for my kids' college education, my mortgage.' That's when people get really kinda funky, if you screw with their livelihood."

"Did people get funky when you screwed with their livelihood?" I asked Sherron.

"Well, for me it was different. Cynthia Cooper at WorldCom they did, because Scott Sullivan was tryin' to hide his mess in a goodwill write-off that was coming up and expected by the market. And she forced it to be recognized. And so different employees did blame her. For me, the company had imploded, executives were blaming Andy Fastow, the CFO, and that didn't ring true. We all knew it was a wider rot. So when Congress found my memos, released 'em to the press, I got a lot of support. Because now there was a sense that justice was gonna be done, that the people responsible were not gonna get away with it. Too many executives met with people, didn't put it in writing, or used language that could be read either way. Enron tried to put that spin on what I was sayin' to Ken Lay, but if you read it, it's pretty black and white."

"What about at the time?" asked Paul. "Who knew in August, when you sent him the email? Did other co-workers know you had done that?"

"A few. Just a small handful."

"Those that would have been supportive to you?"

"Well, like, Jeff McMahon was supportive at first, but when Ken Lay didn't listen, he dropped me in the grease. I said in our book, *Power Failure*, that it was the weirdest thing, because I really felt that this was financial statement fraud on a level that would kill the company, and I saw executives fighting to be in the wheelhouse. Elbowing their way to be captain of the *Titanic*."

"And they should have known very well where things were headed," said Paul.

"Yeah. You need to be manning the lifeboats. Who cares who's captain of this boat! But it shows to me how much people drink the Kool-Aid and really get caught up, and don't see the dangers. But my main point is, you can't really regulate this stuff from the outside very well. The companies hired really great value-at-risk folks, risk managers, internal-audit control folks. They know, from inside, where the dangers are. And *Margin Call* is a great movie, if you haven't seen it. It was by a first-time director, first-time screenwriter. I need to write the guy. He's absolutely brilliant. So we saw it in the movie theaters, *loved* it. It looks like it represents Lehman, but I think it's more about Merrill Lynch. It's got Stanley Tucci, Kevin Spacey, Jeremy Irons, Demi Moore. It's got this incredible cast. And we bought the DVD when it came out, and lookin' at the extras? The guy's dad was the value-at-risk guy at Merrill Lynch for thirty-nine years. It's amazing. It's got a lot of symbolism. There's a twentysomething kid that's just always saying, 'What do you think So-and-so makes? What'd you make last year?' And he wants to have a discussion with his boss on how he spent the millions he made, and he's just, you know, in it for himself. And then it's got some age politics, 'cause a younger guy jumps over an older guy, it's got some sex politics, 'cause Demi Moore kinda squished Stanley Tucci's character. It's got it all."

"You should write the guy and say, 'A really great movie—Sherron Watkins,'" I suggested. "Then he can put that on his publicity."

"On his Amazon page," she said. "I need to write a review on Amazon. It's *really* good. But people knew what was happening. Their value-at-risk people figured it out. But they don't get listened to early enough and often enough, because the CEO wants to hear how we swing for the fences and make the stock price double. So it'd be a simple law, cash only, and you can still use stock options for the lower levels if you want, and repeal that '93 act."

"Is there any chance of this happening?" Paul asked.

"Well, part of the problem is the way the Republican Party has taken over the airwaves with Fox and talk radio, where there's this idea that if you try to mess with people's salaries you're envious, you're jealous. They earned it. You're a socialist. It's a combination of messing with the American Dream—I may be a blue-collar worker, but my grandchild might be a CEO—and 'Well, look what actors make, look what ballplayers make.' But it's not the same thing. The CEO hires the benchmarking company, the consulting firm that determines he's underpaid, and he's the chairman of the board, so he's their boss even in the boardroom. It's not the same thing at all. And, they can not perform and still get paid."

"So ultimately it's about human nature," I said.

"Yeah. And we need all these checks and balances in place, and we've messed it up. We've put such a carrot out there with these stock options. We wrote this silly law, and started this whole stock option craze that has fouled the waters."

"Inadvertently, right?"

"Inadvertently."

"It seemed like a good idea at the time."

"Mm-hmm."

"And that was Clinton."

"Mm-hmm."

"We've just had an election. What's going to be the effect on these kinds of matters of this election and its result?"

"Well, I have no idea. I hope that Obama might listen to Paul Volcker and do something about it. But I would say Obama's gonna be lookin' at immigration and health care."

"So these issues are gonna get on the back burner and not get addressed?" said Paul.

"Pushed aside. Dodd-Frank was supposed to address it, and the Volcker Rule. But what happens first is, the business lobbying effort tries to kill any regulation. When they see that they can't kill it, then they make it *this* thick. Dodd-Frank is supposedly *this* thick. There's this famous divorce lawyer here in town. He had this socialite come, 'Woe is me, woe is me,' divorcin' her rich husband, and she's not gonna get anything, because he had her sign this ironclad prenup, so she just knows she's toast. And he says, 'Well, sweetie, we don't know that for sure. Let me just ask you one simple question: How many pages is your prenup?' She says, 'Oh, it's ironclad. It's a hundred and twenty-five pages.' He says, 'No sweat, sweetie. I'll getcha all ya need. If it was two pages, we'd be in trouble.' Well, Dodd-Frank is supposed to prevent speculative investing. And look at Chase. They had, what, a six-billion-dollar loss this past summer? And they said that it doesn't violate Dodd-Frank, it's like a hedging strategy? I'm sorry."

"Much of what we know should happen won't happen," I said. "Right?"

"Right."

"Which gets back to your point about how it can't really be regulated from outside."

"Which is why it's important to look at those stock options, it's important to make that something that we address, because otherwise it just doesn't get any better. You need to pick up a *Houston Chronicle* today, because in the business section it's about BP's settlement.[2] You know, where they paid the four billion or something, and admitted criminal negligence? And they hung it on three people: two people that were rig workers, and one here in Houston for obstruction of justice. And the two guys that were rig supervisors, they're flyin' out in the helicopters to live on the rigs, just like the eleven guys that got killed. And they did misread a test, and what they did helped cause it. But it's like Abu Ghraib! It really is from leadership, you know?"

"This was one of the points you made in your speech at the Air Force Academy," I reminded her. "That it really is all about leadership."

"It is. And when we as a society let the bad stuff happen to the privates, we are fouled up."

"Did you ever aspire to be a CEO?"

"When you're working at the company, you want to keep getting advanced," she said. "You know, you see yourself in leadership."

"You talked about how you really wanted to make vice president."

"Well, what happened in '96 was, I saw problems. And it was significant enough for me that I really wanted to get away from that department. And I thought, 'Should I leave?' But I had not made vice president yet. It was more the ego involved, that 'People aren't gonna believe that I'm leaving on my own.' I switched divisions. That comes into play for everyone. But I try to say that to college kids, because they anticipate that they'll have an ethical dilemma, and they'll just leave. But there's so many reasons why you don't. I wasn't married with a big mortgage at the time, but hey, I didn't want to be looked at as someone who was being pushed out. I wanted to get to that next rung on the ladder, and then look to leave. By then, I made vice president and was engaged. So then you're getting married, then you're buying the house. There's so many things they don't consider. You know, it's been eleven years of talking about Enron. I am shocked at college students'

2   "Offshore crews shoulder a new worry: indictments," commentary by Loren Steffy, *Houston Chronicle*, November 21, 2013, p. D1: "'If I were going to go to the heliport tomorrow, I'd sure as hell be thinking twice about it,' [drilling safety expert David] Pritchard said. 'If I'm a company man, I wouldn't want to think my company's going to throw me under the bus, and if I'm a contractor, I'm wondering how I can get insurance.'"

naïveté! They actually think that as soon as an ethical dilemma crosses their lap, they're gonna quit the company or walk out the door or say something. And ninety-eight percent of 'em are gonna be that deer that goes, 'Oh, what's that? That bright light coming down the road?' Ka-boom. They're gonna be run over by that ethical dilemma, freeze in fear, and not do a thing."

"As a college kid, though, you don't anticipate the complexities of life," said Paul. "And also, the ethical dilemma never is a bright light. In your situation you had Arthur Andersen, you had Vinson & Elkins, you had all these people. At some point you also doubt yourself. You're like, 'Wait a second, I see all this, but all of these professionals, they're saying the opposite.' You're like, 'Wait, am I crazy, or is everybody else crazy?'"

"I've never made anywhere near that kind of money," I admitted. "In my fondest dreams, I think if I had a million bucks, I'd just do whatever I feel like doing. Because who needs more than that?"

"I think that's where we've got a problem too," said Sherron, "and why I like these *Hunger Games* books. Because I've got nieces. I call 'em nieces and nephews; I've got twenty-three first cousins, and some of 'em are close in age, so their kids, you know, they'll call me Aunt Sherron. And some of 'em have done mission trips, and they're deciding whether to be a doctor or a dentist, and sometimes they think dentist because of the work they can do in Guatemala on mission trips, with cleft palates and teeth, you know. But they're deciding on a profession based off what good they can do. And I've got others that want to go to UT, get in the business school. 'I want to work for Goldman Sachs.' 'Really? Why do you want to work for Goldman Sachs?'" She left a long pause.

"Well, if you can't think of anything else, then the only reason is the money," said Paul.

"You know, living so close to Rice is great for all sorts of reasons," said Sherron. "Great green space, we have a dog, it's good for football games, fireworks, for the Shepherd music school. And they had their hundred-year celebration, and they had this great light show put on by this German artist team, and they had Chief Justice John Roberts come and speak. And he couldn't talk about past, pending, or future Supreme Court cases." She laughed. "But it turned out to be good anyway. And there were a lot of law students in the audience. And he said, 'You need to ask yourself why you want to be a lawyer. And if the answer is, "I'm not very good at math, and I don't enjoy science," then you're not in the right profession.' There needs to be a reason why you want to be a lawyer. Not just 'The pay's good, and I don't like math.'"

"I'm an attorney," Paul confessed. He had asked me not to tell Sherron, in case it spooked her. "I went to UT Law. But when you're in college, you don't think about these things. It's the special kids that do. I didn't really think about it. I was like, 'Well, I guess I don't have anything else to do.' And I was good at math. I was an economics major, and I just thought, 'Well, law school sounds neat.' Life just kinda swept me away into it. You don't really think about it. But it's good that someone is there telling you to think about it."

"He gave a good speech," said Sherron. "He clerked for Justice Rehnquist, and he said he always left at five or five-thirty. He said, 'If you want to spend time with young children, the thing is, you gotta do it when they're young.' Because all of a sudden they're seventeen, and they don't have time for you."

"Speaking of John Roberts, do you have a view on the difference he made in the Obamacare case?" I asked.

"I think that was very significant," she said. "I appreciate Nancy Pelosi's work in this. In effect, it probably cost her the Speakership. Because as soon as Scott Brown won, I thought, 'Affordable Care Act's dead. It won't pass the Senate again.' She took what the Senate had passed, when Ted Kennedy was still alive, and did some amazing maneuvering to make it into law. And as a result there was some backlash, she lost her majority ..."

"The Democrats lost Congress as a direct result," said Paul.

"Yeah. But she put the good of the country before her own politics. I just saw the Lincoln movie last night. Have you seen it yet?"

"Not yet," I said.

"I'm looking forward to it," said Paul.

"It's incredible. You know, he did some things that were shaky in the law, in order to get some things accomplished. And he knew over time they wouldn't hold up. And the Emancipation Proclamation was actually something that wouldn't work, and it had some circular problems.

He goes into that in the movie. And Nancy Pelosi did something that, in a white-hot light, looked a little bit too scheming. And it was good fodder for gettin' the Tea Party folks really up in arms."

"But she got it done," I said.

"Mm-hmm."

"Do you identify with one or the other of the parties?" I had been wondering. She was from Texas, after all.

"When *Time* interviewed me in 2002, I said I was independent. But no, I'm a Democrat now. The Republican Party, I don't recognize at all."

"Were you a Republican?"

"No. I voted all over the map. I was kind of a careless voter. I mean, I voted for Ross Perot when I was young and stupid."

"And you got to see him again at the Air Force Academy," said Paul.

"Naw, I missed him. He was the day before I was there. I shoulda come in for the whole thing! I really didn't realize how cool it was. But I'm a staunch believer—are we Facebook friends? We should be Facebook friends. Let's make sure we do that."

"Okay," I agreed.

"So the election happens, and I'd just put a Jeremiah 22:16 quote on my Facebook page, and said ''Nuff said.' And the quote is, back in Old Testament times, the prophets are always doin' like this to these kings of Israel, and this one is getting berated by Jeremiah. And he's just focused on building houses. He's building great stuff and wanting to kind of enhance his kingdom. And the words to him are, it was his father or grandfather, I forget, but it was, 'Remember this king; he looked after the causes of the poor and the needy. And didn't it all go well for him? His focus was on the causes of the poor and the needy, and look, he had plenty of cedar palaces and great stuff.' And it goes on to say, 'He defended the causes of the poor and the needy. Isn't this what it is to know me, says the Lord.' So I posted that and said, ''Nuff said.' Well, I have, I don't know, eight hundred friends on Facebook, and you get those little updates on who likes things? I think a hundred and fifty-seven liked Mitt Romney's page and, um, fifteen liked Obama's page. You know, when you get your little friend updates? Well, I live here in this red state, and I go to a Christian family camp that's an evangelical group, active in church. So anyway, the ones that liked Obama's page were high-fivin' that little thing. Well, two vocal Christians, one of 'em said something about the poor around the world. And the other one said, 'Well, what does the Bible say about marriage, abortion and, um, somethin' else, and Israel?' And my response was, 'Look, when God says this is what it is to know him, I'm gonna pay attention to that.' Oh, one of my comments was, they're worried about the fiscal cliff and all that, and I said, 'Didn't you read the passage? If you look out for the causes of the poor and the needy, the other stuff just happens.'

"And I think it was really important in this country for Obamacare to be put into law, so that people truly can get health insurance. I think there are bad things happening to too many people. So I think John Roberts had his own Abraham Lincoln moment, when he decided to do what he did. There's a great line in that movie, where Lincoln says, 'Do you think we choose to be born?' I want to meet the screenplay writer. 'Cause that's a very spiritually deep question. It's a C.S. Lewis talk. If you've ever read *The Great Divorce...*"

"I have," I said. My dad had laid all those C.S. Lewis books on me when I was a teenager.

"At the end, where he has that little odd thing?"

"It's been a long time."

"There's elements to it where you'd almost think there's another realm, and we choose. Do we choose to be born? Are we fitted for the times? And I think Roberts had a moment there, where he was touched by the divine."

"How did your faith change when the Enron thing happened?"

"Well, I grew up Lutheran," she said. "They really hammer home that it's a sin to worry. You know, you're not trusting that God has your back? So I do think I felt I could take a risk, because that was just in my DNA. So it plays an important part, but I really kinda checked the box and put my faith on a shelf. It was certainly there; I've always been a member of a church. But it wasn't, you know, a daily thing. After Enron, through the process and after, it's all real. You know? I don't seek a corporate job, because I want believers to understand that they're seein' this much of it, and they could see so much more. The stuff that has happened to me the last ten years is just amazing. And it just keeps getting better and better. Hebrews 12:1-3: 'We have a purpose, we have a race that we're meant to run.' That's what I think we've lost in this country, is this sense of vocation, this sense of 'I'm here for a purpose.' The whole thing in Matthew 25 is the sheep and the goats. When it's *all* said and done, and I'm pulling up *everyone*, and deciding between those that are going to heaven and those that aren't: sheep and goats. You saw me nekkid, hungry, thirsty, in prison, a stranger, and you did something—come on! You saw me nekkid, hungry, thirsty, and in prison, and you did nothing—sorry. Did you see *The Adjustment Bureau*, with the angels? Matt Damon?"

"No. You're a real moviegoer."

"I like movies. It kind of concludes that it's all a test. And Abraham Lincoln: 'Did we choose to be born?' And for what purpose? It kinda goes to C.S. Lewis. But I think the poor are with us because we're supposed to do something about it."

"Would you feel that your vocation includes blowing the whistle on Enron, like somehow that was something you were meant to do?"

"I don't know. I think I was in the right place at the right time. I had been at Arthur Andersen for eight years, I had seen their culture decline, I saw what was happening at Enron, I knew Andy Fastow, I had worked with him for three years. So I think I was in a unique position to recognize that it was fraud, when others would have comforted themselves with, 'Well, Arthur Andersen's looked at this, it must be okay.' We're all given these things that maybe take us to the next level. And you rise to it, you can feel it's serious, you can feel it's momentous."

"How long did it take you to write that email?" Paul asked. "And did you have any indecision? Did it take a week for you to decide to send it? Did you go back and forth in your mind?"

"I had switched jobs in late June, and looking at this stuff, there were some questionable hedges. And I was tryin' to get my hands around it, tryin' to figure it out. Well, I had finally a three-hour meeting with two business managers in EEF on July 31, when it was apparent that it was fraud. I kept pushing and pushing and pushing, and finally they were just, 'Look, Sherron, give up. We don't really understand how it works. We just assume it does because Arthur Andersen has blessed it, and Vinson & Elkins has blessed it.' I kept asking questions and kept getting the spin, but when I'd poke holes in the spin, they'd try and try and try, and finally they just said, 'We don't get it either.'"

"Well, didn't those guys really know?" asked Paul. "I mean, they shoulda known it was fraud."

"No, they didn't. Not those guys. It was so complicated. During Ken Lay's trial, his defense lawyers stacked up binders, like seven binders, on the witness stand, to say, 'Did you look at any of these before you concluded that it was fraud?' These were the legal documents. It was the silliest, stupidest softball question I've ever seen. They were tryin' to be melodramatic in front of the jury. But I said, 'That's silly! That's like looking at the swindler's plan to weave that cloth for the emperor.' Why look at it? You can see the cloth doesn't exist! It was stupid. But that's part of the fraud. You drown people in the complexity, and they don't read the fine print."

"You'd have to really be probing, and really be pushing and pushing, to reach that conclusion," said Paul.

"Yeah. And I had the advantage of stumbling on the transactions when this action has happened. So I'm going, 'This doesn't make any sense. It would make sense if it was *this*, but not *this*.' And so then they're scratchin' their heads kinda goin', 'Oh, yeah, maybe you're right.' I stumble across the transactions when everything had gone against 'em and they were underwater, and their flaws were apparent. So now people are goin' like this"—she turned her head and held a hand up next to her face—"'cause they don't really want to look. Besides the fraudsters, Vince Kaminski was the only one that looked at it all and said, 'This is ridiculous, and I'm not letting you use my department to value the puts and calls that you're using to structure this.' And he got demoted for it. But I didn't know all that. But anyway, so two weeks later was when Skilling quit, on a Tuesday, August 14. And so I came into the office the next day, wrote the first page, and sent it off."

"Your memo was August 15," I said. "The World Trade Center was blown up less than a month later. You were already in your own maelstrom of Enron, and then this enormous thing clobbers America. How did you weather all of that?"

"Well, I'm sure it made me more paranoid," Sherron said. "Because it was just a very bleak time, where you really question everything. It was an alarming time."

"Where were you on September 11?"

"Watchin' *Barney*, of all things! I had met V & E on September 10; they were starting their investigation. It was disheartening to me, but I had like a three-hour meeting with these lawyers. I had been given no real work. And we had bought our house in 1999, and we had wood floors. We'd had the house for two years, no idea that you were supposed to get a waxer and put wax on these wood floors. So I bought a high-end waxer, and I was takin' a vacation day on September 11 to wax the floors! And my nanny was still coming, I had a two-year-old, and she arrived, and my daughter's up, she's watchin' *Barney*. And my nanny arrives and goes, 'Turn on the news! Turn on the news! There's something happening with the World Trade Center!' She had heard it on the radio on the way. And so I was actually at home, which was good, because had I been at work, they just closed everything and sent everyone home anyway. But it was weird. I was watchin' *Barney*. But it was a bleak time."

"Do you make as much money as you made at Enron?" I asked.

"No. But I'm not working 40-50 hours a week either. I have months where I don't give a speech."

"At the Air Force Academy you said your twelve-year-old thinks you're a stay-at-home mom that travels sometimes."

"Yeah."

"Are you enjoying your life now?"

"Well, yes. And my passion really is adult Christian education. I think there is gonna be a great awakening. And I think this far-right evangelical group is on the wrong path. It's hard to know who's a shepherd and who's a sheep there. I mean, it makes no sense for a strong believer to be anti-immigrant. If you do a word search in Bible software for 'stranger' or 'alien,' it's amazing how many verses there are where God says, 'Treat the stranger or alien that lives among you as if he were one of your own, for you were once a stranger or alien in Egypt.'"

"How do you communicate this with fellow Christians who are right-wing?"

"Um, I don't have it down yet. I won't be effective until it's God speaking through me, and that won't happen until I can feel love for 'em, and I don't feel love for 'em yet. I'm gettin' there. Part of it is realizing many of 'em are sheep, wantin' to fit in, led astray by the wrong shepherd. But my issue with God right now is, I don't know why He loves 'em. Or any of us!"

"Do you get recognized on the street?" I asked her.

"Not usually. It's kinda weird. The rank and file employees were very happy with what I did. And so there's a lot of support with that."

"Do you ever get recognized just by members of the public? 'Oh, that's Sherron Watkins'?"

"It's more like, 'I know you from somewhere.' They think I work at their bank."

"So not exactly celebrity status," chuckled Paul.

"And then, if they keep pushing, I'll say, 'Well, did you keep up with Enron?' and they'll say, 'That's it.' The executives, those that bear some guilt, have had to rationalize it that it was just an overzealous government. So I have less friends now than I did."

"Better friends?"

She hesitated. "Better friends, but it's more a lone path. And it's weird in many ways. I've had many miracles happen. It's impacted my husband probably, 'cause he's seen it, so he's kinda seeking that same path. But you'd expect that it impacts friends and relatives? And instead, if they're not ready to do that, then they kind of—you know. I believe that we can live a life that's a lot more like *The Matrix*. Where you really are in situations where you can say, 'Okay, God, dial me up, what am I supposed to do here?' and you get the instructions. But—I guess I use a lot of movie references."

"You sure do."

"Did you see *The Matrix*?"

"Yeah."

"The first one. At the end, the guy that's being a traitor just says, 'Okay, you're gonna put me in a little pod, but I want to be wealthy, I want to have all the girls, I want to have the cars.' I think he wanted to go to Miami!"

"I remember," said Paul. "He just gave in. It was easier just to give in and live in the pod in this fake existence than to keep fighting."

"I think there's people who remain comfortable. And if you do want to go to the next level, then you do have a vocation, and you're seeking it."

The Matrix reminded me of Paul Farmer's 2003 commencement speech at Harvard Medical School, "If You Take the Red Pill."[3] I told Sherron about it.

"That's an awesome college address!" she said. "But it's spiritual. I mean, I think we are near a great awakening, and there's gonna be more people taking the red pill. But there are those that don't. There are those that want to stay in the pod."

"Including some of your relatives."

"Mm-hmm."

"And my relatives. Present company excepted."

"Well, it's hard to make the decision to take the red pill, though," said Paul.

"It's this great unknown," said Sherron. "It's this leap of faith, but as soon as you do it—it's just like all those Old Testament things: you have to step in the raging river, and *then* the water stops. But I do firmly believe that it won't be long before there are a lot more opportunities for people to take the red pill, and more people will be taking it."

*

Paul and I had one more appointment in Houston, for lunch at Bapsi's house. Bapsi Sidhwa was the distinguished author of *Ice-Candy Man* and other beautifully and pointedly observed novels of lived history in

---

3 "Do we dare take the red pill? A serious question from a guy who is gagging on the red pill and still falling down the rabbit hole. As a character in the film says—he's a bad guy, of course—'Ignorance is bliss.'" The speech is reprinted in *To Repair the World: Paul Farmer Speaks to the Next Generation*, edited by Jonathan Weigel, University of California Press, 2013, pp. 72-86.

Pakistan. She was small and endured physical difficulties because of her childhood polio, but she was shrewd and incisive and very political. I had the impression, from her books, that these traits were not unrelated to her polio, the loneliness she had suffered as a result, and her membership in a vulnerable religious minority. Despite the fact that she was not a Muslim, Bapsi was a vocal Pakistani patriot. She and her husband, Noshir, were Parsis, subcontinental Zoroastrians of Persian origin. Bapsi called them "the dodo birds of world religions"—there are only about 200,000 Parsis worldwide. Her family owned the only

brewery still extant in Pakistan. Noshir was in his eighties and remembered sitting on Mahatma Gandhi's lap as a child; his father had hobnobbed with Gandhi, Nehru, Jinnah and the other great figures who wrested independence for India and Pakistan from the British in 1947. I had been their houseguest a few times. Noshir kept a well-stocked bar, and I enjoyed listening to his stories over whiskey. This time it worked out that I was only able to stop by for lunch, with Paul in tow.

"Ethan, you're looking good," said Bapsi. "How is John?"

"He's well," I told her. "He and I are trying to bring a film about the earthquake in Haiti to TCU. That's what we're working on together now."

I had brought my friend John Singleton, director of International Student Services at Texas Christian University in Fort Worth, to Bapsi's house once. John was an enthusiast of international cinema and held a weekly screening on the TCU campus. Entering Bapsi's house, he had noticed a poster on the wall opposite the front door for the movie *Water* by the Indian filmmaker Deepa Mehta, for which Bapsi had written the accompanying novel. "That's a great film," John remarked innocently. "That's *my* fil-im!" Bapsi exclaimed, and they had been buddies ever since.

"He's still sending me fil-ims," she told me happily.

"He says hello."

We sat down to lunch. "What brought you to Houston?" Paul asked Bapsi.

"In Atlanta I didn't find much happening, as a writer," she said. "Then when I moved to Houston, this place has energy, and things just happened and happened, for me and for Noshir."

I told Bapsi that Paul and his wife, my cousin Cindy, lived in Florida.

"*Why* did it take them *so* long to count the votes?" she asked him. "*Every* time!"

"And you know the language that all of us lawyers create..." he mumbled.

"So you're a lawyer?"

"Yes," he admitted.

"So you're part of the problem!"

"Part of the problem," he posited, "is that whenever you have a controversy, and you try to address it, that creates a new controversy."

"What are you, a Republican or a Democrat?"

"A Democrat," he said. "I don't think Ethan would have brought me on this trip if I were a Republican. He would have left me in a roadside ditch somewhere."

Bapsi turned to me. "Good for you, Ethan. These people act as though *he* lost, and *they* won! And they want us to go over the fiscal cliff!"

"It's like a suicide bomber," said Paul.

"That's an awful comparison," said Bapsi.

"But it's accurate," he insisted.

"So, are you optimistic about America, Bapsi?" I asked her.

"I am," she said. "Because the all-white demographics of the country have changed."

✳

As we drove to Austin that evening, Paul told the story of how he and his young family had managed to survive Hurricane Andrew in Miami in 1992.

"It starts with me in Newport, Rhode Island," he began. "I was up at this thing with some friends of mine from college, and they had gotten a place for a week. It was the end of the summer. These are the days before cell phones and emails, so I hadn't really kept in touch with

Cindy. She was at home with Will. What I didn't know is that there's a hurricane headed towards Miami. And Newport is probably an hour and forty-five minutes outside of Boston.

"I had a flight leaving on Sunday. We went to the beach one last time and then started heading to Boston. We were cutting it pretty close. And as we got into Boston, we ran into some traffic. Got to the airport, had to hustle down the concourse, and I was literally the last person on the plane. They were about to close the door. And my seat was in the last row. As I sat down, the pilot made his announcements and said something to the effect of, 'We're glad that we can get you into Miami before the hurricane hits; this will be the last flight.' And I looked at the person next to me and said, 'Hurricane?' They looked at me like I was the biggest idiot. Here I am, flying into a city that's facing a major hurricane, without any clue.

"So we arrive in Miami and, because I'm in the back of the plane, I'm one of the last people off. I get off, and Cindy's there waiting for me with Will. And she's relieved: 'Oh, thank goodness, you made it.' And at that point I believe I found out that Hurricane Andrew was a Category Four storm, and projected to hit somewhere in Miami-Dade County. Or perhaps Broward. And Cindy had been very nervous. She had packed up all our pets, a cooler, and things we'd need for overnight. She was ready to go. As soon as she got me, we were going to a hotel. At first she had picked a hotel in southern Dade County, near Florida City. She had picked that hotel because they took pets, but a neighbor had told her that it sounded like it was too close to the water. So instead she went in totally the opposite direction and found a hotel in West Palm that took pets, that wasn't close to the water.

"So we went straight to West Palm, checked into our hotel, settled in, and I began watching the news coverage, knowing the hurricane was getting closer and closer to Florida. I pretty much stayed up the whole night. First of all to make sure there wasn't any last-minute change in direction that would shoot it up to Palm Beach. I'd really have to be on alert at that point and ready to take action. But it stayed on its course, heading due west, hitting the south part of Miami-Dade County. It probably hit around 5 a.m., but once I knew it was moving out, off the west coast of Florida, we prepared to head back. And I had seen initial reports that there had been loss of power. There was a lot of damage, but they really didn't talk about how much damage in those initial reports.

"We had heard that Camillus House, the homeless shelter, would need ice. And we knew we would need ice, and we were up in West Palm, where they had electricity. We had a big cooler, so we stopped at a liquor store, got six bags of ice, and immediately headed down back to Miami. And on our way down we're listening to the radio reports. The reports coming in were talking about some really frightening damage, including this report from someone who had flown over in a helicopter, one of the news stations, talking about the devastation looking like a war zone. So we went to downtown Miami to Camillus House, to drop off our ice before we went to our house. And the first thing we see is that downtown looks a little bit battered. On the exit ramp to the main exit to the center of downtown, a huge tree had been knocked over that was blocking one of the lanes. That was our first sign that, 'Wow.' Even though the city of Miami is north of where the destruction sounded like it was worst, it was still pretty bad. The higher buildings had lost a lot of windows on the upper floors. My office, which was on the fifty-second floor of the tallest building in Miami at that time, lost a few windows. One of the interesting stories was that these two adjacent offices had both lost windows, and some of the work from one of the lawyers' office ended up in the office of the other lawyer. So instead of whipping everything out, it kind of mixed everything up.

"In the day or two after the hurricane, we heard that people down in southern Dade County really needed supplies. They were not necessarily prepared. It had been a while since a hurricane had hit, and certainly nothing of this magnitude had hit Dade County, and the response system really was not in place to provide for the needs of these people that didn't have water or shelter. And probably what we did wasn't what would be recommended, certainly not now, but we went to stores up in Broward County and picked up diapers, and different supplies that we thought people would need, and water. And we drove down to the really badly affected areas, to try and see if we could find people that might need some of these supplies. And there weren't police at that point really controlling the situation. I think today, police and other emergency services personnel would have limited the access that people would have. But of course I think there would be a better system for delivering those type of things to people in need.

"We found really horrific devastation. There was one house that had half its roof blown off, and this elderly couple were just sitting there in their garage kind of in shock, not really sure what to do. We left some water with them and drove around and found other people to leave our supplies with. It was really a shocking scene, with houses completely destroyed and pine trees stripped of all their needles, bent over at forty-five-degree angles. And about a week later, I had to go down to the Keys for business. At that point the roads were clear. I had a court case down in Marathon. And I drove down, right by the hotel that Cindy had originally booked. And it's a chilling scene, that makes your hair stand up, when you see that this place was completely destroyed. I can only imagine what it would have been like, with an eighteen-month-old, two dogs, two cats, being in the center of one of the worst hurricanes to hit the United States."

"And you flew in completely clueless."

"Yeah. That's a story we can laugh about now, and my friends like to tease me about how stupid I was. But I fully admit that it was highly irresponsible."

✸

"Carolyn didn't get it," said Kelly the next day. "What she likes is the degree."

"It wudn't about football for me," said Carolyn.

Paul's wife Cindy was at the rented house outside Austin when Paul and I arrived, and their college-age kids Will and Katy, and my other cousin Kelly and his wife Carolyn. My wife Jenny would be flying in from Seattle this evening, Thanksgiving Day. The ladies would pick her up at the airport while the men were at the stadium on the UT campus watching the Texas-TCU game. For several hours before that, though, all of us lounged around in the parking lot as guests of a family Paul and Cindy knew. I had several beers before the deep-fried turkey was ready and was feeling pretty sleepy.

My cousin Cindy had been flower girl at my parents' wedding, in Dallas in 1959. Cindy and Kelly's talkative mother, Jeanene, had been a super-duper real estate agent throughout the long boom of the Dallas-Fort Worth metroplex. We all loved "Nene," and at the moment we were worried about her because she was eighty and suffering a bout of ill health, staying with her sister in Tulsa. Her absence was felt. One of the hopes I had cherished was to spend a day or two with Nene, driving around Dallas, hearing stories of her adventures in real estate.

Cindy taught three-year-olds at an expensive private school in Miami. She had a Ph.D. in early childhood education, so kids and parents called her Dr. Haralson. Her brother Kelly had been a screw-up in his youth, until he met Carolyn. Carolyn was the perfect woman: both a great cook and a really smart accountant. Like Sherron Watkins, she had worked at Arthur Andersen. Carolyn was from Quitman, the same East Texas town as Grandma Casey. Cissy Spacek had babysat her. She and Kelly now lived near Quitman on a chicken farm, supplying several flocks a year to one of the big industrial chicken companies. Kelly was almost never seen in any outfit but jeans and a ball cap. Carolyn was in charge of Thanksgiving dinner, which we were having on Friday because of the Thursday football game.

So we were sitting around in lawn chairs in the parking lot outside the stadium, desultorily watching the daytime NFL games on a big-screen TV running off the power from a customized van, and drinking beer. The Cowboys were playing the Washington Redskins. Kelly was bitching about Tony Romo, the Cowboys' quarterback. Bitching about Tony Romo was a pastime for Kelly. "He completes a lotta passes, but he cain't finish a game!" he cried. Occasionally we had a conversation about baseball, but football interested him a lot more. Kelly followed the Rangers and Mavericks dutifully but, like every other Texan except my father, he was really a football guy. "We haven't won a Super Bowl in so long, I cain't even remember which decade it was," he moaned.

"You can always relive the glory days," I said.

"That gets a little old after a while," he grumbled.

The Cowboys' glory days were the 1970s, the days of Roger

Staubach, Tony Dorsett, Too Tall Jones, and the great coach Tom Landry. What I remembered about the glory days was Kelly's and my grandfather, the bald and taciturn Dallas adman E.E. Rominger, in his easy chair in front of the TV in his living room, saying only "Damn!" or "Hell!" when a Cowboy fumbled or dropped a pass. E.E. Rominger was a man of few words.

Kelly had more to say. Around the time the Cowboys were down 21-3 to the Redskins, he caught me sitting on a cooler taking notes. "You better not be quotin' me over there!" he called. (I thought Kelly hammed up the country boy thing sometimes. Later in the weekend, he told a story about how at his church they had shared "joys and celebrations," and a young girl said, "We have a joy. Our sow had twelve babies yesterday, and we *love* pig meat." A few minutes later he turned to me and asked, "Did you get that for your book, Ethan? About the pig meat?")

Eventually, with the Cowboys trailing 31-3, we took our leave of our tailgating hosts and went inside to find our seats.

"I think Texas should be worried about A&M," Paul was saying to Will as we walked up the ramp. (Texas A&M was in the same football conference, the Big 12, as the University of Texas and its opponent in tonight's game, Texas Christian University.) Will was majoring in business at Florida State. He was small but an excellent athlete; like my father, he had been a high school baseball player. He was blond like Cindy but had kinda Spanish-looking features like Paul, who was half Cuban. Will was quiet and could come across as sullen, unless you took him for who he was and got to know him. I had spent a lot of time with Will in 2004, the year he turned fourteen and I was in and out of Miami en route to and from Haiti. I taught him to play tennis, and he became very good at it very quickly. Leveraging our friendship and my uncle-like status to encourage him to read, I gave him a copy of the tennis player James Blake's inspiring autobiography, *Breaking Back*. Next time I was back from Haiti, I asked how he had liked it. "I don't read books," he explained apologetically. Notwithstanding that, I had grown very fond of Will.

Award-winning country music star Jack Ingram sang a good rendition of the national anthem, accompanying himself on acoustic guitar. "I like Jack," said Kelly. "He's good red-dirt music." Then there was lotsa pregame razzmatazz: a singalong of "Deep in the Heart of Texas," a giant Lone Star flag unfolded dramatically over half the field, dueling UT and TCU marching bands. Kelly was sitting on my left. "The TCU girls are dancing with a lot more vim and vigor than the Texas girls," I observed.

"Maybe this isn't their song," he guessed. "Maybe this is TCU's song."

"Singing 'The Eyes of Texas' *after* the national anthem?!" exclaimed Paul on my right. "What's that all about?" He was ribbing me about my pet peeve: how in Texas, the Lone Star flag is always flown not discernibly lower than the Stars and Stripes and is often also the same size. Other states don't get to do that, and I don't think that's okay.

The big video screen behind the far end zone declared:

"Texas is a state of mind. Texas is an obsession.
Above all, Texas is a nation in every sense of the word."
– John Steinbeck

The imprimatur of a Nobel laureate seemed to suggest that we were supposed to read the passage as some great gem of literary wisdom, rather than as a cheap, pandering throwaway line and a sop to the insufferable *amour propre* of his wife's home state. Paul and I speculated that it must be from *Travels with Charley*, and I confirmed that later when I reread the book.

The UT team knelt in unison in the far corner of the near end zone.

"You see what they're doin'?" said Kelly.

"They're praying," I said.

"Yep."

TCU won the toss and elected to kick off. Texas drove confidently down the field, until TCU intercepted a pass at the six-yard line, then TCU's quarterback completed a 35-yard pass. TCU scored a touchdown on that first drive, after overcoming two fourth downs and a fifteen-yard penalty. Then they kicked off again, and Texas made an impressive 41-yard return. Some guy behind me said, "If he'd a got past that guy, he'd a been gone." In the second quarter Texas blocked a TCU field goal attempt but couldn't get much done when they had the ball. "Ash is really off," said Paul in a tone of concern. Ash was the Texas quarterback. Ash drove the team down the field, but then near the goal line he threw an interception. "They didn't see the safety comin' in," said Paul. "That was just a bad read."

Our area of the upper deck was dominated by purple-clad TCU fans chanting, "*T-C-U Frogs!*" Many of them must have driven the three hours from Fort Worth to be here. At one point between plays the screen showed a longhorn steer standing and munching hay in a pen near the far end zone. The steer was the UT mascot, Bevo. "Tonight marks the 96th anniversary of Bevo's first appearance at a UT football game!" the announcer announced. "As you can see, he's enjoying a special Thanksgiving and birthday hay bale." The crowd cheered.

The second quarter continued in ho-hum fashion. "Aw, geez, *stoopid!*" cried Paul. "Texas is just self-destructing. So, did your dad like TCU?" TCU was my dad's alma mater.

"Yeah, he did," I said.

"He just didn't like Texas." In this case Paul meant not the university, but the whole state. Paul had spent a lot of time smoking cigars and talking politics and religion with my dad, and knew him well.

"Yeah, that's right," I confirmed.

"*Rah, rah, TCU!*" cried our section throughout halftime. "*Rah, rah, TCU!*"

"You deserve a special mention on the thank-you page of my book for setting this up," I told Paul.

"Wow," he said. "That would be nice. But if the Horns lose, I don't want any thank-you. I don't want to be blamed for them losing."

The UT marching band played songs by The Who for its halftime show: "Who Are You?," "Pinball Wizard," then a medley of "I Can See for Miles" and "Won't Get Fooled Again." Then the big screen ran a tribute to Professor Daniel S. Hammermesh for the "Excellence in Academics" award he had apparently just been given by "the Germany-based Alexander von Humboldt Foundation." Professor Hammermesh was the Sue Killam Professor in the Foundations of Economics at UT and author of *Labor Demand, The Economics of Work and Pay,* and (according to his web page) "a wide array of articles in labor economics in the leading general and specialized economic journals." He was bald and elderly and wore a beard and spectacles.

"I wonder if he's a football fan," I wondered.

"I don't know," said Paul. "But all that sounded really boring. So I hope for his sake he is."

The crowd showed more interest in voting on the play of the game. "What would you say is the play of the game?" I asked my relatives.

"Well, to me the play of the game is that crazy fumble," said Paul.

"Yep," said Kelly.

"'Cause it should still be a 7-3 game. To come back from eleven points down, when your offense is not exactly in top form, is a tall order."

Texas kicked off to start the second half, and TCU's guy ran it back sixty yards.

"Everybody thought he was gonna take a touchback," said Paul. "They shoulda stopped him at the ten-yard line. I mean, it was a nice runback, but that was pathetic."

But then Texas intercepted a pass, and Paul and Will exchanged high fives. "All right! Finally somethin'," said Paul.

Ash had been replaced by UT's second-string quarterback but was now back in the game. "Would you have kept the other guy in to start the second half?" I asked.

"Yeah," said Kelly. "But it really dudn't matter, because they both sucked. Just like the Cowboys!"

At the end of the third quarter, the cheerleaders did a perky routine accompanied by the band playing "The Yellow Rose of Texas" in double time. TCU scored another field goal, and our section erupted in a lusty cheer:

T! C! U!
T! C! U!
We're gonna beat the hell outta you!
And you! And you! And you and you and you!

Texas failed to convert a fourth down. Then, with one minute twenty seconds left in the game, UT backup quarterback Case McCoy threw an interception, and it was over. Final score TCU 20, Texas 13.

It was fun, particularly since I really didn't care who won. But the thing about football was that you could have this kind of ending, where everybody just stands around for the last minute or two. My father had once actually timed a sample football game and baseball game, to prove that there's more down time in football.[4]

I don't feel like writing much more about my family, except to say that we had a great time and that Carolyn, with help from Cindy and Jenny, put on a fantastic Thanksgiving dinner on Friday. Will left early to attend his last home football game as an undergrad at Florida State. Cigars were smoked and pictures were taken. "Oh, how cute our boys are!" Cindy gushed when Paul and Kelly and I posed for Carolyn. Paul brought cognac, as he could always be counted on to do.

I did lean on two of my loved ones for purposes of this book. I respected my cousin-in-law Carolyn's intelligence and thoughtfulness, and I wanted to know why she had voted for Romney.

"For me it was all about the economy and finance," she said. "I didn't look at it as a Republican or a Democrat. I just looked at it from who might could be—not who *would* be, but who *might could* be—the peacemaker in D.C. For me it's real scary, where we are as a country with debt. My parents were very frugal, and hardworking, and I can recall so many times, 'We can't afford that, we can't afford that.' And that's so ingrained. And I've just known so many people who on a personal level have excessive debt, either consumer debt where they just run up their credit cards, or they buy houses they can't afford. I think their addiction is consumerism. I personally know several people whose way out is to declare bankruptcy. And I get it as to how the banks made that happen and all, but it's easy to blame the banks. At the end of the day for me, personally, it's about individual accountability." Then she asked me: "Do you see that in our society?"

"Yeah, I do," I said.

"Every dollar we don't spend now is kind of an opportunity-cost analysis."

"Nothing else was as important to you as the fiscal stuff?"

"No. And so much of what you read when you're trying to get to know the candidates is just spin. But I believed what I heard or read

---

4   *Seattle Times* columnist Larry Stone replicated my father's experiment and confirmed his findings in a blog entry, "Let's tell it like it is: MLB baseball has more action than NFL football," The Hot Stone League, *Seattle Times*, December 2, 2011. "I spend many an enjoyable Sunday perched on the couch watching football," concluded Stone. "But for excitement and action, give me a baseball game any day."

about how he was able to find consensus as a governor. And I think that's the most important thing that we need, to get past the gridlock."

"Several people I met in Massachusetts told me that they tend to elect Republican governors, as a way to keep the Democrats in check," I told her.

"And that's the beauty of our system, at least until now," said Carolyn.

"So now that Obama has won, what do you hope for?"

"I'm hoping for some movement by all these rigid Tea Party Republicans, and Boehner's going to have to be a real leader. And I think if they can show some movement away from this stupid decision about no tax increase, if they accept that that's not going to be a workable solution and that they have to compromise, then I'm hopeful that the folks on the other side will move off of their positions. So it's going to be painful for all of us. It's like going on a diet, financially speaking."

"I'm not an economist ..." I said.

"And I'm not either. An economist understands it from a scientific point of view. I just see the numbers."

"... but Paul Krugman claims that the budget or economy of a country is not equivalent to the budget of a household."

"And I understand that. But I don't see many indications that some of the stimulus spending worked very well for us, in terms of the creation of jobs."

"So for you this election really was all about the economy."

"Mm-hmm."

"And you had more confidence in Romney than in Obama."

"Yes."

"Because of the economic policies, or because of the ability to conciliate?"

"Both," she said. "To be quite honest, I'm still figuring out exactly what I believe. I guess my thoughts are evolving. But I guess I'm somewhat old-fashioned in the sense of the place for government and the place for my church. We do year-round food pantry, but for Thanksgiving we like to find a family that's really in need and kind of do a cornucopia for them. And in our rural area it's hard to find a family that needs that, because there are so many government programs. And that's good, I guess, but it's surprising to me."

"Surprising?"

"I guess it's surprising to me that government programs are so far-reaching that there's not some unmet need. And I work for a company that needs to hire people. And people might want a job, but they may not want to do work. And I think the government's made it easier to accept government programs, rather than to make it on your own. I do believe that there's a place for all those programs. I just think we need to reevaluate, I don't know if it's the eligibility, or the length of time. But it's more than just a safety net for a lot of people. It's their way of life. And I don't know that that was the original intent."

"As a Texan, how do you feel about Bush?"

"George? Or Jeb? Or Jeb's son?"

"All of them."

"People don't objectively evaluate the Bushes in Texas. My biggest problem with George W. is the mess he got us into with all the wars. I think he created a big part of the financial problems that we're facing. And I'm a pacifist at heart, and I don't know what situations there could be where war would be the right solution."

"Are you confident that a different Republican president would not be as war-mongering as Bush was?"

"I didn't have that concern with Romney, but I did have that concern with McCain."

I thanked Carolyn and told her she was a good sport.

"I'm a little bit intimidated by the prospect of being interviewed," she confessed. "But I am intent on helping your reader to understand that there might be some people that might have thought that Romney had the better solution. What do you think about this? What percentage of people like me, just the average Jane Doe, actually communicate their opinions to their congressman? Do you think people do that anymore? I truly don't believe that necessarily something's right and something else is wrong. For you to be right, I have to be wrong? I don't like that."

And Katy, Paul and Cindy's daughter, was a freshman at New York University and had endured Hurricane Sandy and its aftermath. I had missed Sandy by a week, so I was eager to hear from somebody who had been there.

"We lost power for a week," she said, riding with me and Jenny in my car on the long drive through the dark countryside to hear a couple of country bands. "And we lost hot water for about five days. For the first day, before we lost power, we made a pillow fort. But then after we lost power, people felt like being happy."

"What was that like?"

"Everyone was really tense and grouchy. You were stuck with the same people for a week. There was nothing to do. My roommate ran to Times Square, to get out and do something. I ended up going to New Jersey for the weekend with some family friends, just to get out and have a home-cooked meal. I'm not a huge fan of Jersey, but that was nice."

"I bet it was nice then," I said.

"Oh yeah. They made salmon, and I was like, 'I love you guys.' On Wednesday night, which was like the night of the storm, my friends and I went out and walked to Washington Square Park. Which my parents didn't know about, because they told me not to do anything stupid. At times the gusts of wind were pretty heavy, so you had to like stand your ground. But mostly it was like a drizzle. But Washington Square Park was decimated, though. There were branches everywhere, and leaves, and trees knocked down. And knocked-over garbage cans. They cancelled classes for that week."

"So what did you do for that week?"

"Mostly found ways to stay busy. As the week progressed, the number of people on my floor got smaller and smaller. People left to go to hotels and their families' homes."

On election night, Katy and some friends had walked to Times Square.

"It was awesome," she said. "I don't know much about politics. It's not on my list of things I find super-interesting. But it was really intense seeing Florida as such a swing state. There was one point I think where they were separated by like four hundred votes. I was like, 'Oh my God, don't let Florida go to Romney!'"

"Were you afraid it would?"

"Yeah. So we were just planning on walking to the Empire

State Building, because they had it lit up with the result from both parties. And then we got to the Empire State Building and we thought, 'Well, we're already here. We might as well keep going.' At least that's what the guys I was with thought. I wasn't there for that thought process. I was like, 'Where are we going?' And they were like, 'Times Square,' and I was like, 'Cool.' I actually found out the result of the election as we were approaching Times Square. My friend D.J., who I guess was getting tweets or texts on his phone, said, 'Obama's been re-elected.' And it was, I guess, just so average. I was expecting to hear an uproar. Because that was how it had been in 2008. So when we finally got to Times Square, we ended up running to where the crowd was, because we didn't want to miss the moment of celebration. And we ended up standing there for like ten minutes after the news had come out, and nothing was happening. And then eventually I guess everyone realized that he had won, and there was this moment where everything changed. There was this group that had music, and they were dancing. And then everyone else joined in and started dancing too. People were chanting, 'Yes we can!' and 'Four more years!' Someone starting singing 'God Bless America.' And at first it was kind of separate, different groups, but then it sort of congregated, and we found ourselves right in the middle of it. People were kind of shoving past us with cameras, in order to take pictures of the dancing. There were so many cameras. There was an overhead camera. I was trying my best to avoid being on camera."

"How come?"

"Well, in case I make a stupid face or something, and it ends up on CNN, that would be unfortunate. So this guy came up to me, and he said, 'Hi, I'm from a Japanese news station. Can I interview you?' And I was like, 'Sure!' He just asked how I felt about it. And I said that I was happy."

"Why did you support Obama?"

"I can't give any good, politically sound reasons. But I think as much as people try to tear him down, I think he has been a good president. And I think things have gotten better in the last four years. And I think now that he doesn't have to be reelected, hopefully he'll do even more."

"Do you remember the 2000 election?"

"Oh, no. I remember going to my friend's mom's house and they gave me a Kerry pin. That was that election, right?"

"No, that was 2004."

Katy was not only perky and pretty but a reader and very bright, plus a lot taller and more alert to the wider world than she had been in 2004, the year I spent a lot of time in Miami with her family. I remembered the evening we went out to dinner in Miami Lakes, and she was incredulous to learn that I had never heard of the tweenybop singing star Hilary Duff. I countered by asking if she had heard of, for example, Gerald Ford. When she said "Who's that?" Paul had stopped her on the sidewalk and delivered an impromptu fatherly lecturette about how she really needed to know who Gerald Ford was, because he had been President of the United States.

"Oh, yeah," she said now. "I remember hearing about Al Gore, but that was it. Anyway, we stayed for longer and just sang, and basked in the energy. Then we got cold, and it was twelve-thirty, and we were tired, so we went home. The next day I had my creative writing class. People were talking about their election night stories. And a girl told how she fell asleep on her friend's floor, and this guy woke her up and told her that Romney had won. And the whole room kept it up for like fifteen minutes. And then they told her, and she was like, 'I hate you all.'"

"Yeah, that's like waking up in an alternate universe," I said.

"And then I told about how we walked to Times Square, and everyone was like, 'Wow, that's great!'"

＊

Somewhere in Texas there's a point where the South ends and the West begins. I think it's somewhere between Austin and Amarillo. I might have driven past it in the dark. Maybe there's a plaque marking it, like the plaques one sees all around Texas.

At the end of the Thanksgiving weekend, on Sunday, November 25, I dropped Jenny at the airport then swung back around to head north. I got off the freeway as soon as I could and picked my way north and west on two-lane highways, what in Texas are called farm to market roads. It was what I had been craving and seeking, after weeks of

maxing out on human contact: to be entirely alone, somewhere in the
middle of America. It was sad but sweet, a balm, high lonesome.

This part of Texas was little towns strung along the highways at
intervals of many miles, with a whole lot of farmland in between. They
had all seen better days, and it seemed an open question, in such dry
country, whether such towns should have been here in the first place.
In one, somewhere along U.S. Highway 183, as I slowed approaching
the downtown traffic light, I saw a sign in removable letters bearing the
latest civic information:

PRAY FOR RAIN
26 JH CROSS PLAINS T6
27 V GUSTINE T5
NEIGHBORHOOD
WATCH MAY UMC 6:30

By 7 p.m. I was in Hamlin, which had a Sonic drive-in, a Subway—
both were in many towns where other chains never ventured—the de-
funct-looking storefront office of *The Hamlin Herald*, and a motor inn

whose name I didn't catch,
though I did notice the red
neon VACANCY sign. If
it wasn't exactly inviting, at
least it was there, by the side
of the road. I thought about
stopping. I wanted to stop. I
needed to rest. I even nursed
a notion that I might stay
two or three nights in such a
town, for no particular reason but just to get to know it for itself. It
wasn't a fantasy; it was something I could have done. Here I was. Maybe
I should have done it. There are a lot of things I should have done.

By 8 p.m. Hamlin was far behind me, and I still had a long road
ahead. The town of Spur had the Spur Motel and a Dairy Queen that
was open. I have a nostalgic fondness for Dairy Queens, ever since the
summer of 1987, when near-daily free Blizzards were a fringe benefit of my job driving a school bus pulling a trailer full of canoes into

the Boundary Waters of northern Minnesota from a boys' camp near Superior, Wisconsin. But my digestive system could no longer handle a Blizzard. And I was putting on weight, what with all the hours behind the wheel and convenience-store Dr. Peppers and bags of chips. I hit the 289 loop around Lubbock from the east after driving quite a few miles in the dark through little places with names like Acuff and Roosevelt, keeping a close and anxious eye on my gas gauge, on a farm to market road that had me wondering whether I might be headed into New Mexico. I found a gas station, then swung around the bright lights of Lubbock and kept on, due north towards Amarillo: addicted to forward movement. I was glad enough to be alone and in cell phone silence, but I was also deeply fatigued, and not just from this particular long day of driving. I missed my wife, again. I missed my parents and brother. I missed the warm and friendly cousins I had just left behind. I missed my life in Seattle. For that matter, I missed a great many friends and acquaintances and homes away from home, all around America and the world.

Knowing so many people in so many far-flung places was a treasure one acquired by traveling as much as I had done. But, like any treasure, it had a cost. My world had expanded greatly, and by the same token it had become attenuated. No matter who I was with, I felt the pang of someone else's absence. No matter where I was, I missed home. I had set out to become a certain kind of writer and person, and that's pretty much who I had become, but not without regrets.

One of my role models was a British foreign correspondent and travel writer named Gavin Young. Young was still coming through Bangkok, and writing books at a hotel in Chiang Mai, in 1997 when I interviewed him for *The Nation*, the better of Bangkok's two English-language dailies. He was tall and stout but seemed surprisingly frail when I shook his hand in the lobby of the Dusit Thani hotel. In the piece I published I wrote of finding new poignancy in one of Young's own favorite passages from Joseph Conrad, the one in *Youth* about "the triumphant conviction of strength, the heat of life in the handful of dust, the glow in the heart that with every year grows dim, grows cold, grows small, and expires, too soon, too soon—before life itself." One thing Young and I agreed on was that there was never any greater writer or traveler than Conrad. And, like both him and me, Conrad had left home. "Physically it's getting a bit late," Young acknowledged when I quoted that passage to him. I flattered him subtly by suggesting that he had something else in common with our mutual hero: he had had two distinct careers: as a foreign correspondent for *The Observer* and then, starting in his forties, a new career writing fine and fond travel books with titles like *Slow Boats to China* and *Slow Boats Home*.

"If you're a war correspondent as I was, you go to war after war after war," he told me. "In the end you get fed up with seeing the agony: refugees, killing, fear everywhere about you. It's a very good thing to be traveling with ships, without any worries about refugees or wartime or anything."

I fancied myself already grizzled then, or at least seasoned. I was thirty-one years old. By contrast Gavin Young, sixty-nine when I met him, really had seen it all. But he had asked for it. Growing up in Cornwall, he had felt the call of the sea. As a young man in Arab lands, he had known Ian Fleming and the legendary traveler Wilfred Thesiger. He had been friendly with Graham Greene. In his book *In Search of Conrad*, he had written that Conrad taught him that "there really is no question of choice when a romantically inclined young man is faced with adventure and life on one hand and a battened-down existence on the other."

"Is there as much adventure and life to be had today as there was in Conrad's day, or your own?" I asked him. It wasn't just an interview question; I needed to hear his answer.

"It was much easier to get an adventurous job when I was younger," he said. "It's very difficult to become a journalist now, I think."

"Do young people read Conrad anymore?"

"Well, I hope so. You do, don't you?"

"I'm not so young anymore."

"You're younger than me."

I see now that I was young then, after all. Now is when I'm not so young anymore. For me there truly had been no question of choice, yet I fear I can't evade responsibility for the fallout. Do we choose to be born? Do we choose to journey through this world? The most distinct impression Young's personality left on me, reinforced by things

I learned later about his personal life and arrangements, was of deep-seated loneliness. He had friends, colleagues, liaisons literally all over the world. He was gregarious. I introduced him to an Indian couple I knew in Bangkok, and the next Christmas he stayed with them in Calcutta. He had many, many friends but, I think, very few intimates. He had no home.

From Amarillo the next morning I drove north, north, north, relentlessly due north on U.S. 287. The Texas and Oklahoma panhandles were a bleak region, at a bleak time of year. Tumbleweed tumbled across the highway in front of me. A billboard promoted the town of Dalhart with the slogan, complete with quote marks,

"Closer to Your Destination"

I could have jigged northwest on U.S. 87 through Dalhart, into the northeast corner of New Mexico, and from there up into Colorado on I-25. That would have been the shorter route on this second long solo driving day in a row, but it seemed inelegant, because I would be heading down into New Mexico later from Colorado Springs. And I was intrigued by the flat nothingness of eastern Colorado. And I wanted this solitude for as long as I could have it; soon enough I would be among people again. For one thing, my mother had lots of people lined up for me to meet in Colorado Springs, where I would be staying nearly a week.

The Springs had burgeoned in the quarter-century my folks had lived there, and not in a good way. It was one of the Western places that suffered what Coloradans call "californication," the overflow of Americans from wherever who had heeded the siren call of California, reached that promised land, but then fled the smog and property taxes and each other to end up in Seattle or Colorado Springs. The Springs had grown on me over the years, but it also had just plain grown. That sort of thing happened to a lot of places. I thought of something my father had said in a letter back in the nineties, when I was still gallivanting around Asia and he had gone to Dallas to bury my grandmother: "I'm sure glad I don't live in Dallas. It seems to be just people and buildings, neither of which are very interesting."

But Colorado Springs and all its people and buildings were still many miles ahead of me today. In Cactus, Texas, the Cactus City Hall was a single-story aluminum-sided shed, very temporary-looking, with the fire department tacked onto one side. On the other side of the road, the Cactus Elementary School was built of plain cinderblock. I guessed that it was a school because I saw the backstop for a ball field, then confirmed it when I saw the name on a wall in small letters. Cactus looked like the haphazard rudiments or vestiges of a town, more aluminum structures and some older small houses, many with windows boarded up. Further north in Stratford I stopped for gas and went inside to pay, because I wanted to use the restroom and buy a Dr. Pepper. As I signed my charge slip the young man behind the counter said, to no one in particular, "Know why I don't like this wind? Cuz I got a big gap in mah door, and mah landlord won't fix it, and it blows dust inside, all over mah house."

"Is it more windy today than usual?" I asked him.

"No sir. This is common."

It was sunny, but it was cold. I got back in my car. The Dalhart billboard prompted maudlin musings about where exactly my destination was, anyway. I drove north and further north. The road crossed a  series of rivers, most of them completely dry. The Canadian. The Beaver. The Cimarron. The Arkansas—pronounced, as anyone from this part of the country knows, with the final s and with the stress on the second syllable. These were the rivers that Augustus McCrae and Woodrow Call and Pea Eye and Deets and Newt and Lorena the pretty young whore who wanted Gus to take her to San Francisco, and the varmint Jake Spoon, and Po Campo the cook, and Dish Boggett and Needle Nelson and the other hands had crossed with the herd they drove north from Lonesome Dove way down in South Texas all the way to Montana, in the last moment before the frontier closed. Jenny and I had read the book aloud to each other as we drove east across Montana, Wyoming, and South Dakota, a long time ago now.

I drove north some more, and then more, and confirmed that eastern Colorado looks a whole lot like western Oklahoma. I went through a couple more towns. Then, about ten miles northwest of Kit Carson on highways 287 and 40, I passed a sedan of a certain type and glimpsed the telltale official logo on its side. I glanced down at my speedometer and saw the number 77. Sure enough, when I looked back up at my rearview mirror, I saw his red taillights come on. Then he turned around, then his cherries began flashing. I pulled over and rolled down my window.

"Good evening, sir," said the young man in uniform, just like on a TV show or something. "I'm Officer Suchandsuch with the Blahbitty-blah. How you doin'?"

"Fine," I said.

"Where are you headed?"

"Colorado Springs."

"For business or pleasure?"

I wondered how much of my very long story he needed to know. "A bit of both," I said. "My parents live in Colorado Springs, but I'm on a long trip around the country."

"The reason I stopped you is your speed," he said. "The posted speed limit here is sixty-five. I clocked you goin' seventy-six. May I see your license, registration, and proof of insurance?"

I handed over my license and insurance card and fished in the glove box. "It's a rental," I told him.

"If I could see the rental agreement then please," he said.

He was correct and polite, even pleasant. He was the first human company I had had since the gas station back in Stratford, Texas. He went back to his car and took a while, which I figured meant I was getting a ticket.

While he was doing whatever he was doing back in his car, I remembered my last ticket, in September 2009 heading east with my friends Todd Shea and Lanny Cordola somewhere in central California to pick up I-5 south, because we had woken up that morning in Santa Clara and were running late for a thing that afternoon in Orange County. It was one of those two-lane highways through the middle of nowhere where, morally, there's no damn good reason anyone should ever have to go less than eighty but, legally, the speed limit is fifty-five. I had been busted for something like twenty-two over, my ticket was for more than three hundred dollars, and I had to take a dumb online class to keep my insurance from going up. Todd was a big, loud dude, a personality who took up a lot of space both figurative and literal while saving lives in earthquake- and flood-affected areas of Pakistan. Lanny was a longhaired Angeleno, a rocker who hung out with members of Guns 'n' Roses and had guest-starred on two episodes of *Full House* because he was pals with John Stamos. Lanny and Todd had made a music video with the Pakistani singer Atif Aslam in the embattled Swat Valley, to promote peace. Both were lovely souls and great friends of mine, and notwithstanding the ticket and the fact that we did arrive late in Mission Viejo anyway, it was a happy memory.

I had driven more than 15,000 miles from Seattle without a ticket. I was musing about how I was going to pay this one, and whether I could write it off as a legit business expense, when the cop returned to my side window.

"Here's a card with my name and number on it, in case you have any questions about this traffic stop," he said. "Just ask that you watch your speed."[5]

"Thank you *very much*," I said sincerely.

"You bet," he said as he turned to walk back to his car.

I pulled away from the shoulder and set my cruise control to exactly 65 miles per hour. A few miles later I turned west onto state highway 94 and saw a sign:

Colorado Springs 92
No services next 70 miles

The two-lane highway was completely unlighted, and I was driving into the sunset. It was one of those all too infrequent moments when one's quotidian awareness is offered a direct confrontation with the

---

5   The card identified him as Trooper C.L. Warren of the Colorado State Patrol, employee number 9228.

motions of the heavenly spheres, when the sun and the earth display their relation to each other against a landscape one cannot fail to notice and appreciate, when all the activity and effort that life entails seem to dissolve into so much sound and fury in the irrelevant background against the mere unmediated fact of existing on a planet. This was not something one could easily put into words, or really wanted to. I had felt it faintly many mornings long ago, as my trans-bay commuter bus from Berkeley emerged from the island tunnel and descended into San Francisco. Watching the sun sink into the Gulf of Mexico from a hotel balcony in Naples, Florida. Riding shotgun in a U-Haul, four long days from Seattle to Anchorage, deeper into autumn each day, then through a blizzard in the Yukon. On the short evening flight north from Colorado Springs to Denver to connect to wherever I was headed next, following the Front Range with my eye as the sun fell behind it and the golden light deepened and the shadows lengthened over the plains to the east. Gaping down at the enormous summit of Nanga Parbat on the flight from Islamabad to Skardu. Lovingly tracing the coastline of Haiti, at the end of the flight from Miami. To know the planet in such ways at such moments is grace, but what does it mean? But is that even a question worth asking?

My father had made a good career and a very rich life out of an unceasing and firmly committed search for meaning. He would tell you that the search, however long or thorough, is necessarily inconclusive, but he had opted for it and drew his vocabulary from ancient and venerable traditions. But as implicitly as I admired and respected him, I had leaned against that option. Partly this had been in reaction to the ways Christianity had been co-opted and abused politically in America during my lifetime. But I also just didn't buy the bit about one particular guy dying on a cross, thereby redeeming the rest of us. That, or at least the things people made of that, seemed like a self-inflicted distraction. Surely more to the point was to live well in this world, while we're here. My father might say that it isn't an either/or, that the metaphors and paradoxes are worth exploring. Fine. But I had crafted my adult purpose out of witnessing and narrating facts and events, and trying to leave meaning to take care of itself.

Asians always ask your religion, and in Asia I had developed a habit of saying that my religion is journalism. Where my father's religion and mine might meet was in something he had told me: "None of it means anything unless it agrees with experience." This to me was the nut graf. I tried to express it in the way I ended my introduction to *Sharing the Good News: Sermons through the Church Year at the Parish of Our Saviour*, my father's greatest hits collection compiled by his Colorado Springs parishioners on the occasion of his retirement. "The most profoundly spiritual experience I've ever had was also the most vividly physical," I wrote: "the sensation of being alive and aware on a celestial orb, as two other orbs passed each other before my eyes, at Angkor Wat in Cambodia in October 1995."

> Words are inevitably inadequate, but what I feel I learned from the solar eclipse I witnessed is the reality of the link between the concrete and the ineffable: everything is connected to everything else; the experience *is* the meaning, and vice versa.

> When I told my father this, he told me how deeply he had enjoyed several weeks he spent one summer sitting on the deck in the wee hours, watching Venus move across the big sky above the Great Plains that stretch from directly below my parents' house all the way to the Mississippi River. Same planet, same universe, same true experience, and I cherish the connection. On those mornings, in the very moment of his profoundly felt experience of himself as a minute but significant locus of the universe's self-awareness, my father would have been smoking a cigar and—whether consciously or not, it doesn't matter—composing his sermons.

✳

While I was driving due west those last seventy lonesome miles toward Colorado Springs and my parents' house, the sun had been sinking behind the mountains, and it now was completely dark. Reaching Ellicott just before six o'clock, I pulled over in a park to write some notes. And then, after savoring a complete lack of network coverage the whole long day from Amarillo, my cell phone rang. I picked it up. "Hi, Dad," I said.

"It's Mom, calling from Dad's phone."

"Hi, Mom."

"Where are you?"

"Ellicott, about twenty miles east."

"Then you'll be about forty-five minutes."

"I hope not," I said. "The sign said like twenty-two miles."

"Well, hurry up!"

"Is it bedtime or something?" My parents were early-to-bed people.

"No, it's not bedtime, but we want to put dinner in. We have a nice barbecue."

I was back in the world of other people and obligations. I hurried up, past Peterson Air Force Base on Highway 24, straight into downtown Colorado Springs, left around the equestrian statue of General Palmer, the city's founder, then past familiar car dealerships and motels on South Nevada, under I-25, past more motels and fast food. I had driven this particular strip many times over the years, but I had never before driven most of the way around America to get here. The neon headdress of the Indian chief at the Chief Motel flashed on and off on my right. Then I passed this part of town's landmark McDonald's, turned right going uphill just past Safeway, and I was home. Well, not exactly home, but close enough.

After six days here, my father would be driving with me as far as Los Angeles. He came out to the driveway now to help me carry things in. He looked inside my car. "Well, I can't go with you!" he exclaimed. "There's no space!"

CHAPTER 7

HITTING HOME

"They just fired the University of Colorado football coach," said my mom the next morning.

"Did he do something bad?" I was thinking of Jerry Sandusky at Penn State.

"Yeah!" my dad called from the kitchen. "He didn't win. That's the cardinal sin."

My parents were opposites in many ways. Dad liked to sit on his deck and read books while smoking a cigar and/or sipping whiskey. The nature of his work had forced him to be social, but he couldn't be forced to enjoy it. He was, as I once heard my mother observe, an introvert who taught himself to be an extravert. The decline and fall of the Episcopal Church had coincided more or less exactly with his career. The new prayer book, women priests, a gay bishop, right-wingers seceding to affiliate with Anglicans in Nigeria, all came during his time. Not all Episcopalians liked all these new changes, or each other. My dad sucked it up and toughed it out as a working rector until he could retire and say the hell with it all, as the factions fed off their vitriol toward each other and destroyed the church from within.

"I went to the Episcopal church in Greenville, South Carolina," I told him.

"They left," he said. His diocesan geography was slightly off target: Greenville was in the Diocese of Upper South Carolina, which had stayed in the church. It was the other half of South Carolina that had seceded. "It's just nuts! It's crazy. The Episcopal Church is falling apart. Her Highness and her minions are always goin' on about how they

300

want the Episcopal Church to be this big, inclusive tent, where every-body can belong—as long as they don't disagree with *them*."

Another thing Dad found hard to bear with good grace was Colorado's obsession with football. "It's like Jeff Wooddell," he said. Jeff was a tall folksy fellow with a mustache, a doctor, friend, and former parishioner. "This time of year he gets all wrapped up in the Broncos. I just cannot *imagine* driving to Denver to watch a *football* game." Then again, Dad had trouble imagining many good reasons to drive the tedious and congested ninety minutes or more to Denver, which he called "a dud of a city."

Mom, by contrast, was the Super Civic Lady of Colorado Springs, moreso than ever in retirement. She had been principal of two different grade schools, one of which, Antelope Trails Elementary, she actually founded in a new subdivision at the north end of town. She had been on the board of the public library for a decade, and president part of that time. She was a Rotarian. She taught graduate courses in elemen-tary education. She was on committees and boards, she was a museum docent, and more often than not she was off to Aspen or Santa Fe or Dollywood for some conference or seminar. When I was a kid she would bring home to Oconomowoc t-shirts from faraway places like St. Louis and Anaheim. These days she sent me fridge magnets. You really couldn't keep up with all the stuff she was involved in, so I didn't try. I just lived with the knowledge that, at any particular point in time, she was involved in something.

She had almost more meetings set up for me this week than I could handle, and she was urging me to attend today's City Council meet-ing, where the major issues voted on would be panhandling downtown and the controversial practice of hydraulic fracturing, or fracking, for oil and gas within city limits. She briefed me on the council members. One was a 33-year-old woman named Brandy Williams, who had in-troduced herself to Mom during her election campaign. "She had her little campaign name tag on, and she walked up to me and said, 'Mrs. Casey, you were my principal when I was in the fifth grade.' So we have a little hug whenever we see each other. She and Val Snyder were the two who took time, after they were elected, to come and learn about the needs of the Pioneers Museum." Mom was on the museum's board, of course. "Then there's a blonde. Lisa—it's a Polish name, or one of those countries up there. And she's pretty conservative."

Dad was sitting in his red leather chair doing a crossword puzzle. He pointed his pencil at Mom: "*She'll* tell you what's good and what's bad."

"How's your crossword puzzle?" I asked him.

"Pretty good. It's Tuesday, so it's still easy."

"Oh, is that the way they work?" said Mom. "They get harder?"

"Yeah. I don't like the *way* in which they get harder by Thursday and Friday. He gives you these clues that are cute."

✳

The City Council meeting opened with a long invocation by a woman who was some kind of Buddhist minister or priestess. "The light in this building is so radiant that it spills out into downtown Colorado Springs," she said. "And let this light expand to the south, all the way to Fort Carson. And to the west. All directions. We've made a full circle. And we ask that the work of the City Council meet the needs of all of the citizens of the great city of Colorado Springs. May all beings be free from all troubles of mind and body. May all beings be at peace. May all beings be free." This was followed by the Pledge of Allegiance, and the council got down to business. The room was jam-packed with members of the public who would have a lot to say several hours later about fracking and panhandling.

The council president, Scott Hente, started by inviting the public to comment on subjects not on the meeting agenda. "And let me tell you right now, folks," he added, "this is gonna be a long meeting, and I'm gonna hold everybody to three minutes."

The first citizen to stand at the mike in the aisle was Marie Rodriguez Diaz, who pleaded for "fair practices for rap artists."

"Could you be a little bit more specific?" asked council member Bernie Herpin.

"It's kind of a stereotyping situation," explained a rapper named Knox, taking over the mike. "Rap music is more than just music. It's become a culture. I myself am a military veteran. These are just your average everyday Americans who just happen to do this type of music."

"I'm still unclear on who's saying you can't do hip-hop music in Colorado Springs," said Herpin.

Next a woman advocated "meatless Mondays" as a way of combatting global warming. "Communities encourage their populations to not eat meat on Mondays," she said.

"I'm here to talk about marijuana," said David Matthew James, who owned a real estate company. "When tenants want to grow medicinal marijuana, where do I stand on that?" In the election just past, Colorado and Washington State had passed measures decriminalizing marijuana use.

"As you know," replied President Hente, "our current laws are in direct conflict with the federal laws. I think I can give you a very direct 'We don't know yet.' Every municipality in Colorado is going to be figuring this out."

After a break, the proposed ordinance to ban panhandling within a specified zone downtown was opened for discussion. "Again, I have to emphasize the fact that I'm strictly going to adhere to the three-minute limit," said Hente.

Steve Saint, executive director of the Pikes Peak Justice and Peace Commission, asked: "How do we bring our sense of compassion and justice into a solution framework, rather than keeping it in an argument framework? The main reason I oppose this ordinance is that it's not a solution; it's kind of a regulatory approach. There are a lot of people on the street who need our help, not our scorn."

Someone from the American Civil Liberties Union added, "Once you start talking about zones, there's really nothing to talk about, because it's really a non-starter when you're talking about civil liberties. The ACLU on the local and state level is totally committed to challenging this ordinance."

"This is totally unconstitutional," asserted a woman with long black hair. "It violates one's right to free speech. Out of sight, out of mind is not a solution." Business and political interests were pushing the ordinance and other changes downtown partly in hopes of attracting tourists. "That is not the reason I don't come downtown," said the woman. "I don't go downtown because I don't want to be on security cameras all the time. Nobody wants to go somewhere where we feel like they're in a correctional facility."

Mayor Steve Bach sat in front and a little to one side. He was tall, dark and handsome, and well coiffed in a Ted Baxter-like kind of way. "I'm told by our police chief that most panhandlers are not homeless, they're professionals," he said. "They're seeking tax-free dollars to feed a drug and alcohol habit."

Riffing on that claim, a man in a maroon "ARREST BUSH" t-shirt said, "Church can be a good thing or a bad thing just like any other drug, depending on how you use it. I'm sure that everyone in this room has used drugs at one time or another. Including church."

"Because the approach you've taken is precisely legal doesn't make it right," warned a thin man in a tan sweater.

"All I hear from this government is that smaller government is better," said the Rev. Roger Butts. "The only place where more government is better is in trampling the poor. And so I ask you: Where does it end? Where will the next zone be?"

"What we have today is pathetic, and it's shameful," said a white-haired man in support of the ordinance. "There's plenty of other cities around the United States, that I've been to, that you've been to. They don't tolerate it, and neither should we." And another man who identified himself as a business owner said: "It really is disruptive."

The ordinance banning panhandling in the downtown zone passed, eight to one.

Then the fracking debate began. The city attorney pointed out that the state was suing the city of Longmont for having banned fracking within its limits. "There's no easy solution or no easy way forward if this ordinance is not implemented," he warned.

One issue was water quality sampling. "I personally don't feel that it's frequent enough," said council member Brandy Williams.

"What's our ability to enforce?" asked council member Tim Leigh. "What happens if we find there's something wrong with the water?"

A citizen named Laurel Biedermann said, "You've been told over the past several months that the oil and gas industry can police itself. What you've not heard is the personal accounts of people who have actually been affected by these activities on their property. The council does not need to collaborate with the state and the oil and gas industry in this crime."

The woman with long black hair was back to say, "Last time I checked, hydraulic fracturing is not something that people who want to see a beautiful place are going to want to look at."

"By the way, in Wyoming, smog has exceeded Los Angeles," said another woman.

Council member Tim Leigh then astonished me by saying: "Everybody gets to speak, but it's the same thing over and over. And I hate to say it, but it's almost insulting. The repetition is killing us." The crowd had waited several hours for the opportunity to say anything at all.

"I'm still learning!" called someone from the back of the room.

Perhaps coincidentally, several pro-fracking testimonials came next. "Please do not let the fear-mongering strike a death knell for what could be an economic boon for us," said a man named Tom.

"The oil and gas industry is not our enemy, but it is an opportunity," said a blonde woman. "I feel pretty safe, because one of the things I've noticed is that they seem to improve their regulations on a routine basis. I would really like us to consider not rhetoric but a little bit of reality."

"As a retired Colorado Springs teacher, I appreciate any increase in revenues," said an older woman with a bun. "The increased staff and jobs would fill our schools. I not only look forward to the additional schools growth, but to the tourist growth which we'll see with the additional prosperity."

"You're gonna get jobs," said Chuck O'Riley, controller for a fracking company. "You have concerns, address 'em and move on."

"More oil and gas regulations mean more jobs," asserted a woman in a suit. "We need jobs. This will be a huge windfall to our city and our schools. Don't just fixate on the irrational arguments of drilling opponents."

But the man in the ARREST BUSH shirt asked: "How much water is there in Colorado Springs? Is there enough water to drink? Do we want to use more water for fracking?" And a woman named Elaine Doudna said, "As a student of history, I'm concerned with unintended consequences. There are five million gallons of water destroyed for every well. Well, that brings to mind the utility rates. What are the frackers going to be charged? Will the revenue go to the city? Will residential customers subsidize fracking? And why should I zeroscape? Why should I conserve?"

"I'm here today because I fear that you will listen to the vocal minority, and not do what the people really want," said a woman with short gray hair. "I don't want oil and gas to happen anywhere else, because I care about the earth. And by the way, I'm the woman with the cross, and no one will come between me and my Lord and Savior, Jesus Christ."

The fracking ordinance failed to pass, on a 4-4 vote with one member absent.

*

The next day my mother went with me for lunch with Kristy Milligan, at a coffee shop across the street from the venerable Poor Richard's Bookstore. Kristy was the director of a local group called the Citizens Project, and my mom had been talking her up to me. In a city run by people my mother considered bullies, she was always on the lookout for allies she could work with to nudge it in the other direction. Kristy was an attractive brown-haired woman in her thirties with a lively attitude and, I gathered as we talked, a fair amount of hard experience. I was of an age, now, where meeting people like Kristy was both encouraging and disconcerting: in this case someone a dozen years younger than myself who was running a widely admired civic organization, whereas I felt barely competent to run my own life.

"Twenty or thirty years ago, I guess close to thirty, this community wasn't as divided," Kristy said. "The history of Colorado Springs shows a very strong independent spirit. A lot of people doing great work that's meaningful for community building, and letting their neighbors live in ways that are useful to them, as long as they're not harmful." She told some of the history of the Citizens Project. "In the late eighties we decided to focus on nonprofits, and specifically faith-based nonprofits," she said. By "we" I think she meant the Citizens Project, though she had not been with the group way back then. And by "faith-based nonprofits" I gathered she meant in particular the locally prominent and nationally controversial group Focus on the Family.

Mom remembered that time well from her years as an elementary principal in Academy School District 20. "District 20 public information officer Larry Perkins was sent out to California," she said, "probably for the purpose of talking to them about the benefits of moving into District 20. And I sat there at Mountain View Elementary and watched the warehouses being built. They call it a campus, I think."

"And anecdotally," said Kristy, "District 20 is the school district that struggles the most with church-state separation issues. Jim Daly has

released a new book, called *ReFOCUS*." Daly was Focus on the Family's new president, and the book was part of his attempt to ease the group away from its obsessive opposition to abortion and gay marriage. "It seems to me that there's a shift of significant impact. And I expect that it will ultimately result in his dismissal. This *ReFOCUS* business might be too much too soon." The very public style of Christianity represented by such groups was anathema to Kristy, or at least foreign to her. "Life is a negotiation," she said. "You just figure out what's safe. And what's safe and true for me is that religion is an incredibly private matter. And I never disclose my personal affiliation. And that carries me through pretty well."

"Does anyone ever ask you to disclose it?"

"All the time! A lot of times when people ask me, it's because they're looking for a referral. I do have a sense of the local landscape and 'What is your particular brand of Christianity, and this is where you should go.' Even if it's not somewhere I would ever go. Are you two going to Dan Savage tonight?" The Seattle-based gay sex columnist.

"No, we're invited out to dinner, so we have to do that," said Mom.

"He's speaking at Colorado College. You might consider swinging by. There might even be picketers. I wonder if I should tell you my story."

"Please," I said.

"I was born here, I was raised here, I went to St. Mary's Catholic School, and then I went to Boulder for college. And I never thought I would come back. I was really embarrassed about being from Colorado Springs. When people asked where I was from, I would say, 'South of Denver.' And people would ask where I went to college and I would say Colorado, and they'd say, 'Oh, Colorado College?' I mean, the elitism of the East Coast is mind-boggling. But then I did something that someone who doesn't want to go back to where they came from should never do, and that is quit my job without having something else lined up. The Citizens Project represented something I didn't know existed. They represented a side of Colorado Springs that I wasn't embarrassed about. And I thought, 'I have to stay here.' It was in that moment that I changed my mind."

"Your growing-up time was in the context of the town already having turned right-wing," I said to Kristy.

"Yes. To which I was largely oblivious." She remembered seeing a Focus on the Family highway sign on I-25 with bullet holes in it. "I remember thinking, 'What is this Focus on the Family, and why would anyone want to shoot it?'"

"And that was when I opened Antelope Trails, and I was concerned about Focus on the Family and its impact," said my mother.

"I was really, really unaware," said Kristy, "in the way that young people can be really pissed off, but they can't attach it to a cause. I didn't have the context at all."

"When did you get the context?"

"I don't think I got it until college." One watershed event was a friend's suicide. "It was within weeks of the Columbine shooting."

"Do you know why he committed suicide?" my mother asked.

"I think he was hopeless," said Kristy. "We are raising a culture of kids who are hopeless and shiftless." But through it all, she had found both hope and purpose. "It's in those moments of courage and failure that we find out who we're going to be in the world."

"I remember writing in my parents' handbook, 'Do allow your kids to fail,'" said my mom. "'Don't rescue them.' I had to be that direct."

"I went to Catholic school because I was very, very naughty in public school," said Kristy.

"So was I!" my mom exclaimed. This must have been one reason she liked Kristy. A famous piece of family lore was how young Judy Rominger got kicked out of the choir at the huge and socially prestigious Church of the Incarnation in Dallas for singing "Goodnight Irene" instead of the assigned hymn.

"So did Catholic school fix you, or mess you up, or both?" I asked Kristy.

"It just felt inadequate to me," she said. "I had a lot of great teachers." One time she had had to do a "person report" as an assignment, and her teacher had encouraged her. "She said, 'Listen, you'd be foolish if you didn't pick Susan B. Anthony.' And that was before I was political."

"It's interesting how she saw something in you."

"I really appreciate the Citizens Project for its role in supporting youth," my mom said encouragingly.

"We have an annual Citizens Religious Freedom Institute," said Kristy. "It's Colorado Department of Education certified, so teachers can get contact hours. We do that on an annual basis. We get calls, we get emails, and we take everything seriously. Our most recent one is a third-grade teacher in District 38—so, just north of Focus on the Family. As part of a presentation about world religions, the teacher asked her students to self-identify their religion. And when the time came for the Christians, most kids raised their hands, and there was a loud kind of 'hoo-rah,' and it made one little girl, the only student who had raised her hand as an atheist, feel terrible. And she was bullied so mercilessly, and the administration did so little to stop it, that she withdrew from school. But another kid brought his Bible to school—totally legally permissible—and he was bullied mercilessly. And that's not okay either. A couple of years ago at Halloween, one of the kids dressed up as Hitler and went around verbally abusing all the students who were Jewish. Any time a school decides to hold its graduation in a church, we say, 'Hey! What's up with that?'"

"Could you talk a little bit about the policy that's developed at D-11?" asked my mother. "Because I think that's monumental." District 11 was the largest school district in Colorado Springs. The State of Colorado had passed an anti-bullying measure. All school districts were required to abide by it, but beyond that they weren't required to have their own defined policies. But District 11 had taken the initiative to write a very specific policy prohibiting bullying on the basis of sexual orientation, among other things.

"Any district that elected to codify in their own way an anti-bullying, anti-harassment policy was ahead of the curve and was making a statement about what the values of the school district were," Kristy explained. "This was a really enumerated anti-discrimination policy. And we thought this was going to be a huge fight. But it passed six to one. We were astonished when at the final reading it passed overwhelmingly. A lot of kids came forward and talked about their experiences. We had no reason to believe there would be such overwhelming support."

I asked what she thought accounted for the astonishing result.

"A couple of things," she said. "First of all, when you can humanize an issue and make it about safety and well-being, it makes it more compelling." But another interesting factor was that, unlike Denver and many other large cities, Colorado Springs had not one big school district but multiple districts that competed for enrollment and resources, and enrollment in District 11 was declining. "When you get into a position of scarcity, you're willing to start throwing things at the wall that seem like a good idea, and see what sticks," said Kristy.

In early July, a huge wildfire had burned for more than two weeks, threatening the city and in fact destroying 346 houses and a tourist ranch on the lower slopes of the Front Range, and making national news. It had come to be referred to as the Waldo Canyon fire. It was the most destructive fire in Colorado history, until an even bigger fire destroyed 511 houses a year later. It's hard to measure enormities and natural disasters against each other, especially since anymore they happen so often that they blunt our capacity to be shocked. But when one of them directly threatens people you love, it hits home.

"I think this was a long time coming for our community," said Kristy.

"Do you have a story?"

"I have a funny story. The fire started, and I saw it right away, and it was a really, really upsetting experience. I was driving on Highway 24, and I said, 'That hillside is on fire. And it must be really big, because I can see it.'" She had had her hair in a pony tail, and she could feel in it some sort of lump. "I reached in and I felt it, and it was a beetle."

"And the smoke and the ash," said my mom. "It was absolutely awful."

"It was," agreed Kristy. "And it represented a moment of solidarity for our community. There was like this moment. And I feel like some of it's residually still there. I think we lost some of it during the election."

"It was a wake-up call for us," said Mom.

Kristy had mentioned the election, so I asked her about it. "One of the things that was interesting to me coming into this election was the ability of people to talk their way out of the fact that what they're doing is inherently racist," she said. "People like to test things in Colorado. They like to float ideas. And it's so easy to amend the state constitution, that you're always dealing with something ridiculous. Here locally there were some surprises." One was a pro-law enforcement, anti-gun control thing called Save Our Sheriff. "I don't think that we as a community like to fund things that aren't sexy. But I think Waldo helped make it sexy. I totally voted against it." A big thing in Colorado was the Taxpayer Bill of Rights, or TABOR, which made it difficult to raise tax revenue. "Someone doing a history of Colorado, and specifically of Colorado Springs, would find the connections between TABOR and the roots of conservative Christian ideology."

"I'm proud that both Colorado and Wisconsin went for Obama," I said. "I was worried."

"I think we were all worried, and I think that's part of the story."

After lunch, Mom drove me up to the mountainside neighborhoods where the fire had destroyed whole subdivisions.

"Oh my God, it was scary," she said. "I think I told you that I had a half-dozen friends who lost their homes. And I think you'll see, when we go up there, that rebuilding has begun. But there are some real hassles that people are having with insurance companies."

On the way up Garden of the Gods Road, we passed a strip mall. "There's Dickey's Barbecue, that just came here," she said.

"From Dallas." Dickey's was a famous chain there.

"I went to school with Elizabeth Dickey. I told the owner when I went by to get some barbecue." She turned right on Flying W Ranch Road. "A lot of the ransacking was very distressing."

311

"There was looting?"

"I don't remember details. One of the Kornyenkos had her house looted when they were evacuated. Now, this complex right here was where my friend Sally Creely lived. She's a good friend. She's a sorority sister."

"From Dallas?"

"No, from here. It was Harbor Pines Point. I think Sally said seven units, so that would make fourteen households. And I think one of my Rotary colleagues had the only house standing here. And the issues with a house that's standing is the incredible smoke damage. And all of the fourteen residents had to vote to rebuild or not to rebuild, and it had to be a majority, and they voted to rebuild." Further on, she said: "Oh, that's where my friend Jan Weiland lives, on Tamora Way. And she was evacuated but didn't lose her home."

"So this is roughly Garden of the Gods-type area," I said. Garden of the Gods is an area of beautiful red rock formations on the slopes above Colorado Springs.

"Yeah. Mountain Shadows is what it's called. You see, they put sandbags, not to block the water but to divert it. That's a serious issue, the flooding."

"Is the flooding connected to the fire?"

"Yes, because of the erosion. Boy, the one thing that was so devastating was the very quick change of the wind. That's why there were houses that were standing in neighborhoods, without any other houses around. That was one huge challenge for the firefighters. I think I told you one of my friends lost two houses."

"No, you didn't."

"Her in-laws lived next door, and they died, so she was renting the house. And she's rebuilding both houses."

I got out of the car to take pictures of a cul de sac where at least five houses had burned down completely. "Ethan, there's someone coming, and they don't like people to take pictures," Mom said through the car window. I got back in. "Boy, I recognize the names of the streets, from all the coverage," she said. "Builders are making a bundle. Oh, the stories of what people took with them when they evacuated. Very interesting. Photograph albums, jewelry. I've got another sorority sister who listed everything she took. There was a strip mall somewhere in there, where they set up a center for people who had lost their homes and been evacuated. They tried to bring the community together in a lot of different ways. Because I think a lot of the neighborhoods were very close-knit, and a lot of people are trying to get that back."

"What was your experience like during the fires?"

"Well, we were just glued to the TV and radio and got all the news, and evacuations, and individual stories of people. But it was smoky, and ash in the air, and dirty."

A news item came on the car radio about the national Republican activist Grover Norquist. "Who is this Grover Norquist?" said Mom. (It wasn't a question, but: "Who *is* this Grover Norquist?")

"Yeah, who died and made him boss?" I agreed.

"I got a petition the other day from some Democrats, saying not to pay attention to him anymore. Norquist sounds like Doug Bruce."

"Yeah, on a bigger scale."

"There was an article about him this morning. Where did he come from?"

"Doug Bruce is the guy who does initiatives and stuff?" In Washington State we had our own Doug Bruce, named Tim Eyman.

"Yeah. He thinks government is evil." TABOR, the Taxpayer Bill of Rights, was one of Doug Bruce's things. "It's played havoc with public funding, schools, all public spending," said Mom. "Look it up, and you can get a clearer picture of the constraints he's built in. He's a *nasty* man, I'll tell you that. He used to show up at Library Board meetings."

"When you were president?"

"Yeah. He's just looking for evidence that money's being misspent. And he got it passed because of the conservatives, the Republicans who don't want government services—until they need them."

On the way back south toward home she talked about the Republican mayor, Steve Bach, whom I had seen at the City Council meeting. Bach had become mayor in 2010 by defeating Richard Skorman, the widely admired owner of Poor Richard's Bookstore.

"The first debate that he and Richard Skorman had was in the Broadmoor," said Mom. "And you could see right away that he was right at home in the Broadmoor. All the hand-shaking of the white and rich people." The Broadmoor was the fancy hotel in the fancy Broadmoor neighborhood, the same neighborhood where my father had been rector of the Parish of Our Saviour for twenty-three years until he retired. For two decades, until they moved to a more accessible and manageable house downhill, my parents had had to drive through the Broadmoor neighborhood and past the hotel to get to their house a thousand feet up the side of Cheyenne Mountain. They had watched as the Broadmoor's new management built a fence and in other ways made it more aloof, less welcoming to the wider community, more fortress-like. Ronald Reagan had stayed in the Broadmoor when he came to town as president. "This whole street was lined with Romney signs," Mom told me as we drove through the Broadmoor neighborhood. "It was just suffocating, totally suffocating." My own indelible memory of the Broadmoor neighborhood was of the dinner party I had been forced to attend at one of what my dad called "starter castles," in the front hallway of which were separate life-sized photographs of the father, mother, and teenage son of the family, each shaking hands with President Reagan.

"Bach wants to beautify downtown," Mom said. "Get all the bums out."

"He claimed yesterday that he cares about people," I said.

"Yeah. I'll believe it when I see it."

In the older and more habitable southern part of the city, but socially downwind from the Broadmoor, my mom showed me the Ivywild School, which had been closed and was being converted into a community marketplace. One of the new owners was Mike Bristol of the Bristol Brewing Company, which was moving into the building. "He'll come up with a new beer, and then he'll sell it and give a portion of the proceeds to a particular nonprofit," she said. "He does that all the time. He and the other guy sold Brian Bennett's book about the dogs and the pubs."

"*The Brew Dogs of Colorado*," I said.

"And they had a book signing right there in the brewery." She had given me a copy of the book, along with a really nice long-sleeved t-shirt bearing the slogan:

DOGS
BEER
COLORADO …
It doesn't get much better
www.BrewDogsbook.com

"They bought this facility from District 11 when they closed the school because of declining enrollment and the aging of the neighborhood," Mom told me. "D-11 closed about four or five schools that year, and people in the neighborhood were just sick, because it's such a stunning facility. And Mike and his buddy had to go to the district to buy the building, then they had to go to the city to do the construction. Mike and Amanda are members of Our Saviour. Neat people."

✳

"It kinda gets in your blood, and the power that comes with it," Jan Martin admitted to me in her office early the next morning. Jan was a member of the City Council and a friend of my mother's. "Whenever I feel tired, I think of Judy," she told me. Jan was a vibrant white-haired woman and, like Kristy Milligan, a relatively rare breed: a Colorado Springs native. "When you go to events everybody wants to talk to you, and you kinda get caught up in that," she said. "You just hope that people who have a solid moral core will make decisions. I've been a lifelong Republican, but the local Republican Party held a forum for all the City Council candidates, and they didn't even invite me."

"Would you mind being quoted saying that?"

"Oh no," she said. "It's a fact. I've refused to change parties, because I've always held out hope that they'll move back toward the center. But I'm a thorn in their side. It feels to me that we're more polarized and more political than we've ever been in my lifetime."

I told her that I had sat through the entire long City Council meeting two days earlier. "It had some of the most difficult topics, all bunched into one meeting," she reflected. On fracking, she told me, "I had asked for several things: water monitoring, air monitoring, the ability to use our own inspectors." The state was discouraging municipalities from regulating fracking. "This is a real state-city issue," said Jan. "And I would love it if the state would provide water monitoring and air monitoring and provide inspectors. I voted against it for that reason. I voted no because I didn't feel we had the safeguards that we only owe our community. Colorado Springs is a home-rule city. This basically preempted our ability to do that. I'm not opposed to fracking.

I just want to be sure that it's regulated adequately. Until I have some assurances on that, I just can't support it."

On the meeting's other big issue, panhandling downtown, she said, "I wish the public could be there to hear what we hear. We really are trying to revitalize our downtown. And the business owners are telling  us that it's hampering their ability to do business. I work downtown, and I haven't seen a problem to the extent that they say. They say this is what they need to prosper. I'm prepared to say, 'Okay, here you go, now go prosper.'" New security cameras were also being installed, at a cost of $200,000. "Our problem has been that there's no enforcement. And that will hold true here also."

"Can't you instruct the police department to do that?"

"Well, we have. We went through an economic downturn several years ago, and while we haven't cut police officers, we haven't been filling vacant positions. This year, as the economy continues to turn around, we're hiring fifty new police officers. We're heavily sales-tax dependent. So we fell harder and faster than most communities, but by the same token we're coming back faster."

My mother had brought me to Jan's office but had to rush off soon because of some other thing she was involved in. "We really don't want to admit that we have poverty, and we want to push it out of sight," she put in.

"We were on Fox News the other night," Jan told us. "But the issue was Salvation Army bell-ringers." In order to outlaw panhandling, they had had to write a law that also forbade the Salvation Army from soliciting donations on city sidewalks. "The only way we could do it was to draw a wider net. So you should have seen the emails that I was getting yesterday, from all around the country."

316

My Seattle friend Dennis had seen Jan in an online video about Colorado Springs politics. "My friend is very left-wing, and he was very impressed with you," I told her.

She laughed. "Don't tell the Republicans!"

Jan had also been covered in *The Guardian* and on the NPR show *This American Life*. "They tend to come to me because I try to be the voice of reason," she said.

"Is Colorado Springs a small town or a big city?" I asked her.

"We are becoming a big city," she replied, "but we've always said we have a small-town mentality. In the West we've tended to grow out, because we have the land, and it's so much cheaper to build on the fringes. You know, Colorado Springs is two hundred square miles now. And that presents real problems for public safety, both police and fire. And public transit, because there's no density. The best way for us to grow is east. However, what we're seeing in the north is that we've really leapfrogged the Air Force Academy."

"When you go north you become part of the greater blob up towards Denver," I pointed out.

"We are about to widen the Interstate from north of town to Monument," she told me.

"What I think They should do is run a train." It occurred to me as I said this that Jan herself was one of They, at least notionally.

"Oh, I've wanted that for so long," she said with feeling. She had spent time in New Mexico, which had a rail system running south to north the full length of the state, and she had a vision to extend that through Colorado. "It would have connected from New Mexico to Wyoming. But it would cost several billion dollars to build a rail. And I don't think there's any heart for it."

I told her I had been startled by her colleague Tim Leigh's outburst in the City Council meeting about how it was "insulting" to him when members of the public expressed their views on issues of public concern in a public meeting. That caused her to reminisce.

"The Pioneers Museum is how I got my start in politics," she said. "There was this cranky old man who basically told us to shut up and sit down. And I was so offended. I thought, 'This goes against everything I think government should be about.'"

I asked her for the full story.

"I was sitting on the Pioneers Museum advisory board," she told me, "and the county announced their plan to build a new eight-story courthouse on Tejon, directly across the street from the museum. The museum's director, Matt Mayberry, asked Chuck Murphy and myself to look into the plans and see if there might be alternative locations. Chuck and I attended a county commissioners meeting to express our concern about the location of the building, and we were treated very harshly by the commissioners and at one time told to 'sit down'. We left the meeting very frustrated and decided to do a recall of two of the commissioners. Hundreds of local citizens came to assist us with the recall and, although we weren't able to collect all the required signatures to pursue the recall election, the county began to work with us to consider alternatives to the eight-story building. In the end, the county agreed to build a two-story entrance, set back from the street, and a six-story adjoining structure on the Cascade side, rather than on Tejon.

"One of the main issues, and how this all got started, was that having an eight-story building at street level on Tejon, directly across the street from the museum, would impact views of Pikes Peak from the museum. The solution that was agreed on removed the concern, and today you can clearly view Pikes Peak from the steps of the museum, as well as the statue of Kathryn Lee Bates that had been placed on the museum grounds to commemorate the writing of 'America the Beautiful' at the top of Pikes Peak.

"This was my first encounter with local politics, and not only did I realize how much I enjoyed making a difference from a grassroots level, but I was also pretty good at it. It was about four years later I made the decision to run for City Council, as I hoped to continue to make a difference in the community, and City Council was where the buck stopped. I never walk out and look across the street that I don't think, 'This was a citizen-led initiative.' My own legacy in my mind will be that. And most people don't even know that it happened. We were fools trying to save a view. For a statue, no less. I would wake up in the morning during that time and I would just bounce out of bed. I couldn't wait to get more signatures!

"I really am a pretty normal person," she added. "I was born and raised here. I really feel we're always on the verge of becoming something great, and we never quite get there."

"Hopefully the new people who come will go to the museum," I suggested.

"Absolutely," she agreed. "When I grew up here in the fifties, there were 40,000 people in Colorado Springs. And now there are 400,000. So just in my lifetime alone, that's the growth we've seen in this city. It's quite remarkable. We have five major military installations, and part of what comes with that is transience. My dad was a car dealer, and around the dinner table we'd talk about the economy. And I was a young woman in a town full of soldiers. And we used to complain about all the GIs, and my father would always say, 'Don't you ever complain about the military in Colorado Springs, because that's what puts food on your table.' And I think he was probably right."

I asked her about the Waldo Canyon fire.

"I tell you, anybody who was here that night and saw that fire come over that ridge and towards the city will never forget that experience," she remembered. "I live over in Garden of the Gods, so I had a really close view. And just not knowing where the fire was going to go. But you know, sometimes tragedy brings out the best in people. All of your political differences go away when you work together to deal with tragedy."

"That fades after a while," I said.

"Yes, it does. And it's interesting to see how quickly we go back to life as normal."

"Nine-eleven is the ultimate example of that," I suggested.

"It's a little bit like a death in your family," said Jan. "If you've ever lost a close loved one, it literally changes your view on life. But you soon find yourself back in your normal routine. To me, though, it's good to know that we have that goodness within us. It's good to know that it's there to be tapped. But we're all frustrated that we can't get to our elected officials in Washington, and we tend to take a lot of that angst locally. I've spoken to our congressmen and senators, and I've said that if they do dumb things in Washington, it impacts me in Colorado Springs, because people can get to me. It's probably the distrust in government that often happens on a national level that impacts me. Because then people don't trust me."

The City Council had term limits, and Jan had two years left before she had to step down. "It's a very liberating feeling," she said. "But you still want to end well. I'll still be careful of what I say and do. But there is a real freedom in knowing that you don't have to run again. I'm seeing the money drive the local politics, and that really concerns me. And I'm seeing that happen on the national level."

"Do you mind if I ask who you voted for in the presidential election?"

"I did vote for Obama," she said. "As a Republican, I really can't support what is considered an extreme conservative approach. It's one of the reasons I'm considered a RINO"—Republican in Name Only. "The party is just too extreme for me right now. Four years ago, we had a small group called Republicans for Obama. And some people wanted to do that again this time. And I said, 'You know, that doesn't really work around here.' So we took a different approach; this time we put on a seminar about the Affordable Care Act. We wanted to show how issues affected people, versus the rhetoric."

"Where is the Republican Party headed now?"

"Colorado Springs locally has been known for rather extreme politics. And I have no reason at this point in time to think that that will shift, based upon this recent election. Yeah—I just don't know what to say. I just don't anticipate a shift toward the center."

"Locally?"

"Locally."

"What about nationally?"

"I actually think there will be a shift toward moderation nationally. I'm also pleased to see that some of the Republican elected officials are willing to consider options, even though they signed the no-tax pledge." She herself had signed no such thing. "I owed it to the community to make decisions based on what's best. This will be an important time for people to look back, I really believe. And I hope it will be for the Republican Party."

"This is a perpetually interesting town," I remarked to her. Colorado Springs, by this point, had been exasperating me from afar for more than half my life.

"It is," she agreed. "There are days. The meeting the other day was long and hard. There are days when I get discouraged. I've never had a job before that I couldn't quit, and this is it. So I'll continue to work hard through the end of my time."

✳

I wasn't able to meet Richard Skorman, the longtime owner of Poor Richard's Bookstore who had cemented his reputation as a civic leader by making a credible run for mayor against Steve Bach in 2010, but on Saturday morning I spoke to him by phone for nearly an hour while he walked his dog.

"It is a funny place," he said. "It's not easy to categorize. There's a lot of strong voices on both sides. In some ways I always feel we're on the front lines here, because the issues are so clearly drawn. So it makes people express themselves. The newspaper, *The Gazette*, has always been genuinely libertarian. There's that sort of Western libertarian philosophy here: live and let live. Until World War II, Fort Carson, Camp Carson, was a place where interracial couples came to live, because they could feel accepted here. The gay issue wouldn't have been a big issue, because of that libertarian streak. It's not that judgmental conservatism. There have been several pro-life initiatives, and even those have failed in El Paso County."

Notwithstanding the town's reputation as a bastion of right-wing Bible bashers, only 37 percent of Colorado Springs residents belonged to a religious congregation, versus fifty percent nationwide. "But there are loud voices in the community that don't have anything else to identify themselves with. The problem is that the local Republican Party has gotten taken over by them. So the candidates, if they want to run on the Republican side of things, they have to pledge allegiance to social conservatism, whether they believe it or not." On the other side of the spectrum, he singled out the Citizens Project, which he called "probably the largest grassroots, local diversity rights group in the country, I would think, with as many as two thousand contributors."

"My theory is that there's so much retired military here, and they tend to be conservative as it is," he said. "And Colorado Springs has attracted older people disproportionately. These are people who've seen government at its worst. If they were going to use that as a model for government, they would want it to be a government they would want to pay taxes to. People distrust government, so it's not easy to fund proper government functions. The other problem with Colorado Springs is that it's so transient. Not only do you have people who are distrustful of government, but they're new here. In fact, it's even difficult to get 'em to plant trees in their homes. And then you have the whole western half of the city, that has a high concentration of more progressive, moderate people, artists. And then you have the outdoor culture. Think about how conservative and anti-tax we are, and yet we were willing to tax ourselves to preserve open space. You ask people why they're here, and 95 out of 100 would say because they love the land and the outdoor life. There's probably twenty people, if you look in the Yellow Pages, that practice acupuncture."

Colorado Springs had a high education level and a high level of library use. "We've also been categorized as one of the more dog-friendly cities. So it's a conundrum. If you look at my election, when I ran, I got very few precincts east of Union, and I won almost every one of 'em to the west. It's almost like two cities. You don't have the industry here. You don't have that sense of permanence that you get with the blue-collar population. And you don't have the minorities, though the Hispanic population is growing. The message against me was I want big government, I wanted to raise your taxes, I had a radical gay agenda, all those things. I told audiences, 'Hide your wallet, I'm coming into the room!'"

"Are any of those things true?" I asked.

"Well, I'm a business person; I want efficient government. But I also want good government. I've never hidden the fact that I'm pro-gay rights. And I pissed off the gun nuts, because we have an open-carry law that makes it hard to get the gangbangers off the streets. As long as you don't have the gun loaded, you can carry it openly. In fact, there was a guy who walked into a City Council meeting and just unloaded it. Sat next to the Boy Scouts. This is libertarian philosophy gone awry. They're so afraid of losing their rights to purchase and bear arms. To me it's not a valid argument. And I wasn't afraid to talk about these things. It was a funny election, because it didn't matter. It just became black and white. There was some voter suppression going on. But I'm glad I ran, just to stir the pot and talk about issues that otherwise wouldn't get talked about. But I'm not sure I'd run again, unless I had a good chance of winning. It was very heartwarming."

I asked him about the local politics of fracking.

"Out of sight, out of mind," he said. "If it started happening in their neighborhood, they'd be outraged. It's in a big, empty part of the city that nobody really cares about. It's not easy for local government to have much control. There's also high unemployment, and people want to create jobs. I'm passionate about greenhouse gases and burning coal and all that, but most people aren't there yet."

"Why did you come here in the first place?"

"I grew up in Akron, Ohio," he said, "with terrible weather and no outdoor life, and the Cuyahoga River catching on fire. So I applied to Colorado College. It afforded me an opportunity to start a nice business. I also think that politically, when you make a difference, you make a bigger difference than you would in a place where people are more like-minded. It was a place where not much was being done. It's been a great ride, because I love local politics. It's real nuts and bolts."

Part of the paradox was that Colorado Springs was a great place to be, but it shouldn't have been there in the first place.

"We built a city that we should have never built, because we don't have water," said Richard. "We import eighty percent of our water from two hundred miles away, and we have lots of erosion. If you look at where Fountain Creek flows into the Arkansas River, it's a brown stream flowing into a clear stream. A lot of built environment is where the urban environment meets the wildland. And we built a city on the cheap. And we created so many impervious surfaces, that so much of our topsoil washes away. Half of that water that we import two hundred miles is to water our landscapes, to keep 'em green. It's a Western problem; it's not only a Colorado Springs problem. It'll be interesting to see, as global warming creeps upon us, how we deal with that. All throughout the West, we've built too many houses and structures in the woods. And the natural fires have been suppressed. And the beetle kill has been another problem. Colorado Springs is really ripe for a huge flood disaster. That's a whole nother issue. You have an 18,000-acre burn scar, in the midst of all this population, and forty percent of it is like Teflon. The mudslide potential is huge. There was so much help given for the victims of the fire, and that's a wealthy neighborhood, well-insured. But very little for restoring the land. It's that typical transient philosophy of the West. It's going to take a disaster for us to realize that we have a flood potential.

"We built our city," he said, "like most cities in the West, right up against the mountains, without thinking of how it would impact us in the future. And the car culture is a big part of it too. You have a whole built landscape that's completely dependent on cars. It's hard to deliver services to that big of a geographic area. The other time bomb that's ticking is that a lot of us Baby Boomers aren't going to be able to drive."

✳

The Pioneers Museum was having an annual open house, its biggest event of the year, that afternoon. Walking in the front entrance of the grand old stone building downtown, my mother and I were greeted by her fellow board member Amber Ptak.

"Your mom's a hotshot around town," Amber said to me. "I don't know if you know that."

"I get that impression," I said.

Mom and I walked around, taking in the exhibits and the vibe. "This is about fossils in the Pikes Peak region," she said, pointing at one exhibit, "and it's done by three fourth-grade classes." It was crowded, and there were lots of young families. Christmas carols were playing. Another exhibit was about Charles Schultz, the cartoonist: "He lived here for a year." We ran into a man I knew and liked, an Our Saviour parishioner named Darryl Thatcher, manning a table. "I've been a docent for six years," said Darryl cheerfully, "and I do various and sundry things. And this is by far the biggest day of the year, in terms of people showing up."

"This was the old county courthouse," Mom told me. "They preserved the safe."

On the third floor, we ran into a woman named Barbara Ackerman. "We supervised teachers at CC together," said Mom.

She pointed. "This is Palmer here. I get Penrose and Palmer confused. They did very different things." It was Palmer, General Palmer that is, who founded Colorado Springs in 1871, whose equestrian statue I had driven around on my way into town. The display included a letter Palmer had written to his fiancee on July 28, 1869: "I am sure there will be a famous summer resort here soon after the railroad reaches Denver."

"We have an incredibly extensive collection," said Mom proudly. "And Leah, whom you met, is the curator of the collection."

A volunteer named Pat Wilkins showed us a gaudy beaded dress. "This was made specifically to be worn in the Buffalo Bill Wild West Show," she said. "So it's not as old as some of the other items, but it's stunning. It's totally beaded front and back." When she noticed that I was taking notes, Pat added: "Are you looking for in-depth information? Because there are printouts. They're made for the docents. Whole sheafs of them. Your mom's on the board; you could get them from Leah."

I took a brochure from another woman pitching memberships at a table. "May I take one?" I asked.

"Sure! We have special rates today. I'm not sure what they all are!"

"This is the courtroom?" I asked Mom as we entered the largest room on the second floor.

"Yeah, we have public lectures in here," she said.

When she introduced me to museum director Matt Mayberry, a cheerful plump man with a camera around his neck, Mom told him: "Ethan's waiting for Jerri."

"Yeah, she's the celebrity," I said. Jerri Marr was the National Forest Service supervisor who had catapulted to local prominence with her televised daily briefings during the Waldo Canyon fire.

"She is," agreed Matt. "You know, one of the most interesting stories that came out of the fire was how, when she was running the press conferences, everyone seemed to relax a little. She was able to control things, just by her demeanor. There are times in life when you see leadership in action, and that's what she did. She was calm, and she was able to bring some levity to a very serious situation. I knew people who would tune in just to watch her."

"When we went up to the Flying W Ranch, they had set up five stations," Mom remembered. "Each station related to one aspect of the environment that was affected by the fire. One station was the Flying W Ranch, and if you want more information, you can go to their website. And one station was on the effect of the fire on water. And Jerri spoke to us, and she has a very strong theme of 'We're all in this together.' She lives in Pueblo. She spoke to us, and she finished, and they put a little stool up for her to get down from the pickup truck, and she fell. And she pointed to the reporter with the TV camera and said, 'Don't record that!' Got a big laugh."

We walked around some more. "Ethan's going to interview Jerri Marr," Mom told a woman named Megan.

"Does she know?" Megan asked.

"Yeah, she does," said Mom. "I don't want to bug her."

"Well, she's going to be the grand marshal of the parade later, and I think she has something else. So you might want to bug her again."

So we did, and I went into a side room and sat down with her for about ten minutes, which was all she had to spare. She was a very ordinary-looking youngish black woman, but she exuded an indefinable yet undeniable charisma. She and her sidekick, Smokey the Bear, had been mingling with the public. Smokey sat down now too and took off his head to reveal his  true identity as a young black man, her nephew. He looked hot and sweaty.

"When did you first learn about the fire?" I asked Jerri.

"The day of the fire," she said. "I just left one fire and went to the other one."

"Did you know it was going to become as big as it did?"

"You never know how big a fire is going to be. It was one of those perfect-storm fires. Just by knowing where the fire was, you knew it had the potential, with conditions and locations at risk. So you just had to stay focused."

I asked her why she did what she did.

"I went into this job to be a servant," she said. "It's a public service job. To be a guardian of our natural resources is such an honor in itself. It was all of us working together as one team that really made the difference. When I look back on this fire, I think of that. I didn't even know it was on national TV until later. But I felt it was really important for people to hear directly from the forest supervisor, rather than a public affairs spokesperson. Hindsight, looking back, I think that was the smartest decision we could have made. People compliment us. And I say, 'Hey, we're a government agency.' Any time someone wants to compliment a government agency, I say, 'Hey, we'll take it!' We were able to have a positive effect on the community. And a positive effect on the country. Because people were pointing at us and saying, 'Hey, they're not rattled.' By saying thank you and encouraging us, that says that we're doing something right. It's kinda like *Sesame Street*: 'Who are the people in your neighborhood?' You remember that?"

"You seem to be able and willing to handle the public role with aplomb," I said admiringly.

"It's part of the job," she said. "Part of being in leadership is connecting with the public. A public servant should be able to connect with the public."

Back in the car, I told Mom what Jerri had said about people not being rattled.

"Oh, I think we were," she demurred. "We were all so scared."

Passing a statue at the corner of Colorado and Tejon, she pointed it out and said, "There's Penrose. He's not on a horse like Palmer. Palmer had a terrible accident. That's what killed him. He lived for a while, but he was paralyzed."

"What kind of accident?" I asked.

"He fell off a horse."

We saw a matinee of *Lincoln* that afternoon, my parents and me and their friends Janet and Jerry Hurst. Janet and Jerry were both lifelong Coloradans and my parents' oldest and closest friends in town. They had been among the parishioners who staunchly and crucially stood by my father way back in 1986-87, when he first showed up and made enemies among the old guard of Broadmoor Episcopalians by doing things like changing the vestment colors for Advent from blue to purple (or vice versa; I forget which, and it doesn't matter), but mostly just by being the new guy.

Like my mom, my dad didn't tolerate bullies, though he did tell me later that if he was ever going to drop dead of a heart attack, it would have been during that period. He waited them out until most of the biggest bullies took their ball and stormed off downtown to Grace Episcopal, whose right-wing rector, Don Armstrong, later pleaded no contest to felony theft charges involving the mishandling of several hundred thousand dollars in church funds. The Grace crisis brought a flow of refugees in the other direction to Our Saviour, where under my father's leadership they were welcomed and given comfort.

The scene from the movie that was on my dad's mind during dinner at Chopstix, the foursome's Asian restaurant of choice, was the one near the end where Lincoln refuses to negotiate with Confederate vice president Alexander Stephens. "I think Obama has an opportunity to stare 'em down," he said.

I told Janet and Jerry about my conversation with Jerri Marr and showed them pictures on my phone of her and of Sherron Watkins, the Enron whistleblower.

"She was strong when we needed strength," said Jerry about Jerri. "What I appreciate is that she was doing her job."

"Okay, you showed us your celebrities, we've got to show you ours," said Janet, and whipped out her phone to show off Beatrice, their new granddaughter.

"Back in the fifties," Jerry remembered, "we had a police chief named Dad Bruce. If there was a black or homeless guy—literally, black or homeless—they'd give him a bus ticket and send him up to Denver. I'd like to think that we've moved beyond that."

✳

"My kind of town," said Dad as we turned off I-25 and headed through Walsenburg. "I'd go nuts after a while, though, I'm sure."

"Because you enjoy the social whirl of Colorado Springs?"

"No, I don't enjoy the social whirl. I just like to have a good bookstore."

This part of southern Colorado was my dad's idea of getting away from it all. Walsenburg was an old Western town, easy to romanticize. It had a Safeway and a nice municipal swimming pool, an old high school and a few downtown buildings in stone that stood as reminders of the long-ago time when Americans had enough optimism to put a town in such a place. A left fork a few miles west would take you to the quaint and artsy smaller town of La Veta, and from there the road wound uphill to the Cuchara Valley. My parents had inherited my grandparents' cabin, and they had expanded it, built a deck, and enjoyed a lot of time there. It was a very fortunate coincidence, when they left Wisconsin in 1986, that they had ended up only two hours from Cuchara.

I had cherished a notion that I might stop there for a few days. The cabin unfortunately now had satellite TV and high-speed Internet, which it wouldn't if I were in charge, but it was still a refuge, as far away from it all as one was likely to get anymore. I had guessed that by this point in my trip I would be burned out, drained, overloaded. I was right about that, but if I was going to be home for Christmas, pushing the pause button at Cuchara was not an option. So, after passing the small hospital outside Walsenburg where my Grandmother Rominger had died, we took the right fork to stay on Highway 160 and drove around Cuchara to the west.

My father pointed to the mountains in the distance.

"You see? Trinchera and the West Peak don't have any snow on them."

"Trinchera has snow," I said.

"Some, but it's usually totally covered in snow this time of year." My parents paid close attention to winter snowfall, because it had a lot to do with whether they would have to worry about water shortages in the summer.

We turned south at Fort Garland, toward San Luis and Costilla just over the state line. "This is our corridor to safety," said Dad. "We'd be surrounded in Colorado, if it weren't for New Mexico." Our destination for today was Santa Fe. If we had stayed going west on 160 we would have hit Grandview just south of Durango, and from there we could have headed south and west to Farmington. The map down that way was replete with place names familiar from Tony Hillerman novels: Shiprock, Window Rock, Mexican Water, Chinle.

"I hate having to make choices," I sighed.

"Well, that's the way life is," he said. Being both a dad and a preacher, he had an ingrained habit of saying things like this, especially for saying exactly this. "Did I ever tell you about the sermon I read about the guy who couldn't make choices?"

"No."

"I can't remember whose sermon it was. Whoever it was, the guy the sermon was about was his college roommate. And he was one of those super-smart guys, who could have been a brilliant academic in physics or literature or whatever else. But he couldn't choose, so he killed himself."

At the convenience store in Costilla, Dad stood outside smoking a cigar while I used the restroom. He came in as I was buying a box of granola bars and a bag of trail mix.

"Why don't you buy a Twinkie too?" he said.

"These are good for you," I protested. "They don't make Twinkies anymore, anyway."

"Somebody'll start making 'em," the lady behind the counter assured us.

"No, they're going to keep making them," said my father. "I read something."

Back in the car, I asked to borrow his Mentholatum. My lips and skin always dried out in Colorado. Mentholatum had always been a staple in my parents' household. There was always a jar next to Dad's living room chair, one on the bedside table, one in the car.

"There's a problem," he said, handing me his small jar now. "I can't find it anymore in this size. All I can find is the big ones, or tubes. And the tubes I can't put in my pocket, because they leak. And the big ones are too big to put in your pocket. So I have a couple of these left, and what I do is, I buy a big one and I transfer it to this one. I just remembered to do that, before this trip."

"Maybe it's just a temporary shortage," I suggested.

"Well, it's been some time," he said. "So if you see any, you might want to go ahead and grab a couple."

"It's a different world here than Massachusetts or South Carolina," I mused as the vast landscape rolled past us.

"It sure is, isn't it? A different world entirely. I remember some trips out this way and into Arizona as a kid, and even more arid than this, and being kind of fascinated, 'cause it was so different from what I was used to."

We had lunch in Taos, then drove southwest on Highway 68 toward Santa Fe. We made a short side visit to the Santuario de Chimayo, an adobe church and shrine built in the early nineteenth century, when New Mexico was part of Mexico. "There are churches like this all over Mexico," my dad whispered inside the sanctuary. In his sixties he had made a project out of learning Spanish, and in recent years he and my brother had made many trips together to Mexico. He whispered again: "Another mistake of Vatican II was to pull the altar away from the wall."

"To make it more democratic?" I whispered back. In Taos we had seen a sign urging us to celebrate "50 years of Vatican II."

"Yeah. And I'll give you several theological reasons later."

A special thing at Santuario de Chimayo was holy dirt. In the gift shop you could buy little Ziploc-type plastic bags to hold it. A sign warned:

> Please! Do not throw
> Holy Dirt on floors
> or statues.
> Thank you.

In the dark, low side room next to the sanctuary, many photographs were tacked to bulletin boards along both walls. A sign explained:

> Many visitors to the Santuario leave photos of their loved
> ones. Please pray for those whose pictures you see here.

One photo was captioned:

> Mark A. Mora is Station in
> Afghanistan & Pakistan. Mark
> is 21 years old, has 2 kids
> Miguel & Monica ages 5 & 3 yrs old.

Another was of a young woman in uniform, holding an automatic rifle:

> Thank you Lord Jesus Christ
> FOR HER SAFE RETURN
> 2 TOURS – IRAQ

"You know what's one of the saddest things about our country today?" said my father back outside.

"What's that?" I knew what he was going to say, because he had been saying it for years.

"That we have a mercenary army. They're not Hessians, they're our own folks, but still."

During my week in Colorado Springs I had shown my trip slides to a group of cadets at the Air Force Academy. "That came up in my talk with the cadets," I said. "Several of them made a point of bringing that up. They said that we're a country of three hundred-plus million people, and a very small percentage are in the armed forces. They're concerned that they're being kept apart as a separate caste, that civilians don't understand their experience or perspective."

"One thing I know," said Dad, "is that if we had had a draft, we wouldn't have gone into Iraq."

I bought a couple of fridge magnets, a holy dirt bag, and a booklet telling Santuario de Chimayo's story. As we were driving away we saw a sign:

WE SHIP CHILE

"Holy chili," I said.

"That's one thing the Catholics know," said Dad admiringly. "They know how to market their church."

Along the road back to the highway were scattered small adobe houses and trailers. And a billboard:

Disability Denied?
Social Security or VA
Helen Lopez, Lawyer

And, back on the highway, a sign:

Santa Fe Opera
5 miles

"Have you heard of the Santa Fe Opera?"

"No," I said.

"It's a pretty big deal, I guess, for people who like opera. We had friends from Our Saviour who would come down for it. It's outdoors;

you'll see it up here on the right. I'm sure I'd like it too, if I could stand opera."

In Santa Fe we checked into the La Fonda hotel on the plaza, and the next morning after breakfast we walked around. Going down in the elevator to check out, Dad said, "I hope they keep these old elevators when they do the renovation." The elevator had beautiful wooden doors and trim.

"Surely they will," I said. "That's part of the point of a hotel like this."

"If they were truly old-fashioned they'd still have the lady," he said.

"You mean to operate it?"

"Yeah. You probably never saw an elevator like that, did you?"

"Nope."

"I saw 'em in Dallas when I was a kid, when I'd go downtown with Mother. It was one of the jobs black ladies could do. She had to make sure the elevator ended up even with the floor, and not a foot above or below, and things like that."

Santa Fe was quaint but neither of us was particularly interested in all the artsy stuff, so we gravitated first to the state capitol building and then back to the Collected Works bookstore. I saw a copy of *Bloodlands* by Timothy Snyder, the professor I had met at Yale who grew up in the suburbs of Dayton, Ohio. I had turned my dad on to Snyder's books. "Did you read *Bloodlands*?" I asked him.

"I did," he said. "Or rather, I got halfway through."

"Ran out of steam?" That he had done so would put the book in good company; he had also run out of steam, more than once, less than halfway through *The Brothers Karamozov*. On the other hand, a few years ago he had read all of *War and Peace* (and for a while after that said, about any world event, "It's just like Napoleon invading Russia!").

"Well, it's one atrocity after another," he said now about *Bloodlands*. "I can see how, if you're into documenting all the atrocities, you'd want to read it. But otherwise, you're like, 'I get it!'"

"Well, I read his other book," I said. "So I don't think his feelies will be hurt if I don't get around to reading this one."

At a five and dime on the plaza Dad bought Aleve and took one, because he had a stiff neck. "I'm supposed to take it with a full glass of water," he observed, too late.

"But you took it anyway," I said.

"Yeah. And in fact it's kind of lodged in my throat. Maybe it'll melt."

"Maybe there's a bubbler," I said, using the Wisconsin word for a drinking fountain.

"You don't see outdoor bubblers as much anymore," he reflected. "I wonder why. Used to see 'em all around Dallas when I was a kid. Oh, in fact, there's one over there. Let's see if it bubbles."

It didn't.

"We stopped havin' 'em around the time we stopped being able to put 'White' and 'Colored' signs on 'em."

I laughed. "No, they had them more recently than that, at least in Wisconsin."

At the door of the cathedral at the upper end of the plaza, an Indian man and woman greeted us pleasantly, and the woman handed me a brochure on the cathedral's history. We walked in and sat in a pew.

"I didn't finish my theological argument for why moving the altar was bad," said Dad. "You rightly pointed out that it made it more dem-ocratic. The Protestants in England moved the altar all the way down here, into the congregation, as if we're all just sittin' around havin' a chummy Last Supper with Jesus."

"What's wrong with that?"

"Nothing, except the chumminess. I mean, what Vatican II and the Episcopalians and all the others have done in the last fifty years is make us chummy with God. What Lincoln said in the movie the other night about what the prophet said three thousand years ago—*that* God

doesn't exist anymore."

"Or that God still ex-ists, but we don't want to know it," I said, to egg him on.

"Yes!" he exclaimed.

"On the other hand, all the fire and brimstone from the right-wingers gets a bit much," I said.

"Yes, it does," he agreed.

We had left I-25 way back in Walsenburg to take more remote and interesting highways further west. We picked it back up here in Santa Fe, heading south and west as far as Bernalillo. At exit 252, there was an animated multi-colored billboard. "That sign is totally out of place," I said.

"Yes, it is. What is it, a casino or something?"

I put on my glasses. "Yes," I said. "Casino Hollywood."

"Godamighty."

We got off the Interstate onto Highway 550 to head northwest toward Farmington. In Bernalillo we crossed the Rio Grande.

"Boy, they've got their share of casinos," said Dad.

"They're everywhere," I said. I meant everywhere around the United States. The only casino I had actually been inside was the Potawatomi Casino right in the middle of the city of Milwaukee. It had felt weird, breathing secondhand smoke for the first time in years and seeing all the zombies jerking off the one-armed bandits. "But here, I guess they've got so many Indians."

"Yeah. That's how they get back at us."

At Cuba, about sixty miles past Bernalillo and just under halfway to Farmington, he told me the full story of the time the infamous Casey Family Volvo had broken down, very close to here.

"We were on our way back to Cuchara," he said. "And we decided, rather than stay on the main road, to cut across this way. And so we decided to go on a road—I'll have to look on the map later and see if it shows it. But it was a paved road. No, it was unpaved. And it was late afternoon, we got pretty much up on the pass, and the car died. It was the Volvo station wagon that we had, and it just died. And the reason it died was the fuel injection system. We didn't know that at that point. And we didn't have any cell phones, of course, and all we could do was sit on the road and wait for someone to come by. And a couple groups came by that couldn't help us. One group was too drunk. The third truck that came by, a pickup, was a local farmer and rancher and his wife, and his relatives from the Midwest, who were visiting and had been fishing. I remember that. And they stopped, and I think we had to turn the car around, and they tied our car to their truck and pulled us six or seven miles to their house."

"Were they white or Indian?" I asked.

"They were white. When we got back to their house, the first thing they offered us was an Old Milwaukee beer. And I remember that because we were from Milwaukee, and I said, 'I know Old Milwaukee beer!' And they fed us dinner and offered us a place to stay for the night. But we just decided to sleep in the car, because there wasn't much room in their house. And the next morning, the farmer tried to see if he could fix my fuel injection, but he was unsuccessful, so he took me into Cuba to see if we could get a tow truck, which we did, and he towed us all the way to Albuquerque."

"You skipped over the part about the legal hearing."

"Yeah. The single licensed tow truck guy at the time was busy. He was out on a call. So I was invited to testify at a hearing for this other guy who was seeking a license. They asked me, 'Have you ever needed a tow in Cuba?' And I said, 'Yeah, right now.' And we exchanged Christmas cards with them for years after that. I don't remember their names. Mom might."

"That's a neat story," I said.

"Yeah, it is. It's one of two or three times where we've been rescued by a good Samaritan. You remember the story about Mom?"

"Down by Pueblo?"

"Yeah."

("I was following Dad down to Cuchara," Mom told me later. "It was a late Friday afternoon. Not dark, but late afternoon. And I ran into a dead animal that had already hardened, and that blew out the tire, but without any danger. A couple stopped behind me and offered to drive me to Pueblo to get a new tire. But I couldn't find my wallet, so they had to pay for it. And of course I paid them back. They were Hispanic, and there was a huge picture of Jesus on the hood of their car. And Dad has made a big deal out of that in sermons, because that's so obviously the message of Jesus: to help people in need.")

"This really is a handsome landscape," said Dad as we continued rolling toward Farmington.

"Yes it is," I agreed. "And we don't belong here."

"No, we don't. We're in an alien land."

"Hard to believe there's a town up ahead."

"Yeah. And I'm surprised that there's a four-lane road here. I've been to Santa Fe two or three times in recent years, but I haven't been out to this part of the world in forty years."

We got to Farmington around three o'clock and found the Comfort Inn. It was windy and chilly; it was December now, and we were at 5,400 feet. As we were getting our stuff out of the car, the wrapper of my most recent York Peppermint Patty blew out the passenger-side door and away. I looked for several minutes but couldn't find it. "How bad is that?" I asked my resident expert.

"Well, from a moral theology point of view, if you can't find it, you don't have to."

"How hard am I required to try?"

"Depends on how holy you want to be."

We had beers and dinner at the Three Rivers Brewhouse, then back at the Comfort Inn we went out to the parking lot to smoke cigars, out of the wind behind a big truck. "Do you remember when we parked our U-Haul truck at the Holiday Inn in Milwaukee?" Dad asked me.

"That was my first big adventure." My very first road trip: just five-year-old me and my dad, on the road in a loaded U-Haul from New Hampshire to Wisconsin. It was also my first international adventure, because we had taken the shortcut between Buffalo and Detroit through Canada.

"We stayed two or three nights in the Holiday Inn before we could move into our house."

"Just you and me, right?"

"Just you and me. And I parked the U-Haul in the Holiday Inn parking lot, and they were looking for us, for whoever owned the truck that was taking up three or four of their parking spaces. And I remember that when we checked out, they were displeased about that."

We were back on the road early the next morning. "You know," said Dad, "driving out here with you guys in that Volvo was pretty stupid. Of course, I understood from the advertisements that Volvos were indestructible."

I insisted on making a right turn several miles out of the way to see the Four Corners Monument, which I remembered from way back when, maybe from that same ill-fated Volvo trip. I overshot it at first and went several miles into Colorado and had to turn around. No other tourists were at the monument, but a Navajo was manning one of the booths selling magnets, shot glasses, and so forth. "Welcome to New Mexico," he said.

"I was just in New Mexico," I said. "It was nice."

"New Mexico's a get-along state," he remarked.

I was browsing among his wide selection of Four Corners magnets. I turned one over: MADE IN CHINA.

"Those are all four-dollar magnets," said the Indian. "And this one's a five-dollar magnet. Have you ever been here before?"

"Way back when I was a kid," I said. "At least thirty years ago."

"This card shows how it was then," he said, pointing to one of the many postcards on a rack. "In '91 they renovated it and made it like this." He showed me another postcard.

"I don't remember all these stalls," I said. "I remember it was open, like on this card."

"Yeah. They put up wooden stalls, like these"—he pointed at a card. "But it's hard to maintain the wood stalls, with water and all. So they built these."

I bought the five-dollar magnet. "I'll take the card too," I said, meaning the old one showing the pre-1991 setup.

"This is what it woulda been like when you came here," he said. "Do you have a quarter?"

"Sorry," I said. "I have one in the car."

"I'll just give you that."

"Thank you."

His cell phone rang. "Thanks for comin' today," he said genially, and I went on my way.

And then we drove, and we drove, and we drove some more. West on 160 through Mexican Water, south on 191 through Round Rock and Many Farms, through the otherworldly red desert landscape. We drove through Chinle disdaining fast food, looking out for a down-home-style diner. We didn't find one. What we found instead were a strip mall, a Burger King, and an A & W. We were both hungry and

I was feeling lightheaded, but driven forward by the urge fostered by being behind a steering wheel on a straight road in a remote place. Twenty-odd miles later, something dawned on me.

"What did I miss out on by not stopping at Canyon de Chelly?" I asked.

"Well, what's surprising about it is the size of the ruins, how extensive they are," said Dad. "It's like Mesa Verde."

"Aw. We shoulda stopped. I'm kicking myself."

"Do you want to go back?"

"Do you mean that?"

"Not really. I can tell you this too, though. It's interesting to see the ruin of one house, but after that it's like, 'This was the kitchen.' And then, 'This was the kitchen of this house,' and then, 'We think that maybe this might perhaps have been used for religious purposes.' It's like going to the Mayan ruins in Mexico with Aaron. He wants to see each one. I found them interesting too, at least for the first fifteen or sixteen."

We were headed now toward the Hopi mesas. Dad had been in these parts as a young teacher when, as I remembered it, he had been befriended by an old man named Homer Honyumptewa. I remembered, or thought I did, meeting Homer myself at some point, but I was vague on how or why or when.

"I don't remember much about Homer himself," Dad told me. "But when I was teaching at Mount Hermon in Massachusetts, during the summers I was part of the Mount Hermon summer school. They had short summer programs for the kids, and you could create your own. One of the things I wanted to do was open up the world to kids. I don't remember how I heard about Ben Priest, but I did. Probably the headmaster at Mount Hermon knew the headmaster at Colorado Academy. And Ben and I created this summer program, where I took some kids from the Mount Hermon

summer program to Colorado Academy, which is in Littleton or Engle-wood—it's still there—and some kids from Colorado Academy joined too. Ben Priest knew Homer, and he was a student of Anasazi and Hopi culture. And we spent a week

at Colorado Academy doing class work, studying and reading about the Hopi and the Anasazi, and then we spent a week or so traveling and living at the Second Mesa. Homer was our host and, as I said, the Octave of the Second Mesa."

Father Octave Lafontant was a Haitian Episcopal priest my father had worked with for many years, a wizened, staunch, and shrewd leader of men, a mensch of his country and community and brother of the equally impressive Fritz Lafontant, visionary founder of the Partners in Health compound at Cange. "And of course it opened up my world more than it did the kids'. That was all new to me. Ben opened all that to me, because while I went to the Southwest as a kid, I don't remember going to the mesas."

"You would have been in your late twenties." Twenty years younger than I was now.

"Yeah. I'm pretty sure you were already born. It was when I was teaching at—"

"St. Mark's?" St. Mark's was the Episcopal school in Dallas, where I was born in 1965 during my parents' two-year abortive attempt to give Texas another try.

"No, because St. Mark's was before Mount Hermon. We all went out and spent that week in Denver, then you and Aaron and Judy went down to Cuchara, and I went to the mesas with the kids."

"So it might have been in '68," I suggested.

"Yes, it might have been. Because I was teaching at Mount Hermon in '68. That was the year Peter Amram and I won Gill County for Clean Gene. Peter and I were in touch again this year, because Peter sent me an email to see how things were in Colorado politically."

The Hopi live on three distinct mesas formed by millennia of erosion, above the desert plain of the Navajo Reservation. The Hopi have been on the mesas for many hundreds of years and are ethnically distinct from, and not especially friendly with, the Navajo. We drove up to the flat top of the First Mesa, parked, and walked around. The few people there were quiet but assertive, somehow, about offering their shawls and trinkets for sale. They made us feel welcome, but I felt shy, and my nosy reporter's instincts failed me. I sensed that to get to know these people who were just there at home minding their own business would take more time than I had, as well as a different approach. And who was I to decide that they would want to be known, anyway? The old lady and her grown son who sold Dad a thirty-dollar shawl and me a twenty-dollar wooden kachina fridge magnet were friendly, but I felt rude just for being there. What business did I have being there? We remarked on the old photograph of a young man in military uniform on the wall. The old lady's son said that the man in the picture was his uncle, who had been drafted to serve overseas in World War II, but that he hadn't talked much about the experience after he returned. "All he said was, 'War no good. Don't go,'" remembered the Hopi soldier's nephew.

Back at the car I told Dad, "That's the most expensive fridge magnet I've ever bought."

"Well, in places like this, not the touristy places, I figure it's just money I'm leaving here," he said. "One of the reasons it's so hard not to buy anything is they're so damn nice. You wouldn't call 'em pushy. The thing that's interesting to me is that these people have been here for I don't know how long. They weren't put here for our benefit. I wonder what Romney had to offer these folks."

On the Second Mesa we looked around at the old photographs on the walls of the Hopi Cultural Center, and I bought a DVD and a book. Dad inquired after Homer Honyumptewa, and the woman at the register speculated politely about who he might have been related to and on which mesa. "He would have been an old man when I was here," he told her. "Nearly fifty years ago." And then, on the Third Mesa at Old Oraibi, the oldest continuously inhabited settlement in North America, a school bus stopped and deposited a boy. The boy was impassive but not shy, and showing us around the village was his idea. His name was Terrance, age ten.

"I'm in fifth grade," he told us, "and I'm learning Hopi from my uncles and them. In the kachina time, the kachinas come, and they dance. And then we send them home to the San Francisco Mountains down by Flag." An older man was working outside one of the houses. "He's my uncle too," said Terrance. "That's an old house, but it's still inhabited. A lady lives there. I'm related to her. We're all related somehow."

He took us behind the village to where the mesa sloped away to the south. He pointed.

"That's the old church, that got struck by lightning long time ago. Nearby it is where we go to pray. We take some feathers, only us boys, and we point them at the sun, and we ask them to help us and stuff."

"How far away is your school?" I asked him.

"I go down there, to Kykotsmovi. We call it K-town for short. We have ten villages." He named them.

"Where do you get water?" asked my father.

"We have a building, and there's water there, with a faucet."

"A well."

"Yes. But long time ago we had to haul water."

My father pointed to the southeast. "Are those your fields over there?"

Terrance pointed in the other direction, to the southwest. "Those are our fields down there. We grow corn and beans and squash. Long time ago we didn't have no rides, and we had to walk down to the fields and back up. Now we have cars."

"Do you ever have too little water?" asked my dad. Anyone living in the Southwest, Hopi on the mesas or Anglo in Colorado Springs, had to know and worry about water.

"No, we have water," said Terrance.

"So you get enough rain or snow?"

"Yes."

"Does it snow here, Terrance?" I asked.

"Yes, it snows," he said. "And we go sledding. And we come back all wet. And then our moms and dads say, 'That's why you shouldn't have done it.'" He grinned.

"All moms and dads say that to their kids," said my dad.

"We kids are all bad," said Terrance.

"No, you're not bad," I assured him.

"Where are you from?" he asked.

"I'm from Seattle."

"And I'm from Colorado," said my dad. "Do you know where Seattle is?"

"No," said Terrance.

"Well, I'm sure you know where Colorado is. It's just over there." He pointed to the northeast. "We can probably see it from here. Seattle is –" He paused. "Do you know where California is?"

"Yes," said Terrance. He didn't seem sure, though.

"Well, Seattle is way north of California."

"Oh."

"Seattle is very far away," I confirmed.

Terrance walked us back toward our car. "Long time ago there used to be twenty-three kivas, but they fell down. Now we have three kivas." We stopped beside his house. "That's the end of the tour," he announced, with another grin. We thanked him, and my father slipped him a few dollars. "That's for school or something," he said.

From the woman in the little gift shop in Old Oraibi I bought a $125 wooden kachina figure and asked if I could take her phone number and call her sometime to ask some follow-up questions. "Sure," she said. Her name was Michele. (It's a good thing I got her number because later, in our room in Tuba City, I realized that I had left my credit card with her. She was kind enough to mail it to me in Seattle. "With anyone else I wouldn't have felt comfortable doing that," Dad commented approvingly.)

"I'm driving around the United States," I explained to Michele. "I'm visiting many different communities, and I'm writing a book about the country at this moment. I think the election we just had was very significant ..." I trailed off, because she didn't seem interested in the election. While she wrote her name and phone number on a slip of paper, I continued: "I've visited so many interesting communities on this trip, but the different communities don't know much about each other. And none of the rest of us know much about the native communities."

She looked up at me across the counter and smiled. "We Hopi, we just do what we do," she told me. "And if people don't know us, we like it. The world can just go by, and we're here, and we live our life."

"I guess that's why you went up on the mesas in the first place," I said.

"Yes," she said. "And it's why we live way out in the desert!"

Heading west again, starting downhill, we could see miles away in the distance below us the lights of a town. "There's Tuba City," said Dad. "It's like coming down the mountain from Mirebalais to Port-au-Prince." Then a few minutes later he said: "Want some perspective on the day?"

"Sure."

"If we'd gone to Canyon de Chelly, we wouldn't have met Terrance."

"Yeah, that's right," I said. There was something about Terrance. "Funny how things turn out."

＊

In the diner at the Quality Inn Navajo Nation in Tuba City, Dad reminisced about the couple times he had gone to Phoenix for job interviews, only to realize that it wasn't a place he and my mother would want to live. "And then there was the time when I was at St. Mary's and I had the opportunity in Alabama," he said. "And your mother said, 'I'm not living in Alabama.'"

"I remember hearing about that one," I said.

"Part of the attraction was that the Bishop of Alabama at the time—I can't remember his name—was one of the good guys. But we wouldn't have been happy in Alabama. The South is a strange place. It's almost as strange as the Mormons."

"So you were never 'into' being from Texas?" I asked, just to hear what he would say.

"No!" he exclaimed. "It was Hicksville. I remember I wrote a letter once to the *Dallas Morning News*. They were having some kind of movement about becoming a 'world city.' They were talking about wanting to be all cosmopolitan and everything. And I asked how Dallas could be a world city, when it was still a segregated city."

"When was this?"

"It was in the fifties, right during the Martin Luther King time."

"You were a kid!"

"Yes."

"Was your letter published?"

"Yes, it was. I kept it and still have it, but I don't know where it is. If I find it, I'll send you a copy."

"Please do," I said. "But my favorite of your letters is the one you wrote to the *Oconomowoc Enterprise*." As I remember it, that was the one he wrote during a mayoral election, when our neighbor Mr. Mc-Garvey was running yet again against Mrs. Whalen, and my dad just couldn't take it anymore. And, as I remember it, the letter went something like this:

> To the editor:
>
> I understand that there's a new group called the Concerned Citizens of Oconomowoc, which advocates maintaining and upgrading city property. I share that laudable goal. I also understand that the Concerned Citizens of Oconomowoc support a certain candidate for mayor. As a concerned citizen of Oconomowoc, I would like to say that that candidate lives three doors down from me, and that if he's concerned about maintaining city property, he might want to start by maintaining his own.

Mrs. Whalen had laughed when I told her that story back in September in Oconomowoc. "Is that letter apocryphal or real?" I asked my dad now. I'm pretty sure it's real, because I remember how awkward and infrequent our neighborhood ballgames became afterward.

"I don't know," he said. "You're the one who remembers it. I don't."

We spent two nights in Phoenix and a night in Kingman, and we toured Hoover Dam, which is really something to see. Dad was in a valedictory mood, observing that Hoover Dam and other great engineering projects like the Golden Gate Bridge had been built right around the time he was born. "Of course the whole selling point was that the dam would provide water to the whole Southwest for infinity," he remembered. Then we drove around Las Vegas and down into California on I-15. We ate lunch and bought some spiced beef jerky at the Alien Fresh Jerky store in the desert town of Baker, drove through Barstow and along the northern edge of Edwards Air Force Base, then spent the night in Lancaster, with a view from our room of the ballpark of the Lancaster JetHawks minor-league baseball team.

"I think there are a lot of parallels between now and the Civil War," said Dad over dinner at the Black Angus Steakhouse. "Not in the details so much, but in the sense of a watershed moment. Now it's not so obvious, but because of the demographic shifts it's substantial. I don't think the Romney types and the white Southern folks are prepared for a brown America."

"Well, that's too bad for them," I said.

"I think they can still create some pain, but I think the game's over," he said, not without pleasure.

"And in a sense it came suddenly."

"Well, in one sense. But if your eyes were open, you could see it coming. The world's a-changin'."

"And that's good," I suggested.

"Yeah, it is. Grandmother Casey would approve, by the way. You know what my father's response to all this would be?" His father had been a great absence in my father's adult life. "I think it would be the same as Lincoln's to that black woman on the porch."

Dad's original idea had been to go with me all the way to San Francisco, then ride a train back to Denver, but inconvenient train schedules and prohibitive fares put the kibosh on that romance. I would be dropping him off at LAX the next day. Before I did, I needed to hear him tell me about his own early road trips. It seemed a key, somehow, to whatever it was that drove me. You have to learn all the history you can, when you can, because you never know when you'll no longer have the opportunity.

"At some point," he obliged me in Lancaster over our complimentary continental breakfast, "we got in the habit of taking the two weeks Dad had for vacation and taking trips all over the country. I remember we went to Santa Monica, and what's that island called out there?"

"Catalina Island?" I guessed.

"Catalina Island. And Knott's Berry Farm, and all across the deserts of the Southwest. I remember Knott's Berry Farm was a big deal to my mother. She had heard of it. It was Route 66, no Interstate. Which meant, by the way, that we always did these trips at forty-five miles per hour. That was the default speed limit. And lots of flat tires. Probably not as many as the Joads, but still. Another was southwest from Dallas to Monterrey, Mexico. All these round trip, in some way or another, not necessarily just coming back the same way."

"Your dad was okay with doing all the driving?"

"It was the only possibility. Mom didn't have a license. Besides that, he was male. He was also our on-board mechanic. Another was to Florida. We went to St. Augustine, I remember. I got stung by a jellyfish swimming at the beach. And Key West, where we thought about flying to Havana, just to say we had been to Cuba. But we didn't, for some reason. It may have been the cost, or it may have been because one of us was afraid to fly. Another was to New York City. I could almost date this one, because the primary memory I have of the trip is that we were staying in a hotel downtown, and I went from the hotel by subway to Yankee Stadium for a night game. I must have been thirteen or fourteen years old, to watch the Yankees play the Indians—the Indians being my team. Herb Score was the pitcher for the Indians."

He had once told me that major league baseball was "a million miles away" from Texas in those days. "We followed the Texas League, with teams in Dallas, Fort Worth, Oklahoma City, Houston, San Antonio, Shreveport, and El Paso. The nearest major league team was St. Louis, and I still remember the days of *delayed* radio broadcasts." The Dallas Eagles of the Texas League had a promotion called the Knothole Gang. "They distributed free passes to the churches, and when you went to Sunday School on Sunday, you could pick up your pass and see a game that week. If you didn't go to Sunday School, you were out of luck that week. I went to Sunday School a lot." He may not have liked Texas, but he did remember nostalgically the America he had grown up in. He once told me that John Grisham's beautiful non-thriller *A Painted House* accurately depicts the world he came from, right down to scenes of the family listening

to Cardinals games on the front porch. I had listened to plenty of ball-games myself, Bob Uecker and his sidekicks doing play-by-play and color for the True Blue Brew Crew I loved so much, on the front porch at 400 South Silver Lake Street in Oconomowoc.

"Do you remember who pitched for the Yankees?"

"No, but I remember who the catcher was."

"Berra?" I guessed. "Campanella was with the Dodgers. Dickey?" No, Dickey was back in the thirties.

"Nope. Elston Howard. Probably I remember that because he was maybe the first black player I'd seen in the major leagues because—although I can't remember who won the game, although probably it was the Yankees, because I was doomed to be disappointed—I think it was a low-scoring game, 3 to 2 or something, and I believe that Howard hit the home run that made the difference."

"So it had to have been after 1948?"

"Yeah, it had to be after '48 because of Jackie Robinson, and because if I had been any younger, I don't think my parents would have let me ride the subway at night by myself."

"Why didn't your father go with you?"

"I don't know! I don't remember that. I just remember that I went by myself. Which was a big deal for me. Another trip was to Canada, but I'm not at all sure where, except that it was probably due north. I remember we went to—what's that city on Lake Superior?"

"Thunder Bay?"

"No."

"Sault Ste. Marie?"

"No."

"Duluth?"

"Yeah. I remember we went to Canada through Duluth. And I remember that we had car trouble in Canada. It was the radiator. And we had to wait while the car got repaired somewhere in Canada, and we hung around this little town."

"That would have been in either Ontario or Manitoba."

"Yeah. One city name that sticks in my mind, although I wouldn't want to swear to it, is Winnipeg. Back then, you could buy little cans of gunk that you put in with the water to seal leaks. I don't know if it did, but enough to get you back home."

"You never got to Seattle."

"No."

"Too far?"

"Yeah. But you just reminded me of another trip. Once we went to Yellowstone Park. About all I remember from that trip is that we got to Yellowstone late and we spent the night in the car, parked right at Old Faithful, and watched it erupt I think two or three times during the night."

"What was the importance of these trips to you?"

"Well, before we get to that, do you know about my trip with the YMCA when I was nine?"

"With the slot machine."

"Yeah. This would have been in '46 or something, because I remember being nine years old. And one thing I remember about the Y is that boys swam in the nude. But it was only later, when I began to study Greek, that I learned that that was a practice that went back to the Greeks. Because the word *gymnas*, from which we derive gymnasium, you'd have to check the exact meaning, but I think it means nude. And the Y always had all kinds of activities and contests and so forth for kids. And one they had that year was that, over a period of weeks, they had a number of things that you had to do, and the winner of that contest won a trip to Yellowstone Park, a YMCA bus trip. And another kid and I tied. The cost of the trip was seventy-five dollars, I remember that. So the Y and our parents somehow agreed that we should both go, and they should split the cost. So both of our parents paid thirty-seven fifty, and we both went. And all the other kids were thirteen or fourteen years old. We were the only ones who were as young as we were. I remember being young enough that the chaperone kept my spending money. And when we got to Pueblo, I think it was, that's when I found the slot machine. And I had a nickel in my pocket from my spending money for a Coke. But I saw the slot machine before I saw the Coke machine. But it wasn't a machine; you'd have a big ice chest. A six-ounce Coke cost a nickel. But it was a nickel slot, so I put the nickel in the slot machine and hit the jackpot. And, like any nine-year-old, I figured that happened every time. And I was gonna multiply my fortune. So I started putting all the nickels back in. All except one."

"You kept one last nickel?"

"I went and bought a Coke. And that cured me of gambling. I've never gambled."

"So you came out ahead."

"Two other things I remember from that trip is that we were gonna go to the top of Pikes Peak, but the bus overheated halfway up, and having breakfast at a little cafe somewhere in downtown Colorado Springs, probably on Tejon or Nevada. I didn't know then, but Colorado Springs was a lot smaller then, and those were the main streets. And I remember there was a jukebox. You remember they used to have little jukeboxes in booths? And one of the songs it played was 'Peg o' My Heart,' which was a Top 40 song at the time, and it was a song that I was fond of. I can still remember the tune. And the other thing I remember from that trip was that I saved a nickel so I could call my folks to pick me up in case they weren't there. But they were."

"So what did these trips mean to you?"

"Well, the importance of the Y trip was that it was the first time I had gone away from home without my parents, which was a real independence thing. The importance of all the trips was that my parents were committed to showing us that the world was bigger than Dallas. It was a big world out there. That's really what it was all about. It says more about my parents than about me."

"But it took."

"But it took, yeah."

CHAPTER 8

HOME STRETCH

As soon as I reached Los Angeles, I knew I had run out of gas. Albeit not literally: on the way down from Lancaster, Dad and I filled up at a 76 station in Santa Clarita. "Could you do without bathrooms in gas stations and cafes and such?" he asked me there.

I thought of all the gas station restrooms of which I had availed myself, all around America. "Nope," I said.

"That's what blacks used to have to do," he said. "Can you imagine?"

I dropped him off at LAX, and abruptly I was alone again. I had just arrived in the most populous state, and I still had most of the fourteen-hundred-mile West Coast ahead of  me, but I had used up my where-withal. Nothing against Califor-nia. As Tom Petty says, "Califor-nia's been good to me/ I hope it don't fall into the sea." But, like Bob Seger, I knew right then I was too far from home. And anyway, as the old Okie says to Jack Burden in *All the King's Men*: "Californy, hit is jes lak the rest of the world, only it is more of hit."

If I had stayed in a soulless chain motel, or camped in state parks as I had been planning to do, I might even so have found more to write about in Southern California. But when I searched on Hotels.com for hotels in my modest price range, what came up was a half-price special on the Queen Mary in Long Beach. So I spent three nights and most of three days on the stately old passenger liner, soothing myself with solitude, cocktails, and vintage wood paneling. It seemed a good omen that one of my favorite novelists, Ursula Le Guin, had met her husband on the Queen Mary; it always feels good and healthy to be in her wise presence.

I looked up a couple of friends, but I really wanted to avoid the freeways, and the best way to do that was to stay on the boat. I wasn't in the mood to learn any more about America, or to meet more Americans. I was reading Robert Harris's erudite historical novel of Rome, *Lustrum*, narrated by Cicero's slave Tiro: "There are no lasting victories in politics, there is only the remorseless grinding forward of events. ... Perhaps Caesar is right—this whole republic needs to be pulled down and built again."[1] And I was, as Paul Theroux puts it somewhere, in retreat from experience. I told myself that the emphasis of my attention didn't have to be proportional to population. And ignoring L.A. would be consistent with the ad hoc decisions I had made along my route to skirt major cities. I hadn't exactly planned it that way, but actually I kind of had. I had spent a couple of days in Chicago, but had found little there to write about. Not that I looked very hard. I had hoped to emulate Theroux's feat of riding the New York subway to its farthest reaches in the outer boroughs. Oh well, I guess he's already done that anyway.[2] I had spent barely two hours in the District of Columbia, for one meeting that turned out to be a dud. Books, plural, could be written about any one of the major cities I had driven past, and for me that was the point: Chicago, New York, and Washington didn't need me to write about them. I figured the same went for L.A.

*

---

1   Caesar strangely echoes Eugene McCarthy (or vice versa). In "Baseball Deregulation and Free Enterprise," *Elysian Fields Quarterly*, vol. 12, no. 1 (Hot Stove League Issue, 1993), McCarthy prescribed a "pure, capitalistic, free enterprise system" for major league baseball, crucially including the proviso that team owners must pay for their own stadiums, then ended by conceding: "If all goes badly, the better choice might be to call off the whole thing as too complicated, outlaw all organized baseball, including the Little Leagues, scatter a few balls and bats and gloves and a catcher's mask or two around, and let the whole process start over again."

2   "Subterranean Gothic," *Sunrise with Seamonsters: Travels & Discoveries* (Houghton Mifflin, 1985), pp. 239-58.

My last bout of reporting had been in Phoenix, where I had spent a couple of days with Dr. Randy Christensen and his colleagues at the UMOM New Day Center shelter on East Van Buren Street and its companion mobile clinic. UMOM was an acronym for United Methodist Outreach Ministries. The mobile clinic was affiliated with the ones I had visited in Detroit and Florida and was partly funded by *American Idol* donations through the Children's Health Fund. Arriving in Phoenix straight from the Hopi mesas via Tuba City had been a shock to the system, but meeting Randy had been energizing and encouraging.

"This is the Cadillac of shelters," he told me. "Most other people are sleeping on the floors. We see a lot of boys, teenagers. The families just tend to dump them and say, 'We gotta take care of the younger kids.' Most of my kids have been in the emergency room six, seven, eight, nine, ten times, and all the research shows that you're gonna spend millions. My main mission now is to get people to see the worthwhileness of these kids. To get people to see that they are worth saving."

Families fortunate enough to secure a living unit at UMOM could stay for up to two years, while they worked with support from the shelter's staff to stabilize their financial situation and enhance their education, skills, and employability.

"So, are you bucking the system?" I asked Randy.

"Yeah," he said. "Early on I used to get frustrated. Now, I still get frustrated, but I don't get as mad anymore."

"Are you political about these things?"

"Yeah. Not something that I set out to do." He was political both at the state level and in Washington, D.C. "When we started telling the story, it had power beyond belief." Randy had gone so far as to tell the story at book length, in *Ask Me Why I Hurt: The Kids Nobody Wants and the Doctor Who Heals Them*. He told me that he and his co-author, Rene Denfeld, had been inspired partly by Tracy Kidder's bestseller about Haiti's Dr. Paul Farmer, *Mountains Beyond Mountains*. Writing the book had been "cathartic," he said. "When my wife was pregnant with the twins, I came home one day after taking care of a girl who had been brutally raped her whole life, and I wanted to tell my wife about it, and she was waiting to tell me that she was pregnant. And I couldn't tell her.

So that's what the book did. But I really wanted to do it in a way that would honor those kids that didn't make it. We tried to tell the story of the kids, but in a way that said, 'You don't have to be a superhero to do this.' The book is filled with my mistakes."

"When you went to medical school, what did you have in mind?" I asked him.

"I thought I was going to be a pediatric cardiothoracic surgeon. And little things began to change. I love pediatrics, I loved what I was doing. It's kind of funny—all of my mentors were these great surgeons.  I actually got asked this year in April to be the director of general pediatrics at Phoenix Children's Hospital. So I thought that while it wasn't my passion, this would be a chance to build a legacy. We were the stepchild for so many years. Now we're the flagship. So when the governor calls and says, 'What is Phoenix Children's doing for the community?' this is what they show them."

But, like all nonprofits, UMOM had been affected by the 2008 financial crisis. "In the late nineties, early 2000s, they were just givin' out money," said Randy. "Now they want outcomes; you have to prove it. I sit on several boards, and all of a sudden people that had $5 million in assets were down to $3 million in assets. The years that were leanest were the years when people were most in need. Now you gotta be a lot smarter about where your money is coming from." The crash had also affected the shelter's clients more directly. "As you start to go west from here, that's where all the housing crashed," he said. "I think some of these schools had like a four hundred percent increase in homeless teenagers. And they can't get to the services, because it's too far."

"It's like any Western city," I said, thinking of Colorado Springs. "It's too spread out."

"Yeah, I think we're the biggest city in the United States now, by area. Access to health care starts with transportation. Just because you have the insurance card doesn't mean you have access."

In addition to the human reasons to alleviate suffering that everyone agrees on in principle but few seem able or willing to prioritize in practice, Randy was assertive about making an economic case for his work. He cited a pregnant woman who had died: "If we would have given her the cheapest of medications, a couple hundred dollars of medications, she'd be alive, the baby would have been born fine, and you would have saved hundreds of thousands of dollars. We're saving money. Really good doctor visits early on save so much. We truly believe in preventive health care. We see that affecting people right out of the womb makes a lifelong difference."

"I get the impression this is the gospel you preach to public officials," I said.

"Yes," he said. "This is the discussion we're having. And again, to be fiscally responsible means you do preventive health care." But behind the health care debate lurked the divisive issue of illegal immigration. "Unfortunately I think there's this perception, especially in Arizona, that all of these people are accessing health care. And the truth is, they're scared. A lot of people ask us what percentage of people who come to the van are undocumented. And the truth is, it's about five percent. So I think they're even scared of us. Part of my own back story is that, although I'm Randy Christensen, my mom was Maria Carmen del Guadalupe Rivera. My grandfather was part Apache. I look at it from a different light. And being in Arizona too, the Native Americans that have been here for years and years and years, you start talking about immigration, and they're like, 'Wait a minute.' I also have a very firm belief that it is my job to take care of the children. And there is never a time when I'll stop and say, 'Does your kid have papers?'"

He sketched a more complex political scenario at the state level than the rest of us tend to see when we look at Arizona from the outside. "Senator Kyl had some connections through his wife to mobile medical care," he said. U.S. Senator Jon Kyl was a Republican, generally considered very conservative. "So early in his career, he helped us to get access to funds and was very supportive. At least we knew where he stood. His office was very well run, incredibly organized. And Congressman Pastor has probably been one of our most incredibly involved officials." Pastor was a Democrat.

"How do you vote?" I asked Randy.

"Democrat," he said. "But I grew up with a very different view of Republicans. I actually aligned myself with them early on. And the fiscal responsibility: I really believe that you show your outcomes." Offering another nuance, he cited Arizona's decision in 1987 to raise the speed limit on its rural highways from 55 to 65 miles per hour. "I liked that as a kid, saying, 'We know what's good for our state.' I suspect that twenty years ago I would have been thought of as moderate, not some ultra-liberal. But we've moved so center-right as a nation. And I believe in universal health care. You should have that as a right. And I think that if you provide that, you'll make our country better."

Randy and his colleagues arranged for me to interview a few of the shelter's residents, including a young black couple, Shaun and Leah Coney, whom I met in their small UMOM apartment.

"It makes me feel good that someone wants to sit down and hear me tell my story," said Leah. "Things were working good until I started having blackout episodes. It turned out I was four months pregnant. Then I fell on my foot wrong and broke it." They lost their house and had to move into a place that cost $200 per week, more than the $800 per month they had been paying in rent. "I just started getting depressed and sad and trying to cover it up, you know, for my babies. And my nurse told me about UMOM. We had to call every day to find out if there was a room here, because at least we had a place to lay our head."

"We did have to sleep in our vehicles about two nights," said Shaun. "That's why I really appreciate here. As a father and as a man, it allowed me to position myself to take care of my family."

Shaun's goal was to get an engineering degree. Leah was a certified nursing assistant with twelve years' experience, earning $14 to $16 per hour. "But I've always wanted to be an RN," she said. "And my personal fear was that I wasn't smart enough to pass the tests. That's where Nurse Kim came in." Kim Williams was on the UMOM staff. "She said, 'I started working on my RN when I was thirty-five.' It took what we was kinda looking at as this embarrassing, dark situation, to this promising dream that's achievable."

"I know it's not solely about the income," said Shaun. "I know it's about budgeting too."

"The budgeting classes have been really helpful," said Leah.

I asked them for their thoughts on the presidential election, which was a month in the past at this point.

"Well, I've thought about sending a letter to Obama," said Leah. "They need to hear more personal stories of places like this. We've met veterans here. They've served for our country, they've done all kinds of things, and they get to a place where they don't know where to go. I'm thankful that UMOM is here, so that people like ourselves can get a step up. Also, with Obama's decision to help with education, it's been  a godsend to us. We're so proud that we're on a path where our children can really look up to us now. I hear my kids talking about college. To hear them talk about college was just awesome to me."

"I have a lot of people say—or not say, but infer—that I voted for Obama because he's black," said Shaun. "That wasn't my reasoning. I think that he's a mirror of hope. I just want to continue to see the follow-through on things. My politics is, 'Just continue to do what you say.'"

I asked them about immigration.

"It's a tough subject," said Leah. "It's a melting pot here, so you get a lot of families that are mixed: some members are legal, and some are illegal. You hear so many stories of people that are illegal and they're gettin' on the system. Something needs to be done. I have some family that's mixed with Spanish, so what do you do if they're here? They need food, but they're illegal, so they're not supposed to be on the system?"

"I have associates that I work with, that are possibly illegal," said Shaun.

"Not possibly," asserted Leah. "They are illegal."

"But it's not like they came across," Shaun objected. "Their parents brought them across. And now they have fear."

"It's complicated," I offered.

"Yeah, when you're dealing with politics, everything is complicated," said Shaun. "But I'm confident that America—I don't mean America, but Arizona—will come up with a solution."

"A lot of 'em are doing automobile work, construction work," said Leah. "And these are high-paying jobs, like $20 an hour. And they pay illegals $14 an hour, which is still pretty good."

"I begin to stop asking questions," said Shaun. "I don't want to know."

"I have a nephew whose father is illegal, and his father was deported," Leah told me. "So now he's without a father, and my sister is raising him as a single mother. But he made that decision to come, she made that decision to be with him, and now there's a beautiful baby as a result. I know that the food banks open their arms to everybody. So what do you do? They're here, they need to eat, and there's so much food that goes to waste every day. I've worked in a restaurant where they throw away food."

"I'm not a politician, I'm not an economics major, so there's some things I may say that will be misinformed," said Shaun. "That's my great disclaimer."

"Just tell your story, baby," Leah exhorted him.

"But I think there are some habits that we've gotten into in America that there's not going to be that middle class," said Shaun. "And that's what America has been built on."

"Sending jobs overseas—ugh," said Leah.

"I don't know the specific definition of socialism, nor economics and all that," said Shaun. "But I think America has created some habits that cater to some specific groups, and I think there should be an equal playing field for all Americans. Now, you could ask, 'Should that be a president's agenda?' But I do think it should be a politician's agenda. They should be for the success of all the people that their position is going to affect."

Their church was a big part of Shaun and Leah's life. "It's a big mixed church," said Leah, "and I like that, because that's the way heaven is going to be. If we don't learn to come together down here, how are we gonna do it up there? Or are we even gonna make it up there? I think that true religion is catering to the widows and orphans.

We always thought we were doing a good deed, and then you find yourself one of the orphans, one of the poor. We heard it in a sermon and it sounded cute, but then you live it, and it's life. It's making us want to do more, and not be afraid to go to the hedges and highways, as the Bible says, and not just stay within the four walls where the good churchy people are. It helped the Bible come alive. You can go to church, and listen to the sermons, but it's so much more outside the four walls. I'd personally like to see a church without walls."

"This really humbled me," said Shaun. "I'm a believer in Christ, and sometimes you get in that mind state that, 'I'm different from that person that don't know.' And there are some differences. But we're all having this human experience. And this helped me in politics, because I look at these people who are illegal, and I think, 'They're human.' I'm not any greater or lesser than anyone."

Another shelter resident, Dawn Valdez, had moved to Arizona with her mother from Dayton, Ohio, and married a Mexican, an "illegal" who became physically abusive. Dawn had also had drug addictions. She was in her mid-forties and had three sons ranging from eleven to twenty-one years old.

"My mom was a letter carrier, and she fell and messed up the cartilage in both of her knees," she told me. "And we came out here because of the better weather. She was a single mom. I know she did the go-go dancing, and she carried the mail, to make sure I didn't go without. But my mom is very bitter about the cards she was dealt. And there was a lot of mental abuse. Boyfriends would break up with her, and she would take it out on me. I can understand now, being a single mom, how some of these things can be done."

"When you're an adult you can understand," I said.

"Yeah, but when you're a kid it hurts a lot," she said. "My stepdad, he's a hillbilly from the hills of Tennessee, and he didn't agree with any of the things I did. And hanging out with black kids, he didn't agree with that at all. He'd say, 'You goin' spook huntin' tonight?' And I'd go, 'Yeah. I'll let you know if I catch one.'"

"How long have you been here at UMOM?"

"Two years."

"Isn't two years the max?"

"Yeah. My exit date is April. I've got my applications in to different housing. I have evictions, and one of them I'm fighting, because I had a restraining order against my husband, and he's the main reason I had to move out of there."

"So the evictions count against you?"

"Oh, yes."

"How?"

"Because you leave before your contract date. So that tacks onto your bill of how much you technically owe the apartment complex. So they charge you for storage and rent. But because I had a restraining order on file with them, we're looking into trying to get that eviction taken off my credit report."

"Was it that eviction that led to your becoming homeless?"

"Sort of. I conned my way into a different apartment complex, and took my abuser back because we had to pay the rent. My husband decided that we were gonna argue just before Christmas 2009. And he took a swing at me. And my son, who's eighteen now, stood up to him, and he said, 'If you hit my mom one more time, I'll kill you.' And my husband looked at me and said, 'You have to make a choice.' And I told him, 'There's no choice to be made. You need to leave.'"

"So then you got a restraining order."

"No, I had the restraining order already. I took him back."

"Do you regret that?"

"Yeah, I do. But in a way, looking back, I don't. Because if I hadn't taken him back, I wouldn't be clean and sober today."

Dawn was doing an internship at Central Arizona Shelter Services (CASS). "Helping people get services," she explained. "If they need a hard hat to do a job, I'll help 'em do that. I'll help 'em with resumes, stuff like that. Those are real homeless people. I mean, we're real homeless people, don't get me wrong. But they sleep on the street and stuff like that. People with serious mental illnesses that can't get help, because they've lost their insurance. It's rough, but I like it."

Arizona's Republican governor, Jan Brewer, was part of the problem. "Her son was in the Arizona State Hospital, right here at 24th and Van Buren," Dawn told me. "And she was one of the biggest advocates for mental health, for making sure they had insurance, until she became governor. And then she said that seriously mentally ill people were draining the budget."

"Why is it important for them to have insurance?"

"Because a lot of them are productive people. They have something to offer society. You get 'em on a regimen, or at least in counseling, and they will be productive people. We don't like Jan Brewer. We don't like Sheriff Joe either." Joe Arpaio was the longtime and controversial anti-immigrant sheriff of Maricopa County, which includes Phoenix.

"These names are nationally recognizable," I said.

"Yeah. Jan and Joe. The two biggest jerks in the world come from Arizona. I don't see anyone else shaking their finger at the president."

"Help me understand what this place is all about," I asked her. "How is it that Arizona produced such people?"

"I don't think Arizona produced them," she said. "I think it's because Arizona is a melting pot of all the other states. What New York used to be for people from all the other countries, I think we're that now for the other states. We've got construction here year-round because of the weather. If you're in construction, you're working three sixty-five."

"What about the immigration issue?"

"My husband was brought here at the age of nine," she told me. "He's lived here all his life, so if he went back to Mexico that would be a foreign country to him. My husband worked for Cox Communications, as an illegal. He's paid taxes. He's done everything that he's supposed to do. It doesn't make sense to me why you punish the kids, the victims. And if Mexico was smart, they would say that if the children are U.S. citizens, they won't take them. That would put the U.S. in a bind, because we'd have all these children with no parents. If you look at the people bummin' money on the street—and this is so sad for me to say—they're Caucasian. Because the Mexicans will pick up dog doo-doo if they have to. My favorite movie is *A Day without a Mexican*. Have you seen it?"

"No."

"It's funny as crud, but it's real. You wouldn't have stuff. We wouldn't have our produce. The lawns wouldn't be getting' done for all these people. Because somewhere the link has stopped with us white people, that we don't do those jobs. I think we're spoiled. I remember working at Walgreen's, and Home Depot was right next to Walgreen's. You didn't see white people standin' out there."

✳

At 11 a.m. on 12/12/12, I sluggishly and reluctantly went ashore from the Queen Mary and got back on the road. I was in no particular hurry this day, and I was determined to get out of greater Los Angeles without going on a freeway. I had long wanted to drive the Pacific Coast Highway, but the first long stretch northbound was anything but scenic or romantic: it was mostly scruffy commercial strips through municipalities whose names were familiar only because the rest of us are forced to be familiar with California: Torrance, Redondo Beach, El Segundo, Venice. Then Malibu, pitching itself as "27 miles of scenic beauty." Then Oxnard, then Santa Barbara, where I stopped for a late lunch.

I had lugged around America a big cardboard box full of books that I intended to read, and of course with all the driving and interviewing and this, that, and the other that I had inflicted on myself or that had come up, I had read almost none of them. Analogous and supplemental to the box of books, I also had a pile of magazine and newspaper articles and printouts that I was working my way through. My wife enjoyed quoting something an old Haji in Kashmir had said to me after the kidnapping by militants of several Western tourists in 1995: "I was thinking yesterday, if Ethan gets kidnap, I will go to the militant group and say, 'Here are his books and papers. He needs these. At least let him have his books and papers.'" Over lunch in Santa Barbara, I was reading from my pile of papers an essay on "Auden and Christianity" in *The New York Review of Books*. The writer, Edward Mendelson, quoted Auden:

> To pray is to pay attention or, shall we say, to "listen" to someone or something other than oneself. Whenever a man so concentrates his attention—be it on a landscape, or a poem or a geometrical problem or an idol or the True God—that he completely forgets his own ego and desires in listening to what the other has to say to him, he is praying.

I took my time over the essay and, if I remember right, the chicken BLT and fries, then I paid the waitress and walked back down the street the way I had come, toward my car. As I walked past the bus stop that before lunch I had passed in the other direction, I noticed a man-shaped lump, lying on the sidewalk beneath the shelter. Was he dead or ill? Was he only sleeping? If so, wouldn't he mind being awakened? Homeless people had habits and routines, and what could I do for or about him, anyway? A group of three people walking past the bus shelter stopped and looked down at him, had a brief discussion among themselves, and walked on. A woman sitting at the shelter, waiting for a bus I guess, faced away from the man lying on the pavement. And I kept walking.

I excused myself to myself and got in my car and continued up the coast. I forgot about the homeless man until I was well up the road and had already booked a non-refundable motel reservation in San Luis Obispo, but then I became swamped with guilt and shame, exacerbated by fatigue. What was the nature and extent of my responsibility toward that neighbor of mine? It was too true that, back in Santa Barbara, I had had nothing to do that was more urgent or important than to notice and concern myself with, pay attention to, that man. And the famous parable was unavoidably on record, rebuking me. Right there and then its very enactment had been right in my face, and I couldn't avoid acknowledging that there was a role I had failed to play. I had missed my cue. All I could do now was write about it, thereby confessing my failure. For whatever good that might do.

I called Jenny.

"Did you miss me?" she asked.

"Yes," I fibbed. Of course I did miss her. But I had called because, in my self-indulgent morosity, in my awareness that I would not turn around and drive back to Santa Barbara, in the attention I was giving to my own ego and desires rather than to the man at the bus shelter, I felt even more lonely than usual.

I stayed the night in San Luis Obispo. I couldn't let myself get back on the road the next day until after I found the Cal Poly store on Higuera Street. I needed to buy some gear there to honor my Seattle friend Pete Sabo, who had traveled with me to Pakistan and Haiti and on the leg of this trip from Miami to Houston, and who was a Cal Poly alum. It was also for Pete's sake that I had driven through Lancaster, where he had grown up. I bought a Cal Poly sweatshirt for Pete and a t-shirt and magnet for myself, had a sandwich, then left town around noon.

I didn't reach Salinas until four o'clock, so I had only an hour or so to visit the National Steinbeck Center. I had planned all along to spend more time there, and had even made appointments with a couple of its staff, which I had to cancel with apologies when it became clear to me that I had neither the time nor the energy to do justice to such meetings. And anyway, I would have had to tell them that I had begun feeling very ambivalent about their local hero. I didn't really have the heart for that, and Bill Steigerwald, the intrepid reporter I had met in Pittsburgh, had already been here, done that, and documented it wonderfully and well in his own road-trip book, *Dogging Steinbeck*. I had been raised, like millions of other Americans of several generations, to admire and even revere Steinbeck, and I was still prepared to call *The Grapes of Wrath*, *Of Mice and Men*, and *East of Eden* all masterpieces. But I was not okay with what I now saw, thanks to Steigerwald, as the fraud Steinbeck had perpetrated with *Travels with Charley*.

I didn't care how famous the guy was or whether he had, deservedly, won the Nobel Prize. I had spent years on the ground all around Asia and in Haiti learning both the craft and the morality of journalism, and I worked very hard to write true stories well. If I had to do that, Steinbeck should too. I was prepared to concede that there are various kinds of truth, but also to insist that writing that claims to be nonfiction must begin and end with factual truth. Every narrative is stylized and selective, and every writer needs a measure of license. But it's not permissible simply to make stuff up and call it nonfiction. And, in his book that was at once padded and oddly short and slight, Steinbeck had gone well over that line.

I toured the very good Steinbeck museum, looked appreciatively at memorabilia and clips from the movies of his books, bought a magnet and a copy of Steinbeck's lesser-known nonfiction book (at least I hope it's nonfiction) *A Russian Journal*, asked a staff member to take my picture standing in front of his legendary camper, Rocinante. But this far down the road on my own American road trip, and having learned the things I had learned from Steigerwald in print and in Pittsburgh,

I was a lot less interested in giving Steinbeck the benefit of the doubt. Steinbeck might well have been a great novelist but, as Grandma Casey would have said, some things are just plain wrong.

Meanwhile, as I drove up the coast, the remorseless grinding forward of events went on. The Republican-dominated Michigan legislature passed anti-union legislation and thousands of protesters, including unionized teachers, occupied the rotunda of the state capitol building in Lansing. A federal report came out predicting that by the year 2060 the Colorado River, which my father and I had crossed at Hoover Dam, would fall short of the demand of the seven Western states that relied on its water by five times the amount consumed by the city of Los Angeles alone. And then one morning I awoke to news that at least twenty-seven people, including eighteen children, had been gunned down at a school somewhere in Connecticut.

I did a couple of things in the Bay Area, but I also cancelled a couple. I was running on fumes now. One of the very first notions I had nursed for this trip had been to spend a day walking east to west, or northeast to southwest, across the city of San Francisco. No way was that going to happen anymore. I spent a couple of nights with my friend Margaret Tamisiea in San Jose. One of many things I found interesting about Margaret was that she was an unapologetic booster for San Jose, which since I lived in the area had overtaken San Francisco in population and was now vying ardently to spend hundreds of millions of public dollars on a new stadium to relocate the Oakland A's, but which still got little respect. Describing her mother lamenting the way of things in *Where I Was From*, Joan Didion writes, "California had become, she said then, 'all San Jose.'" Margaret dismissed such dismissals; her take on her town was cheerfully defiant. Margaret was a cheerful person generally, and it was, well, cheering to be in her company. She took me out to the big downtown display of Christmas trees decorated by Scout troops and school classes. It was unusually cold, almost freezing and, with the plausible-looking fake snow and but for the palm trees, I almost fancied myself home in Wisconsin.

I was in a hurry to get home, but I had set for myself one more task. My friend Kathy Sheetz lived in a historic World War II-era "Rosie the Riveter" cottage in the industrial town of Richmond, at the north end of the East Bay. Way back in Milwaukee I had sought out Moshe Katz for a pro-Israel perspective because I wondered whether my anger over what had been done to Kathy and others on the Gaza flotilla in 2010 had unfairly colored my own feelings. I honestly wanted to hear everyone's story. Now was my opportunity to hear Kathy's.

"All of a sudden you see what democracy is," she told me. "It's not the congresspeople. It's just people out there, pointing the way. Palestinians have been nonviolently resisting for years. They hid cows in the houses so the kids could get milk. They moved the cows around."

"Why did you go on the flotillas?" I asked Kathy.

"As I attended lectures on the Middle East, I became concerned about the unproductive ways the governments were approaching Israel-Palestine," she said. "And listening to long-term human rights activists, I was intrigued by the idea that they were proposing to take a boat into Gaza, simply to shed light on the blockade, knowing that if there were no blockade, the tension between Gaza and Israel would be so much less. So it was worth the effort to go, civil society to civil society, to try this nonviolent action. People say, 'Oh, how naïve.' But I don't know how you get around that."

"Why should you care?" I asked her. "You're not a Jew or an Arab."

"Because as I found out my government's role in funding this forty-four-year occupation, I became concerned about the lack of peace," she said. "What was my government doing? What were we funding?"

The 2010 international flotilla, which included Congresswoman Cynthia McKinney and Irish Nobel Peace Prize winner Mairead Maguire, had been boarded in international waters by the Israeli Navy. "They were really, really rough," said Kathy. "They came on with sound bombs and firing rubber-coated steel bullets. They used tear gas and a dog. And the only thing they told us was, 'Put down your cameras.' Not your guns; your cameras. That was our weapon." Nine activists had been killed, and Kathy was one of hundreds imprisoned in Israel.

"All three of my children tried to contact the U.S. Embassy, and they were told to watch the news," she said.

"Why?"

"Because the U.S. didn't know. And why that bothered me was that I was on a U.S. boat, and I was in international waters, seventy miles from shore. They didn't know what ship I was on, they didn't know if I was dead or alive for two days, and they were told to watch the news. Our closest ally, and they said they couldn't find out if there were any U.S. people. And, in fact, there was a U.S. citizen who was killed."

"The Turkish guy?"

"Turkish-American," she corrected me. "They never acknowledged him. It wasn't until his father came from Turkey about six months later and got a meeting with the State Department, that they had to acknowledge that a U.S. citizen had been killed. There was a congressperson who wanted to arrest us for being terrorists. So you can see how, even though this is trying to open up space to talk about these things, there are other factors that will try to close that space."

"How do you feel about Hamas?"

"This didn't have anything to do with any political groups," she said. "It was people to people. And I'm not a member of Gazan society, so I can't judge their right to rule. They were democratically elected. Even the people I talked to there who didn't support Hamas said, 'Yeah, but they're elected officials.' But I want to reiterate that this isn't to do with any political parties. It's simply that we were invited by civil society organizations."

"How did you get arrested?"

"I wasn't tortured," she said. "I feel uncomfortable talking about it, because my story is inconsequential compared to what happens to the Palestinians, who are put under military detention for years without trial. I was in jail for like four days. Actually, to me it was a very moving story. Because all of the women were put in a new jail in Beersheba. It's in the southern Negev, in the desert. All three or four hundred women were put in there, from all of the seven boats. I met women from all over the world that were on the different boats. There were about ten Americans that were the last to leave. We refused to leave until they told us what happened to an American-Israeli-Palestinian that was on our boat."

"Did they tell you?"

"Eventually we found out. They threatened just to carry us out physically. We're not sure if they told us the truth. Although they said she was freed, we didn't know if that was the truth, and we weren't allowed to see our lawyers. And maybe that wouldn't have made a difference, because the last day the Turkish government was negotiating with the Israeli government to take all of the activists to Turkey."

"Including you?"

"Yeah. Everybody. But the planes wouldn't actually leave until one a.m. the next night, because Turkey was constantly having to update who was getting on the planes, and they wouldn't leave until they had everybody. And Israel wouldn't allow the planes that were sitting side by side on the tarmac to communicate with each other. Each plane had to call Ankara."

"Why?"

"I don't know. So we arrived in Istanbul at three-thirty in the morning. And I think we took the dead with us too. Someone asked us if we wouldn't mind taking a bus just to greet people, to wave to people. Because there were throngs that had been waiting there all day and night. It was a very emotional scene. They were shouting, 'We're all Palestinians now.' They brought us there, they had us all checked out by doctors, access to psychologists. I don't know how they did it, hundreds of people. It was very well organized. They put us up in hotels, and we could arrange to go home at any time we wanted. Which was very nice of them too. They didn't say, 'You're going now.' They said, 'Whenever you're ready, make your arrangements.'"

"At Turkish government expense?"

"I believe so. I think it's super-important to say that I was on a U.S.-flagged boat, and that our government never acknowledged that. All that Barack Obama said was that he was sorry there was loss of life, but Israel has the right to defend itself. He never said anything about U.S. citizens. There's another thing that I think you should include, and that's that every boat that I've been on, the path of the boats never went anywhere near Israel. They went from Cyprus or Greece south, through international waters, to Gazan waters. That's why we consider ourselves kidnapped. We were taken to Israel at gunpoint. Not only that. They tried to make us sign papers when we were deported saying that we entered Israel illegally."

"Did you sign the papers?"

"No. An Israeli reporter called me, because I was one of several people whose bank cards were used by the Israeli Defense Forces. My statements showed that mine was used only to buy beer. Other things were declined, but they did use it to buy beer from a machine. About forty dollars' worth. Bank of America figured out that this didn't seem right and cancelled my card. And these were the dates that I was in jail. We're leaving the world a very dangerous place. This can't be good for America, and it sure isn't good for Israel. Our hope was that it would open up political space, so that people can talk about these things. I now see that we might be on the cusp of something."

"The cusp of what?"

"That's a hard thing to articulate right now. We're finally able to reflect on what is and has been happening there. We're on the cusp of understanding our role, the United States' role."

✳

Not only John Steinbeck but even the mighty Bill Steigerwald, dogger of Steinbeck, had rushed home in the end, and now I could appreciate why. "At last, at 1:30 in the morning, at the end of a 19-hour and 809-mile day, I entered my dark house and carefully slipped into bed with a sleeping woman I assumed was my wife," writes Steigerwald. And I had logged several thousand more miles than either of them, not that it's a competition. I had seen a lot of America, to be sure, but I had left vastly more of it unseen. I guess I got a kinda representative sampling. Anyway, I got what I got. I didn't fail, but I succeeded in getting only a severely abridged version of the absurdly ambitious story I had assigned myself to get. Which is just as well, since who would have time to read the unabridged version?

As I drove around America, I had kept a growing mental list of all the places I had not gone: the notoriously impoverished Pine Ridge Agency in South Dakota (but I would have told a similar story, probably less well, to the one told by Chris Hedges and Joe Sacco in *Days of Destruction, Days of Revolt*); Springfield, Illinois, where a relative of Jenny's was a street cop; across the Upper Peninsula of Michigan and the Mackinac Bridge (I had reluctantly eschewed that scenic route in favor of Cincinnati); Richmond, Virginia, where I had friends; San-ford, Florida, hometown of Trayvon Martin and George Zimmerman; Stuttgart, Arkansas, hometown of Clyde Edwin Pettit, a mentor to me in Bangkok and author of the letter that compelled Senator J. William Fulbright to reverse his position on Vietnam and of the masterpiece *The Experts: 100 Years of Blunder in Indo-China*; Quitman and Dallas; the godforsaken desert outpost of Yuma, Arizona, hours from either Phoenix or San Diego and only a few miles north of the Mexican bor-der; the Andre Agassi College Preparatory Academy in Las Vegas, which I had wanted to visit since reading Agassi's fascinating autobiography.

But you can't go everywhere, and you almost always end up some-where other than where you planned or expected. That's the way life is, as my dad would say. During the long hours behind the wheel, espe-cially in the later stages of my long road trip, I had entertained myself by imagining that, when I got to Seattle, I would not stop but turn right and go around America all over again, with a completely differ-ent itinerary. All the driving did put one in a kind of reverie or trance state, in which one could in fact almost take such a conceit seriously. One's car became one's world, or home. But in my lucid moments I knew that was all it was: a conceit to play with and dismiss. And I was exhausted. Still, the notion was not without a certain appeal.

From Richmond at the top of San Francisco Bay, I headed east toward Sacramento and then up Interstate 5. I stayed overnight in Redding and took aim the next morning for Corvallis, Oregon. I stopped in Mt. Shasta and again in the town of Weed, where I bought a t-shirt and several magnets for myself and friends. "Do you sell weed?" I asked the guy.

"No," he said. "There are a couple of dispensaries in Mt. Shasta, but we don't sell any here."

"It's non-medically legal in Washington now," I remarked.

"Yeah, you guys and Colorado."

In Corvallis lived my friend Dana Warren. Dana had been my downstairs neighbor for a year in Seattle, and he and I had become pals, but we both had gotten too busy to stay in close touch. He insisted that I was welcome in Corvallis, notwithstanding that his wife was about to give birth. But I made the boneheaded decision to go up into Oregon on the smaller, rural U.S. 97, east of the Cascade Mountains. ("Why do you always have to do things the hard way?"—Ethan's dad; "When given a choice, take the pretty route"—Moshe Katz's mom.) I figured from looking at the map that I could cut over on Highway 58 to pick up the Interstate just south of Eugene. But it had started raining while I was still in the mountains in California, and soon after I  crossed into Oregon I found myself in the middle of a full-blown blizzard. It was the only bad weather I encountered anywhere along my route. I had been too long in warm places and had forgotten what December could be like in the Northwest. At times I was the only car on the road, crawling forward on snow with almost no visibility. When I had phone reception, I called Dana. He went online and called me back.

"Highway 58 is socked in," he told me. "The webcam on 58 isn't showing any cars."

There was one more road I could try to take over the Cascades, U.S. 20, but soon I realized that that would be a very bad idea. "I'm sorry we weren't able to pull it off this time," said Dana when I called him again.

I was under the spell of forward movement, though, and I kept going until I slid on ice in Redmond, Oregon. There was a Motel 6 on the other side of the road, and I took the hint. The next morning was clear, and I headed north on rural highways, through Madras and The Dalles, then along the astonishingly beautiful Columbia River valley on I-84. Once I turned north on I-205 at Portland, I needed no further directions. I knew my way home. A couple of hours later I was seeing signs telling me I was almost there:

Entering
Nisqually Basin

Entering
Pierce County

It was just after four o'clock when I went through Tacoma, and I found myself in a rush-hour traffic jam. Which was a drag, but at least it was the last such drag I would have to deal with en route. I wouldn't be en route much longer. Then I was past the Tacoma Dome and on the tedious last stretch past RV dealerships and billboards up toward Seattle. And soon I was at my own front door: "Hi, Honey, I'm home!"

✳

At the end of the road, after the whole story has been told, all the leaving and returning on which I spent so much time and energy is nothing new under the sun, no more than the latest paragraph in the long and inconclusive picaresque tale of a restless species. So be it. I put 18,213 miles on my rental Prius and spent $1,446.09 on 398.332 gallons of gasoline (for 45.72 miles per gallon), plus lodging, sandwiches and power bars and Dr. Peppers, and miscellaneous costs. I accumulated an assortment of souvenirs: a pile of newspapers from towns and cities coast to coast, a "Let's Be More Than Summer Friends" tote bag from Provincetown, a t-shirt from Doe's Eat Place in Greenville, Mississippi, a purple ball cap from Wiley College in Marshall, Texas where, when a student asked if I had spoken at other HBCUs, I had committed the blunder of saying, "What's an HBCU?"[3] A heavy iron garden sculpture of a snail made from castoff farm machinery parts, which I had lugged all the way from Clyde and Nancy Wynia's Jurustic Park in Marshfield,

3 HBCU = historically black college or university.

Wisconsin. Fridge magnets galore. And stories and memories to last a lifetime.

Christmas with the in-laws, a couple weeks of downtime, and then the follow-up ordeal of writing this book, which took me the first eight months of 2013. When I needed a break from writing, I dug up turf in my new backyard, planted shrubs, and built three raised vegetable beds. I discovered that establishing a garden is a lot like writing a book, in the sense that there's only so much you can accomplish on any given day, and to get the whole thing done you have to be both assiduous and patient and use the passage of time to your advantage. I went out of town three or four times for speaking engagements during the spring. Over beers in the Detroit suburb of Redford Township in May, after a poetry slam in the basement of his church, Pastor Jeff Nelson asked me how the book was going. I moaned and groaned about how little progress I was making, but told him I was determined to publish in the fall. He endorsed that schedule and, whenever I felt discouraged after that, I motivated myself by remembering Jeff's words: "You gotta ship." He was right. The idea was to catch history on the fly, and to trust that whatever happened to be happening while I happened to be traveling would both be timely on publication and echo forward in overtones that would remain interesting and meaningful. And indeed, when Edward Snowden revealed the National Security Agency's program of mass surveillance, I could already hear overtones in the title I had chosen long before I began the trip.

I was ready to sit still for a while. But history doesn't sit still. In early July, when the unresolved revolution in Egypt erupted in fresh spasms of repression and violence, my father sent me an email. "This all started in January 2010, when I was having a cup of coffee in a McDonald's in Fort Worth while waiting for you," he remembered.

"Right!" I emailed back. "Except it was January 2011." Just before I went to Pakistan, just before the occupation of the Wisconsin state capitol building in Madison.

"It has been only two and a half years? Feels like three and a half to me."

"Well, it's been an action-packed time, which makes it seem longer. I don't feel like I've really had a chance to catch my breath since 2001."

"Sometimes you just have to make yourself catch a breath." (That's the way life is.) "By the way, maybe I shouldn't have had that cup of coffee. It's that old flower-in-the-cranny principle. If I hadn't had the cup of coffee things would have been different, just as if Napoleon hadn't invaded Russia he wouldn't have been defeated." In *All the King's Men*, the great American political novel I devoured three times while in college in my dad's vintage Modern Library edition that I still possess, Robert Penn Warren's narrator, Jack Burden, asks: "But is any relationship a relationship in time and only in time? I eat a persimmon and the teeth of a tinker in Tibet are put on edge. The flower-in-the-crannied-wall theory. We have to accept it because so often our teeth are on edge from persimmons we didn't eat."

One of the motivating premises of my project had been that America was not separate or different from the rest of the world. I had proven that, at least to my own satisfaction. And I had seen for myself that while the United States, plural, might be in some sense a single country, they are also an archipelago of disparate communities. Whether the center would hold was an open question. As things got uglier in Egypt, with a military takeover and then hundreds killed in raids on encampments of ousted President Morsi's supporters, I remembered the patronizing "Cairo in the Midwest" *New York Times* headline about the Madison capitol occupation of two and a half years earlier, and the defiance and hope expressed by both the citizens who had challenged Governor Walker and those who had overthrown President Mubarak, and I wondered: If things were turning out this way in Egypt, how could we expect them to turn out in Wisconsin?

Home is where the cat is. My cat Cleo, and my wife Jenny, had waited months for me to come home. Over the long years of my adult life I had become at home in the world, but I could only be in one place at a time, and the only place I wanted to be now was home in Seattle, over which I prefer, as Steinbeck daintily put it, to draw a veil. There's a lot more where this book came from, but I hope you get the general idea. This is the trip I took; this is the story I'm in a position to tell. During the months I was writing it, I glanced often at the wall opposite my dining table, at a faded picture, in a simple wood frame, of a boy and his dog lying under a tree. It's a relic of my Grandmother Casey, and accompanying the idyllic old-timey picture is a poem that might be a prayer:

A LITTLE ROCK

I wish I was a little rock
A-sittin' on a hill.
Doin' nothin' all the day
But just a-sittin' still.

I wouldn't eat, I wouldn't sleep,
I wouldn't even wash;
I'd just sit still a thousand years
And rest myself, b'gosh!

Acknowledgements

Thanks first and foremost to Jenny and Cleo for tolerating my absence, and especially to Jenny for her loving and steadfast support for this and all my plans and schemes except the truly hare-brained ones. Chapters 6 and 7 of this book stand as chapter-length expressions of love and appreciation for my parents and all my other wonderful relatives. My brother, Aaron Casey, invited me on that terrific trip around Central Europe in the summer of 1990, and has otherwise generally shared with me the long, rolling road trip called life for nearly half a century. (Aaron was born on the day Martin Luther King, Jr. gave his "I Have a Dream" speech, whose fiftieth anniversary is one week and two days from the day I write this.)

A few other people deserve special thanks: Brian Seredynski, my administrative and marketing assistant during the second half of 2012, was right there with me throughout both the planning and the execution of the trip and gave me crucial support both logistical and moral, as well as savvy advice, on a daily basis. Elaine Haywood rescued me at the last minute by volunteering to do crucial audio transcription when I needed what little time I had left to finish actually writing the book. Bill Steigerwald proved a kindred spirit, a real journalist of rare integrity and intelligence, a sensitive and shrewd reader and editor, and a colleague to cherish during the ordeal of putting a book like this one to bed on deadline. Pete Sabo cropped and edited the photographs in this book with his usual thoughtfulness and quiet aplomb. Dennis Rea and Eric Amrine in Seattle and Ariba Khan in Milwaukee gave me early, active, staunch, and ongoing encouragement.

A trip and book like this one are all about people and stories, so the friends and well-wishers who actively stepped up to share contacts deserve special mention, especially Elliott Attisha, Fawad Butt, Kathleen Conway, Ariba Khan, Paul Rogat Loeb, Gigi Pomerantz, Jeb Wyman, and Glenn Yarnell. Jenny (from Seattle to Milwaukee), Pete Sabo (from Miami to Houston and Galveston), Paul Haralson (a fun side trip to Galveston, then from Houston to Austin), and Dayle Casey a.k.a. Dad (from Colorado Springs to Los Angeles) kept me company and shared the driving along parts of my route.

I'm also grateful to friends old and new who shared their homes with me in many towns and cities all around America: Bry in Madison, Kamal and Ariba in Milwaukee, Fawad and Amber in Chicago, Josh and Courtney in Cincinnati, Tom and Sarah in Redford Township and Kate in Ann Arbor, Mr. and Mrs. Hatmaker and Julia in Harrisburg, Rachel and Bill and Thomas in Massachusetts, John and Courtney in Connecticut, Asma and Imtiaz in New York, Jerry and Annmarie in Havertown, Angie and Ben in Vienna, Charles and Ghislayne in Greenville, Nadeem Iqbal and family in Cary, Tami and Luke in Buford, Aniqa and Aamer in Macon, Rubina and Sajid in Orlando, Paul and Cindy in Miami, Todd and Crystal in New Orleans, Mom and Dad in Colorado Springs, Margaret in San Jose, Kathy and Steve in Richmond, California. Dana and Julie would also have hosted me, if only I hadn't driven east of the Cascades!

I hereby officially don't thank Paul Haralson for getting our tickets for the Texas-TCU football game on Thanksgiving Day, because I don't want him to blame me for him getting blamed for Texas losing (see Chapter 6). I do thank him for a lot of other things, though.

Ethan Casey is the author of *Bearing the Bruise: A Life Graced by Haiti* (2012), praised as "Heartfelt" by Paul Farmer, and of *Alive and Well in Pakistan* (2004), called "Intelligent and compelling" by Pakistani novelist Mohsin Hamid and "Wonderful ... a model of travel writing" by Edwidge Danticat. He has also written *Overtaken by Events: A Pakistan Road Trip* (2010) and is co-author, with Michael Betzold, of *Queen of Diamonds: The Tiger Stadium Story* (1991).

He edited, in collaboration with Jay Rosen and the New York University Department of Journalism, *09/11 8:48 a.m.: Documenting America's Greatest Tragedy*, the first book-length collection of writings published about the September 11, 2001 terrorist attacks, about which John Sutherland wrote in *The Guardian*: "[Casey and Rosen] have functioned like conductors of an orchestra, blending others' talents into unity. One is obliged to think analogically, because there has been nothing quite like this before."

Ethan Casey speaks often to university and high school students, civic and religious groups, and other audiences around North America and elsewhere. To contact him or purchase his books, visit:

www.ethancasey.com

www.facebook.com/ethancasey.author